# TRANSNATIONAL LEGAL PROCESSES AND HUMAN RIGHTS

*Isaac Newton said: 'If I have seen further (...) it is by standing upon the shoulders of giants.'*
*To Eva and Fotis for allowing me to see further.*
– Kyraki Topidi

*For my boys, whom I love so dearly*
– Lauren Fielder

# Transnational Legal Processes and Human Rights

*Edited by*

KYRIAKI TOPIDI
LAUREN FIELDER
*The University of Lucerne, Switzerland*

Routledge
Taylor & Francis Group
LONDON AND NEW YORK

First published in paperback 2024

First published 2013 by Ashgate Publishing

Published 2016
by Routledge
4 Park Square, Milton Park, Abingdon, Oxon OX14 4RN

and by Routledge
605 Third Avenue, New York, NY 10158

*Routledge is an imprint of the Taylor & Francis Group, an informa business*



Publisher's Note
The publisher has gone to great lengths to ensure the quality of this reprint but points out that some imperfections in the original copies may be apparent.

**British Library Cataloguing in Publication Data**
Transnational legal processes and human rights.
1. Human rights. 2. International law--Interpretation and construction.
3. Culture and law.
I. Topidi, Kyriaki. II. Fielder, Lauren.
341.4'8-dc23

**The Library of Congress has cataloged the printed edition as follows:**
Transnational legal processes and human rights / by Kyriaki Topidi and Lauren Fielder.
pages cm
Includes bibliographical references and index.
ISBN 978-1-4094-4818-1 (hardback) 1. Human rights. I. Topidi, Kyriaki, editor of compilation. II. Fielder, Lauren, editor of compilation.

K3240.T7265 2013
341.4'8--dc23

2012030432

ISBN: 978-1-4094-4818-1 (hbk)
ISBN: 978-1-03-292353-6 (pbk)
ISBN: 978-1-315-54983-5 (ebk)

DOI: 10.4324/9781315549835

# Contents

## PART II: THE PROTECTION OF CULTURAL DIFFERENCE WITHIN HUMAN RIGHTS TRADITIONS



## PART III: TRANSNATIONAL ECONOMIC ENTITIES, HUMAN RIGHTS AND CULTURAL IDENTITY

# List of Contributors

**Ali Abid**, JD Candidate, John Marshall Law School, Chicago. Mr Abid is the Lead Articles Editor for the *John Marshall Law Review* and President of the American Constitution Society.

**Deval Desai**, JD. Mr Desai works for the Justice Practice Group of the World Bank. He attended Harvard Law School and Oxford University. He researches in the area of business and human rights. He has written for the Human Rights Program at Harvard Law School.

**Lauren Fielder**, JD, LLM. Professor Fielder teaches African Law, Protection of Vulnerable Groups and Transnational Litigation at the University of Lucerne, where she is the assistant director of the Transnational Legal Studies Program. She writes and speaks about human rights issues in Africa. She studied at the University of Texas in Austin.

**Barbara Grabowska**, MLaw. Ms Grabowska completed her legal studies at the University of Warsaw. She works for the Helsinki Foundation for Human Rights.

**Ehsanul Haque**, Professor Haque is Associate Professor in the Department of International Relations at the University of Dhaka, Bangladesh and Adjunct Professor at East West University. His specialty is South East Asian Affairs. He teaches courses on global politics, political thought in international relations, diplomacy, ethnicity and nationalism, and protracted conflict. He is a Fulbright Scholar.

**Ruth Hargrove**, JD. Professor Hargrove received her JD *cum laude* from the University of San Diego in California. She is a Professor at California Western School of Law. She teaches Juvenile Law at her home university and Comparative Juvenile Law around the world. Before becoming a professor, she was a practicing attorney for 20 years, with her primary focus on juvenile justice.

**Marian Kokeš**. Mr Kokeš is assistant to the Czech Constitutional Court's Vice-President Eliska Wagnerova.

**Piotr Mikuli, PhD**. Dr Piotr Mikuli is a constitutional lawyer and an adjunct professor in the Chair of Comparative Constitutional Law of the Jagiellonian University in Cracow. He is the author and co-author of a number of publications dealing with Polish and foreign constitutional issues.

**Robin Palmer**. Mr Palmer is Director of the Institute for Professional Legal Training, a training and research institute affiliated to the University of Kwazulu–Natal, South Africa. He is a national and international consultant in the fields of justice sector reform, new innovations in truth verification, applied management systems, forensic investigation and training as well as general and applied skills training. He has consulted for various bodies (including UNDP, UNODC, EU, OSI) in Africa, Asia and Europe.

**Carole Petersen**, JD. Professor Petersen received her law degree *cum laude* from Harvard. She also holds a post doctorate diploma from the University of Hong Kong. She is the Director of the Matsunga Institute for Peace and Conflict Resolution and Associate Professor at the William S. Richardson School of Law at the University of Hawaii. She teaches International Law, Human Rights and Equality and Non-Discrimination. She has authored numerous books and articles on human rights and equality.

**Roberta K. Thyfault**. Professor Thyfault received her JD *cum laude* from the California Western School of Law. She is Professor at California Western and teaches legal writing and legal skills. Before becoming a professor, she practiced as a criminal appellate attorney.

**Kyriaki Topidi**, PhD. Dr Topidi is a Senior Lecturer and Senior Researcher at the School of Law of the University of Lucerne. She teaches and researches on religious rights and has a background in human rights, minority protection and EU law. She has published widely in these areas.

**Angelica Tsakiridis**, JD. Ms Tsakiridis is Corporate Counsel and Global Trade Compliance Officer for a major Japanese company in San Francisco. She is also Adjunct Professor at the John Marshall Law School in Chicago, teaching International Trade and Development.

**Mark E. Wojcik, JD LLM**. Professor Wojcik received his JD *cum laude* from the John Marshall Law School and his LLM from New York University. He is director of Global Legal Studies in the John Marshall Law School and has taught extensively in foreign countries. He holds leadership roles in numerous legal organizations and associations. He teaches International Law, International Human Rights and International Criminal Law and is the author and co-author of numerous law review articles, book chapters and books.

# Foreword

The increasing research focus on the various legal and *de facto* processes involved in the transference and migration of human rights norms and systems between international bodies, countries, multinational commercial and humanitarian non-state actors is timely, as the stage has been reached where there is little dispute about the universality of core human rights norms, and the consequent duty to promote and entrench these norms.

Since the debate about the desirability and content of human rights has been substantially concluded, the next stage is the methods whereby these rights are transferred and adopted, to be followed by the final stage, a focus on the effective enforcement of these transferred and adopted rights.

In this book, selected important processes of this second stage of transnational transference and adoption of human rights norms are discussed in three parts: the evolution of human rights in transnational legal settings; the effect of religious and cultural differences in this human rights transference process; and a consideration of the role of commercial entities in this process.

The premise from which these contributions proceed is the general international acceptance of, and the promotion of, the ideal of achieving international compliance with the so-called International Bill of Human Rights, that is, the Universal Declaration of Human Rights (UDHR, 1948); the International Covenant on Civil and Political Rights (ICCPR, 1966); and the International Covenant on Economic, Social and Cultural Rights (CESCR, 1966).

These foundational human rights instruments are supplemented by various optional protocols and seven core international human rights treaties: the International Convention on the Elimination of All Forms of Racial Discrimination (ICERD, 1965); the Convention on the Elimination of All Forms of Discrimination against Women (CEDAW, 1979); the Convention against Torture and Other Cruel, Inhuman or Degrading Treatment or Punishment (CAT, 1984); the Convention on the Rights of the Child (CRC, 1989); the International Convention on the Protection of the Rights of All Migrant Workers and Members of their Families (ICRMW, 1990); the International Convention for the Protection of All Persons from Enforced Disappearance (CPED, 2006); and the Convention on the Rights of Persons with Disabilities (CRPD, 2006).

Against this background, the contributions to the book provide a useful platform for developing a more systematic approach to analyzing and evaluating the impacts of various kinds of interventions and processes involved in the transference of human rights.

When considering the issue of human rights transference, three important themes may be noted: the incremental nature of most of the processes; the interrelationship between, and reinforcing effects of, many of apparently disconnected processes; and the unintended consequences that flow from some attempts at human rights transference actions.

Most of the processes discussed are incremental in the sense that what may be seen as considerable progress in one context may be taken for granted in another. For example, although the equality of rights between men and women in most European countries is taken for granted, progress in the recognition of the equal property and inheritance rights of men and women in many countries in Africa would be considered a major breakthrough.

In addition, the growth in the international recognition of social and economic rights was built on the initial acceptance of basic first-generation rights such as the right to dignity, equality and the right to life. For example, "poverty," which has historically been view merely as a socio-economic condition, is increasingly been viewed as a human rights violation. This recognition in turn reinforces the concept of a rights-based economic development model, and the consequent external and internal pressure on governments to prioritize development to eliminate poverty as a human rights violation. Thus this "rights-based" development movement centralizes human rights as the starting point in the making and implementation of government policy, as it establishes minimum standards of material and social well-being as human rights.

An example of unintended transference of human rights norms is the recent decision by the African Union (AU) to move a summit meeting from Malawi to Addis Ababa in Ethiopia, after new Malawian President Joyce Banda refused to guarantee that Sudan President Omar El-Bashir would not be arrested in Malawi in terms of the International Criminal Court indictment pending against him. Although her predecessor, and many other members of the AU, are signatories to the Rome Statute obliging them to arrest persons in President El-Bashir's position, very few ever had intentions of implementing any international legal obligations that did not suit them politically. The sudden death of the previous Malawian president resulted in a new president willing to carry out her country's international legal obligations, resulting in severe embarrassment for the AU, and reinforcing her country's support for bringing human rights violators to justice.

A very powerful recent example of human rights transference is the rape trials held in the Eastern Congo, where the central government of the Democratic Republic of Congo, the United Nations, the International Bar Association and the Open Society Foundation cooperated to establish and run criminal trials of militia commanders who ordered or fail to stop incidences of mass rape in the Eastern Congo. The convictions of many of these human rights perpetrators have resulted in a measure of emotional and material compensation for the victims, and has sent out the message that nobody is beyond the reach of the law. A consequence will hopefully be to reduce future acts of impunity, thereby providing tangible protection and justice for the vulnerable and powerless.

A vital lesson from the Eastern Congo rape trials experience is the centrality of principles of good governance and the rule of law in ensuring a sustainable environment for the transference and subsequent protection of human rights, whatever the mode of transference.

While there is no generally agreed-upon precise definition of "good governance," and the term itself is often criticized for operating in a liberal Western ideological paradigm, the United Nations suggests eight core characteristics of "good governance," namely governance that is subject to the rule of law, and is consensus-based, participatory, accountable, transparent, responsive, inclusive, equitable, effective and efficient.

The rule of law is the only real guarantor of good governance, meaning accountable, participatory, predictable and transparent public administration. The efficacy of the "rule of law," is, in turn, determined by the effective functioning of the monitors and guarantors of the rule of law: the courts; the police and other law enforcement agencies; the Prosecuting Authorities; the public anti-corruption and good governance institutions; civil society monitoring agencies; legislative oversight mechanisms; and, as always, the media.

One of the biggest human rights challenges is the consistent violation of international social and economic rights, such as the right of access to housing, healthcare services and social security, the right not to be arbitrarily deprived of property, and the futility of rights transfers where the gains of such transfers cannot be realized on a sustainable basis.

Any progress made in transferring and entrenching human rights norms or cultures will be unsustainable without protection and enforcement in an environment of good governance underpinned by the rule of law.

Finally, the various topics on the transference of human rights covered in this book provide a natural bridge to the third stage alluded to above: the focus on remedies that ensure the sustainability of transferred human rights, or stated differently, the transference of remedies for addressing human rights violations. As has been seen, no real remedies are possible in an environment lacking good governance under the rule of law. Given this qualification, any rights transferred or adopted can be better realized where there is a practice of rights enforcement and a general culture of respect for human rights. By way of example, areas that could be prioritized are the effective enforcement of human rights judicial decisions, effective transitional justice implementation mechanisms, and the accountable monitoring of human rights treaties and instruments.

The problem with enforcing judicial decisions on human rights issues is worldwide. In Africa, in 2000 the African Commission on Human and People's Rights found the government of Mauritania responsible for massive human rights violations, including the expulsion of more than 70,000 black Mauritanians into Senegal and Mali. To date, despite the Commission's ruling, only a fraction of this number have been allowed back into Mauritania, and nobody has been brought to justice for human rights abuses in this regard. In 2005, in the case of *Yean and Bosico v Dominican Republic*, the Inter-American Court of Human Rights held that the Dominican government violated the American Convention on Human Rights with racially discriminatory citizenship policies, yet the Dominican government subsequently made these policies *more* restrictive. In *D H and Others v Czech Republic* (2007), the European Court of Human Rights held that the segregation of Roma in Czech schools violated the European Convention on Human Rights, and ordered the Czech government to end these practices and compensate the plaintiffs. The government's response was merely to rename the special Roma schools, but they retained their segregationist practices.

An area where the transference of human rights practices would be particularly apposite is in the field of transitional justice, which includes a range of judicial, quasi-judicial and related approaches to addressing past human rights violations. Like constitutional borrowing, the borrowing and adaptation of, for example, Truth Commission legislation and practices, has proved to be useful to break cycles of violence following political transitions from repressive regimes.

In summary, the topics covered in this book address a vital and developing area of international human rights jurisprudence, and the work also provides a solid basis for further research in the field of transnational legal processes and practices to advance and entrench human rights norms, cultures and practices.

Robin Palmer
*Director of the Institute for Professional Legal Training*
*University of KwaZulu-Natal, Durban, South Africa*

# Acknowledgements

This volume is the result of collective efforts. We would like to thank in particular the University of Lucerne School of Law and its Faculty Manager Marcel Amrein for giving us the opportunity to organize the colloquium that gave birth to this book.

We are also very grateful to the then Dean of the Law School of the University of Lucerne, Prof. Dr Regina Aebi-Müller for her support in our activities in the same respect.

Special thanks also go to Prof. Dr Alexander H.E. Morawa for encouraging us to pursue our work at the Chair of Comparative and Anglo-American Law.

Finally, but by no means less importantly, we are grateful to Ms Uta Dietrich for helping us realize our projects on a daily basis. Without her, much of this would simply not have been possible.

KT/LF

# Chapter 1
# Introduction

Kyriaki Topidi and Lauren Fielder

## The Dialectics of Human Rights Protection in Globalized Legal Spaces

The transference or movement of human rights norms goes hand in hand with globalization. As the world becomes smaller, the migration of human rights ideas increases. This volume sets out to explore these transnational legal human rights processes. National and international contexts are becoming essential in exploring and understanding developments in human rights. Research has amply demonstrated how both law(s) of the nation-state, from the bottom, and international regulations, from the top, interact so as to give shape to the features of the various systems of human rights protection that operate in the different parts of the world.[1] "Movements" of norms are therefore not a new phenomenon, nor are they the exclusive research area of lawyers.

At the outset, it is useful to explore the meaning of transnational legal process. Koh's definition of a transnational legal process as "a process whereby public and private actors, including nation states, corporations, international organizations, non-governmental organizations, and individuals interact in a variety of fora to interpret, enforce, and ultimately internalize rules of international law"[2] is one that captures the spirit and underlying perception of this volume. Koh's analysis of the four core characteristics of transnational legal processes reflects well the common themes of this book: first, it is becoming increasingly difficult to distinguish the respective remits of domestic and international law;[3] second, non-state actors are active contributors in shaping human rights norms;[4] third, movements of norms from the national to the international level operate in both directions;[5] and finally, transnational legal processes produce law that requires states to comply with it.[6] In

1 Sally Engle Merry made this argument as early as 1992 in 'Anthropology, Law and Transnational Processes', *Annual Review of Anthropology*, 1992, 21: 357–79 at 357.

2 Harold Hongju Koh, 'Transnational Legal Process After September 11th', *Berkley Journal of International Law*, 2004, 337, at 339.

3 Harold Hongju Koh, 'Transnational Legal Processes', *Nebraska Law Review*, 1996, 75: 181 at 184.

4 Ibid.

5 Ibid.

6 Ibid.

this sequence of developments what remains contentious and largely unchartered for both lawyers and non-lawyers are the patterns of internalization of norms.[7]

Classic internalization occurs either horizontally or vertically. *Horizontal* internalization consists of inter-governmental fora such as conferences or summits that aim to promote compliance with international law.[8] *Vertical* internalization happens when state or non-state actors interact with a violating state nationally or internationally to induce compliance.[9] Legislation, executive action and judicial interpretation, methods that recur in this book, belong to the latter category. It is legal internalization that represents the center of gravity of our work.[10]

This volume aims to revisit some of the issues resulting from these transnational "movements" in order to map their routes and reflect on the variety of the patterns of interaction of both rules and systems. From colonialism to the challenges faced by contemporary multicultural states as a result of migratory movements, we discuss how norms and, in some cases, entire legal systems have been giving shape to local and supra-national human rights legal orders. The parameters of interactions between the local, national and transnational systems are based on two assumptions: first, the different levels of legal systems of rules and norms are not isolated from each other. They are instead complementary and mutually constitutive. Second, in order to give an accurate reflection of the legal movements, informal ordering systems (also referred to as "private governance") must be accounted for.[11] A characteristic illustration of this trend is the often-discussed involvement of states in various international economic arrangements and international laws affecting local cultures.[12] The World Bank, transnational corporations and the International Monetary Fund, as well as systems of patents, copyrights and trademarks, continue to shape human rights as experienced and practised within local legal orders.

In this book, we are equally interested in the role that institutions, (legal) actors and networks have increasingly assumed in re-shaping and transforming human rights. In this respect, transnational human rights networks, as a form of cross-border collective action, must be also added to the list of formations likely to promote compliance with universally accepted norms.[13] Although transnational activism is not the strict focus of this book, contributions nevertheless address

7 Caöeb J. Stevens, 'Hunting a Dictator as a Transnational Legal Process: The Internalization Problem and the Hissène Habré Case', *Pace International Law Review*, 2002, 24(1): 190, at 198.

8 Ibid. at 199.

9 Ibid.

10 We follow Koh in understanding *legal* internalization as the process by which 'an international norm is incorporated into the domestic legal system and becomes domestic law', although we do not exclude the opposite route of a human rights norms moving from the domestic to the international.

11 Merry (1992), op. cit., at 358.

12 See Chapters 11 and 12.

13 In fact, the obstacles, challenges and significance of these forms of transnational organizations have since the late 1990s become the object of a distinct area of interdisciplinary

the special role played by the legal community and civil society in enforcing human rights domestically. In the light of the discrepancy between qualitative and quantitative studies on the question of whether transnational activism has improved human rights, with the former arguing for an improvement and the latter against it,[14] the need for a more nuanced approach is evident.

The relation between state law and other normative orders is precisely the meeting point of the 11 case studies included in this collection. In their distinct ways, the chapters engage with the "vulnerability" of the local and/or the national to external normative influences. In essence, we are dealing with the different facets of a post-modern understanding of legal pluralism: a type of pluralism born out of the co-existence of the various legal systems operational at a given point in time and space and within a very specific social context,[15] which also needs to be taken into account. The cultural framework, in some cases, has a decisive effect not only on legal procedures but also on the actual content and interpretation of rights.[16]

Methodologically, transnational processes observed in the area of human rights inevitably relate to the study of dispute processing and conflict resolution. These discrepancies are most often the product of the clashes between the different rules emanating from each legal system. Most often, transnational and domestic orders mirror political struggles with multiple local actors competing for national expertise.[17] These clashes illustrate well the multidimensional character of human rights as the object of transnational legal processes.

Another recurring angle of enquiry regarding transnational legal processes and human rights concerns indigenous rights. Indigenous populations have often framed their human rights claims utilizing transnational human rights legal arguments and discourses. From land claims to questions relating to resources as well as sovereignty issues, transnational contexts have proved a recurring pattern for putting forward indigenous cases, as case law from the United States, Canada, Australia or South America shows.

An essential underlying assumption, or at least common understanding, in a significant number of pieces contained in this volume, accepts or suggests that ultimately international human rights law is what we make of it and remains an evolutionary and dynamic normative project.[18] The question of faith in and

---

research through the essential work of Margaret Keck and Kathryn Sikkink, *Activists Beyond Networks in International Politics*, Cornell University Press, Ithaca, NY, 1998.

14 See for example, E. Hafner-Burton and K. Tsutsui, 'Human Rights in a Globalizing World : The Paradox of Empty Promises', *American Journal of Sociology*, 2005, 110(5): 1373–411.

15 Merry (1992), op. cit., at 358.

16 The area of scholarship labeled as critical legal studies focuses on how (and why) law maintains power relationships (cf. Sally Engle Merry (1992), op. cit. at 361).

17 Gregory Shaffer and Mark Pollack, 'Hard vs Soft Law: Alternatives, Complements and Antagonists in International Governance', *Minnesota Law Review*, 2010, 94: 706.

18 Stevens, op. cit., at 192.

compliance with treaties remains for states an open academic debate,[19] introducing gradually a "new sovereignty" for states that are entering a complex web of international connections and transactions that guides their treaty behavior.[20] This book, however, does not focus *stricto sensu* on efficiency or on state interests. Instead, it looks at norms following the Chayes and Chayes triangular framework of efficiency, interest and norms guidance of states' compliance. The geographical and thematic richness and diversity of the contributions do not of course ignore these considerations, yet the chapters do not address them in a frontal manner: they are interested in the content of the norms and how legal and institutional processes affect human rights protection. Ultimately, however, the process becomes successful from a normative perspective only if the norm is supported beyond and outside parliament or courtrooms.

In the light of these considerations, one of the main goals of this book is to respond to the need to provide adequate empirical evidence as to how legal internalization occurs, a place where a gap currently exists in academic scholarship. Moreover, as transnational legal norm conveyance remains unsystematic and heterogeneous across states, especially since national contexts "block, adopt, translate or appropriate a transnational legal norm,"[21] the theme of this book presents itself as timely.

Contributions in this volume use both a *static* as well as a *dynamic* conception of transnational law, depending on the context. For the strictly legal studies, authors reflect on transnational situations, which involve more than one jurisdiction (static).[22] For the chapters with a more socio-legal methodological approach, transnational law is viewed as a source of legal change within a given legal system that consists of legal norms as imported/exported across frontiers (dynamic).[23] Transnational law is also quite predictably affected by political, economic and social forces, which in some cases make it difficult to evaluate the influence of law and distinguish it from other factors.

In sum, transnational legal norms, owing to the fluidity and complexity of transnational legal processes, are dynamic, multi-layered and complex. The studies

---

19 See the seminal work of Abram Chayes and Antonia Handler Chayes, 'The New Sovereignty: Compliance with International Regulatory Agreements', 1995, 4. For them, efficiency, interest and norms guide states' compliance with treaty regimes.

20 Thomas Risse and Kathryn Sikkink, 'The Socialization of International Human Rights Norms into Domestic Practices: Introduction', in *The Power of Human Rights: International Norms and Domestic Change*, Cambridge University Press, Cambridge, p. 5.

21 Gregory Shaffer, 'Transnational Legal Process and State Change: Opportunities and Constraints', Legal Studies Research Paper Series, Research Paper no. 10-28, University of Minnesota Law School, 2011, at 3.

22 Harold Koh, 'International Law as Part of our Law', *American Journal of International Law*, 2004, 98: 43, 53, especially the reference to Phil Jessop's definition of transnational law as 'events that transcend national frontiers'.

23 Shaffer (2011), op. cit., at 7–8.

in this volume illustrate how transnational legal norms are created, evolve and are practised. They propose to do so through individual case studies on legal change.

As a group, these studies emphasize amply the heterogeneity of transnational legal processes that present multiple actors involved, institutions and at times even parallel processes in competition in a given context. Finally, the effects of transnational legal processes are context-specific and in direct relation to domestic legal systems, political circumstances and cultural norms. These studies provide the necessary background to appreciate the complexities of the phenomena analyzed.

Towards these aims, the collection of chapters is organized in three parts: the first part includes five chapters that problematize the broader normative validity as well as the ways in which human rights norms have evolved essentially as they become applied at the national level. The reception of human rights principles and methods of application are not unhindered, and two cases relating to the same country (Chapters 3 and 6) give accounts of the arguments and strategies for resistance. The second part of the book relates to one of the most pronounced features of any and every human rights regime: the protection of cultural difference. From religion and gender equality to the viability of human rights protection per se, the four chapters of this part take a *tour d'horizon* of the wide issues that present themselves when discussing human rights protection on a global scale. The third and final part of the volume looks through its two chapters at the ways in which transnational economic entities, part of the above-mentioned web of "private governance," look at human rights and cultural identity through the lens of the notions of market, interest and economies, and how any potential clashes affect, and in some instances complement, transnational legal processes.

The issues that the authors in their contributions place emphasis on are varied and complex. They all accept, however, the challenges of the study of transnational legal processes in the narrower national confines.

## The Collection of Transnational Legal Narratives

Colonialism, as the archetypical transnational process, in the area of human rights, represents the starting point of the journey in this book. Haque's discussion on universal human rights and cultural relativity relates to the broader question of the modalities for the coexistence of very different legal systems through colonial reformulation. It is also linked to the paradoxical epiphenomenon of colonial legal transformations creating written, although more abstract, human rights standards in systems where the pre-colonial spoken and more thoroughly interpreted norms produced concrete outcomes.[24]

More specifically, the first contribution of this part of the book engages with the important and recurring question of the cultural universality of human rights as a paradigm. This analysis represents a necessary prerequisite in order to then

24 Merry (1992), op. cit., at 365.

analyze specific legal environments of human rights construction and evolution. It sets the platform for the consideration of specific ways in which human rights move transnationally or in some cases fail to do so.[25]

Haque is right to remind us that international law relating to human rights is "not a value-neutral ideology."[26] It represents the reflection of what he calls "a moral touchstone," yet at the same time it is a "method of evaluation" for states and their institutions. Universalism, as discussed by Haque, qualifies human rights as being inherent and intrinsic to humanity. This assumption should *a priori* facilitate transnational legal processes concerning them as all human beings on this planet share them. The obligation incumbent upon states to promote and protect those rights remains consequently constant for all states, regardless of cultural and/or socio-political considerations.

The counter-argument to this approach openly questions the global validity and the broad claim to universality of human rights. One point of sharp attack is predictably directed at the "inordinate individualism in Western human rights doctrine."[27] The ascendancy of cultural relativity that proposed to shape human rights according to customs, values and the broader background of a particular culture has resulted in the fragmentation of human rights. In turn, the nature of human rights as context-specific renders them complex (if not unsuitable) normative constructions or the transnational process.

One of the solutions in order to reconcile the two otherwise incompatible viewpoints rests with the Rawlsian concept of "overlapping consensus."[28] This option leads to agreement on the norms without necessarily agreeing on why these are the "right" norms. In that respect, culture, with its dynamic, evolving and adjustable features, cannot always be an obstacle to the universality of human rights, provided that "an open and un-coerced cross-cultural dialogue" is put in place.[29]

The concepts of dialogue, deconstruction and reconstruction of power relations, as well as internationalized norm creation and national implementation, as discussed in this chapter, describe and are linked to parts of the transnational legal process. Universal human rights are thus the archetype of a transnational legal process in action with a "common humanizing focus" that places the individual at the center of public policy.[30]

The contribution of Ruth Hargrove and Roberta Thyfault is the first of two chapters dealing with obstacles to transnational legal processes as they affect domestic rights protection. This contribution is valuable in that it shows the unique way in which transnational law process work between foreign law and

25 See Chapter 3 for an example of resistance to transnational legal processes.

26 See Chapter 2.

27 Ibid.

28 Ibid.

29 Ibid.

30 Ibid.

constitutional jurisprudence in the United States. The contributors examine the impact of and resistance to the use of foreign law in US Supreme Court cases where juveniles challenge their sentences of death and life without parole. The chapter traces the Court's juvenile punishment cases, examines the backlash against the Court using foreign law in its decisions and discusses why this use of foreign law in juvenile punishment cases conflicts with principles of American democracy.

The authors use as their case study several juvenile punishment cases where the Court used "evolving standards of decency analysis" to interpret the Eighth Amendment prohibition of cruel and unusual punishment. This is a three-part analysis of the views of Americans, the Court and foreigners. Through a line of cases that the authors use, we can see how foreign law has taken a larger share of importance in this analysis, leading to greater Constitutional protection for juveniles convicted of crimes. However, this has caused a tremendous backlash, as the American public is wary of the views of foreigners and of foreign law taking precedence over public opinion. We can see how domestic law has evolved through transnational legal processes, taking account of the negative backlash arising out of these changes.

This evolution and backlash was particularly apparent in the *Roper v. Simmons* case and its aftermath. Justice Kennedy, the author of the majority, was criticized so heavily for this use of foreign law that members of a conservative group called for his impeachment. Congress attempted to pass federal legislation making the judicial use of foreign law impeachable, although the Supreme Court held this to be an unconstitutional violation of the separation of powers. Congress was successful in reigning in the Supreme Court's use of foreign law in its use of the issue as a litmus test for every post-*Roper* Supreme Court nominee.

The authors then explain the reasons for this backlash, particularly that it is undemocratic and a violation of America's sense of exceptionalism. Explaining further, the authors say that the Supreme Court imposed foreign views on an electorate that had rejected those views. The chapter concludes with a warning that "while the Court should be free to consult any source, including foreign sources, for empirical information, it should use the foreign law with caution, and with an appreciation of its historical, political, and cultural context."[31]

The next chapter, by Barbara Grabowska, explores how human rights norms are transmitted into relations governed by private law and examines how growing obstacles to norm transference are created by the expansion of companies and corporations. Grabowska presents this issue of horizontal effect using examples from three legal systems: the German *Drittwirkung*; the European Convention on Human Rights and Strasbourg Court's case law; and European Union law.

Grabowska presents horizontal effect as a result of Ulpian's division of public and private law and explains that the horizontal effect of human rights on private law is a way to guarantee human rights protections and constitutional values

31 See Chapter 3.

by using constitutional law, which she describes as direct horizontal effect, and private law tools, or indirect horizontal effect.

After examining the concept of horizontal effect in detail in the three legal systems described above, Grabowska considers how the three methods discussed impact constitutional law in Poland. She specifically considers anti-discrimination law as the strongest reflection of EU directives. Grabowska explains that

> The European Court of Human Rights and its case law have quite high authority and its jurisdiction seems to be an effective remedy for changing Polish law and practice in the field of human rights. However, it does not apply human rights horizontally. It rather uses the doctrine of positive obligations to examine the scope of responsibility of the State and to consider if there was a violation of human rights.

In examining this issue, Grabowska analyzes a case applying constitutional rights in a damages case in Poland based on discrimination against a disabled person denied access to a supermarket.

Jurisprudence of the Polish Constitutional Court not recognizing Article 32 as a source of the subjective right to equal treatment has caused most scholars to agree that constitutional rights cannot be applied directly or indirectly in private law in Poland. However, arguments can be made that "at least indirect horizontal effect of human rights is possible or needed."

In continuation of the spirit of the work of Grabowska, Marian Kokes and Piotr Mikuli remain geographically anchored in Central and Eastern Europe. They discuss how constitutional courts in the Czech Republic and Poland use subsidiarity when applying the European Convention on Human Rights. Their point of departure assumes a direct linkage between the national and European levels of human rights protection. This bond is nevertheless problematic from the point of view of the legal incorporation of the Convention and situations where the international human rights treaties guaranteeing individuals rights come in conflict with domestic law. Kokes and Mikuli provide a meticulous account of the processes of incorporation of the European Convention on Human Rights (ECHR) in both of the countries studied. In the case of the Czech Republic, the issue of a possible conflict between a human rights treaty and the Constitutional Court has not been resolved yet. The prevailing approach so far has been for the Court to provide a corrective to the international normative text in cases of conflict, even if, as Kokes notes, it is very accommodative in essence to the international treaty concerned, resulting in further confusion as to what human rights are and whether any distinction should be maintained between self- executing and non-self-executing rights. The case of Poland is similar in that constitutionally international norms included in agreements and incorporated in the domestic legal order become norms of internal and universally binding law in the country. In cases of conflicts between the national and international provisions, the Polish constitution suggests a conflict resolution mechanism that relies on interpretations that avoid the direct consideration of the conflict. In this context, the question of the weight of the ECHR is analyzed with respect to the direct, and just as importantly, the indirect ways in which it influences national adjudication. Empirically, the authors look at the constitutional courts' case law when dealing with principles emanating from the Convention and the jurisprudence of the Strasbourg court. They explain how the supra-national norm acts as "a shadow constitution" in both countries considered.

In terms of transnational legal processes, this study showcases an example of "transfer" of human rights norms that happens with minor obstacles and judicial resistance. It is interesting to note the compatibility of the notions of *constitutionality* with *conventionality* (referring to the ECHR) in that respect. It is also worth inquiring as to the extent to which such unconditional "import" of the interpretation of human rights is without dangers.

At the other end of the spectrum, Wojcik is the second to address obstacles to transnational legal processes, again in the context of the United States, in his chapter about legislative attempts to prohibit the use of international law and Islamic law in US courts. It is also an interesting counterpoint to Ali Abid's contribution. Wojcik explains how globalization necessitates the increasing use of foreign law in US courts. Examples include transnational contract disputes, family law matters involving custody or visitation rights of parents and children in different countries, and other criminal and civil litigation matters that may touch upon involving some substantive provision of international or foreign law. In many cases, this is not controversial. However, some courts in the United States may find themselves at the center of political controversies entirely unrelated to the actual type of transnational disputes that end up in court. In some states, proposed legislation – and even amendments to state constitutions – have been introduced to restrict the sources of law that courts may consider in cases brought before them. Some proposals seek to limit the ability of courts to consider "foreign" and "international" law. Remarkably, some proposals even purport to preclude state courts from considering treaties ratified by the United States (which, under the US Constitution, are to be considered as Supreme Law of the Land and controlling over inconsistent state laws). Other proposals go even a step further, prohibiting US courts from considering not only international and foreign law in general, but in particular from considering "Islamic law" or "Shari'a law." The proponents of proposals to ban US courts from considering "Islamic law" or "Shari'a law" allege that there is a campaign of "creeping Islam" that will infect the state and federal courts.

Supporters of these proposals play on the fear and confusion of Americans concerning Islamic fundamentalists. Wojcik's chapter uses Oklahoma's recent state constitutional amendment banning state courts from using international or Islamic law as a case study. Wojcik begins with the background to citing international and foreign law in US court decisions. He highlights four examples of US Supreme court decisions that cited foreign law, igniting controversy amongst Americans. He points out that the controversy is not limited to decisions of the US Supreme

Court, citing a Massachusetts state court case that was criticized for the same reason. Wojcik then moves on to attempts to prohibit the use of Islamic law in US courts, focusing on Oklahoma. He looks at the legislative history and the resulting challenge in the US federal court, which found that the amendment prohibited the amendment from taking effect. Finally, Wojcik's contribution makes observations on the trend in the United States to oppose the use of foreign law and the implications for the transnational legal process.

Carole J. Petersen's contribution explores how the treaty body reporting process influences transnational legal processes. Petersen uses the reporting process in Mainland China and Hong Kong as her case study. She explains that, while China has a history of resistance to human rights monitoring, it has ratified six of the nine United Nations Core Treaties, each with reporting requirements. In addition, China is increasingly involved in the United Nations. Petersen posits that, if the reporting process is effective, then there should be meaningful exchanges and improvements in human rights as a result of the government's dialogues with treaty bodies. Petersen compares the reporting process in Mainland China and Hong Kong, pointing out that the separation of the reporting process between the two provides a useful comparison in the impact of human rights treaties.

The second part of Petersen's chapter briefly introduces the UN system of human rights treaties and the treaty-monitoring bodies. In this section, Petersen highlights the importance of the treaty monitoring process, stating that the reporting process is the chief international enforcement mechanism. We can also see the place of non-governmental organizations (NGOs) in the transnational legal process of human rights norm creation, as treaty-monitoring bodies depend upon NGOs to raise issues that governments would prefer to ignore. The third section discusses Hong Kong, noting the constitutional significance of human rights treaties but focusing primarily on the reporting process. Petersen shows in this section how the International Covenant on Civil and Political Rights (ICCPR) has been instrumental in influencing the domestic rights framework, because the courts enforce it and "government lawyers readily acknowledge that a local law must be declared invalid if it cannot be interpreted in a way that is consistent with the ICCPR." The women's movement is a good example of this. Petersen also shows places where international law does not have an impact on domestic law in Hong Kong, such in the case of sexual minority protection. The next section discusses the situation in Mainland China, analyzing the government's approach to the reporting process and the reasons why international human rights treaties still have less impact in Mainland China than in Hong Kong. Petersen asks

> how should the treaty-monitoring bodies assess China's reports and its progress since it began participating in the reporting process? On one hand, there is no question that the quality of life has improved in the past 20 years for a large percentage of China's population. The majority of citizens also enjoy greater freedom and access to information than they did in the 1980s. However, there are still many sensitive topics that cannot be freely discussed and the government

> does not hesitate to assert its control over political dissidents and others who challenge the one-party state.[32]

She also points to violations of the rights of minority groups. She then explores the very important question of whether China's participation in the UN treaty process is making a difference in the human rights of political dissidents and concludes that very little difference can be observed. However, Petersen believes that China's position of the Convention on the Rights of Persons with Disabilities (CRPD) may be an important change for the better and calls for further study of the treaty's implementation in China.

Peterson concludes her contribution with the observation that Hong Kong and China should continue to submit separate reports. She states that the separate treaty monitoring process has given the people of Hong Kong assurance that their autonomy has some meaning. Her outlook on China is more dismal, as she states,

> it is far more difficult to draw conclusions on the impact of transnational human rights processes in Mainland China. On one hand, China should be congratulated for ratifying treaties, especially for ratifying the CRPD quickly and without reservations. However, Beijing's decreased reliance on reservations does not necessarily reflect a greater intent to comply with treaties. It may be that the Chinese government now perceives the international reporting process as being fairly weak and that it has therefore adopted a new strategy – one of ratifying without reservations and then simply denying that any conflicts exist between treaty obligations and the government's practices and policies. It falls to the treaty-monitoring bodies to seek a broad range of information from NGOs and to continually remind Beijing of its obligations.

The contribution by Ali Abid is the second chapter dealing with anti-Islamic sentiment and is concerned with the human rights implications of defamation resolutions submitted to the United Nations Human Rights Commission. These resolutions are in response to the media's supposed hostility to Islam. Abid points out that Western states oppose the resolutions as threats to the freedoms of expression and religion, while states defend the resolutions and their domestic blasphemy law by alluding to Islamic law's supremacy over international law. He raises the following questions in conjunction with his inquiry: (1) whether the resolutions do indeed violate freedoms protected under international covenants; (2) whether the resolutions might actually support domestic blasphemy laws and what the consequences might be; (3) and – perhaps most importantly – whether anti-blasphemy or defamation of religion laws are actually condoned within Islamic theology.

Abid proposes that these resolutions be opposed on two fronts: appealing to international human rights and arguing against them from within Islamic tradition.

---

32 Chapter 7.

His chapter shows how the two can work together to influence and enhance rights in both traditions. The second section of this chapter outlines the history of the defamation resolutions and their content. Abid then illustrates how the resolutions are in contravention of the right to freedom of expression guaranteed internationally. The fourth section enters into a case study of the blasphemy laws of Pakistan, how and why they were adopted, and their consequences. The fifth section examines the place of religious plurality and respect towards non-Muslims in Islamic theology and how Islamic theology has developed historically with respect to these ideas. Finally, Abid proposes that opponents of the defamation resolutions argue by using the Islamic tradition and addresses certain objections regarding comparative ethics and the ability to affect change within a tradition from the outside.

The value of Abid's inquiry is that it examines how religious law in general and Islamic law in particular influences human rights law, especially where state powers use religious authority to consolidate state power, as Abid shows with the example of General Zia's rule in Pakistan. Abid also explains how a binding international instrument prohibiting blasphemy would legitimize these state laws and cast Islam as a religion opposed to pluralism and make Islam more open to criticism that Islam is incompatible with human rights – the very thing the resolutions seek to remedy. Abid concludes by stating that

> the anti-defamation resolutions represent a fascinating moment in comparative ethics and transnational legal processes. These resolutions explicitly seek to govern dialogues across religious communities on an international arena. They set against each other alleged principles of Islam with those of international human rights and subject them to a vote. The cause of this seeming conflict has been the product of many centuries of debate within the Islamic world and a lack of dialogue between the Islamic world and the West. It is in this moment that we should take up with renewed sincerity an effort to understand and to speak into each others' religious traditions so that the divisions we see in the world may start to mend.[33]

The following chapter in the same section of the book is a contribution on the protection of difference within human rights traditions, and focuses on human rights in Africa. Lauren Fielder's study examines the transnational legal processes involved in transferring international human rights norms to constitutional law in African states. It does this by examining how constitutional courts in African enforce gender equality. Fielder specifically looks at how constitutional courts balance the right to gender equality and the right to culture and custom. She points out that, in Africa, a strong tradition of custom (a right found in many African constitutions) intersects with international human rights obligations, this tension manifesting itself in many situations, such as inheritance, child marriage, bride

33 Chapter 8.

price, divorce law and polygamy. In fleshing out how the courts deal with this tension, the chapter looks at the international human rights obligations to gender equality that most African states have signed up to, then examines the right to culture and explains how it conflicts with these rights. In doing so, Fielder argues that culture is an irreducible social good with great value and significance to Africans. Next, the legitimacy of the transnational process of the application of international human rights by constitutional courts is examined. Human rights transference is problematic in the African context because of the colonial history and the related fear that the application of human rights threatens culture. Finally, the chapter examines traditional African values and explores how courts may be able to incorporate them into their decisions to harmonize the right to culture with international human rights law. Examples of typical African values include dignity, community orientation, the concept of duties and *Ubuntu* (humanity towards others). This is a valuable contribution to this volume, because it illustrates how transnational legal processes work in two directions: international law influences constitutional and customary law, while customary law can shape human rights. Fielder concludes by saying that

> African courts can add legitimacy to their decisions when balancing the right to culture and the right to gender equality by interpreting their international human rights obligations in the light of long-standing African values. Courts can borrow from the decisions of other State constitutional courts in making this interpretation, building a pan-African jurisprudence that will further stabilize constitutionalism in the region and finally give Africa a place at the table in the development of global human rights law.[34]

The final chapter focusing on the ways in which human rights are shaped through transnational legal processes, returns to religious identity, but this time in the field of education in European classrooms. Kyriaki Topidi looks at the legal situation in education with regards to the protection and promotion of religious diversity. The author assumes that human rights are not fixed constructions that are included on our legal systems by agreement. She then demonstrates through her empirical analysis of the Swiss and British systems of adjudicating religious identity conflicts in the classrooms why transnational law and transnational legal processes have become necessary to address these conflicts. To do so, her discussion is theoretically pinned between the concepts of *legal pluralism* and *constitutionalism* in order to show the benefits and limitations of these options as applied in practice. At the outset, and on a preliminary basis Topidi also includes the necessary background on state neutrality and secularism.

In terms of the broader focus of this volume, she reaches a conclusion, sourcing her observations from both domestic and European case law on the matter of the revisiting of international law in order to formulate a new understanding of

34 Chapter 9.

universal claims that places religion at its center. The classic judicial responses to claims related to religious symbols or exemptions, for instance, are inconsistent and unsatisfactory from both an individual and a collective rights perspective. In her view, legal pluralism and all direct or indirect attempts to introduce it in the European continent demonstrate precisely the intensity of transnationalization of law, the increasing number of (conflicting) authorities in action within the European legal sphere on religious rights and the effects of legal fragmentation brought about as a result of migration in Europe. This type of legal fragmentation suggests an equivalent type of fragmentation within each European state, as the Swiss and British case studies, among others, show. Indirectly, thus, diasporic or other social spheres call more and more for transnational responses to religious identity claims in multicultural social settings.

The final part of the book looks at how economic entities influence the transnational legal process of human rights norm creation. The contribution by Deval Desai is a study of agreements between transnational mining companies and indigenous communities. His work shows how these economic agreements are part of the process of norm creation in the sphere of indigenous rights and global governance for mining companies. In particular, Desai's work shows how agreements influence international theory and practice and also state law concerning indigenous rights to share the benefits of mining. It is a valuable contribution to the study of intersections between negotiated agreements and indigenous rights.

Desai explains how the economic agreements have embedded their narratives in the judicial imaging of indigenous peoples, citing the famous Awas Tigni case. He defines what these agreements are and places these agreements in two discursive frames: (1) the Rousseaulian *homme sauvage*; and (2) the idea of indigenous ties to land as a rights- or claims-based discourse. Desai then illustrates how the "indigenous rights professional" is a central interlocutor that shapes the discourse as well. This is important to our study, as we see how individuals (or NGOs as the case may be) influence transnational legal processes. Desai goes into great detail, setting forth narratives of law, narratives of actors and narratives of the indigenous rights professional shaping this process.

Desai's conclusion offers the following observations: mining agreements may become the norm; mining agreements have an embedded narrative of indigenity; law is not always good, and agreements have (identity) politics; the politics of an agreement is not always desirable, giving rise to strategic implications; the indigenous rights professional has a vested interest in deploying agreements; and these vested interests can be to the detriment of the indigenous community.

Angelica Tsakiridis, the contributor of the last chapter, continues this theme: how economic entities affect the process of norm creation. Tsakiridis looks at the devastating effects of multinational corporate actors on Angola and the problems of domestic efforts to police these actors. Her solution is a valuable and novel one: the internationalization of constitutional law. Tsakiridis describes internationalizing constitutional law as a process by which international human rights protection is expanded and strengthened by developing a constitutional law program that includes these protections. This transfers international human rights protections to the domestic law framework, making multinational corporate actors more vulnerable to censor when they violate human rights as part of their economic activities. This greatly expands the enforceability of human rights protections, thus impacting standards of corporate responsibility. We can see here several layers of transnational legal processes at work.

The contributor uses as a case study,

> atrocities committed on a massive scale during Angola's 21-year civil war between Angolan state and quasi-state ("rebel") actors. There, [multinational corporations] in the oil and gas industries directly and indirectly sanctioned and facilitated human rights atrocities against Angolan citizens, including rape, torture, displacement and extrajudicial killings, financed through direct and indirect payments to remain in the country and in joint ventures with Angola's parastatal oil corporation "Sonangol".[35]

She also compares these problems with inadequate legal structures in the United States to combat these problems (such as corruption and other corporate abuses).

The chapter then focuses on a theory of universal responsibility as its basis for the internationalization of constitutional law she describes. This could be accomplished by creating systems that recognize a cause of action against multinational corporate actors and impose liability on these actors for violation of these laws, and by cultivating a jurisprudence of international law that recognizes those claims. Tsakiridis points out that there is a connection between political instability, corruption and human rights abuses, and shows how multinational actors' involvement in a community compounds this corruption, human rights violation and therefore, instability, necessitating a more robust solution.

Her conclusion is that constitutionalization of human rights in accordance with existing legal frameworks (such as the International Criminal Court, The European Court of Human Rights and the Inter-American Court of Human Rights) is the solution to corporate abuses by multinationals. She explains that these existing fora should maintain diversity, and, with the appropriate measures to constitutionalism human rights claims brought against MNCs, have real power to administer meaningful consequences for violations. This collaboration will encourage local actors who are historically disenfranchised and therefore unengaged in traditional models for international planning and policy-making. Effective, international accountability models must be rooted in ethnically, socially, politically and economically diverse norms and expectations, in order to support transparent and fair outcomes, and these fora connect victims to the wider world.

Overall, this volume has the ambition of pushing the discussion on transnational legal processes and human rights a step further by sourcing itself from a rich

35 Chapter 12.

diversity of legal systems, a variety of perspectives and an extensive list of human rights concerned in each case.

# PART I
# The Construction and Evolution of Human Rights Norms in Transnational Legal Settings

Chapter 2

# Universal Human Rights and Cultural Relativity: Conflict or Reconciliation?

Ehsanul Haque

## Introduction

The philosophy of human rights occupies a characteristic, decisive role in the contemporary world as it entails a vision of justice. Although disagreements, controversies and divergences play out in the human rights discourses, the concept is cogent in its broad appeal, devising a yardstick for monitoring, assessing and judging the relationship between national governments and their citizens, whereby governance is meant to add to the dignity of human beings, not to abuse them.

As a matter of fact, human rights are a set of protections and entitlements held by all members of the human species – regardless of race, class, gender, sexual orientation, cultural background or national origin (Frezzo 2012). Human rights are intrinsically *individualistic* – they are rights exercised by individuals in relation to, even against, the state and society (Donnelly 1984). Such rights can be "the language of the victims and the dispossessed" (Donnelly 1998: 20). They are seen as a benchmark for all countries – strong and weak, large and small. The human rights regime pushes states to recognize and support individual and group agency by treating *all* as worthy of respect and dignity and fair treatment (Mertus 2003). The attainment of human rights is *political* as human rights translate, reflect and challenge claims to power; and *nonviolent* as they are propagated and enforced through a regime of international norms, ideas, beliefs and treaties (Baxi 1999, cited in Mertus 2003).

The approach to human rights, primarily a legal one, strives to be nonpartisan, nonparochial or neutral among conflicting political cultures and ideologies (Beitz 2001). However, international law relating to human rights is "not a value-neutral ideology; historically, it is rooted in revolt against the barbarism human governments are universally capable of" (Li-ann 2004: 41). Human rights are thus dignity- and autonomy-enabling rights intended to fulfill a dedicated commitment to the equal worth and dignity of each and every individual (Donnelly 2003). In the contemporary world, human rights instruments are used as immense and compelling bodies of law against modern states' incursions into civil freedom and liberties.

It is axiomatic that human rights represent a common element in an array of views about social justice and political legitimacy found among the world's multitude of cultures (Beitz 2001), and human rights law adheres to the vulnerable individual's protection, recognizing that the state can both safeguard and intimidate its people. It seeks, through a range of international standards and external modes of accountability, to advance and guard human dignity, through the legal technique of "rights" or justiciable entitlements asserted against the modern state (Li-ann 2004). The basic tenet of human rights, thus, epitomizes a moral touchstone – a criterion of appraisal of domestic institutions, a standard of aspiration for their reform and a method of evaluation for the policies and practices of international economic and political institutions.

As opposed to the stereotypical image of human rights as universal, there has been a fierce debate as to whether moral values are universal or relative/specific to the culture they are found in. In recent years, this debate has featured in the pronouncements of statesmen, the writings of academics and arguments and counter-arguments advanced by the human rights advocates/activists and cultural relativists. Opponents have challenged the oft-presumed universal character of human rights, arguing that the meanings, nuances and validity of human rights are relative to particular cultural, social and political contexts. Arguably, the universalist vs. relativist debate has been dauntingly complex and ostensibly unending.

The focus of this chapter falls on the controversies and debates concerning universal human rights vs. cultural relativity. It showcases and compares the dominant views relating to universalism and cultural relativism, identifies the strengths and weaknesses of both ideals, fleshes out the core issues of the debate between the two doctrines, and finally highlights the prospects of reconciliation between the two seemingly competing and opposing theories.

## Framing an International Human Rights Regime

International concerns for human rights did not actually coalesce until the end of World War II as a response to the outrageous denials of rights that were evident during the war. Post-war visionaries with much determination and dedication thus set out to champion the cause of international human rights as never before. The global community witnessed the beginning of a formal recognition of the human rights regime and in 1948 the United Nations General Assembly unanimously and unequivocally adopted the Universal Declaration of Human Rights (UDHR). This Declaration is regarded as one of the most extensive guarantees of human rights worldwide. It begins by stating that the recognition "of the inherent dignity and of the equal and inalienable rights of all members of the human family is the foundation of freedom, justice, and peace in the world" (Preamble, UDHR). The Declaration marked the beginning of the end to triumphant statism in world history (Booth 1999) as it brought the individual to the center. The idea was that, at least theoretically, states would no longer be allowed to cloak with a veil of sovereignty the actual treatment of their citizens. By launching a human rights revolution, the UDHR assumed political, moral and legal connotation and it propelled human rights from the margins of international relations to one of its central pillars (Lauren 2008). In any case, the UDHR is not technically binding in the manner of an international treaty; it is only a recommendation with no provisions for compliance and enforcement. However, it has had considerable impact on thinking at the global level and has validated concerns with human rights; it has even been incorporated into the national constitutions of several countries (Barash and Webel 2002).

A range of worldwide legal instruments have been built on the UN Charter and the UDHR, including an array of covenants, conventions, treaties and declarations of diverse legal meanings – all intended to further clarify the concept of human rights. The UDHR along with two milestone covenants – the International Covenant on Civil and Political Rights and the International Covenant on Economic, Social and Cultural Rights (both adopted in 1966 and entered into force in 1976) – are collectively referred to as the International Bill of Rights, which constitutes an authoritative catalogue of globally recognized human rights. They prevent governments from interfering with freedom of thought, conscience and religion, and from engaging in brutal activities such as torture (Musalo 2010). Beitz (2001) classifies the rights laid out in these documents and states that internationally recognized human rights fall into the following categories:

1. Rights of the person refer to life, liberty, and security of the person; privacy and freedom of movement; ownership of property; freedom of thought, conscience and religion, including freedom of religious teaching and practice "in public and private"; and prohibition of slavery, torture and cruel or degrading punishment.
2. Rights associated with the rule of law include equal recognition before the law and equal protection of the law; effective legal remedy for violation of legal rights; impartial hearing and trial; presumption of innocence; and prohibition of arbitrary arrest.
3. Political rights encompass freedom of expression, assembly, and association; the right to take part in government; and periodic and genuine elections by universal and equal suffrage.
4. Economic and social rights refer to an adequate standard of living; free choice of employment; protection against unemployment; "just and favorable remuneration"; the right to join trade unions; "reasonable limitation of working hours"; free elementary education; social security; and the "highest attainable standard of physical and mental health".
5. Rights of communities include self-determination and protection of minority cultures.

Other international agreements have elaborated and enlarged the scope of human rights in areas such as genocide, slavery and forced labor, racial discrimination, apartheid, discrimination against women, and the rights of children.

There is much agreement that the contemporary international human rights regime has profoundly been influenced by Western philosophical traditions and ideas. The Western conception of human rights has several manifestations: (a) *individuality* – each human being is considered to be a separate, distinct whole; (b) *moral agency* – each person is a free, autonomous agency; (c) *moral equality* – each individual is deemed inherently equal; (d) *rationality* – each individual has access to reason; and (e) *individual integrity* – each person inherently possesses dignity concomitant with his or her individuality (Skubik 1992).

## The Core of Universalism and its Appeals

If human rights are entitlements one possesses by dint of being human, these are then obviously universal in nature and scope (Li-ann 2004). In actuality, the universal recognition and acceptance of human rights as a method for accomplishing human dignity is maximally undisputed and well recognized. Universalism suggests that human rights are inherent in the individual, regardless of his or her nationality, ethnicity or socio-economic status. From this standpoint, human rights are *not* granted either by the state or law; rather such rights are intrinsic in humanity. Every individual is born with the same rights, making human rights *absolute* for all human beings. The UDHR, at its core, supports the idea that there are certain universal human rights that the international community has accepted (Harrelson-Stephens and Callaway 2007). Nearly all UN human rights documents/instruments, explicitly or implicitly, assume the universal character of human rights, their indivisibility and equal importance.

More than six decades after the UDHR was drafted, there arises a legitimate question whether people around the world think that the Declaration still reflects a universally accepted notion of human rights. According to one group of experts, the validity and relevance of the UDHR continues to be widely and decidedly reaffirmed based on two beliefs: (a) that human rights and freedoms are innate in the nature and dignity of each human being; and (b) that there is a strong urge for a globally accepted set of basic ethical standards and principles that is unvaryingly applicable to all cultures, religions and political systems. In fact, the efforts of the UN, in close collaboration with national governments, courts of law and civil society activists, as well as national, regional and international human rights institutions, have effectively built a *global constituency* in support of the UDHR principles (World Federation of United Nations Associations 2008). A shared comprehension of human rights norms, principles and current debates is, hence, crucial for their full realization and with this vision the UDHR was adopted as the first global proclamation that acknowledged the universality of human rights. This document is now considered one of the solid pillars of international human rights law.

The moral fiber and resolve of the UDHR was reaffirmed in the Vienna Declaration, 1993. The Declaration affirms that the universal nature of these rights and freedoms is "beyond question." The universality of human rights is asserted as the basis for the obligation incumbent upon states to promote and protect those rights. The Declaration also affirms that all human rights are not only universal and indivisible but are also interdependent and interrelated, and that it is the responsibility of states, regardless of their political, economic and cultural systems, to promote and protect all human rights and fundamental freedoms. Nevertheless, the attainment of these rights and freedoms varies from society to society.

## Contesting Universalism

Response to universalism from people belonging to other cultures is sometimes apathetic, albeit many Westerners presume that the former would endorse their steps favoring global human rights. This has resonance with the "moral arrogance" of the West that drives Westerners to export the Western version of human rights to other societies (Barash and Webel 2002: 446). Detractors, being wary of Western intentions, claim that universalism evokes colonial practices and add that one group assumes superiority over the other and bases its values, ethics and power on that assumption (Ife 2001; Harris-Short 2003). On the "imperialistic character" of universal human rights, Ignatieff (2001: 102) gives his version in the following words:

> Human rights doctrine is now so powerful, but also so unthinkingly imperialist in its claim to universality, that it has exposed itself to serious intellectual attack. These challenges have raised important questions about whether human rights norms deserve the authority they have acquired: Whether their claims to universality are justified, or whether they are just another cunning exercise in Western moral imperialism.

Then again, Ignatieff (2001) believes that, although inordinate individualism in Western human rights doctrine has been a subject of much controversy and criticism even in the West itself, universal human rights are not only popular; they are also indispensable because they defend and protect individuals against group authority.

Since human rights in today's world are interpreted, publicized, promoted and championed by the world's leading political, economic, military and cultural powers, the entire notion of human rights has become "ideologically hegemonic" in global society (Donnelly 2007). Consequently, the contemporary international human rights regime has, to a great extent, been shaped and influenced by the Western world, which explains the dominance of the liberal democratic traditions in the literature and practice of human rights in comparison to inadequate coverage of the issue in the non-Western world.

Critics and skeptics claim that human rights are a Western construct that does not fit well with societies based on different values and traditions. Such a position is generally held by the non-Western world, but interestingly, related views are held by few in the West as well. In 1947, the American Anthropological Association issued the following "Statement on Human Rights" that was submitted to the UN Commission on Human Rights, cautioning about the risks of incorporating Western cultural values into the Draft UDHR:

> It will not be convincing to the Indonesian, the African, the Indian, the Chinese, if it lies on the same plane as like documents of an earlier period. The rights of man in the Twentieth Century cannot be circumscribed by the standards of any single culture or be dictated by the aspirations of any single people. Such a document will lead to frustration, not realization of the personalities of vast numbers of human beings. (American Anthropological Association 1947: 543)

Brown (1992: 110) regarded the UDHR as "unwieldy, cumbersome and often self-contardictory in its specific provisions." In fact, the UDHR is the product of such a period when the UN was dominated by the West, and thus quite understandably the Declaration mirrored a Western conception of human rights couched in their language. The drafters of the Declaration, enthused by the spirit of creating an ideal world, believed that the Western philosophy provided the most appropriate framework for a universal code and thus, ought to be extended to the rest of the world. However, in 1948 the vast majority of Afro-Asian countries were under Western colonial tutelage and, with the attainment of their independence, the legitimacy of that assumption of the West came under attack, resulting in the contention that there is more than one value system and giving rise to skepticism as to whether a universal consensus on human rights is a viable idea. It is claimed that even now these countries of the global South have little voice and choice in the human rights deliberations largely influenced by Western perceptions and priorities.

There are allegations that advocates of universalism, by and large, propagate Western moral standards, and thereby any attempt to establish or impose universal human rights standards amounts to cultural imperialism. It is against this backdrop that several brands of human rights have emerged – Asian values, African values and Islamic values (Harrelson-Stephens and Callaway 2007) – making human rights a fragmented issue. Another critical view suggests that international human rights norms are little more than legal pronouncements – the high-handed dictates of the powerful nations of the world, engaging in modern "colonization" impose their standards on less powerful nations (Musalo 2010).

## The Ascendancy of Cultural Relativity: "De-Westernizing" Human Rights?

The essence of cultural relativity implies that the ingredients of a culture are not dependent on any absolutes outside that culture and above all other cultures. Instead, they vary in line with the background and development and natural habitat of the particular culture. "Ingredients" refer to social customs, religious rituals, mythology and attitudes towards nature and other peoples (Ruggiero 1992). In addition, each culture or society possesses its own rationality, coherence and set of values (Booth 1999). In this sense, the idea of human rights itself is "a historically circumscribed and context-bound phenomenon" (Rao 1995: 168). In the words of anthropologist Kluckhohn (1944: 43):

> The principle of cultural relativity does not mean that because the members of some savage tribe are allowed to behave in a certain way that this fact gives intellectual warrant for such behavior in all groups. Cultural relativity means, on the contrary, that the appropriateness of any positive or negative custom must be evaluated with regard to how this habit fits with other group habits.

Thus, cultural relativism – as posited against universal values – is the idea that each culture is to be evaluated on the basis of its own values and norms of behavior and *not* on the basis of those of another culture. Simply put, proponents of cultural relativism contend that one culture's practices and beliefs should not be judged by the standards of another. The fundamental principle out of which cultural relativism emerges is – "judgments are based on experience, and experience is interpreted by each individual in terms of his or her own enculturation" (Herskovits 1973: 15). As a result, people in different cultural settings and with different social standings think and act differently (Mannheim 1936). Put differently, cultural relativists claim that fundamentally different standards of morality, practices and belief systems operate in diverse cultures and they cannot be measured with a yardstick alien to them. Cultural relativism thus holds that there *is* a basic incommensurability between the value systems of different cultures (Edgar and Sedgwick 2002). Moreover, cultural relativism not only stresses morals, ethics and values; it is also related to the judgments of time and space and volume, and contrasts in perception and cognition, as well as conduct (Herskovits 1973). Each culture is to be looked at in terms of its own structure and values instead of being judged by the standards of any other civilization acclaimed as absolute (Kroeber 1950). Bozeman (1971) puts forward several views that are worth mentioning: (a) there exist fundamental differences between Western legal theories and cultures and those of Africa, Asia, India and Islam; (b) in order to fully comprehend a culture, one must be a product of that culture; (c) even if a culture were to borrow a concept from another culture, that concept's meaning would be filtered through the first culture's unique linguistic–conceptual culture; (d) there can be no universal meaning to a moral value; and (e) a universal text on values would not enjoy widespread support.

Unlike universalism, cultural relativism is the assertion that human values are context-specific and hence their interpretation, promotion and implementation are subject solely to the cultural norms and specificities of the society concerned (Pollis and Schwab 2000). In human rights discourses, cultural relativism typically "appears as a substantive normative doctrine that demands respect for cultural differences" (Donnelly 2007: 294). The notion of cultural relativism further suggests that local cultural traditions – religious, political and legal practices – determine the existence and scope of civil and political rights enjoyed by individuals. However, cultural relativists see other cultures, not as "wrong," but as "different," and they assert that we cannot regulate and control social behaviors. For that reason, cultural relativists argue that what one society calls a human rights violation, another might regard as a legitimate cultural practice. Therefore, Ignatieff (2001) emphatically states that human rights processes, policies and practices should not undermine traditional cultures and norms. It is in this context that, although states formally recognize the value and appeal of universality, they proclaim that a country's human rights situation should not be judged in total disregard of its historical, cultural and national conditions. For example, in the 1993 Bangkok NGO Declaration of Human Rights, the East Asian leaders acknowledged and accepted the universal validity of human rights, but argued that these needed to be well defined, balanced and weighted in the light of local history, culture and religious backgrounds (Parekh 2000, Iovane 2007).

## Against Cultural Relativism

Fierce criticisms are leveled against cultural relativism by many analysts. Müllerson (1997: 73), for instance, writes: "although there may be no human rights paradise in the world, there are quite a few human rights hells where none of the rights and freedoms solemnly proclaimed in the UN documents are applied in practice." Hartung (1954: 118) denounces the theory of relativism while he states:

> Cultural relativity is flying under false colors; it claims to be empirical but is illogical; it claims to be objective but is surreptitiously moral; it claims to be reasonable but elevates irrationalism; it claims to be scientific but prevents the development of an experimental science of sociocultural conduct.

At its most extreme, cultural relativism contends that there is no superior, international or universal morality, and that the moral and ethical rules of all cultures merit equal respect (Kottak 2000). Booth (1999) labels cultural relativism as one of the "tyrannies" in the world, tyrannizing human rights, and asserts that such practices reduce/weaken social and political explanations of culture. He further maintains that relativism overstates the self-contained nature of societies and, by producing and privileging traditionalism, favors elites to the detriment of the interests of the mass of people. Zechenter (1997) is scathingly critical of the relativist theory as most of its formulations are contradictory and tautological, tending to legitimize the dysfunctional beliefs and customs of non-Western cultures while silencing nondominant voices in those societies. She holds a circumspect view that, if relativism were to undermine the universalist foundations of international human rights law, culturally sanctioned breaches of individual rights would be validated and hence individuals would stay unprotected against rulers, governments and others in power. However, playing down traditionalism does not mean brushing aside traditions, as in modern societies the role of traditions cannot be discounted.

In the contemporary world, human rights campaigners and practitioners contest many of the precepts of cultural relativism. In fact, the very idea of human rights questions the validity and full implementation of cultural relativism by invoking a realm of justice and morality beyond particular countries, cultures and religions. Human rights, as seen by the universalists, are vested in individuals and these rights are *not* mundane laws that specific governments merely formulate and enforce – rather they are seen as *inalienable* (nations cannot either abridge or abrogate them) and *international* (wider than individual nations and cultures). Within the state-based framework of mainstream human rights, the "culture defense" sounds shaky when placed in the context of urbanization, industrialization, the rapidly expanding bureaucratic machinery, communication systems that greatly enhance state control, and systems that link national economies to the global economy (Rao 1995).

Deplorably, the doctrine of cultural relativism has been manipulated and capitalized on by some countries and their leaders to legitimize their egregious and horrendous violations of human rights, although such malpractices leave out any philosophical or cultural justification. Scruton (1994: 32) observes: "in argument about moral problems, relativism is the first refuge of the scoundrel" (cited in Müllerson 1997). It is true that, for many "scoundrels," relativism is a convenient pretext for the disavowal of human rights as an alien concept. In such cases, sovereignty is often used to shield regimes that breach both ethical self-determination and most internationally recognized human rights (Donnelly 2007). For example, under the rubric of "Asian values" (which hold the primacy of group rights over individual rights), countries like Singapore, China and Malaysia have for long argued that they have a distinctive historical and cultural legacy and thus that their core values are at variance with Western conceptions of democracy and human rights. Attempts to "impose" Western values or to claim their moral superiority are bitterly criticized as "cultural imperialism" and a sign of disregard for these Asian civilizations and heritages. While justifying their authoritarianism, these countries further argue that some of the political and civil rights found in the international human rights doctrine – mainly freedom of expression and political participation – are incompatible and incommensurate with traditional Asian political beliefs, which value social harmony over public dispute and the collective pursuit of shared interests over the individual pursuit of private interest (Iriye and Goedde 2012, Beitz 2001). Thus, the leaders of these countries are apt to reject any criticisms of their human rights records as unwarranted interference in their domestic affairs because, as they claim, their distinct cultures do not support such interventions. As another illustration, women in many societies are unable to define what constitutes "culture" – laws/customs are introduced that violate women's rights but they are defended by their societies on cultural grounds. So, while it may be true that restricting education for women has historically been part of some cultures, that does not justify the continuation of that practice (Campbell et al 2010).

It goes without saying that one of the positive aspects of relativism is its recognition and respect of cultural plurality. However, the relativists' indifference to and unconcern about horrendous practices such as genocide, cannibalism and torture, and other atrocious approaches to human beings, must not be connived with.

## Interface between Universalism and Relativism: The Controversy and Discourse

On the surface, human rights do not appear to be neutral because they conflict with practices endorsed by one or another of the world's major conventional beliefs and moralities. As we have seen, human rights academics have advanced opposing theories of rights that compete for primacy. The most passionate debate among human rights adherents center on the dichotomy between the divergent positions held by the universalists and cultural relativists. The resulting tension continues to engulf the human rights agenda across the world.

While the adoption of the UDHR knits the states of the world together and aims to address human rights issues under one umbrella, it does so in political and moral senses – the legal weight it carries is not a heavy one. In addition, when challenging the universality of human rights, the developing countries tend to advance three key arguments: (a) they had little/no opportunity to give inputs to the drafting of the UDHR owing to their colonial status at that time; (b) the rights outlined in the declaration are ethnocentric, echoing Western conceptions and leaving out non-Western views on human rights; and (c) excessive emphasis has been put on the rights of the individual, often at the expense of the rights of groups and collectivities. As a result, states seek alternatives to the universal model of human rights (Harrelson-Stephens and Callaway 2007).

The global community witnesses cultural practices that lead to the perpetuation of a debate on sovereignty and the universality of human rights. In the twenty-first century, many states still perceive the human rights regime as "an assault on their sovereignty, and many societies see this as a threat to their way of life" (Harrelson-Stephens and Callaway 2007: 9). When enumerating the linkage between culture and universal human rights, two contrasting views appear. The first does not recognize that there is any nexus between the two, upholding a view that internationally recognized human rights solely flow from international legal instruments and can be preserved regardless of cultural variation according to existing international jurisprudence. The second discards universal human rights as being a Western construct imposed on the populations of the South. Some academics maintain that neither of these positions is correct as "no culture has a monopoly on human rights" (El Obaid and Rehman 2002: 1) and the notion of human rights is so extensive that it cannot be situated entirely within a single cultural tradition at a particular moment of history (El Obaid and Rehman 2002).

Cultural relativists make a case that rights and moral values cannot be established universally and thus human rights are not necessarily universal. It follows that the concept of universal human rights is far-fetched as the human rights movement has been driven by wealthy and powerful Western nations who have defined human rights in terms of the cultural tenets relevant in their own societies. The relativists argue that, as cultural norms significantly vary, Western standards should not be applied to non-Western cultures (Campbell et al., 2010). Conversely, the zealots of universal human rights assert that universality does not presuppose uniformity – the ideal signifies that such rights would be based on universally recognized and accepted principles that transcend cultural or religious diversities/boundaries. Universalism is, therefore, at the root of modern international law holding that there is an underlying human unity that entitles all individuals, irrespective of their cultural or regional antecedents, to certain basic minimal rights and that individual human beings have specific rights simply by virtue of being human (Zechenter 1997, Campbell et al. 2010). However, it is presupposed by the universalists that non-Western cultures will evolve by degrees, creating a space for universal doctrine of human rights to prevail. Therefore, a rigid approach to universality is likely to backfire. In turn, cultural relativists are at times unyielding and obdurate, assuming the fixity and irreversibility of traditional culture (Pollis 2000).

From the preceding analysis, it is clear that, in universalism, an individual is a social unit, possessing inalienable rights, and driven by the pursuit of self-interest. In the cultural relativist model, a community is the basic social unit. Concepts such as individualism, freedom of choice and equality are absent in a community. Incontestably, cultural relativism is somewhat problematic and vulnerable to abuse; however, universalism in its current form is not a panacea to the world's problems. Universalism, as the allegation runs, is used by many Western states to negate the validity of traditions and customs in the non-Western world. Proponents of universality maintain that the human rights that have been guaranteed in international treaties and conventions are universal, applicable to all countries, and should prevail even when they are at odds with cultural or religious practices. In contrast, advocates of cultural relativism reason that permitting international/universal norms to override the dictates of culture and religion is a violation of state sovereignty. In 1993, the former foreign minister of Singapore, Wong Kan Seng, in a statement at the UN Conference on Human Rights in Vienna, pronounced that "universal recognition of the ideal of human rights can be harmful if universalism is used to deny or mask the reality of diversity" (cited in Müllerson, 1997: 79). Evidently, the universalist approach to human rights was soft-pedaled in that conference when China, Malaysia, Singapore, Indonesia, Iran and Syria vociferously assumed a cultural relativist position by assailing the UDHR, and subsequently the final document included a clause stating that the global human rights standards should be tempered with "regional peculiarities and various historical, cultural and religious backgrounds" (Henkin et al. 1999: 112, Iriye and Goedde 2012). However, there has been a plethora of discussions and debates on the possibility of reconciliation between the two competing beliefs.

## Towards an Uncoerced Reconciliation between Universalism and Relativism

The foregoing discussion begs a fundamental question – how can the contending claims of cultural relativism and universal human rights be reconciled avoiding tensions and putting down dissensions? The discussion, of course, does not imply that the conflict is absolute and that there is no space for mutual inspiration and overlapping of categories that could be articulated for the purpose of consensus. It is true that neither universalism nor cultural relativism is immune from misinterpretation and political manipulation. We live in a world of cultural difference where the appeal of universalism is strong and sustainable and the philosophy of human rights suggests compromise instead of conflict for a better and more just world.

As regards a genuine, unforced international consensus on human rights, Taylor (1999) agrees with what Rawls (2005) illustrates in his *Political Liberalism* as an "overlapping consensus," with different groups, countries, religious communities and civilizations, reaching an agreement on certain norms that ought to govern human behavior. As stated by Taylor (1999: 124): "each would have its own way of justifying this from out of its profound background conception. We would agree on the norms while disagreeing on why they were the right norms, and we would be content to live in this consensus, undisturbed by the differences of profound underlying belief." In effect, convergent norms would be justified in very different underlying spiritual and philosophical outlooks. These cultural overlappings are universally shared categories that may be considered as social constructs that stem from common approaches to common problems that are encountered by different cultures (Wiredu 1996).

Even though vast differences exist in ideologies, levels and styles of economic development, and patterns of political evolution, practically all states today have adhered to the human rights standards articulated in the UDHR and the International Human Rights Covenants. The concept of human rights is, in reality, a reformulation of justice for the individual in a particular context. Donnelly (1984: 414–15) rightly observes:

> While human rights – inalienable entitlements of individuals held in relation to state and society – have not been a part of most cultural traditions, or even the Western tradition until rather recently, there is a striking similarity in many of the basic values that today we seek to protect through human rights. This is particularly true when these values are expressed in relatively general terms. Life, social order, protection from arbitrary rule, prohibition of inhuman and degrading treatment, the guarantee of a place in the life of the community, and access to an equitable share of the means of subsistence are central moral aspirations in nearly all cultures.

Moreover, Donnelly (2007) sensibly writes that the past legacies of colonialism demand both prudence and sensitivity on the part of the Western world when they advocate universalism vis-à-vis clashing cultural values. Mere exercises of universalism that permeate Western norms and values would meet "understandable suspicion, even resistance" (Donnelly 2007: 304).

To many analysts, cultural, religious or other traditions are not insurmountable impediments to a universal acceptance of basic human rights and their implementation as cultures and values are fluid, and with this flexibility arises the possibility of devising a truly universal approach reflecting the values of both worlds. Culture is resilient, capable of changing and making adjustments, although changes occur gradually compared with rapid changes in the economic and political spheres of society (Müllerson 1997). Thus, variations in cultural values and traditions do not *always* constitute obstacles to the universality of human rights. As Rao (1995: 172–3) maintains:

> In any event, culture is not a static, unchanging, identifiable body of information against which human rights may be measured for compatibility and applicability. Rather, culture is series of constantly contested and negotiated social practices whose meanings are influenced by the power and status of their interpreters and participants. Furthermore, culture is only one constituent part of the complex web of power relationships that circumscribes our existence.

Over time cultural values and traditions embrace accommodation and adaptation. Donnelly (2008) holds a view that cultures are astoundingly accommodating, adding that, although core values are invariable, those values, as the Western example illustrates, can be associated with diametrically opposed social practices – racism no less than equality; self-determination no less than imperialism. Almost every culture in the past was involved in practices that today we would consider gross and systematic violations of human rights. In addition, societies themselves change, bringing positive elements for delivering justice and dignity for all humanity. As Hobsbawm (1994: 9) observes: "in the 1980s, socialist Bulgaria and non-socialist Ecuador had more in common than either had with the Bulgaria or Ecuador of 1939" (cited in Müllerson 1997).

In the age of globalization, countries are experiencing sweeping transformations and adaptations. Indeed, globalization processes, driven by the rapid development of new information and communication technologies, are often perceived to be eroding cultural diversity, making the preservation of such diversity imperative. Unless the major civilizations of the world enter into a meaningful and result-oriented dialogue with each other, not only will the cultures face threats to their existence but also the fundamental rights of the human beings are likely to wither away.

Parekh (1999) states that, if universal values are to garner widespread support and enjoy democratic backing and be free of ethnocentric biases, they should arise out of an open and uncoerced cross-cultural dialogue. A cross-cultural dialogue and harmonious interaction should be promoted among individuals and groups having plural, varied and dynamic cultural identities as it will signify the common core of acceptable human rights.

In the same vein, intercultural promotion of human rights should be bolstered as it is one of the most effective means of resistance against the abuse of people. However, this requires the formulation of human rights based on the values of individual cultures and the opening of dialogue among them. Tensions between cultures and communities can be eased through dialogue, campaign, education and training and a willingness to learn from and to be respectful and tolerant of others. In today's world, there are plenty of spaces, places, structures and methods for intercultural dialogue. Such dialogue attempts to identify the current social norms through critical discussion/reflection and create new ones that might be shared by individual cultures in a universal way. The significant feature of the intercultural dialogue is the effort to ascertain a variety of transcultural features in common which can be shared by all cultures and therefore by the entire human civilization (Hrubec 2010). On many occasions, intercultural dialogue "requires a deconstruction and reconstruction of power and power relations" (Karsten and Küntzel 2006: 10). Such a dialogue is not the exclusive domain of the state or civil society – it requires cooperation and calls for the co-creation of something new that can be commonly shared.

In fact, human rights and cultural diversity are intertwined and co-constitutive – full respect for human rights creates an environment for, and is, a guarantee of cultural diversity; simultaneously, sensitivity to issues of cultural legitimacy will facilitate the implementation of human rights as understood by the universalists. Cultural diversity can only thrive in an environment that safeguards fundamental freedoms and human rights, which are universal, indivisible, interconnected and interdependent (Shaheed et al. 2010). Although different cultures have different norms and values, there are more resemblances between multiplicity of cultures than a cursory glance would reveal (Müllerson 1997). As Walzer (1994: 8) notes: "every human society is universal because it is human, particular because it is a society" (cited in Müllerson, 1997). Therefore, any hard-nosed global approach to human rights regime stubbornly unaccommodative of socio-cultural traditions is unlikely to secure broad support from the world arena.

It should be borne in mind that the universal character of human rights *does not* extend to their forced implementation. Rather, international law lays down a procedure for the accomplishment of international human rights at the national level, allowing states to exercise their sovereign rights while consenting to international monitoring of human rights situations. In fact, norm creation has been internationalized, but its enforcement is left *only* to the sovereign states. Few exceptions – most remarkably genocide, crimes against humanity, certain war crimes, and torture and arbitrary execution – emphasize the almost full sovereign authority of states to implement human rights in their territories as they see fit (Donnelly 2007, 2008).

Today, most states accept the authority of the UDHR. Amazingly, this Declaration has been translated into 337 different languages (Welch 2008) which makes it the most widely translated document in human history. It has become a touchstone for actions by governments, individuals and non-governmental actors. As Halliday (1995) states, most people of all cultures accept some legitimacy for universalism: very few people would argue that torture, starvation, infanticide and slavery can be treated at the same level as welcoming customs or festival arrangements. Indeed, human rights enshrined in the Universal Declaration have stretched in a series of treaties. Today, there are eight core international human rights treaties – on civil and political rights; economic, social and cultural rights; racial discrimination; discrimination against women; torture; rights of the child; migrant workers; and rights of persons with disabilities – which represent an impressive ratification rate.

Nonetheless, because of sharp cultural variations and distinct historical and religious traditions the implementation of some human rights would be challenging in certain countries/regions. However, it would be imprudent to totally depreciate cultural or religious traditions while promoting human rights and these differences *should* be recognized and respected by individual states and international organizations while they advocate human rights. Not all human rights, even those which are embodied in various UN instruments, can universally be accepted by or are equally important for each society (UN 1993). There may be periods in a given society when particular rights are much desired, either because they are manifestly violated or because at a certain level of societal development and implementation of basic rights people start to turn to other rights and freedoms (Müllerson 1997). It seems unavoidable that complexities rooted in the cultural or religious traditions of few societies decelerate the full implementation of international human rights standards. In any case, a considerable time period will be needed by some countries/regions before a realistic compliance with human rights standards is in the offing.

## Concluding Thoughts

As a moral precept, the ideal of human rights is one of the windows through which we envisage a just and fair human order. Based on the ideological commitment to the intrinsic worth and dignity of each individual, human rights specify the conditions under which human beings can live a minimally decent life. To have human rights ethos respected in full is a righteous aspiration to which everyone ought to contribute. Admittedly, international measures for the protection of human rights are meant to supplement, *not supplant*, the domestic system where this falters, in deference to the cynical feature of human experience – the gap between rhetoric and reality, between aspiration, action and actualization.

Indisputably, the question of human rights will continue to demand attention on the future international agenda. Nevertheless, challenges are there: in seeking to impose restraints on public and private power holders, human rights law seems chimerical – a grandiose ideal in an imperfect world. Nonetheless, whatever the disagreements are, human rights share a common humanizing focus – placing individuals at the center of public policy. Supposedly, human rights advocacy stresses that the power, security and economic well-being of states and their ruling elites should be accompanied by a genuine concern for the average citizen and/or the least well-off in political and economic terms (Forsythe 1989). It is in this context that any discussion/debate on the conflicting positions of the universalists and cultural relativists suggests that the two views are not as antithetical and incongruous as is often thought by many. As has been indicated, a dialogue between different ethical, religious and cultural traditions can yield universal standards, inasmuch as universal ideal is not immutable or absolute; rather, it is the sequel/progression of the interlocution based as much on complementarity as on commonality (Camilleri 1994).

## References

American Anthropological Association. 1947. Statement on human rights. *American Anthropologist*, 49(4), 539–43.

Barash, D.P. and Webel, C.P. 2002. *Peace and Conflict Studies*. Thousand Oaks, CA: Sage.

Baxi, U. 1999. Voices of suffering, fragmented universality, and the future of human rights, in *The Future of International Human Rights*, edited by B.H. Weston and S.P. Marks. New York: Transnational Publishers, 101–56.

Beitz, C.R. 2001. Human rights as a common concern. *American Political Science Review*, 95(2), 269–82.

Booth, K. 1999. Three tyrannies, in *Human Rights in Global Politics*, edited by T. Dunne and N.J. Wheeler. Cambridge: Cambridge University Press, 31–70.

Bozeman, A. 1971. *The Future of Law in a Multicultural World*. Princeton, NJ: Princeton University Press.

Brown, S. 1992. *International Relations in a Changing Global System: Toward a Theory of the World Polity*. Boulder, CO: Westview Press.

Camilleri, J.A. 1994. Human rights, cultural diversity and conflict resolution: The Asia Pacific context. *Pacifica Review*, 6(2), 17–41.

Campbell, P.J., Mackinnon, A. and Stevens, C.R. 2010. *An Introduction to Global Studies*. Oxford: Wiley-Blackwell.

Donnelly, J. 1984. Cultural relativism and universal human rights. *Human Rights Quarterly*, 6(4), 400–19.

Donnelly, J. 1998. *International Human Rights*. Boulder, CO: Westview Press.

Donnelly, J. 2003. *Universal Human Rights: In Theory and Practice*. New York: Cornell University Press.

Donnelly, J. 2007. The relative universality of human rights. *Human Rights Quarterly,* 29(2), 281–306.

Donnelly, J. 2008. Relativity and the universal declaration. *eJournal USA* [Online], 13(11), 33–7. Available at: http://www.america.gov/media/pdf/ejs/1108.pdf#popup [accessed: 10 October 2010].

Edgar, A. and Sedgwick, P. 2002. *Cultural Theory: The Key Concepts*. London: Routledge.

El Obaid, A. and Rehman, I.A. 2002. Universality of Human Rights and Cultural Relativism [Online]. Available at: http://www.equitas.org/english/programs/downloads/ihrtp-proceedings/23rd/Rehman-El-Obaid-Ang.pdf [accessed: 15 October 2010].

Forsythe, D. 1989. *Human Rights and World Politics*. Lincoln, NE: University of Nebraska Press.

Frezzo, M. 2012. Introduction, in *Sociology and Human Rights: A Bill of Rights for the Twenty-First Century*, edited by J. Blau and M. Frezzo. London: Sage, 3–14.

Halliday, F. 1995. Relativism and universalism in human rights: The case of the Islamic Middle East. *Political Studies*, 43(Supplementary Issue 1), 152–67.

Harrelson-Stephens, J. and Callaway, R.L. 2007. What are human rights? Definitions and typologies of today's human rights discourse, in *Exploring International Human Rights: Essential Readings*, edited by R.L. Callaway and J. Harrelson-Stephens. Boulder, CO: Lynne Rienner, 4–10.

Harris-Short, S. 2003. International human rights law: Imperialist, inept and ineffective? Cultural relativism and the UN Convention on the Rights of the Child. *Human Rights Quarterly*, 25(1), 130–81.

Hartung, F.E. 1954. Cultural relativity and moral judgments. *Philosophy of Science,* 21(1), 118–26.

Henkin, L., Neuman, G.L., Orentlicher, D.F. and Leebron, D.W. 1999. *Human Rights.* New York: Foundation Press.

Herskovits, M.J. 1973. *Cultural Relativism: Perspectives in Cultural Pluralism.* New York: Vintage.

Hobsbawm, E.J. 1994. *The Age of Extremes: A History of the World, 1914–1991*. New York: Vintage.

Hrubec, M. 2010. Preconditions of an intercultural dialogue on human rights. *Veritus*, 55(1), 183–205.

Ife, J. (2001). *Human Rights and Social Work: Towards Rights Based Practice.* Cambridge: Cambridge University Press.

Ignatieff, M. 2001. The attack on human rights. *Foreign Affairs*, 80(6), 102–116.

Iovane, M. 2007. The universality of human rights and the international Protection of cultural diversity: Some theoretical and practical considerations. *International Journal on Minority and Group Rights*, 14(2/3), 231–62.

Iriye, A. and Goedde, P. 2012. Introduction: Human rights as history, in *The Human Rights Revolution: An International History*, edited by A. Iriye, P. Goedde and W.I. Hitchcock. Oxford: Oxford University Press, 3-24.

Karsten, A. and Küntzel, B. 2006. *On Intercultural Dialogue.* Forum on Intercultural Dialogue. Council of Europe, Strasbourg, 22–26 November

2006 [Online]. Available at: http://www.ifuw.org/uwe/docs/coe-intercultural-dialogue.pdf [accessed: 5 October 2010].

Kluckhohn, C. 1944. *Mirror for Man.* Greenwick, CT: Fawcett.

Kottak, C.P. 2000. *Cultural Anthropology*. New York: McGraw-Hill.

Kroeber, A.L. 1950. Anthropology. *Scientific American*, 183(3), 87–94.

Lauren, P.G. 2008. The universal declaration of human rights: Launching and sustaining a revolution. *eJournal USA* [Online], 13(11), 3-7. Available at: http://www.america.gov/media/pdf/ejs/1108.pdf#popup [accessed: 10 November 2011].

Li-ann, T. 2004. Pragmatism and realism do not mean abdication: A critical and empirical inquiry into Singapore's engagement with international human rights law, in *Singapore Year Book of International Law*, Vol. 8. Malaysia/Singapore: Gaunt, 41–91.

Mannheim, K. 1936. *Ideology and Utopia: An Introduction to the Sociology of Knowledge.* London: Routledge.

Mertus, J. 2003. The new U.S. human rights policy: A radical departure. *International Studies Perspectives*, 4(4), 371–84.

Müllerson, R. 1997. *Human Rights Diplomacy*. London: Routledge.

Musalo, K. 2010. When Rights and Cultures Collide [Online]. Available at: http://www.scu.edu/ethics/publications/iie/v8n3/rightsandcultures.html [accessed: 10 October 2010].

Parekh, B. 1999. Non-ethnocentric universalism, in *Human Rights in Global Politics*, edited by T. Dunne and N.J. Wheeler. Cambridge: Cambridge University Press, 128–59.

Parekh, B. 2000. *Rethinking Multiculturalism: Cultural Diversity and Political Theory*. Cambridge, MA: Harvard University Press.

Pollis, A. 2000. A new universalism, in *Human Rights: New Perspectives, New Realities*, edited by A. Pollis and P. Schwab. Boulder, CO: Lynne Rienner, 9–30.

Pollis, A. and Schwab, P. 2000. Introduction, in *Human Rights: New Perspectives, New Realities*, edited by A. Pollis and P. Schwab. Boulder, CO: Lynne Rienner, 1–8.

Rao, A. 1995. The politics of gender and culture in international human rights discourse, in *Women's Rights, Human Rights: International Feminist Perspectives*, edited by J.S. Peters and A. Wolper. London: Routledge, 167–75.

Rawls, J., 2005. *Political Liberalism*, New York: Columbia University Press, 385 et seq.

Ruggiero, V.R. 1992. *Thinking Critically About Ethical Issues.* London: Mayfield.

Scruton, R. 1994. *Modern Philosophy*. London: Sinclair-Stevenson.

Shaheed, F., Muigai, G., Manjoo, R, Muñoz Villalobos, V. and Jahangir, A. (2010). Human Rights Are Essential Tools for an Effective Intercultural Dialogue. Statement by a group of United Nations experts on the World Day for Cultural Diversity for Dialogue and Development, 21 May [Online]. Available at: http://www2.ohchr.org/english/issues/cultural_rights/docs/statements/Statement_cultural_diversity21052010.doc [accessed: 25 September 2010].

Skubik, D.W. 1992. Two perspectives on human rights and the rule of law: Chinese east and Anglo-American west. *World Review*, 31(2), 28–45.

Taylor, C. 1999. Conditions of an unforced consensus on human rights, in *The East Asian Challenge for Human Rights*, edited by J.R. Bauer and D.A. Bell. Cambridge: Cambridge University Press.

UN. 1993. Report of the Regional Meeting for Asia of the World Conference on Human Rights (Bangkok, 29 March to 2 April 1993) – Bangkok Declaration. UN Doc. A/CONF.157/ASRM/8 of 7 April 1993.

Walzer, M. 1994. *Thick and Thin: Moral Argument at Home and Abroad.* Notre Dame, IN: University of Notre Dame Press.

Welch, C. 2008. The universal declaration of human rights at sixty. *eJournal USA* [Online], 13(11), 3–7. Available at: http://www.america.gov/media/pdf/ejs/1108.pdf#popup [accessed: 10 October 2010].

Wiredu, K. 1996. *Cultural Universals and Particulars: An African Perspective.* Bloomington, IN: Indiana University Press.

World Federation of United Nations Associations. 2008. Report on the Global Online Dialogue on the Universality of Human Rights, presented in Paris, 3–5 September at the DPI/NGO conference [Online]. Available at: http://www.un.org/dpi/ngosection/annualconfs/61/pdfs/WFUNA_report_on_th_%20RTD_dialogue_on-HR.pdf [accessed: 2 October 2010].

Zechenter, E.M. 1997. In the name of culture: Cultural relativism and the abuse of the individual. *Journal of Anthropological Research*, 53(3), 319–47.

# Chapter 3

# The Impact of, and Resistance to, the Use of Foreign Law on Juvenile Punishment in the United States

Ruth Hargove and Roberta Thyfault*

## Introduction

This chapter examines the impact of and resistance to the use of foreign law[1] in US Supreme Court cases where juveniles have challenged their sentences of death and life without parole.[2] The impact of foreign law and the conflict over its use is best illustrated by three such cases decided less than two decades apart.[3]

In each case, the juvenile challenged his sentence under the Eighth Amendment to the US Constitution, which bans "cruel and unusual punishments."[4] When Kevin

---

* The authors would like to thank California Western School of Law for its support. In addition, they are grateful to California Western Law School Professors Leslie Culver, Floralynn Einesman, and Michael Yu for their support, ideas, and commentary. They also thank Professor Mark Wojcik from John Marshall School of Law for his review and comments.

1 As Professor Buys notes, "foreign law" and "international law" are distinct concepts. "Foreign law" consists of "foreign statutes or codes and decisions by the national courts of foreign countries." "International law" refers to "international treaties or conventions, customary international law, general principals of law, and the works of jurists or scholars." Cindy G. Buys, *Burying Our Constitution in the Sand? Evaluating the Ostrich Response to the Use of International and Foreign Law in U.S. Constitutional Interpretation*, 21 BYU J. PUB. L. 1, 4, 6 (2007). For simplicity, when this chapter refers to "foreign" law," it includes "international law" because courts and commentators often use those terms interchangeably.

2 When this chapter uses the term "juvenile," it means a person who is under eighteen. *See* Roper v. Simmons, 543 U.S. 551, 568 (2005) (holding that the Eighth Amendment to the United States Constitution forbids executing anyone under 18). *See also* U.N. Convention on the Rights of the Child, *opened for signature* November 20, 1989, 1577 U.N.T.S.3, art. 1 (prohibiting the imposition of a sentence of life without possibility of parole, or death, against juveniles younger than 18). For the complete text of the Convention on the Rights of the Child, see Office of the United Nations High Commissioner for Human Rights, http://www2.ohchr.org/english/law/pdf/crc.pdf (last visited May 10, 2012).

3 *See* Stanford v. Kentucky, 492 U.S. 361 (1989); Roper v. Simmons, 543 U.S. 551 (2005); Graham v. Florida, 130 S. Ct. 2011 (2010).

4 U.S. CONST. amend. VIII.

Stanford challenged his death sentence in 1989 for a killing he committed at age seventeen,[5] Justice Antonin Scalia, the Court's leading critic of using foreign law to decide domestic issues, authored the plurality opinion, joined by, among others, Justice Anthony Kennedy.[6] The plurality rejected foreign law and upheld the death penalty for juveniles as young as sixteen.[7]

Sixteen years later, in 2005, Donald Roper challenged his death sentence for a murder he had committed at seventeen.[8] This time, Justice Kennedy championed the use of foreign law, reversed *Stanford*, and categorically abolished the death penalty for all juvenile offenders under eighteen.[9] The resulting outcry included calls for Justice Kennedy's impeachment, Congressional threats to impeach *any* judge who used foreign law, and death threats to two justices.[10] More nuanced critics questioned whether Justice Kennedy had used foreign law to replace US Constitutional principles.[11]

Nonetheless, five years later, in 2010, when Terrance Graham challenged his sentence of life without parole for a robbery he committed at age sixteen, Justice Kennedy used foreign law to abolish life without parole sentences for all nonhomicide juvenile offenses.[12]

This chapter traces the US Supreme Court's juvenile punishment cases, examines the backlash against Justice Kennedy's use of foreign law, and discusses why many view his use of foreign law in juvenile punishment cases to conflict with principles of American democracy.

## The Eighth Amendment's Evolving Standards of Decency and the Conflict Over Using Foreign Law to Determine it

The text of the Eighth Amendment comes "directly from the English Declaration of Rights of 1688, and the principle it represents [is traceable] to the Magna Carta."[13] It applies to the states through the Fourteenth Amendment.[14] However,

5 Stanford was seventeen years and four months old when he and an adult accomplice killed Stanford's brother in law. Stanford v. Kentucky, 492 U.S. 361, 365 (1989).

6 Justice Scalia announced the judgment of the Court and delivered the opinion of the Court with respect to Parts I, II, III, and IV-A, and an opinion with respect to Parts IV-B and V, in which the Chief Justice Rehnquist and Justices White and Kennedy joined. Stanford v. Kentucky, 492 U.S. 361, 364 (1989).

7 Stanford v. Kentucky, 492 U.S. 361, 380 (1989).

8 Roper v. Simmons, 543 U.S. 551, 555 (2005).

9 Roper v. Simmons, 543 U.S. 551, 579 (2005).

10 *See infra*, *Roper:* The Conservative Backlash.

11 *See infra*, Understanding the Resistance to Foreign Law.

12 Graham v. Florida, 130 S. Ct. 2011, 2034 (2010).

13 Trop v. Dulles, 356 U.S. 86, 100 (1958) (footnotes omitted).

14 U.S. CONST. amend XIV; *see* Robinson v. California, 370 U.S. 660, 667 (1962) (recognizing that the Eighth Amendment applies to states through the Fourteenth Amendment).

the Supreme Court has long recognized that the Eighth Amendment's words are imprecise and "their scope is not static."[15] Since 1958, when the Court decided *Trop v. Dulles*, the Court has held that a punishment is cruel and unusual if society's "evolving standards of decency" say it is.[16] The "evolving standards of decency" test sees the Eighth Amendment as "progressive,"[17] recognizing that contemporary society may reject a punishment that was accepted when the Framers wrote the Bill of Rights.[18] As *Trop* recognized, "[t]he basic concept underlying the Eighth Amendment is nothing less than the dignity of man."[19] Thus, "[t]he Amendment must draw its meaning from the evolving standards of decency that mark the progress of a maturing society."[20]

The Eighth Amendment is therefore viewed through a contemporary lens and concerns questions of human dignity that appear to transcend national boundaries.[21] Consequently, Eighth Amendment cases have become one flashpoint for the recent conflict among the judiciary, Congress, and the public over the propriety of using foreign law in constitutional analysis.[22] Supreme Court justices who favor consulting foreign law look to the laws and practices of other countries to provide empirical data concerning the evolving standards of decency.[23]

The Court's use of foreign law is not new.[24] More than fifty years ago, when the Court first articulated the "evolving standards of decency" test in *Trop*, the

---

15 Trop v. Dulles, 356 U.S. 86, 100–01 (1958).

16 Trop v. Dulles, 356 U.S. 86, 101 (1958).

17 Weems v. United States, 217 U.S. 349, 373 (1910).

18 Weems v. United States, 217 U.S. 349, 373 (1910); *see also* Thompson v. Oklahoma, 487 U.S. 815, 822 and n. 4 (1988) (the Constitution's drafters delegated to future judges the task of interpreting the Eighth Amendment guided by the "evolving standards of decency" test).

19 Trop v. Dulles, 356 U.S. 86, 100 (1958).

20 Trop v. Dulles, 356 U.S. 86, 101 (1958).

21 *See* Trop v. Dulles, 356 U.S. 86, 100 (1958); *see generally*, David J. Seipp, *Our Law, Their Law, History, and the Citation of Foreign Law*, 86 B.U. L. Rev. 1417, 1442 (2006) ("American law . . . has always allowed some core universality, some morality or sense of justice that transcends U.S. boundaries."); Jacob J. Zehnder, Note, *Constitutional Comparativism: The Emerging Risk of Comparative Law as a Constitutional Tiebreaker*, 41 Val. U. L. Rev. 1739, 1758 (2007) (noting the Court has cited to foreign law in decisions involving human rights ); Ruth Bader Ginsburg, *A Decent Respect to the Opinions of [Human]kind: The Value of a Comparative Perspective in Constitutional Adjudication*, 64 Cambridge L.J. 575, 585 (2005), *available at* http://www.cpl.law.cam.ac.uk/CLJ_Ruth_Ginsburg_SDWL2005.pdf (Justice Ginsburg's speech to the American Society of International Law, acknowledging *Trop*'s recognition that the "dignity of man" is central to Eighth Amendment analysis).

22 *See infra, Roper*: The Conservative Backlash.

23 *See infra,* Understanding the Resistance to Foreign Law.

24 *See, e.g.* Wilkerson v. Utah, 99 U.S. 130, 134–37 (1879) (looking to, *inter alia*, the practices of other countries to hold that punishment of death by shooting passed Eighth Amendment muster); Weems v. United States, 217 U.S. 349, 391–96 (1910) (analyzing

plurality and dissent considered foreign law in the challenge to a federal law that punished wartime deserters with denationalization.[25] In overturning the law, the plurality noted "the civilized nations of the world" were in "virtual unanimity" against denationalization. [26] The dissent relied on the *practices* of other nations to reach the opposite result.[27]

The Court's reference to foreign sources caused little debate until Justice Kennedy switched his position on the issue, authoring several opinions on hot-button social issues that relied on foreign law.[28] Justice Scalia has become the most vocal judicial and extrajudicial critic of using foreign law to interpret the US Constitution.[29]

## The Evolving Standards of Decency Factors: American Consensus, Foreign Views, and Independent Judgment

Thirty years after deciding *Trop*, the Court applied its reasoning when William Wayne Thompson challenged his death sentence for a murder he had committed at age fifteen.[30] To determine whether Thompson's death sentence was constitutional, the Court examined standards of decency by considering (1) American consensus, (2) foreign views, and (3) the Court's independent judgment.[31] Justice John Paul Stevens wrote for the Court and Justice Scalia for the dissent. Justice Kennedy

---

English predecessor to Bill of Rights to determine whether a punishment was cruel and unusual); Trop v. Dulles, 356 U.S. 86, 102 (1958) (considering "the international community of democracies" when determining whether punishment was cruel and unusual); Coker v. Georgia, 433 U.S. 584, 596 n. 10 (1977) (noting "[i]t is thus not irrelevant here that out of 60 major nations in the world surveyed in 1965, only 3 retained the death for rape where death did not ensue"). *See also The Use of International and Foreign Law in Interpreting the U.S. Constitution*, Am. Const. Soc'y for L. & Pol'y, *available at* http://www.acslaw.org/files/intl%20law%20study%20guide%201-18-06.pdf, at 5 (last visited May 10, 2012) (noting "[t]he practice of looking at foreign and international law has a particularly strong tradition in the Eighth Amendment context, going back to one of the first cases challenging punishment as 'cruel and unusual'").

25 Trop v. Dulles, 356 U.S. 86, 101 (1958).

26 Trop v. Dulles, 356 U.S. 86, 102 (1958).

27 Trop v. Dulles, 356 U.S. 86, 126–27 (1958) (Frankfurter, J., dissenting).

28 *See infra, Roper*: The Conservative Backlash.

29 *See, e.g.* Thompson v. Oklahoma, 487 U.S. 815, 869 n. 4 (1988) (Scalia, J., dissenting); Stanford v. Kentucky, 492 U.S. 361, 369 n. 1 (1989) (plurality); Lawrence v. Texas, 539 U.S. 558, 597–98 (2003) (Scalia, J., dissenting); Roper v. Simmons, 543 U.S. 551, 622–28 (2005) (Scalia, J., dissenting). *See also* Justices Antonin Scalia and Stephen Breyer, *Discussion at the American University Washington College of Law: Constitutional Relevance of Foreign Court Decisions* (January 13, 2005), http://domino.american.edu/AU/media/mediarel.nsf/1D265343BDC2189785256B810071F238/1F2F7DC4757FD01E85256F890068E6E0?OpenDocument.

30 Thompson v. Oklahoma, 487 U.S. 815, 818 (1988).

31 Thompson v. Oklahoma, 487 U.S. 815, 822, 830, 833 (1988).

was on the Court, but took no part in the decision.[32] The Court held that executing juveniles under the age of sixteen was cruel and unusual.[33]

Justice Stevens first looked to see if Americans had reached a consensus as to the juvenile death penalty, expressed through state laws and jury verdicts.[34] Even though the majority of states set no minimum age for executions, Justice Stevens said these states did not favor executing juveniles. Their failure to set a minimum age showed only that they had not considered the issue, as it was "self-evident" that executing children was "unacceptable."[35] Justice Stevens found Americans had reached a consensus against the juvenile death penalty, because the eighteen states with a minimum death penalty age had set it at or above sixteen.[36] Further, no state had executed any juvenile under sixteen in forty years.[37] Therefore, legislation and practice proved that executing fifteen-year-olds "is now generally abhorrent to the [community's] conscience."[38] The Court found the American consensus "consistent with the views . . . expressed by . . . other nations that share our Anglo-American heritage, and . . . the leading members of the Western European community."[39]

Although the Court acknowledged foreign views, these views could only confirm an American consensus, which itself was entitled to heavy but not dispositive, weight.[40] Rather, the ultimate judgment as to the constitutionality of the sentence belonged to the Court.[41] The Court exercised its judgment by determining if the death penalty was proportionate to the crime. The Court reasoned that the death penalty was only proportionate if it served the death penalty's goals of retribution or deterrence.[42] Because fifteen-year-olds were neither as culpable as adults nor as likely to consider the consequences of their conduct, the plurality concluded that executing them for murder was disproportionate punishment.[43]

In dissent, Justice Scalia raised three broad objections to the plurality's analysis. First, he asserted that, under his originalist view, the Eighth Amendment's meaning had remained static since its drafting. Therefore, the proper question was whether the Framers would have considered Thompson's punishment cruel and unusual.[44] Justice Scalia answered this question in the negative, noting that, historically,

32 Thompson v. Oklahoma, 487 U.S. 815, 818 (1988).
33 Thompson v. Oklahoma, 487 U.S. 815, 838 (1988).
34 Thompson v. Oklahoma, 487 U.S. 815, 823 (1988).
35 Thompson v. Oklahoma, 487 U.S. 815, 827–28 (1988).
36 Thompson v. Oklahoma, 487 U.S. 815, 829 (1988).
37 Thompson v. Oklahoma, 487 U.S. 815, 832 n. 37 (1988).
38 Thompson v. Oklahoma, 487 U.S. 815, 832 (1988).
39 Thompson v. Oklahoma, 487 U.S. 815, 830–31 (1988).
40 Thompson v. Oklahoma, 487 U.S. 815, 830–31, 833 (1988).
41 Thompson v. Oklahoma, 487 U.S. 815, 833 (1988).
42 Thompson v. Oklahoma, 487 U.S. 815, 836–38 (1988).
43 Thompson v. Oklahoma, 487 U.S. 815, 834–35, 838 (1988).
44 Thompson v. Oklahoma, 487 U.S. 815, 864 (1988) (Scalia, J., dissenting).

juveniles had been executed for crimes they had committed when they were under sixteen.[45]

Second, looking to *Trop*'s "evolving standards of decency" test, Justice Scalia disagreed that Americans had reached a consensus against the juvenile death penalty.[46] In particular, he thought Justice Stevens was wrong to find the nineteen states with no minimum execution age were against the juvenile death penalty.[47] Moreover, Justice Scalia believed the Court was wrong to substitute its judgment for that of American society. According to Justice Scalia, the "majority of the small and unrepresentative segment of our society that sits on [the] Court" should not make moral judgment as to what is cruel and unusual.[48] The Court's role was only to determine what the Eighth Amendment meant when it was drafted, or, at most, to determine the evolving standards of decency held by American society.[49] Moreover, Justice Scalia objected to the use of foreign law, because "where there is not first a settled consensus among our own people, the views of other nations, however enlightened the Justices of this Court may think them to be, cannot be imposed upon Americans through the Constitution."[50]

The Court in *Thompson* expressly left open the question of whether executing juveniles between the ages of sixteen and eighteen was cruel and unusual.[51] The Court resolved this issue a year later, in *Stanford v. Kentucky*, when it considered two cases. In one, the juvenile was four months past his seventeenth birthday when he committed capital murder; in the other, the juvenile was sixteen and a half.[52] Juries sentenced both to death.[53]

Justice Scalia wrote the Court's plurality opinion, joined by, among others, Justice Kennedy.[54] Justice Scalia noted that the sentences would have been constitutional when the Framers adopted the Eighth Amendment because even seven-year-olds could have theoretically been executed then.[55] He then addressed the juveniles' contentions that their sentences were unconstitutional under current standards of decency.[56] In applying the evolving standards of decency test, he focused solely on whether Americans had reached a consensus against the juvenile death penalty. This inquiry required neither independent judicial analysis nor any consideration of foreign law. The only inquiry was an "objective" one that

---

45 Thompson v. Oklahoma, 487 U.S. 815, 864 (1988) (Scalia, J., dissenting).
46 Thompson v. Oklahoma, 487 U.S. 815, 864–68 (1988) (Scalia, J., dissenting).
47 Thompson v. Oklahoma, 487 U.S. 815, 867–68 (1988) (Scalia, J., dissenting).
48 Thompson v. Oklahoma, 487 U.S. 815, 873 (1988) (Scalia, J., dissenting).
49 Thompson v. Oklahoma, 487 U.S. 815, 873 (1988) (Scalia, J., dissenting).
50 Thompson v. Oklahoma, 487 U.S. 815, 868 n. 4 (1988) (Scalia, J., dissenting).
51 Thompson v. Oklahoma, 487 U.S. 815, 838 (1988).
52 Stanford v. Kentucky, 492 U.S. 361, 365–66 (1989).
53 Stanford v. Kentucky, 492 U.S. 361, 366, 367 (1989).
54 Stanford v. Kentucky, 492 U.S. 361, 364 (1989).
55 Stanford v. Kentucky, 492 U.S. 361, 368 (1989).
56 Stanford v. Kentucky, 491 U.S. 361, 369 (1989).

determined the will of the electorate.[57] Foreign law was irrelevant because "it is *American* conceptions of decency that" control.[58] Justice Scalia concluded that Americans, who expressed their will through state laws, believed that the death penalty for those as young as sixteen conformed to their conceptions of decency. Therefore, the penalty was constitutional.[59]

Justice Scalia's victory in *Stanford* was short lived. Four years later, the Governor of Kentucky commuted Stanford's death sentence to life in prison without the possibility of parole.[60] Moreover, just sixteen years after the Court decided *Stanford*, it overturned *Stanford* entirely in *Roper v. Simmons*.[61]

## *Roper v. Simmons* Reconsiders and Rejects *Stanford v. Kentucky*

Christopher Simmons was seventeen when he and two friends committed a home invasion burglary and killed the terrified homeowner by throwing her, duct-taped and bound, off a bridge to drown.[62] A jury sentenced Simmons to death.[63] When his case reached the Supreme Court, Simmons urged the Court to reverse *Stanford*.[64] Simmons probably recognized that the time was ripe for the Court to do so.

The Court had recently reversed *Penry v. Lynaugh*,[65] which it had decided on the same day in 1989 that it had decided *Stanford*. In *Penry*, the Court had found no Eighth Amendment bar to executing the mentally retarded.[66] However, in 2002, the Court reversed *Penry* in *Atkins v. Virginia*, finding that "standards of decency" had evolved to prohibit executing the mentally retarded.[67] All three factors of the evolving standards of decency test were met: the nation had reached a consensus against executing the retarded;[68] the world community "overwhelmingly disapproved" of the practice;[69] and the Court independently determined that

57 Stanford v. Kentucky, 491 U.S. 361, 369–70 (1989).

58 Stanford v. Kentucky, 492 U.S. 361, 369 n. 1 (1989).

59 Stanford v. Kentucky, 492 U.S. 361, 369–80 (1989).

60 *See* Roper v. Simmons, 543 U.S. 551, 565 (2005).

61 Roper v. Simmons, 543 U.S. 551, 578 (2005).

62 Roper v. Simmons, 543 U.S. 551, 556–57 (2005).

63 Roper v Simmons, 543 U.S. 551, 558 (2005).

64 Roper v. Simmons, 543 U.S. 553, 559–60 (2005).

65 Penry v. Lynaugh, 429 U.S. 302 (1989).

66 Penry v. Lynaugh, 492 U.S. 302, 340 (1989).

67 Atkins v. Virginia, 536 U.S. 304, 320 (2002).

68 Atkins v. Virginia, 536 U.S. 304, 313–17 (2002).

69 Atkins v. Virginia, 536 U.S. 304, 316 n. 21 (2002). Chief Justice Rehnquist thought that reliance on foreign laws was "antithetical to federalism." Atkins v. Virginia, 536 U.S. 304, 322 (2002) (Rehnquist, C.J., dissenting). Justice Scalia's dissent also objected to using foreign laws. He found irrelevant "the practices of the 'world community,' whose notions of justice are (thankfully) not always those of our people." Atkins v. Virginia, 536 U.S. 304, 347–48 (Scalia, J., dissenting).

neither retribution nor deterrence were served by executing those whose reduced mental capacity limited their culpability.[70] Justice Kennedy had joined in the *Atkins* majority, signaling that he might be ready to reverse his position in *Stanford*.[71]

In *Roper v. Simmons*, he did so, ruling that the death penalty for those under eighteen is cruel and unusual punishment.[72] When Justice Kennedy wrote the majority opinion in *Roper v. Simmons*, he returned to the three-part "evolving standards of decency analysis" that examined the views of the American people, the Court and the world community.[73] However, he was quickly accused of misrepresenting the data on American consensus, ignoring the objective evidence on the proportionality analysis,[74] and giving too much weight to foreign law.[75]

As to American consensus, although fewer than half of the states banned the juvenile death penalty, and only four had banned it since *Stanford*, Justice Kennedy nonetheless saw a slow, but growing, movement among states to abolish the juvenile death penalty.[76] However, he appeared to shift the juvenile's burden to prove consensus against the juvenile death penalty to the state's burden to prove

---

70 Atkins v. Virginia, 536 U.S. 304, 319–20 (2002).

71 Atkins v. Virginia, 536 U.S. 304, 305 (2002).

72 Roper v. Simmons, 543 U.S. 551, 578 (2005).

73 Roper v. Simmons, 543 U.S. 551, 561–64 (2005).

74 *See* Roper v. Simmons, 543 U.S. 551, 588, 598–604 (2005) (O'Connor, J., dissenting); Roper v. Simmons, 543 U.S. 551, 609–22 (2005) (Scalia, J., dissenting).

75 *See* Roper v. Simmons, 543 U.S. 551, 622–28 (2005) (Scalia, J., dissenting).

76 Roper v. Simmons, 543 U.S. 551, 564–67 (2005) (pointing out that thirty states have abolished the juvenile death penalty; twelve of those states totally abolished it outright and the other eighteen specifically excluded juveniles from the death penalty). The dissent notes, however, that the twelve states that completely abolished the death penalty should not be considered proof of those states' disregard for the death penalty applied *specifically* to juveniles. Roper v. Simmons, 543 U.S. 551, 610–11 (2005) (Scalia, J., dissenting). *See generally* Roger P. Alford, *Roper v. Simmons And Our Constitution In International Equipoise*, 53 UCLA L. Rev. 1, 5 (2005) (noting the Court's focus on "the number of states that had abandoned the death penalty altogether combined with those that [had] maintained it but excluded juveniles from its reach").

a consensus for the death penalty.[77] Regardless, the consensus factor was not dispositive, because the Court was required to exercise its "independent judgment."[78]

The Court conducted a proportionality review to inform its judgment and reasoned that youth reduced culpability in *Roper* just as mental retardation had reduced culpability in *Atkins*.[79] Juveniles are more impulsive and less risk-averse than adults, which reduce their culpability for their crimes.[80] Nor would a death sentence deter juveniles, because they rarely think of the consequences of their actions.[81] Even if they *did* consider consequences, life imprisonment without the possibility of parole remained a deterrent, as it is "a severe sanction, in particular for a young person."[82]

Responding to Justice O'Connor's criticism that seventeen-year-olds are unlike mentally retarded offenders, who are "*defined* by precisely the characteristics which render death an excessive punishment,"[83] Justice Kennedy acknowledged that the rare seventeen-year-old could be depraved enough to deserve the death penalty.[84] However, the death decision could not be left to jurors because the crime's gruesomeness might so prejudice them that they could not consider youth's mitigating nature. Thus, under its independent analysis, the Court concluded that neither retribution nor deterrence could justify imposing a death sentence on juvenile offenders.[85]

---

77 Roper v. Simmons, 543 U.S. 551, 567 (2005); Roger P. Alford, *Roper v. Simmons and Our Constitution in International Equipoise*, 53 UCLA L. Rev. 1, 6–7 (2005). As Justice Scalia noted in dissent, fewer than fifty percent of the states banned the juvenile death penalty, and the American people had explicitly disapproved of an international ban on the juvenile death penalty. *See* Roper v. Simmons, 543 U.S. 551, 609–15 (2005) (Scalia, J., dissenting). Further, the United States refused to ratify the United Nations Conventions on the Rights of the Child because Article 37 explicitly prohibited juvenile execution. Moreover, the United States had ratified the International Covenant on Civil and Political Rights subject to reservation to execute any person except a pregnant woman, including juveniles below the age of eighteen. *See* Roper v. Simmons, 543 U.S. 551, 622 (2005) (Scalia, J., dissenting) (citing Senate Committee on Foreign Relations, International Covenant on Civil and Political Rights, S. Exec. Rep. No. 102–23, at 11 (1992)).

78 Roper v. Simmons, 543 U.S. 551, 564 (2005).

79 Roper v. Simmons, 543 U.S. 551, 568–75 (2005).

80 Roper v. Simmons, 543 U.S. 551, 570 (2005).

81 Roper v. Simmons, 543 U.S. 551, 571–72 (2005).

82 Roper, v. Simmons, 543 U.S. 551, 572 (2005).

83 Roper v. Simmons, 543 U.S. 515, 602 (2005) (O'Connor, J., dissenting) (citing Atkins v. Virginia, 536 U.S. 304, 318 (2002)).

84 Roper v. Simmons, 543 U.S. 551, 572 (2005). However, Justice Scalia observed in dissent that the unusual circumstances of this case justified the jury's death verdict. Justice Scalia noted, with no small irony, that Simmons had in fact considered the consequences of his actions before he terrorized and tortured his victim, as he had told his friends that, as minors, "they could 'get away with it.'" Roper v. Simmons, 543 U.S. 551, 622 (2005) (Scalia, J., dissenting).

85 Roper v. Simmons, 543 U.S. 551, 572–74 (2005).

Finally, Justice Kennedy looked at foreign laws to confirm the Court's conclusion.[86] Unlike the previous cases, which had looked to foreign views to confirm an American consensus, here Justice Kennedy used foreign law to confirm the *Court's* judgment.

Justice Kennedy wrote that the United Nations Convention on the Rights of the Child (CRC), an international treaty that forbids the execution of juveniles, confirmed that standards of decency had evolved to require America to ban the practice.[87] The United Nations General Assembly had adopted the CRC in 1989.[88] Article 37 provides, in part, that "capital punishment . . . [may not] be imposed for offences committed by persons [under] eighteen."[89]

Noting that all 194 members of the United Nations had ratified the treaty, except Somalia and the United States, the Court concluded, "the United States now stands alone in a world that has turned its face against the juvenile death penalty."[90] Justice Kennedy emphasized that "[t]he opinion of the world community, while not controlling our outcome, does provide respected and significant confirmation for our own conclusions."[91]

Justice O'Connor dissented because she did not believe a national consensus had developed since *Stanford*,[92] nor did she believe that the death penalty was always a disproportionate sentence for juveniles.[93] Nevertheless, Justice O'Connor took pains to note that foreign law could be relevant to determine the evolving standards of decency.[94] Justice O'Connor believed that "the existence of an international consensus of this nature can . . . confirm the reasonableness of a . . . genuine American consensus."[95] The problem in *Roper*, according to Justice O'Connor, was that there was no consensus to confirm.[96]

Justice Scalia's dissent was more impassioned. He accused the majority of usurping the role of state legislatures and then supporting its view with foreign law.[97] He said that the majority had discarded American views as "irrelevant," while "the views of other countries and the so-called international community

86 Roper v. Simmons, 543 U.S. 515, 575–78 (2005).

87 Roper v. Simmons, 543 U.S. 515, 575–78 (2005). *See also* United Nations Convention on the Rights of the Child, *opened for signature* November 20, 1989, 1577 U.N.T.S. 3, art. 1 (defining a juvenile as anyone under 18).

88 United Nations Convention on the Rights of the Child, *opened for signature* November 20, 1989, 1577 U.N.T.S. 3, art. 1.

89 United Nations Convention on the Rights of the Child, *opened for signature* November 20, 1989, 1577 U.N.T.S. 3, art. 37.

90 Roper v. Simmons, 543 U.S. 515, 577 (2005).

91 Roper v. Simmons, 543 U.S. 515, 578 (2005).

92 Roper v. Simmons, 543 U.S. 515, 588–98 (2005) (O'Connor, J., dissenting).

93 Roper v. Simmons, 543 U.S. 515, 598–04 (2005) (O'Connor, J., dissenting).

94 Roper v. Simmons, 543 U.S. 515, 604–05 (2005) (O'Connor, J., dissenting).

95 Roper v. Simmons, 543 U.S. 515, 605 (2005) (O'Connor, J., dissenting).

96 Roper v. Simmons, 543 U.S. 515, 605 (2005) (O'Connor, J., dissenting).

97 Roper v. Simmons, 543 U.S. 515, 615, 622–28 (2005) (Scalia, J. dissenting).

[took] centerstage."[98] Justice Scalia was also outraged because the Court's decision forced the United States to comply with the CRC, a treaty it had explicitly refused to ratify.[99]

Justice Scalia thought the majority had cherry picked foreign law; he therefore invited the Court to consider the world's views on Americans' rights to jury trial and freedom of speech, press and religion.[100] If the Court did not want to reconsider those issues in light of world opinion, it should stop relying on foreign law to resolve other domestic issues, because "[t]o invoke alien law when it agrees with one's own thinking, and ignore it otherwise, is not reasoned decisionmaking, but sophistry."[101]

Justice Scalia predicted that *Roper* heralded the end to sentences of life without parole for juveniles because, in addition to banning the juvenile death penalty, CRC Article 37 bans sentences of juvenile life without parole.[102] Only five years after *Roper*, the Court was faced with this issue when Terrance Graham asked the Court to abolish juvenile life without parole sentences in nonhomicide cases in *Graham v. Florida*.[103]

Graham was sixteen when he was tried as adult for, and convicted of, attempted armed robbery.[104] He served a year in a detention facility and, only six months after his release, went on a one-night robbery spree.[105] He was nineteen when the state court sentenced him to life without possibility of parole.[106]

The Supreme Court reversed his sentence, ruling that life without parole for juvenile nonhomicide offenders was cruel and unusual punishment.[107] Justice Kennedy, writing for the majority, applied the Eighth Amendment criteria. As in

98 Roper v. Simmons, 543 U.S. 515, 622 (2005) (Scalia, J. dissenting).

99 Roper v. Simmons , 543 U.S. 515, 622–23 (2005) (Scalia, J. dissenting).

100 Roper . Simmons, 543 U.S. 515, 624–27 (2005) (Scalia, J. dissenting).

101 Roper v. Simmons, 543 U.S. 515, 627 (2005) (Scalia, J. dissenting).

102 Roper v. Simmons, 543 U.S. 515, 623 (2005) (Scalia, J., dissenting) (citing to United Nations Convention on the Rights of the Child, *opened for signature* November 20, 1989, 1577 U.N.T.S. 3, art. 37).

103 Graham v. Florida, 130 S. Ct. 2011, 2020 (2010). *See generally* Leslie Patrice Wallace, "*And I Don't Know Why It Is That You Threw Your Life Away": Abolishing Life Without Parole, the Supreme Court in* Graham v. Florida *Now Requires States to Give Juveniles Hope for a Second Chance*, 20 B.U. Pub. Int. L.J. 35 (2010).

104 Graham v. Florida, 130 S. Ct. 2011, 2018 (2010). In Florida and many other states, the District Attorney has discretion to treat juveniles over 14 as adults for purposes of charging and trying them in adult court. *See* Graham v. Florida, 130 S. Ct. 2011, 2030 (2010).

105 Graham v, Florida, 130 S. Ct. 2011, 2018–19 (2010).

106 Graham v. Florida, 130 S. Ct. 2011, 2020 (2011). Graham technically only received a life sentence along with a fifteen-year sentence, but because Florida had eliminated its parole program, a life inmate could only be released through executive clemency, so Graham was effectively sentenced to life without parole. Graham v. Florida 130 S. Ct. 2011, 2020 (2010).

107 Graham v. Florida, 130 S. Ct. 2011, 2034 (2010).

*Roper,* however, he looked to foreign law not to confirm an American consensus, but to confirm the Court's own judgment. He first examined whether an American consensus existed against the penalty. Although seventy-four percent of the states allowed juveniles to be imprisoned for life without parole, Justice Kennedy found its imposition rare, concluding that a national consensus existed against it.[108] Justice Kennedy next examined whether the sentence was proportional to Graham's culpability. Graham's age, reduced moral culpability and capacity for change undermined the efficacy of any legitimate penological goal, so the sentence was disproportionate to his crime.[109] In a categorical blow to the sentence, Justice Kennedy found this true not just for Graham, but for all juvenile nonhomicide offenders.[110] As to the third factor, Justice Kennedy again found "overwhelming" international "confirmation" for the decision.[111] He noted that the United States was the only nation that imposed life without parole sentences on juveniles.[112] Justice Kennedy acknowledged that foreign law did not bind the United States on this issue, but said that foreign law supported the Court's conclusion.[113]

In *Graham,* Justice Scalia's fear that *Roper* heralded the demise of juvenile life without parole was unrealized. Although the international community categorically condemned life without parole for *any* juvenile crime, *Graham* left states free to impose that penalty on juvenile killers.[114] In 2012, the Supreme Court limited states' ability to impose life without parole even on juveniles convicted of murder. The Court ruled that state laws that impose a *mandatory* sentence of life without parole on a juvenile convicted of murder are unconstitutional under the Eighth Amendment. The Court did not prohibit such a sentence, but said the court had to weigh aggravating and mitigating factors before imposing such a sentence. The Court also warned the states that such sentences should be rare. The Court's ruling did not refer to foreign law. *See* Miller v. Alabama, 132 S. Ct. 2455 (2012).

---

108 Graham v. Florida, 130 S. Ct. 2011, 2023–26 (2010).

109 Graham, v. Florida, 130 S. Ct. 2011, 2026–30 (2010).

110 Graham v. Florida, 130 S. Ct. 2011, 2030–33 (2010). Chief Justice Roberts concurred that Graham's life sentence violated the Eighth Amendment, but saw no reason to extend that limited ruling to cover all juveniles. Graham v. Florida, 130 S. Ct 2011, 2036–43 (2010) (Roberts, C.J., concurring).

111 Graham v. Florida, 130 S. Ct. 2011, 2033–34 (2010).

112 Graham v. Florida, 130 S. Ct. 2011, 2033 (2010).

113 Graham v. Florida, 130 S. Ct. 2011, 2034 (2011). None of the concurring or dissenting justices addressed the majority's use of foreign law.

114 Graham v. Florida, 130 S. Ct. 2011, 2034 (2010).

## ***Roper*: The Tipping Point for the Conservative Backlash against the Influence of Foreign Law**

By the time Justice Kennedy wrote *Roper*, Justice Scalia had already excoriated him two years earlier for his opinion in *Lawrence v. Texas*.[115] There, Justice Kennedy had used foreign law to overturn a state statute that criminalized homosexual sodomy as unconstitutional under the Fourteenth Amendment.[116] Justice Scalia's dissent predicted a "massive disruption of the current social order"[117] by a Court that had relied on "foreign views."[118] In a similar vein, Justice Scalia later characterized Justice Kennedy's *Roper* opinion as a "diktat," invoking an image of an America defeated by foreign law.[119]

Justice Scalia's criticism of *Lawrence* and *Roper* provided ammunition for conservative groups that called on Congress to impeach Justice Kennedy for citing foreign law.[120] Just a month after the Court decided *Roper*, members of a conservative group met in Washington to, among other tasks, remediate "'Judicial Tyranny'."[121] One speaker advocated for Justice Kennedy's impeachment because Justice Kennedy had used foreign law to "uphold . . . Marxist, Leninist, and satanic principles."[122] Some who occupied an even more distant fringe took things a step further: Justices Ginsburg and O'Connor were singled out for their support of foreign law and were targeted with Internet death threats.[123]

115 Lawrence v. Texas, 539 U.S. 558 (2003).

116 Lawrence v. Texas, 539 U.S. 558, 572–79 (2003).

117 Lawrence v. Texas, 539 U.S. 558, 591 (2003) (Scalia, J., dissenting).

118 Lawrence v. Texas, 539 U.S. 558, 598 (2003) (Scalia, J., dissenting).

119 Roper v. Simmons, 543 U.S. 551, 628 (2005) (Scalia, J., dissenting). A diktat is defined as "a harsh settlement unilaterally imposed (as on a defeated nation)." MERRIAM-WEBSTER, http://www.merriam-webster.com/dictionary/diktat (last visited May 12, 2012).

120 Dana Milbank, *And the Verdict on Justice Kennedy Is: Guilty*, WASH. POST, April 9, 2005, at A3, available at http://www.washingtonpost.com/wp-dyn/articles/A38308-2005Apr8.html (noting that Michael P. Farris, chairman of the Home School Legal Defense Association, said Kennedy "'should be the poster boy for impeachment' for citing international norms in his opinions").

121 Dana Milbank, *And the Verdict on Justice Kennedy Is: Guilty*, WASH. POST, April 9, 2005, at A3, available at http://www.washingtonpost.com/wp-dyn/articles/A38308-2005Apr8.html.

122 David J. Seipp, *Our Law, Their Law, History, and the Citation of Foreign Law*, 86 B.U. L. REV. 1417, 1442 (2006) ; Dana Milbank, *And the Verdict on Justice Kennedy Is: Guilty*, WASH. POST, April 9, 2005, at A3, available at http://www.washingtonpost.com/wp-dyn/articles/A38308-2005Apr8.html.

123 David J. Seipp, *Our Law, Their Law, History, and the Citation of Foreign Law*, 86 B.U. L. REV. 1417, 1420 (2006) (citing Gina Holland, *Justice Ginsburg Reveals Details of Death Threat*, ASSOCIATED PRESS, March 15, 2006).

Congress reacted to Justice Kennedy's use of foreign law by proposing federal legislation making judicial use of foreign law impeachable.[124] The House introduced the "Constitution Restoration Act"[125] and similar legislation repeatedly in 2004 and 2005. The proposed legislation mimicked Justice Scalia's criticism, ordering judges to refrain from consulting foreign law unless necessary to understand the "original meaning" of US law.[126]

However, even Justice Scalia, the most vocal critic of using foreign law in constitutional analysis, recognized that Congress's attempt to choreograph judicial reasoning itself violated constitutional principles of separation of powers, and he responded to the blaze he had helped to ignite. In 2006, he publicly chastised Congress for meddling in the Court's decision-making process.[127] This failed to several members of the House of Representatives who, in 2009, drafted a resolution to "prevent the misuse of foreign law in Federal courts" and generally prohibit any judge from deciding a case on "the authority of foreign law."[128] In 2011, Florida Representative Sandy Adams sponsored a bill with similar language.[129] This bill, like all Congressional attempts to punish the judiciary for considering foreign law before it, failed.[130]

Congress has been more successful in trying to limit judicial use of foreign law in another context: Congress has subjected every post-*Roper* Supreme Court nominee – Chief Justice John Roberts, and Justices Samuel Alito, Sonia Sotomayor,

---

124 *See* Lisa Sofio, Note, *Recent Developments in the Debate Concerning the use of Foreign Law in Constitutional Interpretation*, 30 Hastings Int'l & Comp. L. Rev. 131, 132–33 (2006) (noting several attempts Congress made to restrict the judicial use of foreign law).

125 The Constitution Restoration Act of 2004, H.R. Res. 3799, 108th Cong. (2004).

126 *See, e.g.*, American Justice for American Citizens Act, H.R. 1658, 109th Cong., § 3 (2005) (forbidding any court from employing any law of "any international or foreign state except for the English constitutional or common law or other sources of law relied upon by the Framers of the Constitution of the United States"); S. Res. 92, 109th Cong. (2005) (seeking to bar judges from consulting foreign law except as necessary to ascertain the Framers' intent). *See generally* David S. Law, *Generic Constitutional Law*, 89 Minn. L. Rev. 652, 656 n. 16 (2004) (providing comprehensive list of Congressional attempts to limit courts' use of foreign law).

127 Justice Scalia's remarks came at a public policy forum of the National Italian American Foundation. Charles Lane, *Scalia Tells Congress to Mind Its Own Business*, Wash. Post, May 19, 2006, at A19, *available at* http://www.washingtonpost.com/wp-dyn/content/article/2006/05/18/AR2006051801961.html.

128 H.R. Res. 473, 111th Cong. (2009).

129 H.R. 973, 112th Cong. (2011). The bill proposed amending Title 28 of the United States Code to, *inter alia*, "prevent the misuse of foreign law in federal courts."

130 *See generally* Austen L. Parrish, *Storm in a Teacup: The U.S. Supreme Court's Use of Foreign Law*, 2007 U. Ill. L. Rev. 637, 645, *available at* http://illinoislawreview.org/wp-content/ilr-content/articles/2007/2/Parrish.pdf (discussing Congressional reaction to use of foreign law).

and Elena Kagan – to a new litmus test requiring disavowal of foreign law.[131] Although each nominee agreed that foreign law does not establish precedent that the Supreme Court must follow, Justices Sotomayor and Kagan acknowledged that foreign law might be helpful in learning how other countries had resolved an issue.[132] In fact, Justice Sotomayor joined Justice Kennedy's decision in *Graham*, which relied extensively on foreign law to support the Court's ruling that sentences of life without possibility of parole for juveniles in non-homicide cases violated the Eighth Amendment.[133]

## Understanding the Resistance to Foreign Law: Is it Just Xenophobic or Were *Roper* and *Graham* Undemocratic?

The backlash against foreign law puzzled many commentators, who observed that it is the critical reaction to the use of foreign law that is new, not its actual use.[134] The

---

131 *Transcript: Day Two of the Roberts Confirmation Hearings – Part III*, WASH. POST, September 13, 2005, http://www.washingtonpost.com/wp-dyn/content/article/2005/09/13/AR2005091301210.html (responding to Senator Kyle); *U.S. Senate Judiciary Committee Hearing on Judge Samuel Alito's Nomination to the Supreme Court – Part I*, WASH. POST, January 10, 2006, http://www.washingtonpost.com/wp-dyn/content/article/2006/01/10/AR2006011000781.html (responding to Senator Kyle). *Transcript: Day Three of the Sotomayor Confirmation Hearings, Part II*, http://latimesblogs.latimes.com/washington/2009/07/sotomayor-hearings-complete-transcript-day-3-part-2.html (last visited May 12, 2012) (responding to Senator Coburn; *Transcript: Kagan Confirmation Hearings*, http://www.marylandindependentparty.org/for_discussion/Kagan_confirmation_hearings_transcript.html (last visited May 12, 2012) (responding to Senator Grassley).

132 *Transcript: Day Two of the Roberts Confirmation Hearings – Part III*, WASH. POST, September 13, 2005, http://www.washingtonpost.com/wp-dyn/content/article/2005/09/13/AR2005091301210.html (responding to Senator Kyle); *U.S. Senate Judiciary Committee Hearing on Judge Samuel Alito's Nomination to the Supreme Court – Part I*, WASH. POST, January 10, 2006, http://www.washingtonpost.com/wp-dyn/content/article/2006/01/10/AR2006011000781.html (responding to Senator Kyle). *Transcript: Day Three of the Sotomayor Confirmation Hearings, Part II*, http://latimesblogs.latimes.com/washington/2009/07/sotomayor-hearings-complete-transcript-day-3-part-2.html (last visited May 12, 2012) (responding to Senator Coburn); *Transcript: Kagan Confirmation Hearings*, http://www.marylandindependentparty.org/for_discussion/Kagan_confirmation_hearings_transcript.html (last visited May 12, 2012) (responding to Senator Grassley).

133 Graham v. Florida, 130 S. Ct. 2011, 2017, 2033 (2010).

134 Much has been written concerning the Court's long practice of using foreign law. *See, e.g.*, Cindy G. Buys, *Burying Our Constitution in the Sand? Evaluating the Ostrich Response to the Use of International and Foreign Law in U.S. Constitutional Interpretation*, 21 BYU J. Pub. L. 1 (2007 ) (discussing the heavy influence of foreign law in the United States); David J. Seipp, *Our Law, Their Law, History, and the Citation of Foreign Law*, 86 B. U. L. REV. 1417, 1428–36 (2006); Paul Finkelman, *Foreign Law and American Constitutional Interpretation: A Long and Venerable Tradition*, 63 N.Y.U.

vehemence of the reaction to foreign law has an unmistakable air of xenophobia: death threats, laws threatening judicial impeachment for its use, and descriptions of judges who use foreign law as "satanic"[135] are difficult to cast in a rational light. This section attempts to make sense of the reaction by examining four reasons for it.

First, and most obviously, the complaint about foreign law was at bottom a complaint about the results achieved by its use when it expanded personal liberty. Critics were unhappy that the Court looked to foreign law to expand personal liberties on controversial social issues such as consensual sex between same-sex partners and the death penalty.

Second, conservatives felt betrayed by Justice Kennedy's shift from a supporter of the juvenile death penalty in *Stanford* to its chief abolitionist in *Roper*.

Third, in *Roper* particularly, the Court appeared to give greater weight to foreign law than it had previously, creating a slippery slope that, in elevating foreign law above that of the United States, appears undemocratic.

Finally, the Court's willingness to disregard American views while deferring to foreign ones violates the United States's sense of exceptionalism.

That the criticism is results-based is evidenced by the critics' silence when the Court referred to foreign law in *Bowers v. Hardwick* to restrict personal liberty and uphold a state statute criminalizing intimate sexual contact between same-sex partners.[136] Seventeen years later, the critics vocalized their outrage when the Court used foreign law to reverse *Bowers* and hold that a similar statute was unconstitutional.[137] Justice Scalia's dissent articulated that outrage when he wrote that "'[t]he Court's discussion of these foreign views . . . [was] . . . meaningless dicta. Dangerous dicta, however, since 'this Court . . . should not impose foreign moods, fads, or fashions on Americans.'"[138]

A sense of conservative betrayal may have fueled the backlash. When Justice Kennedy, a President Reagan appointee, cited foreign law, and used that law to expand personal liberties, social conservatives may have felt betrayed.[139] In

---

Ann. Surv. Am. L. 29 (2007) ; *The Use of International and Foreign Law in Interpreting the U.S. Constitution*, Am. Const. Soc. L. & Pol'y, http://www.acslaw.org/files/intl%20law%20study%20guide%201-18-06.pdf (last visited May 12, 2012); *see also* Jeffrey Toobin, *How Anthony Kennedy's Passion for Foreign Law Could Change the Supreme Court*, The New Yorker, September 12, 2005, at 42, *available at* http://www.newyorker.com/archive/2005/09/12/050912fa_fact ("The United States Supreme Court has made references to foreign law since the earliest days of the Republic.").

135 *See supra, Roper*: The Conservative Backlash.

136 Bowers v. Hardwick, 478 U.S. 186, 196–97 (1986) (Burger, C.J., concurring).

137 Lawrence v. Texas, 539 U.S. 558, 571–75 (2003). *See supra, Roper*: The Conservative Backlash for discussion of judicial and extrajudicial reaction to Lawrence v. Texas.

138 Lawrence v. Texas, 539 U.S. 558, 598 (2003) (Scalia, J., dissenting) (quoting Foster v. Florida, 537 U.S. 990 n.* (2002) (Thomas, J., concurring in denial of certiorari)).

139 *See generally* Jeffrey Toobin, *How Anthony Kennedy's Passion for Foreign Law Could Change the Supreme Court*, The New Yorker, September 12, 2005, at 42, *available at*

*Stanford*, Justice Kennedy had joined in Justice Scalia's opinion, which expressly rejected reliance on foreign law.[140] Only 16 years later, he authored *Roper*, which embraced foreign law to an unprecedented degree.[141]

In addition, while reference to foreign law was not new, the weight Justice Kennedy gave it did appear new. Professor Alford notes that *Roper* was "new" in the depth and breadth of its consideration of foreign law.[142] He writes, "[f]or the first time in history, the Supreme Court devoted an entire section of an Eighth Amendment opinion – six paragraphs and just under four pages of the slip opinion – to constitutional comparativism."[143] Chief Justice Rehnquist had foreshadowed the critics' complaint about the use of foreign law in his *Atkins* dissent, even though in *Atkins* the majority had confined its reference to foreign law to a footnote.[144] In *Atkins*, Chief Justice Rehnquist wrote that previous death penalty decisions had referred to foreign law merely to test "'the climate of international opinion,'"[145] and had relied "only on the bare citation of international laws."[146]

Justice Kennedy's heavier reliance on foreign law appears to give it a greater role than it played in earlier decisions. Critics correctly observe that Justice Kennedy used foreign law to confirm the Court's own judgment, rather than to confirm an American consensus.[147] This left Justice Kennedy open to criticism that he had disregarded American views.[148]

Indeed, the evidence of consensus was weak in both *Roper* and *Graham*. Justice Kennedy had found consensus against the juvenile death penalty in *Roper* when fewer than half of the states that permitted capital punishment limited it to those over eighteen.[149] As Justice Scalia wrote in dissent, "[w]ords have no meaning if the views of less than 50% of death penalty States can constitute a national consensus."[150] In *Graham*, Justice Thomas pointed out that Justice Kennedy found consensus against juvenile life without parole sentences even though 74% of the states, "a supermajority," permitted them.[151] As one commentator said, by relying

---

http://www.newyorker.com/archive/2005/09/12/050912fa_fact (noting Justice Kennedy's reliance on foreign sources had prompted a vigorous backlash both on and off the Court).

140 Stanford v. Kentucky, 492 U.S. 361, 369 n. 1 (1989).

141 Roper v. Simmons, 543 U.S. 551, 575–9 (2005).

142 Roger Paul Alford, *Roper v. Simmons and Our Constitution in International Equipoise*, 53 UCLA L. Rev. 1, 8 (2005).

143 Roger Paul Alford, *Roper v. Simmons and Our Constitution in International Equipoise*, 53 UCLA L. Rev. 1, 8 (2005).

144 Atkins v. Virginia, 536 U.S. 304, 316 n. 21 (2002).

145 Atkins v. Virginia, 536 U.S. 304, 325 (2002) (Rehnquist, C.J., dissenting) (quoting Coker v. Georgia, 433 U.S. 584, 596 n. 10 (1977)).

146 Atkins v. Virginia, 536 U.S. 304, 325 (2002) (Rehnquist, C.J., dissenting).

147 Roper v. Simmons, 543 U.S. 551, 575 (2005).

148 Roper v. Simmons, 543 U.S. 551, 622 (2005) (Scalia, J., dissenting).

149 Roper v. Simmons, 543 U.S. 551, 564 (2005).

150 Roper v. Simmons, 543 U.S. 551, 609 (2005) (Scalia, J., dissenting).

151 Graham v. Florida, 130 S. Ct. 2011, 2049 (2010) (Thomas, J., dissenting).

on foreign sources where a national consensus was weak, the Court "started down a slippery slope that gives more deference to foreign laws than it does to state laws."[152]

Justice Scalia argues that this slippery slope has doubly undemocratic results. First, by finding consensus where none existed, the Court disenfranchised the Americans whose views on the evolving standard of decency the Court purported to consider paramount.[153] The Court then added insult to injury by substituting foreign views that were themselves imposed on Europeans by a bureaucratic elite.[154]

The strong reaction to this perceived one–two punch of disenfranchisement followed by imposition of European views, is explained, in part, by Americans' view of themselves as exceptional. "American exceptionalism" celebrates America's unique democratic institutions and justifies its refusal to consider foreign law.[155] The American system is unique because the nation is governed by a Constitution that delegates limited powers to the government.[156] This "clearly set the U.S. governmental system apart from the authoritarian systems of Europe."[157] The Constitution is also unique in its allocation of "sovereign powers among the national government, the states, and the people [which] created a distinctively American system of federalism with no direct foreign analogue."[158]

Critics of constitutional comparativism are thus unmoved by Justice Kennedy's observation in *Roper* that the United States stood alone in a world that had rejected the juvenile death penalty.[159] America's unique system is distinctively responsive to the popular will, unlike the European system, which rejected the death penalty notwithstanding the will of its own people. Judge Posner, criticizing the Court for using foreign law, writes, "the European rejection of the death penalty probably is related to [*inter alia*] the less democratic cast of European politics, as a result of which elite opinion is more likely to override public opinion than it is in the United States."[160]

---

152 Jacob J. Zehnder, Note, *Constitutional Comparativism: The Emerging Risk of Comparative Law as Constitutional Tiebreaker*, 41 VAL. U.L. REV. 1739, 1764–65 (2007).

153 *See* Roper v. Simmons, 543 U.S. 551, 608–22 (2005) (Scalia, J., dissenting).

154 *See* Roper v. Simmons, 543 U.S. 551, 622–8 (2005) (Scalia, J., dissenting).

155 Sarah H. Cleveland, *Foreign Authority, American Exceptionalism, and the Dred Scott Case*, 82 CHI.-KENT L. REV. 393, 393 (2007).

156 Sarah H. Cleveland, *Foreign Authority, American Exceptionalism, and the Dred Scott Case,* 82 CHI.-KENT L. REV. 393, 394 (2007).

157 Sarah H. Cleveland, *Foreign Authority, American Exceptionalism, and the Dred Scott Case,* 82 CHI.-KENT L. REV. 393, 394 (2007).

158 Sarah H. Cleveland, *Foreign Authority, American Exceptionalism, and the Dred Scott Case,* 82 CHI.-KENT L. REV. 393, 394 (2007).

159 *See* Roper v. Simmons, 543 U.S. 551, 575 (2005).

160 Richard A. Posner, *The Supreme Court 2004 Term -- Forward: A Political Court,* 119 HARV. L. REV. 31, 86 (2005).

Likewise, Professor Steiker explains that Americans and Europeans in fact see eye to eye on the death penalty, but America's "political institutions are more responsive to the public will."[161] Although Europeans overwhelmingly support capital punishment,[162] in Europe, political parties select the candidates, protecting them "from hot-button single issues like the death penalty."[163] This contrasts with the American primary system, where a candidate's position on a hot-button issue can lose or win an election. Americans generally require their local, state, and federal representatives to support the death penalty.[164]

Indeed, Americans are particularly populist in criminal matters. The Constitution "ensure[s] state dominance over criminal law. As a result, criminal law-making and law enforcement are understood and experienced in the United States as primarily a state and local concern."[165] Thus, Americans see no reason why the federal government should impede on a state's traditional prerogative to permit the death penalty.[166] Chief Justice Rehnquist expressed this sentiment in his *Atkins* dissent, when he complained that the Court had violated fundamental principles of federalism in striking the law that permitted execution of the mentally retarded.[167]

Steiker observes that American government is also exceptional because "lay participation in the criminal justice system" is much greater in the United States than abroad.[168] No other country gives so much control to criminal trial juries.[169] Thus, Justice Kennedy struck a blow to a core American value when he

---

161 Carol S. Steiker, *Capital Punishment and American Exceptionalism*, 15, http://international-ul.com/pdf/steiker.pdf (last visited May 16, 2012).

162 Carol S. Steiker, *Capital Punishment and American Exceptionalism*, 15, http://international-ul.com/pdf/steiker.pdf (last visited May 16, 2012).

163 Carol S. Steiker, *Capital Punishment and American Exceptionalism*, 16, http://international-ul.com/pdf/steiker.pdf (last visited May 16, 2012).

164 Carol S. Steiker, *Capital Punishment and American Exceptionalism*, 13–15, http://international-ul.com/pdf/steiker.pdf (last visited May 16, 2012).

165 Carol S. Steiker, *Capital Punishment and American Exceptionalism*, 21–22, http://international-ul.com/pdf/steiker.pdf (last visited May 16, 2012).

166 *See* Carol S. Steiker, *Capital Punishment and American Exceptionalism*, 19, http://international-ul.com/pdf/steiker.pdf (last visited May 16, 2012) (pointing out that "[o]ne of the most clearly exceptional aspects of the structure of American government is the . . . direct political accountability of institutional actors within the criminal justice system," as prosecutors and judges are generally elected or "otherwise politically accountable."

167 Chief Justice Rehnquist dissented "to call attention to the defects in the Court's decision to place weight on foreign laws [among other data] . . . in reaching its conclusion . . . [which was] antithetical to considerations of federalism." Atkins v. Virginia, 536 U.S. 304, 322 (2002) (Rehnquist, C.J., dissenting).

168 Carol S. Steiker, *Capital Punishment and American Exceptionalism*, 19, http://international-ul.com/pdf/steiker.pdf (last visited May 16, 2012).

169 Carol S. Steiker, *Capital Punishment and American Exceptionalism*, 19, http://international-ul.com/pdf/steiker.pdf (last visited May 16, 2012).

acknowledged in *Roper* that, while some juvenile killers deserved death, juries could not be trusted to make the decision.[170]

Professor Steiker also theorizes that exceptionalism cuts both ways. She says that "*European* exceptionalism" explains why Europe is unified in abolishing the death penalty while America is not.[171] Steiker explains that Europe's domination by Mussolini, Hitler, and Stalin created a demand to neutralize the state's power to impose death.[172] In contrast, the United States is free from Europe's historical burden, permitting it to maintain "'anti-internationalism'... [in which] 'the United States can pick and choose the international conventions and laws that serve its purpose and reject those that do not.'"[173]

Although principled objections to the manner in which the Court used foreign law exist, it should be noted that the critics who complain that the Court's decisions in *Roper* and *Graham* thwarted the democratic will are not entirely consistent. The conservative members of the Court have not hesitated to overturn the will of the people, as expressed through legislation, when the Court felt constitutionally bound to do so.[174]

Further, Justice Scalia's insistence in *Stanford* that the Court limit itself to an inquiry into American consensus[175] confines the Court to a ministerial role. However, the Constitution does not contemplate that the judiciary defer the

---

170 *See* Roper v. Simmons, 543 U.S. 551, 572–23 (2005).

171 Carol S. Steiker, *Capital Punishment and American Exceptionalism*, 26, http://international-ul.com/pdf/steiker.pdf (last visited May 16, 2012 (emphasis added).

172 Carol S. Steiker, *Capital Punishment and American Exceptionalism*, 26, http://international-ul.com/pdf/steiker.pdf (last visited May 16, 2012).

173 Carol S. Steiker, *Capital Punishment and American Exceptionalism*, 27, http://international-ul.com/pdf/steiker.pdf (last visited May 16, 2012) (quoting Peter J. Spiro, *The New Sovereigntists: American Exceptionalism and Its False Prophets*, FOREIGN AFFAIRS, November/December 2000, at 9).

174 *See, e.g.* Arizona Free Enterprise Club's Freedom Club PAC v. Bennett, 131 S. Ct. 2806 (2011) (declaring unconstitutional provision of Arizona's campaign finance law because law violated freedom of speech under First Amendment); Citizens United v. Federal Commc'n Comm'n, 558 U.S. 310 (2010) (declaring unconstitutional a provision of Bipartisan Campaign Reform Act of 2002 that prohibited corporations from engaging in political speech because law violated freedom of speech under First Amendment); United States v. Morrison, 529 U.S. 598 (2000) (declaring unconstitutional provision in Violence Against Women Act that provided a federal civil remedy for victims of gender-related violence because Congress lacked authority under the Commerce Clause or the Fourteenth Amendment to enact such legislation); United States v. Lopez, 514 U.S. 549 (1995) (declaring unconstitutional the Gun-Free School Zones Act that made it a federal crime to possess a firearm near a school because Congress lacked authority under the Commerce Clause to enact such legislation).

175 *See* Stanford v. Kentucky, 491 U.S. 361, 369–70 (1989).

task of constitutional interpretation to the legislature or the electorate; indeed, constitutional interpretation is vested in the Court.[176]

Several current Supreme Court justices believe that consulting foreign law enhances the Court's ability to correctly apply US law, particularly in areas concerning human rights that transcend national boundaries. In a public speech on the issue, Justice Ruth Bader Ginsburg defended the wisdom of consulting foreign law. She places great "value . . . on comparative dialogue." [177] In her view, "[t]he US judicial system will be the poorer . . . if we do not both share our experience with, and learn from, legal systems with values and a commitment to democracy similar to our own."[178] Addressing the critics, she concedes, "foreign opinions are not authoritative; they set no binding precedent for the US judge."[179] Still, she notes, "they can add to the store of knowledge relevant to the solution for trying questions."[180]

Likewise, Justice Breyer has long defended the use of foreign law to help resolve domestic issues confronting foreign judges. When he debated Justice Scalia at American University, Justice Breyer said, "first, of course, foreign law doesn't bind us . . . [in interpreting] constitutional law . . . But . . . [foreign] judges . . . have problems that often, more and more, are similar to our own . . . 'If here I have a human being called a judge in a different country dealing with a similar problem, why don't I read what he says if it's similar enough? Maybe I'll learn something.'"[181]

---

176 As Chief Justice Roberts recently observed, at least since 1803, the Court has "'recognized that when an Act of Congress is alleged to conflict with the Constitution, '[i]t is emphatically the province and duty of the judicial department to say what the law is.'" Zivotofsky *ex rel.* Zivotofsky v. Clinton, 132 S. Ct. 1421, 1427–28 (2012) (quoting Marbury v. Madison, 1 Cranch 137, 177, 2 L. Ed. 60 (1803)).

177 Ruth Bader Ginsburg, *"A Decent Respect to the Opinions of [Human]kind": The Value of a Comparative Perspective in Constitutional Adjudication*, 64 Cambridge L.J. 575, 578 (2005), *available at* http://www.cpl.law.cam.ac.uk/CLJ_Ruth_Ginsburg_SDWL2005.pdf.

178 Ruth Bader Ginsburg, *"A Decent Respect to the Opinions of [Human]kind": The Value of a Comparative Perspective in Constitutional Adjudication*, 64 Cambridge L.J. 575, 576 (2005), *available at* http://www.cpl.law.cam.ac.uk/CLJ_Ruth_Ginsburg_SDWL2005.pdf.

179 Ruth Bader Ginsburg, *"A Decent Respect to the Opinions of [Human]kind": The Value of a Comparative Perspective in Constitutional Adjudication*, 64 Cambridge L.J. 575, 580 (2005), *available at* http://www.cpl.law.cam.ac.uk/CLJ_Ruth_Ginsburg_SDWL2005.pdf.

180 Ruth Bader Ginsburg, *"A Decent Respect to the Opinions of [Human]kind": The Value of a Comparative Perspective in Constitutional Adjudication*, 64 Cambridge L.J. 575, 580 (2005), *available at* http://www.cpl.law.cam.ac.uk/CLJ_Ruth_Ginsburg_SDWL2005.pdf.

181 Justices Antonin Scalia and Stephen Breyer, *Discussion at the American University Washington College of Law: Constitutional Relevance of Foreign Court Decisions* (January

Legal Analyst Jeffrey Toobin writes that Justice Kennedy became a devotee of examining foreign law only after he had traveled widely in Europe, especially after the Iron Curtain fell.[182] There, he and other jurists responded to the calls of newly formed democracies in the 1980s that sought help in drafting constitutions.[183] Justice Kennedy's work and relationships with foreign lawyers and judges increased his awareness of and appreciation for foreign law.[184] He came to embrace the use of foreign law as a source of information, much like the statistical and social science data amici briefs routinely provide to the Court.[185]

Particularly in matters concerning individual rights, consulting the views of others who share our common humanity might provide useful information.[186] The critics of foreign law overreacted when the Court used foreign law, but its defenders may have understated how it was used, particularly in *Roper* and *Graham*.

## Conclusion

The United States exercised its sense of exceptionalism when it refused to ratify the Convention on the Rights of the Child, and when it expressed a reservation to that part of the ICCPR that abolished the juvenile death penalty. Thus, when Justice Kennedy required the United States to follow the treaties it had rejected, he touched off a firestorm that is at least in part the product of a sense that the Supreme Court had imposed foreign views on an electorate that had rejected those views. That those foreign views belonged to the bureaucratic elite, and not the European people, only added fuel to the fire. In light of America's view of itself as

13, 2005), http://domino.american.edu/AU/media/mediarel.nsf/1D265343BDC2189785256B810071F238/1F2F7DC4757FD01E85256F890068E6E0?OpenDocument.

182 Jeffrey Toobin, *How Anthony Kennedy's Passion for Foreign Law Could Change the Supreme Court*, THE NEW YORKER, September 12, 2005, at 42, *available at* http://www.newyorker.com/archive/2005/09/12/050912fa_fact.

183 Jeffrey Toobin, *How Anthony Kennedy's Passion for Foreign Law Could Change the Supreme Court*, THE NEW YORKER, September 12, 2005, at 42, *available at* http://www.newyorker.com/archive/2005/09/12/050912fa_fact.

184 Jeffrey Toobin, *How Anthony Kennedy's Passion for Foreign Law Could Change the Supreme Court*, THE NEW YORKER, September 12, 2005, at 42, *available at* http://www.newyorker.com/archive/2005/09/12/050912fa_fact.

185 Jeffrey Toobin, *How Anthony Kennedy's Passion for Foreign Law Could Change the Supreme Court*, THE NEW YORKER, September 12, 2005, at 42, *available at* http://www.newyorker.com/archive/2005/09/12/050912fa_fact. An amicus brief is "[a] brief, [usually] at the appellate level, prepared and filed by [a non-party to the action who has an interest in the matter] with the court's permission." BLACK'S LAW DICTIONARY 217 (9th ed. 2009).

186 See Mark C. Rahdert, *Comparative Constitutional Advocacy*, 56 AM. U. L. REV. 553, 655 (2007) (discussing the reasons for and against comparative constitutional analysis and concluding, "there is more to be gained than lost from comparative constitutional analysis").

exceptional in its democratic and populist history, some reaction, if not the vitriol accompanying it, was not surprising.

*Roper* and *Graham* did not replace American consensus with a foreign one, but the Court did give primacy to its independent judgment, not to American consensus, and Justice Kennedy used foreign law to confirm that judgment.

Critics of foreign law are right that European and American experiences are different, historically, politically and culturally. So while the Court should be free to consult any source, including foreign sources, for empirical information, it should use the foreign law with caution, and with an appreciation of its historical, political, and cultural context.

# Chapter 4
# Horizontal Impact of Human Rights – Dialogue Between Constitutional and International Law

Barbara Grabowska

## Introduction: The Origins and Essence of "Horizontal Effect of Human Rights"

This chapter presents the issue of horizontal effect using examples from three legal systems as different ways in which constitutional values (human rights in particular) affect relations governed by private law. This issue is a function of several factors and processes – the development of constitutional law, everyday social life and unavoidable conflicts between human rights and freedoms. The progressive and difficult to contain development of society and social relationships result *inter alia* in the structure of subjects fulfilling public functions. The growing role of private subjects (companies, corporations) causes a real impact on human rights and their structure, and new threats to them.

The issue of horizontal effect of human rights seems to be derived from Ulpian's division of public and private law.[1] The basic feature of public law is that it applies to situations between the state and the individual and is governed by the rule of the subordination of the individual to the state, which owns public power and is entitled in prescribed situations to enforce its decisions (judgments, administrative decisions, etc.). Private law regulates relations between individuals. The concept of the horizontal effect of human rights somehow mixes these two systems into one, although not uniformly. That is why it is often called the privatization of human rights,[2] which should be understood as the impact of constitutional rules (e.g. equality) and human rights on private law. It should be underlined that originally human rights were interpreted as a consequence of public law and were mostly understood as "negative freedoms" – a sphere of life that the state's authorities could not interfere with. Thus human rights were (and still are) a legal means of protection against the omnipotence of the state.

1 Publicum ius est quod ad statum rei Romanae spectat, ius privatum est quod ad singulorum utilitatem.

2 Barak A. 2001, "Constitutional Human Rights and Private Law," in Friedmann D., Barak-Erez D., eds, *Human Rights in Private Law*, Hart, Oxford, p. 13.

One of the reasons for the horizontal approach of human rights comes from the view that human rights can be violated by both the state and by the individuals who should take responsibility for these violations,[3] especially in situations when some public services are supplied by private actors. The second reason for this approach comes as a consequence of the privatization of some public areas of life where the state previously enjoyed a monopoly. The horizontal effect of human rights on private law is a means of guaranteeing a proper level of protection for human rights and constitutional values using constitutional law (direct horizontal effect) or private law tools (indirect horizontal effect).[4]

Chronologically the German approach of horizontal effect of human rights in private law came first. German achievements in this field (as so called Drittwirkung) have had a great impact on its progress and implications for other national legal systems. The second paradigm analyzed in this paper deals with public international law – particularly with the European Convention on Human Rights and Strasbourg Court's case law. The third legal system observed is European Union law – a specific and unique international law system with increasing attention to human rights protection. As a conclusion, I would like to show how those three independent but co-related legal systems dialogue with each other and the impact of this dialogue on Polish law. I will subsequently address the question of whether the horizontal effect of human rights (statutory and judicially) exists in Poland. The vehicle for the discussion of the different approaches of the "horizontal effect" of human rights is the example of the rule of equality (right to equal treatment) functioning in these different legal environments.

## Doubts and Disadvantages of the "Third Party Effect"

The main problem of horizontal effect is that the extended protection against violations of human rights (by private persons) results in the limitation of other people's rights. That is why it is proposed that fundamental rights should have very limited value in private law, especially when using indirect horizontal effect.[5] Moreover, it is argued that the existing private law is already to a very large scale an expression of the values behind fundamental rights. In addition, according to J. Smith, fundamental rights do not offer enough guidance to decide a case. As

3 One aspect of this issue is the responsibility of non-state actors such as transnational corporations under international law. Compare the UN Declaration of 2003 "Norms on the Responsibility of Transnational Corporations and Other Business enterprises with regard to Human Rights," E/CN.4/Sub.2/2003/12/Rev.2.

4 Barak, op. cit., pp. 14, 21.

5 Smith J.M. 2006, "Private Law and Fundamental Rights: A Skeptical View," Maastricht Working Papers, Faculty of Law 8/2006, p. 8; the author states that in indirect effect the rules designed for private relations have priority over fundamental rights and cannot be absorbed by them (but they can still be interpreted in the light of human rights).

an example he presents wrongful birth cases. The third argument is that private parties are not bound by fundamental rights (meaning that they are not addressed to private parties, but to the state). This is closely connected to the division between public and private law and to the fact that private persons do not need to pursue the public interest. It is also a consequence of the fact that the nature of fundamental rights is to control the state's power, not the individual's autonomy.

A good example illustrating the problem is the constitutional rule of equality. In these two legal branches (private and public), the rule of equality has completely different scopes and plays different roles. In public law, it is a general rule that governs the activity of public authorities – the state must not discriminate (treat unequally) between people who are in similar situations (meaning that the similar should be treated similarly). In this field equality is the general rule and discrimination (unequal treatment) the exception. In private law the situation is reversed – freedom of contract is a fundamental element of private relations but it is based on the assumption that one can enter into contract with anybody one wants to. On the other hand, it means that one does not have to make a contract (come into contractual relations) with another person.

As mentioned previously, there are two kinds of horizontal effects: direct effect of constitutional law (public law) rules on private law and indirect effect based on the use of private law tools, by interpreting private law blanket clauses in the light of constitutional supreme rules.[6] Currently the common denominator in the different types of horizontal effect of human rights seems to be the indirect effect understood as a different way of interpreting private law for the purpose of maintaining the "constitutional level" of protection of human rights. It is the best way to apply a rule of proportionality, which is indispensable in resolving conflicts between rights, freedoms and other values.

## Germany – the Doctrine of Horizontal Effect of Human Rights in the Motherland

Germany is thought to be the cradle of the *Drittwirkung* doctrine. This is mostly due to the judgments of the German Constitutional Court in Karlsruhe and the Federal Labour Court. The first judgment was made in 1958 in the *Luth* case, which established the cornerstone for the creation and the further development of the doctrine of horizontal effect of human rights. Erich Luth (the head of the Press Association in Hamburg) called for a boycott of Veit Harlan's new film. Harlan had been the director of anti-Semitic films in the Third Reich. The producer and the distributing company applied successfully for an injunction prohibiting Luth from repeating his statements. However, the Constitutional Court accepted Luth's constitutional complaint. The Court found that the Constitution creates an "objective system of values" that is binding for all public authorities, including

6 Barak, op. cit., pp. 29, 42.

courts, which must solve legal disputes in such manner that their judgments will express this order of constitutional values. Such an approach has been called the "indirect" horizontal effect of fundamental rights since constitutional values are transposed into a private law dispute by private law tools, balancing additionally two constitutional rights – freedom of speech and protection of good reputation. Thus human rights have been indirectly applied to the horizontal relations between two private parties.

In the *Luth* case, the Federal Constitutional Court found that, under the "objective order of values," the freedom of speech will prevail according to the proportionality test created on the grounds of this case and it "will prevail as long as it does not infringe the legally protected interests of another party which take precedence over free speech in the particular circumstances of a case."[7]

One recent important discussion on the scope of application of constitutional rights and freedoms to private relationships took place during the preparation of the Equality Law in Germany.[8] Despite the intensive discussion and strong arguments against the draft, the Parliament accepted it, and the General Act on Equal Treatment (*Allgemeines Gleichbehandlungsgesetz*; hereinafter AGG) entered into force on 1 August 2006. It prohibits discrimination on grounds of race, ethnic origin, sex, religion, disability, age and sexual orientation. The most controversial part of the Act is Part Three on "Protection Against Discrimination Under Civil Law." AGG does not cover all private contracts but only applies in certain situations, such as "bulk business," that typically arise without regard to a specific person in a large number of cases and under comparable conditions (Article 19, paragraph 1, point 1). It also applies to obligations that have as their object private-law insurance (Article 19, paragraph 1, point 2). At the same time, the AGG defines the exceptions from this equality rule (Article 19, paragraphs 2–5) and permissible differences in treatment (Article 20). The scope of the German anti-discrimination law is much wider that the scope of EU anti-discrimination law, which caused doubts as to whether anti-discrimination legislation for non-state actors is appropriate in the German context.[9] The debated point is the issue of possible remedies for breach of the rule of equal treatment, particularly the obligation to contract. Until now, the constitutionality of this remedy has not been

7 Fedtke J. 2007, "Germany. Drittwirkung in Germany," in Oliver D., Fedtke J., eds, *Human Rights and the Private Sphere. A Comparative Study*, Routledge-Cavendish, Abingdon, p. 145.

8 Sommeregger G. 2005, "The Horizontalization of Equality: The German Attempt to Promote Non-Discrimination in the Private Sphere via Legislation," in Sajo A., Uitz R., eds, *The Constitution in Private Relations: Expanding Constitutionalism*, Eleven International, Utrecht, pp. 36–40.

9 Wiemann, J. 2010, "Obligation to Contract and the German General Act on Equal Treatment (Allgemeines Gleichbehandlungsgesetz)," *German Law Journal* 11(10), p. 1132; available at: http://www.germanlawjournal.com/pdfs/Vol11-No10/PDF_Vol_11_No_10_1131-1146_DAAD_Wiemann%20FINAL.pdf

challenged by any judgment of the Federal Constitutional Court. Moreover, there are arguments that claim that such remedy is compatible with German Basic Law.[10]

## The (Lack of) Horizontal effect of Human Rights Under the European Convention on Human Rights

According to the case law of the European Court of Human Rights, the application of the rights and freedoms set forth in the European Convention on Human Rights (hereinafter the Convention) to the relations between two private subjects seems to be impossible, first of all because of the stipulation of Article 1 of the Convention, which is addressed to the States–Parties of the Convention:

> The High Contracting Parties shall secure to everyone within their jurisdiction the rights and freedoms defined in Section I of this Convention.

Second, private individuals are not the actors of public international law. The individual may lodge an application to the European Court of Human Rights but cannot be sued before it on the grounds of the Convention. Accepting the idea of the horizontal effect of human rights and applying it in practice means that certain obligations need be imposed on individuals on the grounds of the Convention. To make them effective, it would have to be possible to defend them before the Strasbourg court.

Nevertheless, there are at least two cases that have dealt with the issue of horizontal effect of human rights in private law and within private relations. The first one was the judgment of *Pla and Puncernau v. Andorra.*[11] The applicant, Antoni Pla Puncernau, was a citizen of Andorra and the adopted son of Francesc-Xavier Pla Pujol, who died in 1996. The Andorran court decided that the applicant, as an adopted child, could not inherit the estate of Mr Pla Pujol's mother, Carolina Pujol Oller. One of the clauses of her last will of 1939 stipulated that her son was to pass on his inheritance to a child or grandchild "from a legitimate and canonical marriage." In the event of failure to satisfy those conditions, the estate was to pass to the children and grandchildren of Ms Pujol Oller's daughters.

Mr Pla Pujol married Roser Puncernau Pedro (the second applicant) and, in 1969, they adopted Antoni (the first applicant). In 1995, Mr Pla Pujol bequeathed the property he had inherited to Antoni, giving Roser a life-interest in the estate. On 18 May 2000, the High Court of Justice of Andorra found that that Antoni, as an adopted child, could not be considered "a child of a lawful and canonical marriage" and could not, therefore, inherit Ms Pujol Oller's estate. The court ordered the applicants to hand over the property to Ms Pujol Oller's

10 Ibid., pp. 1144–5.

11 Judgment of 13 July 2004, application no. 69498/01.

great-granddaughters, deemed to be her rightful heirs. The decision was upheld by the Constitutional Court.

The European Court found that there had been a violation of Article 14 (prohibition of discrimination) read in conjunction with Article 8 (right to respect for private and family life) of the European Convention on Human Rights. The Court decided that the Convention as a living instrument should be read in the light of the present conditions and stated that "where such a long period has elapsed, during which profound social, economic and legal changes have occurred, the courts cannot ignore these new realities."

The judgment was criticized.[12] An interesting and important source of these critiques was the dissenting opinion of Judge Garlicki. He found that "under our case-law it is obvious that there may be certain positive obligations of the State to adopt measures designed to secure respect for Convention rights, even in the sphere of the relations of individuals between themselves." However, he stated that "it seems . . . obvious that the level of protection against a private action cannot be the same as the level of protection against State action" and "what is prohibited for the State need not necessarily also be prohibited for individuals."

The basic argument for this statement is that "every prohibition of private action . . ., while protecting the rights of some persons, unavoidably restricts the rights of other persons." Additionally, Judge Garlicki interpreted the inheritance law specifically, arguing that the "whole idea of a will is to depart from the general system of inheritance, that is, to discriminate between potential heirs." Those private testamentary dispositions should have priority, with exceptions "where the disposition may be said to be repugnant to the fundamental ideals of the Convention or to aim at the destruction of the rights and freedoms set forth therein."

In the opinion of Judge Garlicki, in the circumstances of the *Pla* case, the testarix had taken a decision, "which was perhaps unjust, but cannot, even by present-day standards, be regarded as repugnant to the fundamental ideals of the Convention or otherwise destructive of Convention rights."

In the second "horizontal" ECHR case (*Appleby and others v. United Kingdom*),[13] the Court found no violation of the Convention. The applicants set up an environmental group, Washington First Forum, to campaign against a plan to build on the only public playing field near Washington town center. In 1998, the applicants set about collecting signatures for a petition to persuade the council to reject the project. They tried to set up a stall and canvass views in "The Galleries," a shopping mall in Washington that had become the effective town center. They were prevented from doing so, however, by Postel, a private company that had bought most of the shopping area and had, under domestic law, the power to exclude anyone conducting unauthorized activities on its land.

12 Kay R.S. 2005, "The European Convention on Human Rights and the Control of Private Law," *European Human Rights Law Review* 5, pp. 466–79.

13 Judgment of 6 May 2005, application no. 44306/98.

The manager of one of the shops in the mall gave the applicants permission to set up stands in his store. However, permission was not granted in April 1998, when the applicants wished to collect signatures for a further petition. The manager of The Galleries informed the applicants that permission had been refused because the owner took a strictly neutral stance on all political and religious issues. However, the applicants claimed that other organizations had been allowed to carry out collections and to set up stalls and displays in The Galleries.

The applicant argued that they had been prevented from meeting in their town center to share information and ideas about the proposed building plans. In their opinion, this situation violated their freedom of expression (Article 10) and freedom of association (Article 11). The main problem of the case concerned the issue of the conflict between two rights – freedom of expression and property rights. The Court decided in the circumstances of the case to give priority to the second one, arguing that it was not sure "that there should be automatic rights of entry to private property." Moreover, the Court argued that the applicant had alternative means of communicating their views to the public. In the Court's opinion, the Government had not failed to comply with any positive obligation to protect the applicants' freedom of expression or freedom of assembly.

In the *Appleby* case, the judgment was passed by six votes to one. Judge Maruste presented his partly dissenting opinion in which he asked the question whether "private owners' property rights should prevail over other rights or does the State still have some responsibility to secure the proper balance between private and public interests?" He presented opposite arguments to those accepted by the majority of the Court. First of all, Judge Maruste argued that the shopping mall in this case is the area that "in its functional nature and essence is a *forum publicum* or "quasi-public" space." He did not agree with the statement that "through privatization the public authorities can divest themselves of all responsibility to protect rights and freedoms other than property rights." He found that individuals should be permitted to exercise their rights (such as freedom of speech) on the property of a privately owned shopping center. He did not agree with the situation where certain public services and institutions could be made inaccessible to the public and participants in demonstrations. Finally, in his opinion, the public authorities did not carry out a balancing exercise and did not regulate how the privately owned *forum publicum* was to be used in the public interest.

Perhaps, a new step forward in applying human rights horizontally could be the development of the Court's case law based on Protocol no. 12 to the Convention.[14] Article 1 of Protocol no. 12 states that the enjoyment of any right set forth by law shall be secured without discrimination on any ground such as sex, race, color, language, religion, political or other opinion, national or social origin, association with a national minority, property, birth or other status. Paragraph 2 adds that no one shall be discriminated against by any public authority on any ground such as those mentioned in paragraph 1.

14 Opened to signature in Rome, 4 November 2000.

The explanatory report to the Protocol states that Article 1 raises the "question to what extent Article 1 obliges the parties to take measures to prevent discrimination, even where discrimination occurs in relations between private persons (so-called "indirect horizontal effects")." It also explains that the prime objective of Article 1 is to embody a negative obligation for the parties: the obligation not to discriminate against individuals (point 24 of the Report).[15]

According to Report, Article 1 of Protocol no. 12 is not intended to impose a general positive obligation on the parties to take measures to prevent or remedy all instances of discrimination in relations between private persons. Moreover, Article 1 of the Convention sets a general limit on state responsibility, which is particularly relevant in cases of discrimination between private persons.[16]

In summary, the Report explains that the first paragraph of Article 1 refers to "any right set forth by law." This expression seeks to define the scope of the guarantee provided for in this paragraph and to limit its possible indirect horizontal effects.

Apart from the fact that third-party effect of rights and freedoms in the Convention does not appear in fact in the Court's case law, the Court managed to employ some methods of applying the Convention's values to the private parties. These are the doctrine of positive obligations, the obligation to interpret private law instruments in a manner compatible with the Convention and the requirement of balancing competing rights and public interests in the private sphere. Most likely, Protocol no. 12 will not greatly change these methods and will not establish a new one but may develop them using the rule of equality.

Current developments of the European Convention on Human Rights and Strasbourg case-law show that horizontal application of the Convention is quite similar to the German approach proposed in the *Luth* case, since the Court "has insisted on the duty of the domestic authorities to interpret even private law instruments in a manner compatible with the Convention."[17] However, it is certain that "the Court has never been willing to adhere clearly to the *Drittwirkung* approach."[18] A much more popular and broadly accepted concept that could replace the horizontal application of human rights is the wide scope of positive obligations

15 The Explanatory Report is available at: http://conventions.coe.int/Treaty/en/Reports/Html/177.htm.

16 Point 27 of the Report.

17 Spielmann D. 2007, "The European Convention on Human Rights. The European Court of Human Rights," in Oliver, D., Fedtke, J., eds, *Human Rights and the Private Sphere. A Comparative Study*, Routledge-Cavendish, Abingdon, p. 464.

18 Garlicki L. 2005, "Relations between Private Actors and the ECHR," in Sajo A., Uitz R., eds, *The Constitution in Private Relations: Expanding Constitutionalism*, Eleven International, Utrecht, p. 143.

of the state, for instance, to "provide legislative framework prohibiting private action that violates various rights and liberties guaranteed in the Convention."[19]

## European Union Law and ECJ Case Law – The Relation Between Internal Markets and Human Rights on the Example of the Right to Equality

Under European Union law, equality has been recognized as a universal right.[20] It has also been found to be a general rule of EU law[21] owing to the fact that fundamental rights are an essential component of the general principles of Community law.[22] The rule of equality in the EU legal order has two separate sources. The first is the EU primary law – (Treaty on the Functioning of the European Union and Treaty on the European Union) and the second is the European Convention on Human Rights and the Charter of Fundamental Rights of the European Union (created on the basis of the international instruments and constitutional traditions common to the Member States).

On the grounds of horizontal effects of human rights, the rule of equality is particularly interesting. The widest scope of regulation (containing also horizontal use of the rule of equality) is the main feature of the directive 2000/43[23] (the so-called "racial directive"). According to Article 3 of the Directive, it shall apply to social protection, including social security and healthcare, social advantages, education, access to and supply of goods and services that are available to the public, including housing.

The last issue (access to and supply of goods and services that are available to the public, including housing) is also covered by Directive 2004/113 implementing the principle of equal treatment between men and women in the access to and supply of goods and services. This broad scope of the racial directive is extremely important from the social point of view, especially in the field of elimination of social exclusion, since this directive also applies to wholly internal situations without a cross-border dimension.[24]

In the recent judgment of EU Court of Justice of 1 March 2011 (*Association belge des Consommateurs Test-Achats ASBL, Yann van Vugt, Charles Basselier*

---

19 Ibid., p. 142; X and Y v. Netherlands, judgment of 26 March 1985, application no. 8978/80.

20 Judgment of 12 December 2002, Rodríguez Caballero, C-442/00.

21 Judgment of ECJ of 19 January 2010 Kücükdeveci, C-555/07, Judgment of 22 November 2005 Mangold, C-144/04, paragraph 75; Joined Cases 117/76 and 16/77 Ruckdeschel and Others, paragraph 7.

22 Opinion of the ECJ C-2/94.

23 Council Directive 2000/43/EC of 29 June 2000 implementing the principle of equal treatment between persons irrespective of racial or ethnic origin.

24 Ringheim J. 2010, "The Prohibition of Racial and Ethnic Discrimination in Access to Services under EU Law," in *European Anti-Discrimination Law Review* 10 (July), 13.

*v. Conseil des ministres*, C-236/09) it was found that Article 5, paragraph 2 of Directive 2004/113 is incompatible with Articles 21 and 23 of the Charter of Fundamental Rights and invalid with effect from 21 December 2012. Article 5, paragraph 2 of the directive 2004/113 creates the exemption from the general rule of the prohibition of discrimination based on sex as a factor in the calculation of premiums and benefits for the purposes of insurance and related financial services (Article 5, paragraph 1).[25] It states that:

> Notwithstanding paragraph 1, Member States may decide before 21 December 2007 to permit proportionate differences in individuals' premiums and benefits where the use of sex is a determining factor in the assessment of risk based on relevant and accurate actuarial and statistical data. The Member States concerned shall inform the Commission and ensure that accurate data relevant to the use of sex as a determining actuarial factor are compiled, published and regularly updated. These Member States shall review their decision five years after 21 December 2007, taking into account the Commission report referred to in Article 16, and shall forward the results of this review to the Commission.

The case originally concerned the Belgian Law of 21 December 2007, which implements the derogation provided for in Article 5(2) of Directive 2004/113. The applicants (Association belge des Consommateurs Test-Achats ASBL) brought an action before the Constitutional Court for annulment of the Law of 21 December 2007. The applicants claimed that the Law is contrary to the principle of equality between men and women. The Constitutional Court decided to refer prejudicial questions to the European Court of Justice (ECJ).

This exemption permits proportionate differences in individuals' premiums and benefits where the use of sex is a determining factor in the assessment of risks based on relevant and accurate actuarial and statistical data. In the Court's opinion "Directive 2004/113 is silent as to the length of time during which those differences may continue to be applied, Member States which have made use of the option are permitted to allow insurers to apply the unequal treatment without any temporal limitation." In consequence, the Court found that "there is a risk that EU law may permit the derogation from the equal treatment of men and women, provided for in Article 5(2) of Directive 2004/113, to persist indefinitely."

The *Associate de Belgie* judgment is important because it was based on comparison of the provisions of the directive and the Charter of the Fundamental Rights because recital 4 to Directive 2004/113 expressly refers to Articles 21 and 23 of the Charter. That is why the Court decided that the validity of Article 5(2) of that directive must be assessed in the light of those provisions. It shows the

---

25 Member States shall ensure that, in in all new contracts concluded after 21 December 2007 at the latest, the use of sex as a factor in the calculation of premiums and benefits for the purposes of insurance and related financial services shall not result in differences in individuals' premiums and benefits.

growing role of the Charter and the fact that it can play an important role as a primary EU law in the jurisdiction of the ECJ.

Non-discrimination provisions on the ground of EU law are also contained in the Draft Common Frame of Reference (hereinafter DCFR), prepared finally in 2008 by the Study Group on a European Civil Code and the European Research Group on Existing EC Private Law (Acquis Group). The doctrine of law found that DCFR "deserves admiration for the explicit manner in which it recognizes the relation between contract law and constitutional law."[26] This is because the provisions of DCFR need to be "read in the light of any applicable instruments guaranteeing human rights and fundamental freedoms and any applicable constitutional laws" (Article I-1: 102 (2)).

What is innovative in DCFR is that it is the first comprehensive private law instrument to include rules on non-discrimination.[27] It states that a person has a right not to be discriminated against on the grounds of sex or ethnic or racial origin in relation to a contract or other juridical act, the object of which is to provide access to, or supply, goods or services that are available to the public (Article II-2: 101). The scope of the above prohibition of discrimination is the same as in the EU directives 2000/43 and 2004/113 concerning gender and ethnic and racial origin.

DCFR provides definitions of direct and indirect discrimination. According to Article II-2: 102 (1) of DCFR, "discrimination" means any conduct whereby, or situation where, on the above grounds (gender and ethnic or racial origins) one person is treated *less favorably* than another person is, has been or would be treated in a comparable situation, or in an apparently neutral provision, a criterion or practice that would place one group of persons at a particular disadvantage when compared with a different group of persons. Discrimination also includes harassment on grounds of gender or racial or ethnic origin.[28]

The Draft also provides an exception to the right not to be discriminated which states that unequal treatment that is justified by a legitimate aim does not amount to discrimination if the means used to achieve that aim are appropriate and necessary (Article II-2: 103).

Moreover, Chapter 2 of Book II constitutes a specific (reversed) burden of proof in proceedings (e.g. before the court) concerning discrimination. If a person who considers himself or herself discriminated against establishes facts from which it may be presumed that there has been such discrimination, it falls on the other party to prove that there has been no such discrimination (Article II-2: 105). There is an exception to this rule providing that it does not apply to proceedings

26 Mak Ch., 2009, "Fundamental Righs in DCFR," Centre for the Study of European Contract Law Working Papers Series no. 2009/01, p. 24.

27 Ibid.

28 According to II.-2: 102 (2) "harassment" means unwanted conduct (including conduct of a sexual nature) which violates a person's dignity, particularly when such conduct creates an intimidating, hostile, degrading, humiliating or offensive environment, or which aims to do so.

in which it is for the court or another competent authority to investigate the facts of the case.

Further, Article III–1: 105 states that Chapter 2 (Non-discrimination) of Book II applies with appropriate adaptations to:

- the performance of any obligation to provide access to, or supply, goods, other assets or services that are available to members of the public;
- the exercise of a right to performance of any such obligation or the pursuing or defending of any remedy for non-performance of any such obligation; and
- the exercise of a right to terminate any such obligation.

A probable new step of non-discrimination legislation in EU law is proposal (2008) for a Council Directive on implementing the principle of equal treatment between persons irrespective of religion or belief, disability, age or sexual orientation.[29] The aim of this proposal is to implement the principle of equal treatment between persons irrespective of religion or belief, disability, age or sexual orientation outside the labor market – in social protection, including social security and health care, social advantages, education and access to supply of goods and services which are available to the public, including housing.[30] Moreover, the important factor for passing new anti-discrimination directive should be the fact that EU ratified on 23 December 2010 the UN Convention on the Rights of Persons with Disabilities. The proposal is still being discussed in the Council[31] and it seems that "consensus within the Council . . . appears to be elusive."[32] However, it is correct that "it would be beneficial . . . to consider comparative constitutional law on Drittwirkung . . . since it will soon be necessary to take rights and their vertical and horizontal effects (more) seriously in the EU law order."[33] Originally this statement was addressed to the Court of Justice of the European Union, but it is pertinent to the discussion in the Council of Ministers.

29 COM(2008) 426; 2008/0140 (CNS).

30 According to proposal, in terms of access to goods and services, only professional or commercial activities are covered – not transactions between private individuals acting in private capacity.

31 The current stage of proceedings can observed on the Euopean Parliament website: http://www.europarl.europa.eu/oeil/popups/ficheprocedure.do?lang=en&reference=2008/0140%28APP%29.

32 Bell M. 2010, "Combating Discrimination in Areas Outside Employment: the Anticipated Impact of the Proposed New Directive," in *Expanding Equality Protections in Goods and Services. Irish and EU Perspectives*. The Equality Authority, Dublin.

33 Avabelj M. 2005, "Is there Drittwirkung in the EU Law?," in Sajo A., Uitz R., eds, *The Constitution in Private Relations: Expanding Constitutionalism*, Eleven International, Utrecht, p. 163.

## Poland – Something New in Horizontal Effect?

In conclusion, I would like to consider how the three methods (German, Strasbourg and EU) discussed in this chapter impact constitutional law in Poland, if at all. The strongest impact on the horizontal interpretation of constitutional human rights in Poland is EU law and the best examples of this are anti-discrimination directives, in particular 2000/43 and 2004/113. They were the main reasons (similar to Germany) for the preparation of new legislation in Polish law concerning exclusively the issue of equality law.

The European Court of Human Rights and its case law have high authority and the Court's jurisdiction seems to be an effective remedy for changing Polish law and practice in the field of human rights. However, it does not apply human rights horizontally. It rather uses the doctrine of positive obligations to examine the scope of responsibility of the State and to consider whether there has been a violation of human rights.

In turn, the German legal system is similar to Poland's continental legal system, and German anti-discrimination legislation has a much wider scope than the Polish Act on equal treatment. Germany decided to have a maximalist version of anti-discrimination law, while the Polish parliament (and the government that proposed the bill) chose the minimalistic one. This is probably because most of the constitutional law scholars in Poland find no horizontal effect of constitutional human rights in the private sphere.[34]

In the discussion about the scope of possible application of the rule of equality (Article 32 of the Constitution of Poland) to private law relationships, the Polish Constitutional Court decided that Article 32 does not create a direct subjective law of individual equal treatment.[35]

However, there are cases where argumentation involving the application of constitutional rights has been used in damages actions before the courts in Poland. One such is the case of Jolanta Kramarz, who sued Carrefour Poland for denying her the access to the Carrefour supermarket in Warsaw. Kramarz was blind and in November 2007 she attempted to access to the Carrefour store with her guide dog. The dog was wearing a special sign – "do not caress – I am working." The applicant was stopped at the door entrance by a security officer who allowed entrance "only to the lady who does not need a dog to access the market." The reasons for the denial of entry were based on hygiene grounds and sanitary security. In May 2008, Kramarz (represented by a *pro bono* advocate) lodged a civil complaint against Carrefour Polska Limited Liability Company for personal good breach based on the denial of access because of her blindness. She claimed the ability to access the

34 So far the most important paper on the horizontal effect of rule of equality is the article by M. Safjan, current Judge of the Court of Justice of the European Union: Safjan M. 2009, "Efekt horyzontalny praw podstawowych w prawie prywatnym: autonomia woli a zasada równego traktowania," Kwartalnik Prawa Prywatnego 2/2009, s. 304.

35 Decision of the Constitutional Court of 24 October 2001, no. SK 10/01.

market, 25,000 PLN for the Foundation "Vis Maior" and the publication of official apologies in an important Polish daily newspaper.

The argumentation of the claim was based on the fact that Kramarz was discriminated against. She was treated in the same way as a sighted person, while her situation was different. The guide dog was "replacing" her own eyes. The denial of access violated her dignity and the right of freedom of movement. The attitude and reaction of the security officer humiliated her. The denial of access to dogs was motivated by security reasons, mainly sanitary. The restriction introduced, however, were not proportionate to the goal pursued.[36]

The *Kramarz* case ended with a friendly settlement reached before the Warsaw Regional Court on 28 January 2009. It proved the non-existence of non-discrimination law in Poland, and showed how ineffective the non-discrimination rules really are in cases concerning blind persons.[37]

Unfortunately, similar cases were not a consideration for preparing the draft of the Act on Equal Treatment in Poland. Work on the draft was caused by the need for implementation of the EU anti-discrimination directives, in particular Directives 2000/43 and 2004/113. The Act on Implementation of Certain Provisions of the European Union on Equal Treatment 38 was passed on 3 December 2010, and entered into force on 1 January 2011. Currently, there is no case law based on this Act, but during parliamentary debate on the Act, Polish non-governmental organizations such as Helsinki Foundation for Human Rights and the Polish Society of Anti-Discrimination Law presented critical opinions concerning mainly the scope of the anti-discrimination provisions of the Act and solutions concerning the requirement to establish an Equality Body. The Parliament decided that the Ombudsman shall play the role of the Equality Body required in the Directives; however, the Ombudsman's Office (*Biuro Rzecznika Praw Obywatelskich*) did not receive any additional funds for performing its new duties.

The scope of the Act is based on different discriminatory features depending on the aspect of social life where unequal treatment could appear. Discrimination in access to goods and services available to the public (including housing) is prohibited if it is based on racial or ethnic origin, nationality or sex. However, access to education is secured against discrimination based only on racial or ethnic origin and nationality. It should also be underscored that a number of exceptions from the general rule of equality form the main part of the Act of 3 December 2010, which in fact reverses the scheme of the rule and its exception. Moreover, a case similar to Kramarz, if brought to court, could not find protection on the

36 Pudzianowska D. 2009, "Dyskryminacja osób niewidomych – sprawa J. Kramarz przeciwko Carrefour Polska Sp. z o.o." (sygn. I C 498/08), Niepełnosprawność i Rehabilitacja, nr lipiec – wrzesień.

37 "Blind Woman's Victory in Court Sets Precedent for Non-discrimination," available at: http://humanrightshouse.org/Articles/11468.html

38 Law of 3 December 2010 implementing certain EU regulations concerning equal treatment law (unofficial translation).

grounds of the Act on equal treatment, because disability as a prohibited ground of discrimination is not mentioned in it.

The fact that the Constitutional Court in Poland does not recognize Article 32 of the Constitution as a source of the subjective right to equal treatment has had a great impact on most of the scholars that share the view that constitutional rights cannot be applied directly or indirectly in private law. This has particular importance for rule of equality, which was underlined during the work on the Act on equal treatment.[39] However, it is possible to find arguments saying that indirect horizontal effect of human rights is at least possible[40] or needed.[41] The means to solve the conflict between the rights of individuals is the rule of proportionality.

When answering the question of which approach – German, European Court of Human Rights or EU – has been chosen by the Polish courts and legislators, the answer until now would be none of them. First, there is a lack of merit discussion, and second, there is a fear that applying the rule of equality to private relations would lead to the reality described by Milton Friedman: "a society that puts equality before freedom will get neither. A society that puts freedom before equality will get a high degree of both."

39 Legal opinion of Professor B. Banaszak, available at: http://www.radalegislacyjna.gov.pl/index.php?id=377&id2=375.

40 Safjan M. 2009, "Efekt horyzontalny praw podstawowych w prawie prywatnym: autonomia woli a zasada równego traktowania," Kwartalnik Prawa Prywatnego 2/2009, s. 304.

41 Professor Ewa Łętowska, when talking about "radiation of Constitution" on the other branches of law, argued that generally speaking there is no life without radiation; Łętowska E. 2006, "Promieniowanie orzecznictwa Trybunału Konstytucyjnego na poszczególne gałęzie prawa," in *Księga XX-lecia orzecznictwa Trybunału Konstytucyjnego*, Warszawa 2006, pp. 353–4.

Chapter 5

# The Subsidiary Application of the European Convention on Human Rights by Constitutional Courts in the Czech Republic and Poland

Marian Kokeš and Piotr Mikuli

## Introduction

The aim of this chapter is to discuss the issue of the subsidiary application of the European Convention on Human Rights and Fundamental Freedoms (hereafter "the ECHR") by constitutional courts in the Czech Republic and Poland. By "subsidiary application" we understand the situation in which constitutional judges use a rule or a principle from the Convention as a kind of support in the process of constitutional review.

The ECHR came into being on 4 November 1950. Since this year, there has been an enormous amount of development, and 60 years later and through the case law of the European Court for Human Rights (hereafter "the ECtHR"), the ECHR has become deeply entrenched in the legal orders of the Contracting States. Following the accession to the Council of Europe of former Soviet bloc states, the ECtHR's jurisdiction now extends to more than 800 million people in 47 countries, stretching the length and breadth of the continent and beyond, from Azerbaijan to Iceland and from Gibraltar to Vladivostok. The ECHR and its growing and diverse body of case law have transformed Europe's legal and political landscape, qualifying the ECtHR as the world's most effective international human rights tribunal (Helfer 2008: 126). The ECHR and case law of the ECHR constitute today a "*ius commune*" of the Contracting States to the ECHR for the protection of human rights and fundamental freedoms (Arnold 2007: 4). The main aspect of this point of view is that fundamental rights protection is administered by both national constitutions and the ECHR.

However, this ever closer linkage between the national and the ECHR levels of human rights protection has been accompanied by reservations in many national legal systems, because it is still a matter of domestic law (mostly of constitutional law) to determine, and of domestic courts (in the European space, primarily of constitutional courts) to rule on, the status of international law generally, and on the status of human rights treaties in particular, as well as their effects in domestic law. Generally, the ECHR and Convention rights are domesticated through their incorporation into national legal orders. The ECHR can be domestically effective to the extent that national officials recognize, enforce and give full effect to Convention rights and the interpretive authority of the ECtHR in their decisions. As Keller and Stone Sweet have argued, the ECHR is most effective where Convention rights, *de jure* and *de facto*: (1) bind all national officials in the exercise of public authority; (2) possess at least supra-legislative status (they occupy a rank superior to that of statutory law in the hierarchy of legal norms); and (3) can be pleaded directly by individuals before judges who may directly enforce them, while disapplying conflicting norms. In such position, the ECHR is not subject to the principle of *lex posterior derogat legi priori*, but takes precedence over all conflicting infra-constitutional norms (Keller and Stone Sweet 2008: 683). Therefore the most important question is how states incorporate the ECHR at the constitutional level because the depth and extent of the incorporation process of the ECHR determine and strongly influence the position of the ECHR and Convention rights in national legal orders. A doctrinal understanding of the process of incorporation is an indispensable first step in any attempt to explain the impact of the ECHR on national legal systems (Keller and Stone Sweet 2008: 683). In remarkably similar cases where the international human rights treaties guaranteeing individuals such rights come into conflict with domestic law the question of a reinterpretation of the approach to international conventions on human rights in national legal system gets put on the agenda. In resolving this conflict of two legal norms in particular states, the resolution of the issue of what legal force is accorded to human rights treaties in those legal orders (mostly in constitutions) plays an important role.[1]

## Process of Incorporation of the ECHR into the Czech Republic's Domestic Law

The Czech and Slovak Federal Republic before its disintegration into two separate states ratified the ECHR, including its Protocols, on 18 March 1992. The (Czechoslovak) Federal Charter of Fundamental Rights and Freedoms (Federal Charter),[2] adopted in January 1991, stipulated that "international treaties on human rights . . . ratified and promulgated by the (Federal Republic) are . . . generally binding and have priority over statutes (Article 2)." The Federal Charter thus singled out a specific category of international treaties ("international human rights treaties") and gave them application priority (Bobek and Kosař 2010: 15). After the dissolution of the Federal Republic, both newly emerged states, the Czech Republic and Slovakia, acceded to the ECHR on 30 June 1993 and are bound by the ECHR retroactively from 18 March 1992, the date of the accession of the

1 For more detailed overview of this problematic see Wagnerová (2006: 117).

2 Constitutional Act no. 23/1991 Coll. of 9 January 1991.

Federal Republic.[3] Both the Czech and the Slovak constitutions also introduced provisions similar to the above cited Article 2 of the Federal Charter. The Czech Constitution of 1993 (hereafter "the CC")[4] in Article 10 reproduced the above-mentioned provision of the Federal Charter almost *verbatim* and provided that "ratified and promulgated international treaties on human rights . . ., by which the Czech Republic is bound, *are immediately binding and have priority over statutes*" (emphasis added). Article 10 CC should be read in conjunction with Article 87(1) (a) CC in its original wording, which stipulated that "[The Czech Constitutional Court] has jurisdiction . . . to annul statutes or individual provisions thereof, if they are in conflict with the constitutional act or international treaty under Article 10 CC." Thus, Article 10 CC in its original wording provided that international conventions concerning human rights and fundamental freedoms which have been duly ratified and promulgated and by which the Czech Republic is bound are directly applicable and take precedence over statutes. In consequence, the Czech Republic from the beginning inserted the special category of "international human rights treaties" into its constitution. Human rights treaties were thus accorded a higher legal force than statutes. It should be added that the CC provided that these treaties were referential norms for the Czech Constitutional Court (hereafter "the CCC"; Article 87(1) (a) of the CC in the previous wording; Wagnerová et al. 2007: 320 and Sládeček et al. 2007: 83).

From that point of view it could be stressed that the CC, before the adoption of below-mentioned "Euro"-amendment, belonged to the group of national constitutions that refer to human rights treaties as a separate category accorded a different (higher) legal force than other international agreements, as well as other sources of international law. This solution created in the Czech Republic many potential problems in the practical application of this provision and caused a theoretical conflict between the Czech legal academia, ordinary courts and politicians on the one side and the CCC on the other side. This provision did not resolve the issue of whether human rights treaties had the same legal force as the CC, that is, whether they belong to the "*constitutional order*," and the CCC never expressed an opinion on this point. The CC also did not explicitly designate who should determine, in concrete cases, whether or not an international agreement qualified as a human rights treaty. The problem consists in the fact that not only treaties, such as the ECHR, which were indisputably human rights treaties, but also an ever greater number of treaties such as, for example, the International Covenant on Economic, Social and Cultural Rights (hereafter "the ICESCR") were received into the domestic legal order prior to the adoption of the CC. Thus,

3 Within six months of the collapse of the Czech and Slovak Federal Republic, the Council of Europe's Committee of Ministers reacted by deciding that the Czech Republic and the Slovak Republic were to be regarded as having succeeded to the ECHR retroactively from their date of independence. The ECtHR followed suit by holding the two new states accountable for any breaches committed by the predecessor state.

4 Constitutional Act no. 1/1993 Coll. of 16 December 1992.

none of these treaties was subject to the formal procedure laid down in the CC, and since no other constitutional provision made reference to their classification, it was up to the CCC itself to determine what position it would take on them.

It was not until the 14 March 2001 decision on a constitutional complaint (no. II. US 304/98) that an attempt was made to at least partially cope with this problem. At the same time, however, it did not attempt to resolve the issue of whether the right under Article 6(1) of the ICESCR is indeed a human right. On the contrary, without any more detailed reasoning, it simply declared the entire covenant to be a human rights treaty:

> The ICESCR ranks among the duly ratified and promulgated (No. 120/1976 Coll.) treaties on human rights and fundamental freedoms in the sense of Art. 10 of the CC (as the CCC also established, for example, in its decision, No. Pl. US 35/93). In addition, its direct applicability and precedence over statutes follows therefrom. However, the *direct applicability* of an international agreement, which expresses the fact of its reception (incorporation) into Czech law, must be distinguished from the *direct effect* of that agreement's individual provisions in domestic legal relations. Not all provisions of international conventions under Art. 10 of the CC are also *directly effective*, rather only those which are appropriate and capable of being directly effective.

However valuable is the attempt to distinguish between self-executing (directly effective) and non-self-executing legal norms contained in international agreements, the issue of whether the ICESCR concerns human rights was not argued substantively by the CCC. Otherwise the issue of whether a certain right is self-executing can be posed even in relation to human rights contained in international conventions other than those of the second and third generation.[5]
Indignant reactions were called forth by the CCC's Judgment no. Pl. US 16/99 of 27 June 2001, in which the CCC annulled the entire portion of the Civil Procedure Code (Act no. 99/1963 Coll.) regulating the judicial review of administrative decisions. The CCC decided to annul it because this statute's provisions did not allow for the full review of administrative decisions; therefore, the CCC came to the conclusion that these provisions were in conflict with Article 6(1) of the ECHR:

> The current regulation of the administrative judiciary shows serious constitutional law deficiencies. Primarily, certain activities of the public administration, like its potential inactivity, are not under the review of the judicial power at all. Further, not everyone whose rights may be affected by an administrative decision has the right to turn to the courts. Even if he does have that right, he is not a party to a fully fair trial under Art. 6 par. 1 of the ECHR, although that should be the case in a number of matters. An issued court decision is then final and (with

5 In this respect, procedural rights are typically mentioned, if an institutional mechanism for ensuring such rights is lacking in domestic law. See Kühn (2004: 483).

> the exception of a constitutional complaint) non-reversible, which leads to inconsistent case law, as well as to an unequal position for the administrative body, i.e. to a situation in conflict with the requirements of a state governed by the rule of law. The finality of certain decisions (stopping proceedings) can then even lead to a denial of justice.

The CC and constitutional law were strongly influenced by the adoption of a constitutional amendment that entered into force on 1 June 2002 (the so-called "Euro"-amendment of the CC).[6] The "Euro"-amendment primarily provided for the possibility of the Czech Republic to become a signatory party to an international organization – the European Union (Article 10a CC) – and for a broader opening of the national constitution to European Union Law, but also newly formulated the position of international treaties in the Czech legal order (Article 10 CC), and has influenced the status of the ECHR and other human rights treaties. In other words, the "Euro"-amendment normatively abolished the specific category of "international human rights treaties" that were endowed with a higher legal force than statutes and replaced the old Article 10 CC with the following wording: "Promulgated treaties, to the ratification of which Parliament has given its consent and by which the Czech Republic is bound, form a part of the legal order; *if a treaty provides something else than the statute, the international treaty shall apply*" (emphasis added). In addition to amending Article 10 CC, the reference to international treaties in Article 87(1)(a) CC was modified and from the formal perspective, human rights treaties also ceased to qualify as referential norms for the CCC. Certain authors from the Czech academic sphere maintained the opinion that Article 10 CC theoretically clarified the issue of whether the ECHR belonged to the constitutional order. They clearly said no, *all* international treaties under Article 10 CC, including international human rights treaties, enjoy "only" the priority of application.[7] Finally it made clear that the CCC no longer has the power to review the conformity of statutes with international human rights treaties. It became the task of the ordinary courts to apply the international treaties instead of the statute, if the conditions under Article 10 CC were met (Bobek and Kosař 2010: 15).

The reality is entirely different, however. The issue of a possible conflict between a human rights treaty and the CC has as yet not been resolved and this situation still causes many application problems. The CCC tried to resolve it and

6 The 'Euro'-amendment of the CC was carried out by the Constitutional Act no. 395/2001 Coll., entered into force on 1 June 2002.

7 The application priority of international treaties means that the international human rights treaties were supposed to be applied instead of statutes but were not granted a higher legal force.

completely reinterpreted this part of the "Euro"-amendment. In a proceeding on the abstract control of norms on 25 June 2002 (no. Pl. US 36/01), the CCC held:[8]

> the inadmissibility of changing the substantive requirements of a democratic state based on the rule of law also contains an instruction to the CCC, that no amendment to the CC can be interpreted in such a way that it would result in limiting an already achieved procedural level of protection for fundamental rights and freedoms. . . . The scope of the constitutional order concept cannot be interpreted only with regard to Art. 112 (1) of the CC, but must be interpreted in view of Art. 1 (2) of the CC and must include ratified and promulgated international agreements on human rights and fundamental freedoms. For these reasons Art. 95 (2) of the CC must be interpreted to the effect that a general court has an obligation to present to the CCC for interpretation a matter in which it concludes that a law which is to be used in resolving the matter is in conflict with a ratified and promulgated international agreement on human rights and fundamental freedoms.

Therefore, the CCC concluded that international human rights treaties have "*retained*" their constitutional status. In fact the CCC "*constitutionalized*" international human rights treaties, including the ECHR, and re-read the specific category of "international human rights treaties" into Article 10 CC and treats Article 87(1)(a) CC as if its wording had not changed. Furthermore, the CCC held that the ordinary courts still must refer a clash between an applicable statute and the ECHR to the CCC under the concrete review of constitutionality, which was met with occasional resistance from the ordinary courts (Bobek and Kosař 2010: 16). Despite a criticism primarily from the academic sphere (Kühn and Kysela 2002: 199, Malenovský 2002: 917), the CCC has repeatedly upheld its position and thus the human rights treaties enjoy a higher position in the national hierarchy of sources than envisaged by the text of the CC. In decision no. I. US 752/02 of 15 April 2003 the CCC expressed its view:[9]

> the Czech Republic is bound by the international agreements on human rights and fundamental freedoms, and pronounced an opinion that precedence must be accorded to treaties on human rights. The respect and protection of fundamental rights are defining elements of the substantively understood state governed by the rule of law; therefore, in a case where a conventional obligation protecting a fundamental right exists side by side with a conventional obligation which tends to endanger that same right, the first obligation must prevail. Although after "Euro"-amendment of the Constitution agreements on the protection of human

8 See The Constitutional Court of the CR, 'Selected Decisions 2001–2002, Vol. II' (Linde, Prague, 2003), 157.

9 See The Constitutional Court of the CR, 'Selected Decisions 2002–2003, Vol. III' (Linde, Prague 2004), p. 241.

> rights no longer form an independent category of legal norms with priority in application under the previous wording of Art. 10, nonetheless they are a special group of norms, and at the same time represent a reference point of view, both for the abstract review of norms and for proceedings on constitutional complaints.

This approach whereby the CCC's case law provides a corrective to the normative text, even if very accommodating to international treaty law, is still very problematic, because the CCC still does not draw any distinction between self-executing and non self-executing rights and has not even resolved, in a decision of principle, the issue of what human rights are (Wagnerová 2006: 124).

The CCC's attitude to human rights treaties had consequences for the institution of constitutional complaint. The Act on the CC of 1996 provides in § 72(1) who is entitled to file such a complaint. Under that provision, a constitutional complaint can be filed by an individual or a legal entity who claims that a decision that has entered into legal effect in a proceeding in which he/it was a party, a measure or other intervention by a public authority ("intervention by a public authority") violated his/its fundamental right or freedom guaranteed by the constitutional order. As it was mentioned, the catalogue of fundamental rights and freedoms guaranteed by the constitutional order is contained primarily in the Czech Charter and in the CC. However, in the light of the above-mentioned conclusions, it is not surprising that the CCC includes in this catalogue also fundamental rights and freedoms guaranteed by the human rights treaties, especially the ECHR, by which the Czech Republic is bound, which are *directly applicable* in a proceeding on a constitutional complaint before the CCC (Wagnerová et al. 2007: 319). owing to its "ECHR-friendly" approach, the CCC quashed the decisions of the ordinary courts with the use of conclusions based on an extensive reading of the ECHR and the ECtHR's case law. This applies most for decisions where the CCC interpreted the scope and aspects of the right to fair trial. Thus, the right to fair trial enshrined in Article 36 etc. of the Czech Charter has been often interpreted with accordance with Article 6 of the ECHR, especially within criminal procedure, but also within civil cases, for example, the question of admissibility of evidence (decision no. IV. US 335/05 of 6 June 2006), custody regulation (decision no. I. US 603/07 of 7 June 2007) or non-pecuniary compensation of damages for previous unlawful limitation of personal freedom (decision no. I. US 85/04 of 13 August 2006). In this decision the CCC said that:

> the claim for compensation is constructed not only in the area of simple law, but also by the ECHR, in Art. 5 (5), which is, under Art. 10 of the CC, a directly applicable norm in the domestic legal order of the CR, and which must be given priority in application before statutes. Regardless of how the content of the institution of compensation of damage is treated by the domestic legislature, the case law of the general Courts and the constitutional Court, or domestic civil doctrine, in domestic application of the ECHR one must start with the concept of compensation of damage as it is treated by the national European constitutional

Courts and supreme Courts, whose case law gives rise to the case law of the ECHR. As regards specifically state liability for limiting personal freedom, and thus the relationship of the domestic civil law of offenses and Article 5 (5) of the ECHR, the situation in individual European states is that the classic dogmatics of civil legal institutions gave way to direct application of Article 5 (5) of the ECHR interpreted fully autonomously by the national Courts. The CCC also bases this position on the case-law of the ECtHR which has consistently ruled that the ECHR's institutions can have completely autonomous content and a scope not dependent on their legal classification under domestic law.

## The ECHR and the Polish Legal System

The Polish Constitution of 1997[10] does not refer to any international treaty on human rights as a separate category of normative acts, yet in general terms it regulates the relationship between national and international law. Before the binding Constitution came into force, the status of international law in Poland was quite unclear (Machowicz 2009: 21). The Constitution of 1952 did not provide any method of implementation of international agreements after their ratification. In the period before the systemic transformation, international law was applied only occasionally in the jurisprudence of the Polish courts. The concept of the self-executing norms of international law used by the Polish Constitutional Court (hereafter "the PCC") contributed to the development of the Polish courts referring to international agreements. This had great legal significance in the situation when Poland became a party to many international agreements concerning human rights. The notion of self-executing norms enabled the domestic application of international agreement norms when they were both precise enough to be construed without major difficulties and at the same time detailed in such a way that they could create particular rights and/or duties (Machowicz 2009: 23). The arrangement of the apparent relationship between both branches of the law – international and domestic – was also not covered in the "Small Constitution" of 1992.[11]

The regulation of the status of international law in the current constitution was the consequence of the introduction to the 1997 constitution of the so-called "closed system of sources of universally binding law." According to this concept, only acts explicitly mentioned in the Constitution may constitute the direct basis of somebody's rights and obligations, while others "shall be of an internal character" (such as resolutions of the Council of Ministers and orders of the Prime Minister and ministers mentioned in Article 93(1)). In terms of international law, on the basis of Article 87(1), only ratified international agreements constitute a

10 *Journal of Laws* (1997), no. 78, item 483; *Journal of Laws* (2001), no. 28, item 319; *Journal of Laws* (2006), no. 200, item 1471; *Journal of Laws* (2009), no. 114, item 946.

11 *Journal of Laws* (1992), no. 84, item 426.

source of universally binding law. At the same time, the Constitution distinguishes two kinds of ratified international agreements. The first of these are agreements that were ratified on the basis of the consent expressed in statute; the second are international agreements ratified without such statutory consent. Within the first category a further division exists as the Seym and the Senate may express their consent for the ratification in a normal legislative procedure, that is, by a simple majority of votes (Article 89(1)) or in a special procedure, described in Article 90(2) and (3) of the Constitution.

Article 89(1) enumerates all the cases in which ratification requires a statute to be passed. This procedure is obligatory if an international agreement concerns: peace, alliances, political or military treaties; freedoms, rights or obligations of citizens, as specified in the Constitution; the Republic of Poland's membership in an international organization; considerable financial responsibilities imposed on the state; matters regulated by statute or those in respect of which the Constitution requires the form of a statute. In turn, a statute granting consent to ratification passed in a special procedure is used only when an international treaty transfers the competences of the state power to an international organization or to an international organ. The aim of this provision was to introduce a procedure to join the European Union and to accept all the EU requirements provided in the founding treaties. This special procedure requires a permitting statute to be passed by a qualified two-thirds majority of votes in the presence of at least half of the statutory number of deputies or senators respectively. According to the Constitution, such consent may also be expressed in a nationwide referendum. The hierarchical position of legal norms included in such agreements, at least from the constitutional perspective, is equal to that of norms included in agreements ratified by means of an ordinary statute.

The act of ratification of an international agreement therefore has two meanings. The first, an external one, has an effect within international law, and the second one involves incorporation of the norms of an international agreement within the domestic legal order. As stipulated in Article 91(1), all the ratified international agreements that are promulgated become a part of the Polish legal order and are applied directly unless its application depends on the enactment of a statute. In this way the international norms included in the agreements become the norms of internal and universally binding law (Banaszak 2009: 58). According to the jurisprudence of the PCC, the direct application of an international agreement is possible only when all the normative elements on which such an application depends are defined in this agreement. Among the international agreements that are directly applied in practice, the ECHR as well as other important treaties on human rights (such as International Labour Organization conventions or Hague Convention on the Civil Aspects of International Child Abduction) are some of the most common.

All the international agreements that are concluded other than by ratification cannot constitute a direct applicable source of the law in Poland. They may not, as such, shape the legal situations of individuals without the transformation into the domestic legal order (Garlicki 2009: 140).

The status of ratified international agreements within the Polish system of the sources of universally binding law depends on whether their ratification took place with or without statutory consent. According to Article 91(2) of the Constitution, an international agreement ratified upon prior consent granted by statute shall have precedence over statutes if such an agreement cannot be reconciled with the provisions of such statutes. This is, in a sense, a counterpart to Article 10 of the Czech Constitution after the "Euro"-amendment.

According to Garlicki and Masternak-Kubiak, the process of applying the acts of external law in Poland is much the same as the process of applying the Constitution (Garlicki and Masternak-Kubiak 2006: 175). They distinguish three kinds of such application: (1) the so-called "autonomous application" in which a court applies a rule of international law as the sole basis for a judicial decision – this means that the domestic law does not constitute the ground of its decision; (2) co-application in which a judge uses an international provision as well as a domestic one and thereby creates a legal norm from both of them; and (3) control application, which concerns the resolution of conflicts between a rule of international law and a domestic provision.

In terms of the first form of application of international agreements it should be noted that the normative content of this frequently coincides with constitutional regulations; therefore courts in practice have a choice of which norm is supposed to be the basis of their decision. This situation takes place first of all in the case of human rights agreements. Applying the ECHR requires, to a considerable degree, reference to the jurisprudence of the Strasbourg Court.[12] In practice, the most developed form of judicial application of international agreements is "co-application," which occurs as an interpretative application (Wójtowicz 2004: 326). This means that the courts also apply such agreements indirectly by interpreting domestic law in line with international obligations. Interpretative application is a consequence of Article 9 of the Constitution, which states that the Republic of Poland shall respect international law binding upon it, and the above-mentioned Article 91(1). It should be noted as well that Article 9 is perceived by scholars of constitutional law to be an important element of construing statutes that "enables to cover the constitutional duty to respect not ratified part of international law" (Działocha 2006: 42). It is used first of all in cases of resolutions of international

12 See the judgment of the Supreme Court of 11 January 1995 in which the Court held that 'from the moment of joining the Council of Europe the jurisprudence of ECtHR should be taken into consideration in the process of interpretation of the Polish law' (Garlicki and Masternak-Kubiak 2006: 172). As Machowicz emphasizes, the receptivity of the Polish courts to the jurisprudence of the ECtHR takes two forms: an indirect one (referring to the judgments of the ECtHR through citing the existing Polish decisions in which such judgments have been used) and a direct one (directly referring to international judgments). See Machowicz (2009: 30).

organization or international customary law (Działocha 2006: 42).[13] Thus this provision appears to illustrate the principle of general receptivity of the Polish legal system towards international law (Działocha 1999: 84).

In the above-mentioned control application, in turn, the constitution suggests that courts should resolve conflicts between international law and statutes by discovering interpretations of the provisions that would allow not to decide on the incompatibility of norms. Only when this turns out to be impossible must a judge give the priority to the international agreement ratified with the prior consent expressed in statute (Wójtowicz 2004: 327). The right not to apply a statutory norm that is in conflict with this type of international agreement can be exercised by all ordinary and administrative courts. Nevertheless, regardless of this fact, the PCC, on the basis of Article 188 of the Constitution, is also entitled to decide on this problem within an abstract or incidental control (question of law). However, when it comes to the need to assess provisions of such international agreements in relation to the constitution, it seems that the PCC is the only organ entitled to resolve such a conflict. This observation is the consequence of a premise that ordinary courts do not have the authority to decide on the nonconformity of a statutory provision to the constitution.[14] It derives directly from Article 8(1) and (2) and Article 178(1) of the Constitution. The former states that the constitution shall be the supreme law of the Republic of Poland, and the latter stipulates that judges, within the exercise of their office, shall be independent and subject only to the constitution and to statutes. Being subject to the constitution and statutes also means, it seems, the subordination of judges to international agreements introduced to the Polish legal system by means of ratification concluded with the prior statutory consent or the consent expressed in the national referendum (Błachut and Mikuli 2005: 273). Therefore, in the case of the above-mentioned conflict, an ordinary court must refer to the PCC a question of law concerning the conformity of such international agreements to the constitution on the basis of Article 193 of the Constitution. This means that it should do exactly the same as in the situation when a conflict between a statute and the constitution occurs. However, in the case of human rights treaties, including the European Convention, it is hardly likely that the PCC would decide on their non-conformity to the constitution because an explicit convergence exists between these treaties and the constitutional provisions concerning the freedoms and rights of an individual. Likewise in the Czech Charter, many of the provisions mirror almost literarily the regulations included in the ECHR.

13 See also (Albi 2005: 80).

14 However, this standpoint is controversial and some scholars accept a thesis that an ordinary court may refuse to apply a statute in a concrete case when, according to a judge, it is unconstitutional. See for instance Sadurski (2005: 21). Moreover, the Supreme Court in some rulings opposed the Constitutional Court's monopoly in adjudicating constitutional matters. See the judgment of 7 April 1998 (I PKN 90/98).

As mentioned, neither the ECHR nor any other international acts on human rights constitutes a separate category of the sources of law in Poland. The ECHR was ratified on 19 January 1993, that is, before the Constitution of 1997 came into force. Nevertheless, Article 241 of the Constitution stipulates that international agreements, previously ratified by the Republic of Poland on the basis of constitutional provisions valid at the time of their ratification and promulgated in the *Journal of Laws of the Republic of Poland*, shall be considered as agreements ratified with prior consent granted by statute, and shall be subject to the provisions of Article 91 if their connection with the categories of matters mentioned in Article 89(1) derives from the terms of an international agreement. On this basis, at present, ECHR has an equal status to other international agreements ratified with the prior consent granted by statute according to Article 89 of the current Constitution.

Conventional norms therefore have precedence over statutes in the process of application of the law. The legal state of affairs seems to be clearer than in the Czech Republic as there is no doubt that conventional provisions do not have constitutional status. The Constitution in Article 188(1) stipulates that that the PCC has the competence to verify the compatibility of all the international agreements with the constitution. This means that a constitutional norm makes a reference pattern in the process of judicial review of international agreements. However, it must be emphasized that the PCC is not entitled to question the validity of a ratified international agreement towards the Polish state. This would lead to the undermining of the constitutional principle of respect of international law, as well as Article 27 of the Vienna Convention on the Law of Treaties (Masternak-Kubiak 2003: 302, Grzybowski 2006: 342). The consequence of the PCC's judgment on the incompatibility of the international agreement with the Constitution is only that it is impossible to apply the former within the system of internal law. After the Court's decision the normative conflicts of such kind may be resolved either through the introduction of a specific amendment to the constitution or through renunciation of the international agreement.

In the context of the topic of this chapter, it must be noted that both in the scholarship and in the case law the question was considered of the extent to which an international norm may constitute a basis of review within the institution of constitutional complaint (Masternak-Kubiak 2003: 309). The Polish constitution complaint is defined as follows:

> in accordance with principles specified by statute, everyone whose constitutional freedoms or rights have been infringed, shall have the right to appeal to the Constitutional Court for its judgment on the conformity to the Constitution of a statute or another normative act upon which basis a court or organ of public administration has made a final decision on his freedoms or rights or on his obligations specified in the Constitution. (Article 79)[15]

15 It should be stressed that, in contrast to the Czech Republic, the Polish model of constitutional complaint does not encompass acts of applying the law, i.e. administrative

The issue seems to be quite important, especially as far as human rights treaties are concerned. According to the justification of the judgment of the PCC of 10 July 2000 (SK 21/99), Article 91(1) and (2) does not create any rights and freedoms for an individual, but clarifies only the position of international treaties in the Polish legal system. Simultaneously, the Court expressed its view that the term "constitutional freedoms and rights" used in Article 79(1) also encompasses human rights regulated in the basic acts of international law (i.e. in the ECHR), but only if a complainer refers to such a standardized right included in these acts, which at the same time is provided in the Polish Constitution. Similarly, in the judgment of 7 May 2002 (SK 20/00) the PCC indicated that, for that reason, within the constitutional complaint proceedings it does not make any difference whether some rights arise from the ECHR or not as they are not protected in this procedure. This approach has at least two important consequences. The first is that the constitutional complaint cannot be used in the case of any infringement of rights acquired only by means of international agreements. In this regard, only violation of a constitutional right or a freedom may be treated as a reason for lodging such a complaint.[16] The second outcome of the above-mentioned the PCC judgment is a confirmation that freedoms and rights included in the acts of international law, in contrast to the Czech Constitutional Court's approach, are not part of the constitution.

Nevertheless, irrespective of these arguments, in the process of decoding the meaning of many constitutional human rights provisions, the PCC guides itself by the norms of the ECHR. In this way a reference pattern in the process of constitutional review of legislation is constructed, not only on the basis of the Constitution as such but also on international legal norms as well as the Strasbourg case law. Sometimes, the PCC makes a very direct reference to the ECHR and Strasbourg rulings as an interpretative hint in order to settle a proper meaning of a particular constitutional provision. In turn, other cases refer to international standards in more indirect ways, that is, they are quoted as a certain reinforcement of a PCC standpoint. In the judgment of 12 December (K 32/04) the PCC expressed the conviction that:

> It must be noted that although the Constitutional Court is not competent to execute control of infringements of individual rights in terms of infringements of the Convention, it feels itself bound by the values and standards of this Convention. Therefore, a basis of review applied by the Court is interpreted in the light of those standards and values.

---

decisions and court judgments. The subject of the review is limited to abstract and general acts upon which basis a final decision/judgment has been made.

16 See also the justification of the judgment of the Constitution Court of 31 March 2005 (SK 26/02).

## The Impact of the ECHR and ECtHR's Case Law on the Case Law of Constitutional Courts

As Stone Sweet stated, through incorporation (constitutionalization) the ECHR functions as a "shadow constitution" or as a "surrogate charter of rights," in many states that previously possessed their own judicially enforceable Bill of Rights (for example Belgium, France, the Netherlands and Switzerland; Stone Sweet 2009: 923–44). In other states, where national constitutions already provided for a system of constitutional justice, the ECHR now functions as a "supplement" to national rights protection. This situation is characteristic, for instance, for Germany, Spain, Italy, Poland and also for the Czech Republic. As well as the ECHR being a formal part of the national legal order, the case law of the ECtHR comprises the essential criteria for the interpretation of internal fundamental rights by national constitutional courts. From this point of view the ECtHR plays a "*constitutional role*" because the protection mechanism of the ECHR confers on the ECtHR a "*constitutional mission*" to lay down common principles and standards relating to human rights and to determine the minimum level of protection that states must observe (Stone Sweet 2009: 935). As former president of the ECtHR, Professor Wildhaber, said, the ECtHR sets common legal standards that permeate the legal orders of the Contracting States, standards that influence and shape domestic law and practice in areas such as criminal law, the administration of justice in criminal, civil and administrative matters, family law, property law, etc. (Wildhaber 2002: 161–5). Keller and Stone Sweet defined three different functions of the ECtHR: (1) as a kind of "High Cassation Court" when it comes to procedure; (2) as an international watchdog when it comes to grave human rights violations and massive breakdowns in rule of law; and (3) as an oracle of constitutional rights interpretation when it comes to fine-tuning the qualified rights of Articles 8–11 and 14 ECHR (Keller and Stone Sweet 2008: 687).

Below we will quote some examples of the PCC and CCC referring to the ECHR and ECrHR's rulings.

*Czech Republic*

The CCC often refers to the ECHR when it comes to interpreting the meaning of the freedom to express opinions and the freedom to acquire and to disseminate information (Article 17 of the Czech Charter). In the judgment no. IV. US 23/05 of 17 July 2007, concerned with human dignity and freedom of speech, the CCC claimed that:

> the requirement that critics themselves must prove the facts claimed is a European constitutional standard confirmed also by case-law of the ECtHR (e.g. case Pedersen and Baadsgaard v. Denmark). Other general principles applied in case-law of European constitutional Courts, as well as in case-law of the ECHR, are as follows . . .

Another significant example where the CCC (by using the ECtHR's jurisprudence) interprets individual rights enshrined in the Czech Charter in an extensive manner is the right to respect for private and family life. In the judgment no. II. US 586/06 of 20 February 2007 the CCC had to define and interpret the term "family life" because both Article10(2) of the Czech Charter, and Article 8 of the ECHR speak generally about protection of family life, or respect for family life, without, however, defining in legal terms what they mean by the term "family life." The CCC claimed that:

> The family is a social group of related persons, among whom there are close ties – blood, psychosocial, emotional, economical, etc. Thus although at the level of social reality the concept of family is very changeable (as stated above, the social reality of the family has undergone successive transformations, and through them the traditional European concept of the family has disintegrated more and more noticeably, and legal regulation of the family and family life is necessarily also subject to these transformations), nevertheless it can not be overlooked that the basis of family ties is traditionally precisely the biological bond of a blood relationship between family members. Therefore, on the one hand we can not rule out the fact that legal protection as a family can also be enjoyed by a social group of persons living outside the institution of marriage, or a group of persons not related by blood, among whom there are nonetheless the abovementioned emotional and other ties (persons living together as mates, partners living together with a child that was born to one of the parents from another relationship, etc.). And that scope of the concept of family life also arises from the case law of the ECtHR. . . . On the other hand, that concept of family and family life also assumes the importance of blood ties between family members. In Kroon and others v. the Netherlands the ECtHR gave priority to the biological tie between the father of a child living in a de facto bond with the mother and that child, and denying the paternity of the mother's husband, over the legal situation and the legal construct of the family: "respect" for "family life" requires that biological and social reality prevail over a legal presumption.

Because of the above-mentioned conclusions of the CCC jurisprudence that the human rights treaties enjoy a higher position in the national hierarchy of sources of law, the CCC now (i.e. after the "Euro"-amendment) also has powers to strike down a statute solely for non-compliance with human rights treaties, even if there is no equivalent provision in the Czech Charter (Wagnerová et al. 2007: 321). Thus, the CCC has struck down several statutes for their non-conformity with the ECHR (or with other international human rights treaties[17]). For instance the CCC struck down Article 146(2) of the Code of Criminal Procedure "solely" for

17 For example, the judgment no. Pl. US 31/96 of 9 April 1997 where the CCC repealed Article 171(l)(d) of the Criminal Code 'solely' for inconsistence with the Convention on the Rights of the Child.

inconsistence with Article 6(1) ECHR[18] and § 241(2) of the Code of Criminal Procedure "solely" for inconsistence with Article 5(4) ECHR.[19] In the judgment no. Pl. US 3/09 of 16 June 2010, the CCC quashed § 83a of the Code of Criminal Procedure (that composed conditions for the conduct of police searches of non-housing premises) for inconsistence with Article 8 ECHR and Article 17 ICCPR. The CCC stated that:

> The case of a house search or search of other premises involves restriction of a person's fundamental right to the inviolability of his dwelling, guaranteed by Art. 12 (1) of the Czech Charter, according to which "A person's dwelling is inviolable. It may not be entered without the permission of the person living there." Likewise, Art. 8 (1) of the ECHR guarantees this fundamental right, stating that: "Everyone has the right to respect for his private and family life, his home and his correspondence;" and likewise Art. 17 of the ICCPR guarantees the individual this fundamental right, protecting him from "arbitrary or unlawful interference with his privacy, family, home or correspondence." . . . In contrast to the indicated sub-constitutional definition of the institution of a "dwelling," the case-law of the ECtHR is built on a wider concept of the term for purposes of setting the scope of the fundamental right guaranteed by Art. 8 (1) of the ECHR, and is based on a close connection between it and the right to a private life. The ECtHR identified the wider concept of "dwelling" when interpreting the Convention in the light of current conditions, in accordance with the aim pursued by Art. 8 of the ECHR, i.e. protection of individual's privacy from unjustified interference by the public authorities, because in modern times it is not possible to maintain a sharp spatial division of privacy in premises used for housing and privacy exercised in a person's working environment. Therefore, under the right to respect for one's dwelling under Art. 8 (1) of the ECHR, the ECtHR also includes a requirement for respect for the privacy of a company's headquarters, branches, or the operating premises of legal entities (cf. judgment of 16 April 2002 in the case Colas Est. v. France), office premises (cf. judgment of 25 February 1993 in the case Crémieux v. France, or judgment of 25 February 1993 in the case Miailhe v. France) or attorneys' offices (cf. judgment of 12 December 1992 in the case Niemietz v. Germany). It added that restricting the concept of a dwelling in a manner that would exclude places where one conducts one's profession is not always possible, as it is enough to point to the interconnectedness and impossibility of separating an individual's personal activities from his work activities (Niemietz v. Germany, § 29 and 31).

A separate subject is the proceedings concerning measures necessary to implement a decision of an international Court (also the ECtHR) by virtue of the Article 87(1) (i) CC. Paradoxically and quite disconnectedly, the CCC (through the adoption

18 See judgment no. Pl. US 15/04 of 30 November 2004.

19 See judgment no. Pl. US 45/04 of 22 March 2005.

of the "Euro"-amendment of the CC) was at the same time endowed with a new competence which was introduced by amendment to the Act on the Constitutional Court (no. 182/1993 Coll.).[20] There the CCC should have decided in a criminal matter in which an international tribunal (the ECtHR) found that, as the result of the encroachment of a public authority, a human right or fundamental freedom was infringed in conflict with an international treaty (the ECHR), a petition for rehearing may be submitted against such decision of the CCC under the conditions set down in the Act on the Constitutional Court. If the CCC's judgment is in conflict with the international tribunal's decision, the CCC shall quash that judgment; otherwise it shall reject the petition on the merits. In its new judgment the CCC shall proceed on the basis of the international tribunal's proposition of law. The problem is if the CCC in its new judgment is bound to opinion in judgment of the international tribunal, that is, the ECtHR or not. Many authors prefer a view that the CCC is not bound to that opinion but in its new judgment it should follow and reflect on the ECtHR's judgment. So the CCC could decide as well as before but with respect to opinions and conclusions that are involved in ECtHR's judgment, as it was stated in the decision no. Pl. US 1/09 of 28 July 2009:

> Under § 119b (3) of the Act on the CC, after granting the rehearing, the CCC in its new Judgment proceeds from the legal opinion of the international court, in this given case from the Judgment of the ECtHR dated 24 July 2008 in the case of Melich and Beck v. the Czech Republic, Application No. 35450/04, which declared a violation of the fundamental right of the complainants to a fair criminal trial under Art. 6 (1) of the ECHR, a part of which is formed by the principle of presumption of innocence established in Art. 6 (2) of the ECHR, and the right to have adequate time and facilities for the preparation of defense under Art. 6 (3) (b) of the ECHR.

### *Poland*

In several of its judgments, the PCC considered the significance of Article 38 of the Constitution in the light of the Convention's standards. Article 38 stipulates that the Republic of Poland shall ensure the legal protection of life of every human being. In the case of 23 March 1999 (K 2/98) the Court ruled that this Article should be

20 Section 119 (1) of the Act on the CC provides: 'Should the Constitutional Court have decided in a criminal matter in which an international court found that, as the result of the encroachment of a public authority, a human right or fundamental freedom was infringed in conflict with an international treaty, a petition for rehearing may be submitted against such decision of the Constitutional Court under the conditions set down in this Statute. The Constitutional Court should, thus, open the road to the revision of its own decisions, in the case they resulted in an infringement of human rights guaranteed by human rights treaties, which, however, should allegedly not have been taken into consideration as a referential norm in the original decision on the constitutional complaints.

perceived first of all as a prohibition of deprivation of human life. This prohibition, although not absolute, must be understood in the light of Article 2(2) of the ECHR, which enumerates the exceptional situations when such deprivation may take place. In the above-mentioned Article 38, the PCC also found a positive aspect of the right to live. This notion encompasses the commitment of public authorities to take various actions to ensure the protection of human life. This understanding of Article 38 was also applied in a very well-known case concerning the possibility of shooting down a hijacked aircraft ("renegade" aircraft) that could be used for a terrorist attack (Grabowski 2010: 299–301). The PCC referred to Article 2 of the ECHR as well as many cases of the ECtHR in which it pointed out *inter alia* that, within its jurisdiction, a state has the obligation to assure the security of an individual as well as the obligation to take all available and reasonable measures to protect the right to life. The PCC also took into consideration that the premises of legal admissibility of deprivation of life in the jurisprudence of the ECtHR are interpreted in a very restrictive way and that this court occasionally allows pre-emptive measures to be taken by a state. For these reasons, considering the choice between the life of passengers and the life of others, the PCC stated that the use of the force against a "renegade" aircraft is not in conformity with Article 2 of the ECHR. The PCC noted that the ECtHR is not in favor of any model solution of the conflict of values, that is, public safety and freedoms and rights of individuals, as the required safety degree depends on the circumstances of a particular case.

The PCC, likewise the CCC, also often refers to the ECHR when it comes to interpreting the meaning of Article 54 of the Constitution concerning the freedom to express opinions and the freedom to acquire and to disseminate information along with Article 14 (freedom of the press). In the judgment of 21 April 2004 (K 33/03) the PCC expressed the conviction that the right to acquire information also encompasses any "commercial speech" in the context of consumer's rights. The PCC clearly stated that the same results from the ECHR and "there are no reasons arguing for accepting, on the basis of Article 54, a narrower interpretation of the scope of the protection than exists in ECHR." In the judgment of 5 May 2004 (P 2/03) the PCC argued that, included in Article 54(1) of the Constitution, the freedom to express one's opinions (encompassing the freedom to hold one's opinions and to receive and impart information and ideas without interference from public authorities and regardless of state frontiers) is not absolute and might be subject to limitations. These limitations are laid down in Article 10 of the ECHR in a similar formulation to Article 31(3) of the Constitution.[21]

The PCC generally accepts the Strasbourg standards concerning the freedom of speech in reference to the activities of state institutions and public persons.

21 Article 33(3): "Any limitation upon the exercise of constitutional freedoms and rights may be imposed only by statute, and only when necessary in a democratic state for the protection of its security or public order, or to protect the natural environment, health or public morals, or the freedoms and rights of other persons. Such limitations shall not violate the essence of freedoms and rights."

The PCC agrees that the level of this freedom is definitely greater in relation to public persons than to private individuals. Nevertheless, the PCC in the judgment of 6 July 2011 (P 12/09), did not decide to set aside Article 135 § 2 of the Polish Criminal Code penalizing an offence consisting of insulting the President of the Republic. The Court did not see in this provision any infringements of Articles 54(1) and 31(3) of the Constitution or of Article 10 of the ECHR.

In the judgment of 12 April 2000 (K 8/98) the PCC tried to interpret the meaning of the term "expropriation of the ownership" used in Article 21(2) of the Constitution. The PCC took a stand that this provision had to be understood in a broad way, which is confirmed in the jurisprudence of the ECtHR *inter alia* in the background of Article 1 of the additional Protocol no. 1 to the ECHR. This Article states that "no one shall be deprived of his possessions except in the public interest and subject to the conditions provided for by law and by the general principles of international law." The PCC also referred to Strasbourg case law concerning the deprivation of ownership in terms of the right to compensation, arguing that

> A due, i.e. just compensation constitutes therefore an element restoring a proper balance between the needs arising from the general interest of the society and the requirements connected with the protection of the basic rights of an individual (see the judgment of the ECtHR of 23rd September 1982 – Sporrong Lonnroth). In the light of the jurisprudence of the European Court of Human Rights and of the Constitutional Court not only does a cause, for which the interference is taken to the right to ownership, decide on the admissibility of such interference but also a way of its regulation made by the legislator.

In reference to the right to ownership it is worth stressing that the ECtHR case law served as a strong support in the case of 19 April 2005 (K 4/05) in which the PCC decided that the constraints in determining the rent rate for tenants of accommodation located in private buildings were not in conformity to the constitution. The PCC analyzed the ECtHR's case *Hutten-Czapska v. Poland* of 22 February 2005 (350014/97), in which the provisions for the regulated rents were considered to violate standards for the protection of ownership.

Further examples of a situation when an ECHR provision constituted a direct reference pattern in the process of constitutional interpretation were the judgments[22] in which the PCC considered the content of Article 45(1) of the Constitution conferring the right to a fair and public hearing before a competent, impartial and independent court. The PCC argued that Article 45(1) of the Constitution, to the extent it concerns the right to a court procedure that conforms to the requirements of a fair and public hearing, takes into account the content of the first sentence of Article 6(1) of the Convention. In turn, in the judgment of 18 October 2004 (P 8/04), the PCC indicated that exceptions from the constitutional right to appeal against

22 See judgments of 2 April 2001 (SK 10/00), 7 September 2004 (P 4/04), 19 February 2008 r. (P 49/06) and 18 February 2009 (Kp 3/08).

judgments made in the first stage (Article 78), as part of the right to a fair trial included in Article 6 of the ECHR, had to pass the proportional tests enumerated in the ECtHR case *Werner v. Poland (2003)* (36 EHRR 28). The above-mentioned judgment P 8/04 is also interesting as the PCC took a stance here as to the influence of the ECtHR's approaches when deciding on a particular matter:

> The commitment to take into account a judgement of ECtHR in actions of domestic organs obliges also the Constitutional Court to apply, within constitutional review, such principles and methods of interpretations to moderate any potential collisions between the standards arising from the Polish applied law and those formulating by ECtHR.

Taking this point of view, the PCC argues at the same time that its jurisdiction consists in deciding on the constitutionality of legal norms only, and does not encompass the correctness of their application in individual cases as this matter is the responsibility of ordinary and administrative courts (see the judgment of 7 March 2005, P 8/03).

## Conclusions

As can be seen from the above-mentioned examples, there is a close link between the jurisprudence of the CCC and PCC and standards promoted by the ECtHR. The ECHR has a strong impact on the Czech and Polish legal (constitutional) orders. The CCC's and PCC's "pro-ECHR" stance (Bobek and Kosař 2010: 18–19) is not surprising, since the catalogue of human rights in Poland and in the Czech Republic was to a significant degree influenced by the ECHR. In fact, several definitions of human rights in the Czech Charter of Fundamental Rights and Freedoms and in the Polish constitution mirror almost word by word their equivalents in the ECHR. Thus, in general, the case law of the CCC and PCC is very "ECHR-friendly" and both courts quote the ECtHR's jurisprudence on a regular basis and in an extensive manner when interpreting individual rights. Moreover, in the Czech Republic, thanks to the specific CCC attitude to the described "Euro-amendment," the notion of *constitutionality* in many ways coincides with the notion of *conventionality*.

From its earliest judgments the ECtHR recognized the subsidiary character of the ECHR system, by which it meant that it was primarily for the national judicial authorities to secure the rights enshrined in the ECHR. Thus the ECtHR has always placed its relationships with the superior national (constitutional) courts at the center of the ECHR mechanism. So today, all national high courts have a powerful interest in closely monitoring the ECtHR's activities, and in staying one step ahead of the latter when it comes to developing standards of rights protection.

The approaches of PCC and CCC are no doubt part of a wider tendency of universalization of human rights standards in the contemporary democratic state. This globalized notion of human rights is perceived currently as an important inspiration of democratic legal principles in the modern world. It contributes to defining liberal democracy as such. However, it does not mean that there are no possible dangers in the uncritical taking over of all points of view imposed by transnational institutions. It must not be forgotten that the concept of human rights is a part of the constitutional foundation of the state and constitutes the expression of the will of the sovereign nation. The problem of various interpretations of the rights and freedoms is more evident when it comes to deciding on very delicate matters, from the point of view of a particular society, such as abortion or the attitude to religion. In this context, J. Filip's observation seems to be right that, although the Member States of the Council of Europe should accommodate the high level of jurisprudence of the ECtHR, the latter from time to time should also assess its rights and "take a look outside the ivory tower" (Filip 2010: 376).

## References


Albi, A. 2005. *EU Enlargement and the Constitutions of Central and Eastern Europe*. Cambridge: Cambridge University Press.

Arnold, R. 2007. The Emergence of European Constitutional Law. *Electronic Journal of Comparative Law* 11(3). Available at: http://www.ejcl.org [accessed: 10 July 2010].

Banaszak, B. 2009. *Impact of European Integration on the Law and the Constitutional System in Poland*. Warsaw: C.H. Beck.

Błachut, P. and Mikuli, P. 2005. Uwagi o stosowaniu ustaw przez sądy w przypadku ich kolizji z prawem wspólnotowym [Remarks on Applying Laws by Courts in Case of their Incompatibility with European Law], in *Polska w Unii Europejskij* [*Poland in the European Union*], edited by J. Wawrzyniak and M. Kruk-Jarosz. Kraków: Zakamycze/Kluwer Polska, 267–74.

Bobek, M. and Kosař, D. 2010. The Application of European Union Law and the Law of the European Convention on Human Rights in the Czech Republic and Slovakia – an Overview, Eric Stein Working Paper, 2. Available at: http://www.ericsteinpapers.eu [accessed: 15 July 2010].

Działocha, K. 1999. *Law and Its Sources in the Constitution of the Republic of Poland: The Principles of Basic Institutions of the System of Government in Poland*, edited by K. Działocha. Warsaw: SEJM Publishing Office, 71–88.

Działocha, K. (ed.) 2006. *Basic Problems of Applying the Constitution of the Republic of Poland. Final Research Report*. Warsaw: SEJM Publishing Office.

Filip, J. 2010. Wznowienie postępowania przed Sądem Konstytucyjnym Republiki Czeskiej z powodu uwzględnienia orzeczenia Europejskiego Trybunału Praw Człowieka [Rehearing of a Proceeding before the Constitutional Court of the Czech Republic as the Consequence of the Judgment of the European Court of Human Rights], in *Rada Europy a przemiany demokratyczne w państwach Europy Środkowej i Wschodniej w latach 1989–2009* [*The Council of Europe and the Democratic Transformations in the States of Central and Eastern*

*Europe in the years 1989–2009*], edited by J. Jaskiernia. Toruń: Wydawnictwo Adam Marszałek, 367–77.

Garlicki, L. 2009, *Polskie prawo konstytucyjne. Zarys wykładu* [*Polish Constitutional Law. An Outline of a Lecture*]. Warsaw: Liber.

Garlicki, L. and Masternak-Kubiak, M. 2006. Władza sądownicza RP a stosowanie prawa międzynarodowego i prawa Unii Europejskiej [The Judicial Power of the Republic of Poland and the Application of International Law and the Law of the European Union], in *Otwarcie Konstytucji RP na prawo międzynarodowe i procesy integracyjne* [*Receptivity of the Polish Constitution to International Law and Integration Processes*], edited by K. Wójtowicz. Warsaw: Wydawnictwo Sejmowe, 165–84.

Grabowski, R. 2010. Wpływ standardów Rady Europy na zakres ochrony życia ludzkiego w Polsce w świetle orzecznictwa Trybunału Konstytucyjnego [The Influence of the Council of Europe Standards on the Scope of the Protection of Human Life in the Light of the Jurisprudence of the Constitutional Court], in *Rada Europy a przemiany demokratyczne w państwach Europy Środkowej i Wschodniej w latach 1989–2009* [*The Council of Europe and the Democratic Transformations in the States of Central and Eastern Europe in the Years 1989–1999*], edited by J. Jaskiernia. Toruń: Wydawnictwo Adam Marszałek, 288–304.

Grzybowski, M. 2006. Prawo międzynarodowe i wspólnotowe jako wzorzec i przedmiot kontroli norm [International and Community Law as a Reference Pattern and a Subject of the Control of Norms], in *Księga XX-lecia orzecznictwa Trybunału Konstytucyjnego* [*The Book Commemorating the 20th Anniversary of the Jurisprudence of the Constitutional Court*], edited by M. Zubik. Warsaw: Biuro Trybunalu Konstytucyjnego, 333–51.

Helfer, L. 2008. Redesigning the European Court of Human Rights: Embeddedness as a Deep Structural Principle of the European Human Rights Regime. *European Journal of International Law* 19(10), 125–59.

Keller, H. and Stone Sweet, A. 2008. Assessing the Impact of the ECHR on National Legal Systems, in *A Europe of Rights: The Impact of the European Convention on Human Rights on National Legal Systems*, edited by H. Keller and A. Stone Sweet. Oxford: Oxford University Press, 677–712.

Kühn, Z. 2004. Samovykonatelnost, přímá účinnost a některé teoretické otázky aplikace mezinárodních smluv ve vnitrostátním právu [The Self-Executing Nature, Direct Applicability and Certain Theoretical Issues of the Application of International Agreements in Domestic Law]. *Právník*, 5, 483.

Kühn, Z. and Kysela, J. 2002. Je Ústavou vždy to, co Ústavní soud řekne, že Ústava je? [Is the Constitution Always What the CCC Says that the Constitution Is?]. *Časopis pro právní vědu a praxi*, 3, 199–214.

Machowicz, K. 2009. *Ochrona praw człowieka w Rzeczypospolitej Polskiej na tle standardów europejskich* [*The Human Rights Protection in the Republic of Poland against the Background of the European Standards*]. Lublin: Wydawnictwo KUL.

Malenovský, J. 2002. Postavení mezinárodních smluv o lidských právech v českém právu po 1. červnu 2002 [Status of International Human Rights Treaties in the Czech Law After 1 June 2002]. *Právník*, 9, 917–32.

Mastrenak-Kubiak, M. 2003, *Przestrzeganie prawa międzynarodowego w świetle konstytucji Rzeczypospolitej Polskiej* [*The Respect for International Law in the Light of the Constitution of the Republic of Poland*]. Kraków: Zakamycze/Kluwer Polska.

Sadurski, W. 2005. *Rights Before the Court. A Study of Constitutional Courts in Postcommunist States of Central and Eastern Europe*. Berlin: Springer.

Sládeček, V., Mikule, V. and Syllova, J. 2007. Ústava ČR. Komentář [*The Constitution of the CR. Commentary*]. Prague: C.H. Beck.

Stone Sweet, A. 2009. *On the Constitutionalization of the Convention: The European Court of Human Rights as a Constitutional Court*. Special publication commemorating the 50th anniversary of the European Court of Human Rights/Revue Trimestrielle des Droits de l'Homme.

Wagnerová, E. 2006. *The Direct Applicability of Human Rights Treaties in Venice Commission, The Status of International Treaties on Human Rights*. Strasbourg: Council of Europe Press.

Wagnerová, E., Dostal, M., Langasek, T. and Pospisil, J. 2007. *Zákon o Ústavním soudu s komentářem* [*Commentary on Act No. 182/1993 Coll., on the Constitutional Court*]. Prague: ASPI.

Wildhaber, L. 2002. A Constitutional Future for the European Court of Human Rights? *Human Rights Law Journal* 23(5–7), 161–5.

Wójtowicz, K. 2004. Otwarcie Konstytucji RP na prawo międzynarodowe i procesy integracyjne [Receptivity of the Polish Constitution to International Law and Integration Processes], in *Podstawowe problemy stosowania Konstytucji Rzeczypospolitej. Raport wstępny* [*Basic Problems of Applying the Constitution of the Republic of Poland. Preliminary Research Report*], edited by K. Działocha. Warsaw: Wydawnictwo Sejmowe, 293–324.

Chapter 6

# Legislative Attempts to Prohibit the Use of International Law and Islamic Law in US Courts

Mark E. Wojcik

## Introduction

Federal and state courts in the United States may be called upon to apply the law of other countries in any number of cases: transnational contract disputes,[1] family law matters involving custody or visitation rights of parents and children in different countries,[2] and other criminal and civil litigation matters involving some substantive provision of international or foreign law.[3] Indeed, federal and state courts throughout the United States must regularly consider and apply foreign law sources in cases where the parties have chosen foreign law or when the substantive nature of the dispute calls for the application of a foreign or international source of law, such as an applicable treaty. As a result of increased globalization, the same is true of courts in other countries. Because people do business around the world, there is an ever-increasing need to consider laws from various countries, including

1 A contract for the sale of goods between two countries may involve the substantive law of either country. International treaties may also come into play, such as the United Nations Convention on the International Sale of Goods ("CISG"), 11 April 1980, 1489 U.N.T.S. 3, 52 Fed. Reg. 6262 (1987). Where a dispute arises in such a transaction, the court would accordingly be called upon to apply the law of one country or the other as well as any applicable international law sources.

2 Courts may also become involved in international family law matters such as child abductions by a non-custodial parent.

3 Contracts may stipulate that they are to be construed under the laws of one country or another, and that they should be litigated in those countries. Cases may be filed in one country (such as the United States) to sue for civil wrongs committed in another country (such as Turkey). Arik v. Boeing Co., 2011 IL App (1st) 100750-U (Ill. App. Ct. Jan. 10, 2012) (families of Turkish citizens killed in an airplane crash in Turkey sued for damages not in Turkey but in Chicago at the Circuit Court of Cook County, Illinois). In addition, documents sought in one country (such as the United States) for litigation purposes may be protected by privacy laws of another country (such as bank secrecy laws in Switzerland).

countries with legal systems that may be based at least in part on Islamic law.[4] We also see appropriate moments for US courts to acknowledge when rulings conform with international human rights norms or recent decisions of the various courts of other countries.

Some courts in the United States, however, may find themselves at the center of political controversies entirely unrelated to the actual type of transnational disputes that end up in court. In as many as 20 states, proposed legislation – and even amendments to state constitutions – is being considered or has already been introduced to restrict the sources of law that courts may consider in cases brought before them.[5] These proposals seek to limit the ability of courts to consider "foreign" and "international" law. Remarkably, some proposals even purport to preclude state courts from considering treaties ratified by the United States (which, under the United States Constitution, are to be considered as "Supreme Law of the Land" and controlling over inconsistent state laws, and even inconsistent state constitutions).[6] Other proposals go even a step further, prohibiting US courts from considering not only international and foreign law in general, but in particular "religious law," especially "Islamic law" or "Shari'a law."[7] Approximately 50 countries around the world can be characterized as Muslim states.[8] At least 11 of these 50 countries have constitutions that acknowledge Islam to be a source of national law.[9] The proponents of proposals to ban US courts from considering "Islamic law" or "Shari'a law" allege that there is a campaign of "creeping Islam" that will try to infect the state and federal courts of the United States.

The proposals to limit state courts from considering international law or Islamic law have proven to be popular measures among some voters.[10] For

---

4 See, e.g., Sadakat Kadri, Heaven on Earth: A Journey Through Shari'a Law from the Deserts of Ancient Arabia to the Streets of the Modern Muslim World 6–7, 188 (Farrar, Strauss, and Giroux, 2012).

5 See ABA House of Delegates Res. 113A, at 2 n. 4 (2011) (citing *The Law of the Land*, ABA J. 14 (April 2011)).

6 See U.S. Const. Art. VI.

7 The term "Islamic law" can be defined as: "a body of regulations and codes of conduct which have divine origin and are, in the main, located and locatable in the Muslim scripture, the Qur'an. This body of law is technically known as the *Shari'ah* or in Ibn Khalchun's phrasing, the 'revealed law.' . . . The Islamic law is also a system of duties. It comprises rites, legal and moral obligations all of which are brought together under the same religious command. Islamic law is of and from the Almighty." Oladosu Afis Ayinde, *Victims, Witnesses and Perpetrators: The Poetics of Violence in Islamic Jurisprudence*, in Islam in Contemporary Africa: On Violence, Terrorism and Development 1, 6 (Cambridge Scholars Publishing, 2007).

8 Sadakat Kadri, Heaven on Earth: A Journey Through Shari'a Law from the Deserts of Ancient Arabia to the Streets of the Modern Muslim World 6 (2012).

9 Ibid. at 6–7.

10 Federal legislation to restrict federal courts has also been introduced in the past, but that legislation was considered either unlikely to pass both chambers of the federal

example, measures have been passed in the states of Louisiana,[11] Oklahoma,[12] and Tennessee.[13] Voters in conservative districts in the United States, such as "the Bible Belt," appear to be a special target of these proposals. Political campaigns to pass laws and referenda banning consideration of religious laws (and in particular, "Islamic Law" or "Shari'a Law") have instilled fear and created confusion among voters, who are essentially warned that Islamic fundamentalists are about to take over the courts of the United States and impose rules of Islamic law on unsuspecting US citizens. These political campaigns essentially allege that Islamic activists are waging "lawfare" (a term created to suggest the use of warfare through the US court system). The campaigns fuel the distrust that many Americans have of any foreign authority or foreign legal system. They also prey upon false fears that some domestic courts rule without regard to written statutes, case precedent and fundamental guarantees of freedom and liberty enshrined in the federal and state constitutions. Where voters can be convinced to distrust judges and to fear any foreign or international law, it is easy to see how proposals can succeed in banning courts explicitly from considering foreign law, international law, Islamic law, and Shari'a. The issue is highly charged by the volatile combination of politics, emotion and faith.

This essay explores recent proposals to ban courts from considering categories such as "foreign law," "international law," "religious law," "cultural law," "Islamic law," and "Shari'a law."[14] In particular, this essay examines a state constitutional amendment from America's heartland, Oklahoma. Although the voters of that state overwhelming voted to prohibit their state courts from using international law or Islamic law, the federal district and appellate courts found that identifying a specific religion for disparate treatment violated the Establishment Clause of the US Constitution. Although the particular language of the Oklahoma Amendment was found to be unconstitutional, the issue is unlikely to disappear anytime soon. Attempts to restrict the sources of law that American judges can consider presents an interesting snapshot of a legal system facing extraordinary political challenges to judicial independence and professionalism.[15]

---

Congress or likely to be vetoed by the President if it did happen to pass.

11 2010 La. Acts. 714.

12 Okl. Enr. H.J.R. 1056 (2010).

13 The "American and Tennessee Laws for Tennessee Courts" bill was signed into law on 13 May 2010. 2010 Tenn. Pub. Acts. 983.

14 Following the court decisions that found express references to Shari'a law to violate the First Amendment of the US Constitution, later legislative proposals have instead preferred more general terms. *See, e.g.*, ABA House of Delegates Res. 113A, at 2 (2011). The various proposals have been based generally on model legislation offered by a group calling itself the "American Public Policy Alliance." *See* ibid. at 2–3.

15 *See, e.g.*, ABA House of Delegates Res. 113A, at 3 (2011).

## Background: Citing International and Foreign Law Sources in US Court Decisions

Oddly enough, attempts to prohibit courts from citing particular sources of law evolved as a response to a series of rulings by the US Supreme Court. These rulings advanced particular human rights issues, including decriminalizing gay and lesbian conduct, prohibiting the death penalty for juvenile offenders or the mentally retarded, and ending racial discrimination. Conservative commentators, who misrepresented the methodology used by the US Supreme Court, criticized these rulings because they cited international human rights law treaties and sources of foreign law.

Here are some examples of the Supreme Court decisions that caused conservative commentators so much distress. In each case, the foreign and international authorities were not controlling of the outcome but were cited merely as additional authority.

In *Atkins v. Virginia*,[16] the Supreme Court held that the Eighth and Fourteenth Amendments to the US Constitution prohibited the execution of a mentally retarded person. The Supreme Court reviewed its own precedent as well as the actions of state legislatures across the United States.[17] After finding that there was a national consensus in the United States against imposing the death penalty on mentally retarded offenders,[18] the majority decision noted that "within the world community, the imposition of the death penalty for crimes committed by mentally retarded offenders is overwhelmingly disapproved."[19] The majority did not cite any foreign or international source as controlling its interpretation of the US Constitution. It referred to the foreign precedent only to show that other countries shared the consensus reached in the United States against executing mentally retarded offenders.

In a second example of a case citing foreign authority, *Lawrence v. Texas*,[20] the US Supreme Court struck down sodomy laws as being unconstitutional.[21] In doing so, the Supreme Court overruled its 1986 decision in *Bowers v. Hardwick*,[22] which had narrowly found that the Georgia state sodomy statute did not violate the US Constitution. In *Bowers*, the concurring opinion by Chief Justice Burger had made "sweeping references to the history of Western civilization and to Judeo-Christian moral and ethical standards" condemning homosexuality; the opinion

16 536 U.S. 304 (2002).

17 *See* ibid. at 311–17.

18 Ibid. at 316.

19 Ibid. at 316 n. 21. As support for this proposition, the majority decision cited the *amicus* brief submitted by the European Union.

20 539 U.S. 558 (2003).

21 Ibid. at 578–9.

22 478 U.S. 186 (1986).

failed to acknowledge that other sources went "in an opposite direction."[23] To correct that error, the *Lawrence* Court cited the Wolfenden Report to the British Parliament (which recommended repealing sodomy laws in that country) as well as *Dudgeon v. United Kingdom*,[24] a decision from the European Court of Human Rights, which had ruled five years before *Bowers* that sodomy laws violated the European Convention on Human Rights.[25] The foreign sources were not cited as controlling sources of law and were not used to interpret the US Constitution; they were cited only to refute Chief Justice Burger's claim that there was no authority favoring the privacy rights of gay and lesbian persons.[26] Considering its own precedent in earlier US Supreme Court decisions, the majority decision in *Lawrence* determined that *Bowers v. Hardwick* was no longer good law in the United States.[27] The majority then noted that the European Court of Human Rights and court decisions from other countries were in accord with the Supreme Court's determination that *Bowers* was no longer valid precedent.[28] Those foreign court decisions were not cited to construe the US Constitution; they were cited to show that the decision reached independently by the Supreme Court was in accord with the international human rights standard evidenced in those opinions.

In a third example of a Supreme Court case citing international human rights law, the Supreme Court held in *Grutter v. Bollinger*[29] that the use of race as a factor in student admissions by a public law school was not unconstitutional.[30] The Supreme Court found that "the Equal Protection Clause [of the US Constitution] does not prohibit the Law School's narrowly tailored use of race in admissions decisions to further a compelling interest in obtaining the educational benefits that

23 *Lawrence*, 539 U.S. at 572.

24 45 Eur. Ct. H.R. (1981).

25 *Lawrence*, 539 U.S. at 573.

26 Ibid.

27 *See* ibid. at 576.

28 The majority decision cited decisions from the European Court of Human Rights and referred to cases cited in an amicus brief filed by Mary Robinson and others: "To the extent Bowers relied on values we share with a wider civilization, it should be noted that the reasoning and holding in Bowers have been rejected elsewhere. The European Court of Human Rights has followed not Bowers but its own decision in Dudgeon v. United Kingdom. *See* P. G. & J. H. v. United Kingdom, App. No. 00044787/98, ¶ 56 (Eur. Ct. H. R., Sept. 25, 2001); Modinos v. Cyprus, 259 Eur. Ct. H. R. (1993); Norris v. Ireland, 142 Eur. Ct. H. R. (1988). Other nations, too, have taken action consistent with an affirmation of the protected right of homosexual adults to engage in intimate, consensual conduct. *See* Brief for Mary Robinson et al. as Amici Curiae 11–12. The right the petitioners seek in this case has been accepted as an integral part of human freedom in many other countries. There has been no showing that in this country the governmental interest in circumscribing personal choice is somehow more legitimate or urgent." *Lawrence*, 539 U.S. at 576–7.

29 539 U.S. 306 (2003).

30 Ibid. at 343–4.

flow from a diverse student body."[31] A concurring opinion by Justice Ginsburg and joined by Justice Breyer cited as additional authority the International Convention on the Elimination of All Forms of Racial Discrimination,[32] a human rights treaty ratified by the United States in 1994, as well as the Convention on the Elimination of All Forms of Discrimination against Women,[33] a human rights treaty to which the United States was not a party.[34] She cited those treaties not to construe any provision of the US Constitution, but to affirm that the majority's observation that race-conscious programs "must have a logical end point" was in accord "with the international understanding of the office of affirmative action."[35] Her citations of those authorities were again to show that the result reached by the Supreme Court was in accord with international law, as evidenced here by two international human rights treaties.

*Roper v. Simmons*[36] is another example of a US Supreme Court case that cited foreign or international law. In *Roper*, the Supreme Court held that applying the death penalty to persons who were juveniles at the time of the offense constituted cruel and unusual punishment under the Eighth Amendment to the US Constitution.[37] As it did with its earlier decision in *Atkins*, the majority opinion in *Roper* carefully analyzed the case under its own precedent and "society's evolving standards of decency" evidenced, in part, by state legislation that repealed the juvenile death penalty in various US jurisdictions.[38] It found evidence within the United States of a national consensus against the juvenile death penalty.[39] After holding that the death penalty should not be imposed upon juveniles, the court noted "the stark reality that the United States is the only country in the world that continues to give official sanction to the juvenile death penalty."[40] The majority decision took special care to note that "[t]his reality does not become controlling, for the task of interpreting

31 Ibid. at 343.

32 International Convention on the Elimination of All Forms of Racial Discrimination, Annex to G.A. Res. 2106, 20 U.N. GAOR, 20th Sess., Res. Supp. (No. 14), at 47, U.N. Doc. A/6014, Art. 2(2) (1965). The United States had ratified the treaty with reservations, understandings, and declarations.

33 Convention on the Elimination of All Forms of Discrimination against Women, Annex to G.A. Res. 34/180, 34 U.N. GAOR, 34th Sess., Res. Supp. (No. 46), p. 194, U.N. Doc. A/34/46, Art. 4(1) (1979).

34 *Grutter*, 539 U.S. at 344 (Ginsburg, J., concurring).

35 Ibid.

36 543 U.S. 551 (2005).

37 Ibid. at 573–9. A "juvenile offender" was one who was younger than 18 years of age. See ibid. at 555–6. The Eighth Amendment provides: "Excessive bail shall not be required, nor excessive fines imposed, nor cruel and unusual punishments inflicted." U.S. Const. amend. VIII.

38 See *Roper*, 543 U.S. at 563–7.

39 Ibid. at 564–75.

40 Ibid. at 575.

the Eighth Amendment remains [the] responsibility" of the US Supreme Court.[41] However, the majority decision noted that the Supreme Court had indeed "referred to the laws of other countries and to international authorities as instructive for its interpretation of the Eighth Amendment's prohibition of 'cruel and unusual punishments.'"[42] In that context, the majority decision looked to decisions of other common law countries and decisions from courts of Western Europe, which had all prohibited the juvenile death penalty.[43] It also cited Article 37 of the United Nations Convention on the Rights of the Child,[44] an international human rights treaty ratified by "every country in the world . . . save for the United States and Somalia," which expressly prohibits capital punishment for crimes committed by juveniles under the age of 18.[45] It cited other international human rights treaties to the same effect, including the International Covenant on Civil and Political Rights,[46] a treaty that the United States had signed and ratified (with an applicable reservation), the American Convention on Human Rights[47] (a treaty to which the United States was not a party), and the African Charter on the Rights and Welfare of the Child[48] (to which the United States was also not a party).[49] It also surveyed practices from other countries that had abolished the juvenile death penalty.[50] The majority opinion found it "proper" to "acknowledge the overwhelming weight of international opinion against the juvenile death penalty," and it carefully noted that "[t]he opinion of the world community, while not controlling our outcome, does provide respected and significant confirmation for our own conclusions."[51]

41 Ibid.

42 Ibid.

43 Ibid. at 575–6.

44 U.N. Convention on the Rights of the Child, Art. 37, 20 November 1989, 1577 U.N.T.S. 3, 28 I.L.M. 1448 (entered into force 2 September 1990).

45 *Roper*, 543 U.S. at 576.

46 See International Covenant on Civil and Political Rights, Art. 6(5), 999 U.N.T.S., at 175 (prohibiting capital punishment for anyone under 18 at the time of offense) (signed and ratified by the United States subject to a reservation regarding Article 6(5)).

47 American Convention on Human Rights: Pact of San José, Costa Rica, Art. 4(5), 22 November 1969, 1144 U.N.T.S. 146 (entered into force 19 July 1978).

48 African Charter on the Rights and Welfare of the Child, Art. 5(3), OAU Doc. CAB/ LEG/ 24.9/49 (1990) (entered into force 29 November 1999).

49 *Roper*, 543 U.S. at 576.

50 Ibid. at 577–8.

51 Ibid. at 578. The majority decision went on to say that it was proper to acknowledge values shared by other countries: "Over time, from one generation to the next, the Constitution has come to earn the high respect and even, as Madison dared to hope, the veneration of the American people. *See* The Federalist No. 49, p. 314 (C. Rossiter ed. 1961). The document sets forth, and rests upon, innovative principles original to the American experience, such as federalism; a proven balance in political mechanisms through separation of powers; specific guarantees for the accused in criminal cases; and broad provisions to secure individual freedom and preserve human dignity. These doctrines and guarantees are central to the American experience and remain essential to our present-day

In each of those Supreme Court rulings, the majority or concurring opinion cited to international human rights treaties, including the International Covenant on Civil and Political Rights and the Convention to Eliminate all forms of Racial Discrimination. The United States has ratified both of those treaties, albeit with reservations, understandings, and declarations that rendered those treaties "non-self-executing" in US courts. However, in addition to citing treaties to which the United States was a party, the majority or concurring opinions also cited international human rights treaties that the United States has not yet joined as a state party, such as the Convention to Eliminate Discrimination Against Women, the Convention on the Rights of the Child, and the American Convention on Human Rights.

The Supreme Court decisions did not apply those international human rights treaties to construe the US Constitution. Those human rights treaties (whether ratified or not by the United States) were cited only after the Court had reached its decision based on its own reading of the US Constitution and the applicable US precedents. The additional citations to those international human rights treaties were simply to show that the ruling reached in each case was in conformity with international human rights norms or recent decisions of other courts around the world.[52]

Critics of the decisions falsely stated that the US Supreme Court majorities had invoked international and foreign law to decide questions of law under the US Constitution. The Supreme Court did no such thing. The Supreme Court, in each of the cases cited, reached its decision by applying judicial precedent from the United States. The additional citation to international human rights law treaties did not convert the decision from one decided under principles of US Constitutional Law to one decided under international law.

In addition to criticizing US Supreme Court decisions citing international human rights treaties, critics also attacked certain state court decisions that cited legal developments from other countries. For example, the decision of the Supreme Judicial Court of Massachusetts, when it first recognized a right to same-sex marriage, cited court decisions from neighboring Canada.[53] The court noted that, at the time of its decision, two Canadian provincial courts had recognized the right to

---

self-definition and national identity. Not the least of the reasons we honor the Constitution, then, is because we know it to be our own. It does not lessen our fidelity to the Constitution or our pride in its origins to acknowledge that the express affirmation of certain fundamental rights by other nations and peoples simply underscores the centrality of those same rights within our own heritage of freedom." Ibid.

52 The Supreme Court could have just as easily cited treatises or law review articles in a similar manner. The Court's decision would not have been dictated by what was written in a treatise or law review article, but the Court could have pointed to those sources to show that its result was in conformity with what those sources predicted. Statements that the Supreme Court was applying international or foreign law to rule on an issue of constitutional law misrepresent what the Supreme Court was actually doing.

53 Goodridge v. Dep't Pub. Health, 798 N.E.2d 941 (Mass. 2003); *see also* Mark E. Wojcik, *The Wedding Bells Heard Around the World: Years from Now, Will We Wonder Why We Worried About Same-Sex Marriage?*, 24 N. Ill. U. L. Rev. 589 (2004).

same-sex marriage.[54] The state court in Massachusetts by no measure thought that those Canadian decisions were controlling in Massachusetts; the court cited them only as evidence that the result it had reached under Massachusetts state law was in conformity with recent decisions from another common law country. Yet, critics of the decision pointed to the citation of Canadian decisions with scorn, claiming them to be evidence of the creeping influence of foreign law in the United States.

These critics took issue not with the methodology employed by the courts, but with the outcomes of the disputes resolved by the bench. We know this in part because some critics made their denunciations of the court decisions shortly after the decisions were released; these critics simply did not have time to read the decisions that they were criticizing.[55] In the context of the cases discussed here, the criticism of citing international and foreign law sources ignored two things: first, that the United States had been a party to some of the treaties cited; and second, that all of the citations to international and foreign sources were made to show that the result reached was in conformity with international law or with recent decisions from other countries. The courts did not use those international and foreign sources to decide any constitutional questions under the federal or state constitution; the international and foreign sources were included only as additional citations after the courts had reached their results under the applicable standards of federal and state law.

Critics who claim that the courts are deciding constitutional questions by using international and foreign sources either do not read those decisions carefully enough or purposefully mischaracterize what the courts did in those cases. Often the unwarranted attacks on the judiciary are made for political purposes. In that context, it is easy to see how the next steps were made: critics of using international

---

54 EGALE Canada, Inc. v. Canada (Attorney General), [2003] 13 B.C.L.R.4th 1 (B.C. C.A); Halpern v. Toronto (City), [2003] 172 O.A.C. 276. *See also* Wojcik, *supra* note 53, at 636–45.

55 Any person asked for an opinion about a court decision should take the time to read it before expressing an opinion. If pressed by a journalist for a quote, the person should answer that he or she has not yet had time to read the decision and will not have a comment on it until he or she has had time to review the court's decision and its reasoning. Such an answer would convey the proper respect that we should have for the independence and professionalism of judges. Journalists, for their part, should be wary of reporting any comments from persons who have not read the decision. If a person attempts to make a statement about a court decision immediately after its release, the journalist should ask that person whether he or she has read the decision they are criticizing (or, likewise, praising). If the person answers honestly that he or she has not yet had time to read the decision, the journalist should offer to contact the person the following day. Such an action by journalists would produce more thoughtful commentary about court decisions, help instill respect for the independence and professionalism of judges, and create an ethical standard for journalists by which they would refuse to report the criticism of court decisions that their critics had not even bothered to read.

and foreign law focused their attacks on Islamic law as a specific example of foreign law and the one most likely to elicit a visceral reaction among potential voters.

## Attempts to Prohibit "Islamic Law" in US Courts

Several US jurisdictions have considered (or are considering) legislation to restrict courts from considering not only "international" or "foreign law," but also "Islamic law" or "Shari'a Law." This section examines in depth one of the states (Oklahoma) where a state constitutional amendment was passed. In that state, the constitutional amendment never entered into effect because it was found to violate the federal constitution.

On 25 May 2010, the Oklahoma legislature passed a resolution that directed the Secretary of State of Oklahoma to refer to the voters of Oklahoma a proposed "Save Our State" amendment.[56] The proposed amendment to Article VII of the Oklahoma State Constitution provided as follows:

> The Courts . . . when exercising their judicial authority, shall uphold and adhere to the law as provided in the United States Constitution, the Oklahoma Constitution, the United States Code, federal regulations promulgated pursuant thereto, established common law, the Oklahoma Statutes and rules promulgated pursuant thereto, and if necessary the law of another state of the United States provided the law of the other state does not include Sharia Law, in making judicial decisions. The courts shall not look to the legal precepts of other nations or cultures. Specifically, the courts shall not consider international law or Sharia Law. The provisions of this subsection shall apply to all cases before the respective courts including, but not limited to, cases of first impression.[57]

The House Joint Resolution adopted by the Oklahoma State Legislature also included the following specific ballot language that voters would see when voting on the "Save Our State" proposal:

> This measure amends the State Constitution. It would change a section that deals with courts of this state. It would make courts rely on federal and state laws when deciding cases. It would forbid courts from looking at international law or Sharia Law when deciding cases. SHALL THE PROPOSAL BE APPROVED?[58]

---

56 Without presenting evidence that the state itself was ever in danger, the name "Save Our State" was used for that amendment to invoke the same acronym ("SOS") used by ships in distress, from the phrase "Save Our Ship."

57 Oklahoma House Joint Resolution 1056, adopted 25 May 2010, *as quoted in* Awad v. Ziriax, 670 F.3d 1111, 1117–18 (10th Cir. 2012).

58 Ibid. at 1118.

Before that language went on the ballot, however, the Attorney General of Oklahoma determined that the description was legally inadequate because it did not define for voters the terms "international law" or "Sharia Law."[59] The Attorney General revised the ballot language as follows to include definitions of both terms:

> This measure amends the State Constitution. It changes a section that deals with the courts of this state. It would amend Article 7, Section 1. It makes courts rely on federal and state law when deciding cases. It forbids courts from considering or using international law. It forbids courts from considering or using Sharia Law.
>
> International law is also known as the law of nations. It deals with the conduct of international organizations and independent nations, such as countries, states and tribes. It deals with their relationship with each other. It also deals with some of their relationships with persons. The law of nations is formed by the general assent of civilized nations. Sources of international law also include international agreements, as well as treaties.
>
> Sharia Law is Islamic law. It is based on two principal sources, the Koran and the teachings of Mohammed.
>
> SHALL THE PROPOSAL BE APPROVED?[60]

The term "international law" was thus defined to include customary international law as well as treaties ratified by the United States. The term "Sharia Law" was defined as Islamic law derived from the Koran and teachings of the Prophet Mohammed. The Oklahoma Attorney General did not express any opinion on whether the proposal was constitutional or preempted by federal law.[61] There was no statement that international treaties ratified by the United States are binding on states as "Supreme Law of the Land" under Article VI of the US Constitution,[62] and the Oklahoma Attorney General made no statement as to whether any Oklahoma court had ever had occasion to consider any question that would involve Islamic law.

The voters of Oklahoma were to consider the "Save Our State" ballot measure on Tuesday, 2 November 2010.[63] On the eve of that election, some voters reportedly received automated phone calls about a case from New Jersey, where a trial court judge had dismissed a criminal sexual assault case against a Muslim man. The trial court ruled that the husband lacked the criminal intent to commit sexual assault upon his wife because his "desire to have sex when and whether he wanted to, was something that was consistent with his practices and it was something that was not

59 Ibid.

60 Ibid.

61 Ibid.

62 U.S. Const. Art. VI.

63 *See Awad*, 670 F.3d at 1116.

prohibited."[64] That trial court decision was put forth as an example of what could happen when US courts applied principles of Islamic law. In particular, it was used to show that applying principles of Islamic law would result in violence against women (because the New Jersey trial court dismissed the criminal charge against the husband). What the voters of Oklahoma did not know, however, is that the New Jersey trial court opinion would later be reversed on appeal.[65] The appellate court stated its concern that the trial court judge's "view of the facts . . . may have been colored by his perception that, although defendant's sexual acts violated applicable criminal statutes, they were culturally acceptable and thus not actionable – a view that we have soundly rejected."[66] The appellate court thus not only reversed but "soundly rejected" the trial court's failure to protect the abused wife.[67]

The Oklahoma voters approved the "Save Our State" ballot measure by a margin of 70 percent.[68] The election results would normally have been certified one week later, but for a constitutional challenge filed against the measure.[69] Muneer Awad, an American Muslim living in Oklahoma, filed an action on 4 November 2010 to prevent certification of the election results.[70] He claimed that the "Save Our State" Amendment violated the Establishment Clause and the Free Exercise Clause of the First Amendment to the US Constitution.[71] He stated that the "Save Our State" Amendment singled out Islam for negative treatment and that implementation of the measure would stigmatize him and other practicing Muslims.[72] He stated that the Amendment would prevent the courts of Oklahoma from probating his last will and testament, which contained references to Shari'a principles.[73] He said that the Amendment would limit the relief that Muslims could

---

64 S.D. v. M.J.R., 2 A.3d 412, 428 (N.J. Super. 2010); *see also* ABA House of Delegates Res. 113A, at 3 (2011).

65 S.D. v. M.J.R., 2 A.3d 412 (N.J. Super. 2010).

66 Ibid. at 427.

67 Ibid.; *see also* ibid. at 428 ("the [trial] judge was mistaken in determining not to issue a final restraining order in this matter in order to protect plaintiff from future abuse and in dismissing plaintiff's domestic violence complaint").

68 *See Awad*, 670 F.3d at 1118.

69 *See* ibid. at 1118–19.

70 Ibid. Mr Awad was also Executive Director of the Oklahoma Chapter of the Council on American–Islamic Relations (CAIR). Ibid. at 1119.

71 *Awad*, 670 F.3d at 1119. The First Amendment provides the following protections: "Congress shall make no law respecting an establishment of religion, or prohibiting the free exercise thereof; or abridging the freedom of speech, or of the press; or the right of the people peaceably to assemble, and to petition the Government for a redress of grievances." U.S. Const. amend. I.

72 *Awad*, 670 F.3d at 1119.

73 Ibid.

obtain from Oklahoma state courts.[74] He also claimed that the Amendment would foster "excessive entanglement between the government and his religion."[75]

Mr Awad's complaint focused on the new prohibitions against Islamic law.[76] Based on Mr Awad's complaint, a federal district court granted a temporary restraining order and a preliminary injunction against implementation of the "Save Our State" Amendment.[77] The granting of that preliminary injunction was appealed to the US Court of Appeals for the Tenth Circuit, which concluded that Mr Awad's Establishment Clause claim was sufficient to uphold the injunction.[78]

The First Amendment to the US Constitution provides in part that "Congress shall make no law respecting an establishment of religion."[79] That provision, known as the Establishment Clause, applies to state governments through the Due Process Clause of the Fourteenth Amendment.[80] Where a statute is challenged under the Establishment Clause, the applicable test may be found in one of two Supreme Court cases: the *Lemon*[81] test or the *Larson*[82] test. The *Lemon* test applies to "laws affording uniform benefit to *all* religions, and not to provisions . . . that discriminate *among* religions."[83] The *Larson* test provides that, if a law favors one religion over another, it can survive constitutional scrutiny only if it is "closely fitted to the furtherance of any compelling interest asserted."[84] The Tenth Circuit

---

74 Ibid.

75 Ibid.

76 His complaint might have also challenged the portions of the "Save Our State" Amendment that prohibited Oklahoma courts from considering sources of international law, including treaties of the United States that are binding on Oklahoma under the U.S. Constitution as Supreme Law of the Land. U.S. Const. Art. VI. Perhaps because it could have been more difficult for him to have shown standing to challenge the prohibitions against international law, the complaint was limited to challenging the prohibitions against invoking Islamic law in the courts of Oklahoma.

77 *See* Awad v. Ziriax, 754 F. Supp. 2d 1298 (W.D. Okla. 2010).

78 *Awad*, 670 F.3d at 1119. Because the Establishment Clause claim was sufficient, the Tenth Circuit did not consider Mr Awad's additional claim that the "Save Our State" Amendment also violated his rights under the Free Exercise clause of the First Amendment of the U.S. Constitution. Ibid.

79 U.S. Const. amend. I.

80 *Awad*, 670 F.3d at 1126.

81 Lemon v. Kurtzman, 403 U.S. 602, 612–13 (1971).

82 Larson v. Valente, 456 U.S. 228, 255 (1982).

83 *Awad*, 670 F.3d at 1126 (emphasis in original); *see also* W. Cole Durham, Jr & Brett G. Scharffs, Law and Religion: National, International, and Comparative Perspectives 141 (2010) ("Over time, the *Lemon* test became not only the primary mechanism used by the [U.S. Supreme] Court in establishment cases, but one of the most controversial doctrines in the history of constitutional adjudication.").

84 *Awad*, 670 F.3d at 1126; *see also* Corporation of the Presiding Bishop v. Amos, 483 U.S. 327 (1987).

determined that the *Larson* test applied because the Oklahoma Amendment named the religion of Islam as the specific target of its discrimination.[85]

The federal appellate court determined that the amendment prohibited Oklahoma courts from upholding laws of other states that include Shari'a.[86] The amendment allowed, however, the Oklahoma courts to uphold laws of other states that included the law of any religion other than Islam.[87] Because the amendment discriminates among religions, the court easily found it to be "suspect," and subject to the "strict scrutiny" test to determine its constitutionality.[88] To survive a challenge under the strict scrutiny test, the supporters of a challenged piece of legislation must show both (1) "a compelling government interest" and (2) that the legislation "is 'closely fitted' to that compelling interest."[89] To show a "compelling government interest" in discriminating against a particular religion, the legislation "must address an identified problem that the discrimination seeks to remedy."[90] A compelling state interest must be an "actual" and "concrete" problem, and not just the "[m]ere speculation of harm."[91]

When asked by the federal court to state its compelling interest, the defenders of the "Save Our State" Amendment simply asserted that "Oklahoma certainly has a compelling interest in determining what law is applied in Oklahoma courts."[92] The court acknowledged that interest as "a valid state concern," but found that "this general statement alone is not sufficient to establish a *compelling* interest" of the state government.[93] The court found that supporters of the Amendment could not identify any "actual problem" that the Amendment sought to solve.[94] The supporters admitted that they "did not know of even a single instance where an Oklahoma court had applied Sharia law or used the legal precepts of other nations or cultures, let alone that such applications or uses had resulted in concrete problems in Oklahoma."[95] Because there was no history of harm, the court easily concluded that "any harm Appellants seek to remedy with the proposed

85 Ibid. at 1128. The appellants had attempted to argue that the amendment banned all religious laws from Oklahoma's courts and that Shari'a was named only as an example. *See* ibid. The court rejected that argument because the amendment named "Sharia law" in two places. Ibid.

86 *Awad*, 670 F.3d at 1128–9.

87 Ibid.

88 Ibid. at 1129 (citing *Larson*, 456 U.S. at 246).

89 Ibid. (citing *Larson*, 456 U.S. at 246–7).

90 Ibid. (citing Brown v. Entm't Merch. Ass'n, 131 S. Ct. 2729, 2738 (2011)).

91 Ibid. (citing Consol. Edison Co. of New York, Inc. v. Pub. Serv. Comm'n of New York, 447 U.S. 530, 543 (1980), and Turner Broadcasting Sys., Inc. v. FCC, 512 U.S. 62, 644 (1994)). Additionally, "overly general statements of abstract principles do not satisfy the government's burden to articulate a compelling interest." Ibid. at 1130.

92 *Awad*, 670 F.3d at 1130.

93 Ibid. (emphasis in original).

94 Ibid.

95 *Awad*, 754 F. Supp. 2d at 1308; *Awad*, 670 F.3d at 1130.

amendment is speculative at best and cannot support a compelling interest."[96] Without a compelling interest based on an actual problem, the court noted that "the second step of the strict scrutiny analysis – whether there is a close fit with a compelling state interest – [was] unnecessary and not feasible."[97] The court nonetheless observed that the "Save Our State" Amendment prevented courts not just from "applying" Shari'a but from even considering any of those laws.[98] As stated by the court, "[e]ven if the state could identify and support a reason to single out and restrict Sharia law in its courts, the amendment's complete ban of Sharia law is hardly an exercise of narrow tailoring."[99]

Because he was alleging the violation of a constitutional right, the court concluded that Mr Awad did not need to show "irreparable injury" if the Amendment were allowed to go into effect.[100] The court recognized that damages would be "inadequate or difficult to ascertain" for the governmental condemnation of his religion.[101] The "Save Our State" Amendment – passed by 70 percent of Oklahoma's voters – never entered into effect.[102]

The "Save Our State" Amendment was put before the voters of Oklahoma to remedy a problem that did not exist in that state. Although the proponents knew that no Oklahoma court had ever applied Islamic law or the legal norms of other countries,[103] they created a campaign to confuse and frighten voters. The federal court decision declared the state constitutional amendment to violate the federal constitution. Some observers described the federal court decision as a setback to attempts to pass similar legislation in as many as 20 other US jurisdictions.[104] Although it might be a setback, the ruling did not derail the movement to enact legislation to restrict the kinds of law that courts can consider. Sponsors of

96 *Awad*, 670 F.3d at 1130.

97 Ibid. The court stated that the analysis was "unnecessary" because "both a compelling interest and a close fit are required to survive strict scrutiny." Ibid. The court stated that the analysis was "not feasible" because the court had "no concrete problem or compelling interest to try to fit with the Save Our State Amendment." Ibid. The court stated that "[o]ne cannot try on a glove to see if it fits when the glove is missing." Ibid. at 1130–31.

98 *Awad*, 670 F.3d at 1131.

99 Ibid.

100 Ibid.

101 Ibid. After considering some additional factors, the federal appeals court found that the federal district court did not abuse its discretion in granting an injunction to prevent the "Save Our State" Amendment from entering into effect. Ibid.

102 Although Mr Awad challenged only the prohibitions on citing Islamic Law or Shari'a, the court struck the entire Amendment, including its prohibition on citing international law. *See Awad*, 670 F.3d at 1132 n. 16.

103 Ibid. at 1130.

104 *See* Kari Huus, *Federal Court Deals Blow to Anti-Shariah Efforts* (10 January 2012), *available at* http://usnews.msnbc.msn.com/_news/2012/01/10/10097954-federal-court-deals-blow-to-anti-shariah-efforts?lite.

similar legislation are now simply more careful to avoid explicit mention of Islamic law or Shari'a.[105]

## Infringements of Constitutional Rights

The House of Delegates of the American Bar Association, considering the problem of legislation to restrict courts from considering foreign law, international law, and Islamic law, adopted the following two-part resolution:

> RESOLVED, That the American Bar Association opposes federal or state laws that impose blanket prohibitions on consideration or use by courts or arbitral tribunals of foreign or international law.
>
> FURTHER RESOLVED, That the American Bar Association opposes federal or state laws that impose blanket prohibitions on consideration or use by courts or arbitral tribunals of the entire body of law or doctrine of a particular religion.[106]

The American Bar Association (ABA) policy directly opposes attempts to restrict the sources of law that American courts can consider. It also indirectly supports the independence and professionalism of judges. The ABA policy and its accompanying report recognize that the various legislative attempts to prohibit courts from considering particular sources of law are all attempts to "deny fundamental rights to a group of citizens based on the vote of a state legislature or the results of a state-wide referendum."[107] For reasons identified in part by the ABA report, the various legislative proposals and state constitutional amendments violate several provisions of the US Constitution.

Taken together with the appellate court's decision in *Awad*, we see that proposals to restrict courts from considering international law, foreign law, Islamic law and Shari'a law can be found to violate at least five provisions under the US Constitution: (a) the Supremacy Clause; (b) the Contracts Clause; (c) the Establishment Clause; (d) the Free Exercise Clause; and (e) the Full Faith and Credit Clause.

---

105 *See, e.g.*, ABA House of Delegates Res. 113A, at 3 (2011) (citing *The Law of the Land*, ABA J. 14, 14 (April 2011) (which noted that in "South Dakota, state [Representative] Phil Jensen says he learned from the Oklahoma decision to omit the word Shariah in similar legislation he sponsored . . . In South Carolina, state [Senator] Michael Fair, a sponsor of an anti-Shariah bill in his state, says that he too has heeded the tactical wisdom to 'keep it bland'")).

106 ABA House of Delegates Res. 113A, at 1 (2011).

107 Ibid. at 5.

*Supremacy Clause*

The Supremacy Clause of the US Constitution makes "supreme" the federal constitution, federal laws and treaties made under the authority of the United States. Accordingly, state laws – and even state constitutions – cannot stand if they violate the Supremacy Clause. The Supremacy Clause provides that:

> This Constitution, and the Laws of the United States which shall be made in Pursuance thereof; and all Treaties made, or which shall be made, under the Authority of the United States, shall be the supreme Law of the Land; and the Judges in every State shall be bound thereby, any Thing in the Constitution or Laws of any State to the Contrary notwithstanding.[108]

Legislation and state constitutional amendments (like that passed in Oklahoma) that prohibit courts from applying "international law" would violate the Supremacy Clause. "International law" had been defined in the "Save Our State" Amendment passed by the Oklahoma voters as including treaties entered into by the United States.[109] The Supremacy Clause, by its own terms, states that those federal treaties bind "Judges in every State."[110] By denying judges the ability to consider and apply treaties entered into by the United States, the Oklahoma Amendment violates the Supremacy Clause.

For example, the United Nations Convention on the International Sale of Goods ("CISG"),[111] a treaty ratified by the United States in 1986 and effective in the United States in 1988, is generally considered to be a self-executing treaty that applies directly in state courts without any need for further implementation of legislation.[112] The CISG essentially operates as an international version of the Uniform Commercial Code, although the particular scope of the CISG is much more limited. However, the CISG applies when a buyer or seller in the United States makes a contract with a buyer or seller located in another country that has ratified the CISG.[113] The CISG applies of its own accord to that international sales contract, even if the buyer and seller did not realize that there was such a thing as

108 U.S. Const. Art. VI, § 1, cl. 2.

109 *See Awad*, 670 F.3d at 1117–18.

110 U.S. Const. Art. VI, § 1, cl. 2.

111 11 April 1980, 1489 U.N.T.S. 3, 52 Fed. Reg. 6262 (1987).

112 *See, e.g.*, ABA House of Delegates Res. 113A, at 6 (2011) (citing Delchi Carrier SpA v. Rotorex Corp., 71 F.3d 1024, 1027 (2d Cir. 1995)).

113 *See* CISG Art. 1(a) ("This Convention applies to contracts of sale of goods between parties whose places of business are in different States . . . when the States are Contracting States."). Article 1(b) would also allow the CISG to apply "when the rules of private international law lead to the application of the law of a Contracting State," but the United States took a reservation on that provision. Accordingly, for the United States, the CISG applies to transactions only when both parties are in countries that are parties to the CISG.

the CISG.[114] The buyer and seller are free to modify the CISG and to even exclude its provisions entirely, but they must do so expressly.[115] Accordingly,

> under the Supremacy Clause, a state court faced with a sale of goods dispute governed by the CISG between a state resident and a supplier in, say, France must apply the CISG unless the parties expressly opted out of it, and any state constitutional amendment or statutory provision that prohibited this outcome would violate the Supremacy Clause, which provides that, as a treaty, the provisions of the CISG are "supreme" over state law.[116]

In addition to applying the CISG as a treaty of the United States, a US court would also be charged under the Convention with considering how other countries have interpreted the Convention. The Convention directs that its interpretation be informed by its "international character and . . . the need to promote uniformity in its application and the observance of good faith in international trade."[117]

Other treaties ratified by the United States are also supreme law of the land. When those treaties are self-executing and not in need of further federal legislation to bring them into effect, those treaties and must be applied even at the state and local level. Any state constitutional amendments that purport to abrogate that need to apply federal treaties violate the Supremacy Clause.

*Contracts Clause*

The Contacts Clause of the US Constitution provides that "No State shall . . . pass any . . . Law impairing the Obligation of Contracts."[118] As noted by the ABA in its report, provisions of state law that limit the rights of parties to choose the law of their contracts would violate the Contracts Clause.[119] American courts commonly give great deference to the choice of law in contracts. "Courts, including the US Supreme Court, generally honor the parties' choice of law, unless such law is contrary to public policy, even if doing so results in an outcome contrary to the laws that would otherwise apply."[120] Commercial contracts, particularly those involving cross-border transactions, frequently include a choice of law provision,[121] and

---

114 *See, e.g.*, Usinor Industeel v. Leeco Steel Prods., Inc., 209 F. Supp. 2d 880 (N.D. Ill. 2002).

115 Article 6 provides of the CISG provides that "[t]he parties may exclude the application of this Convention or, subject to article 12, derogate from or vary the effect of any of its provisions," CISG Art. 6.

116 ABA House of Delegates Res. 113A, at 6 (2011).

117 *See* CISG Art. 7(1); *Delchi Carrier SpA*, 71 F.3d at 1028.

118 U.S. Const. Art. I, § 10, cl. 1.

119 ABA House of Delegates Res. 113A, at 6 (2011).

120 Ibid. at 7 (citations omitted).

121 Ibid.

parties to a contract may choose another country's law to govern any disputes that may arise under the contract.

Supporters of the proposals to restrict foreign law may argue that American companies should choose the law of a US jurisdiction for all of their contracts. Although such a "solution" would undoubtedly appeal to most American companies, in a cross-border contract the other party to the contract may want the foreign law to apply. It is no solution to demand only that US law apply in the international business context, and demanding so would either limit the ability of US companies to do business internationally or would increase the contract price substantially over time to accommodate US companies that are afraid of courts in Canada and other trading partners of the United States.[122]

Proposals to restrict foreign and international law may also limit the ability to use international arbitration, or to enforce a foreign or international arbitration award. The inability to enforce an arbitration award would hurt US businesses that succeed in any foreign or international arbitration proceeding and would "seriously impede business and stymie economic development."[123]

Adverse effects could also be felt with non-economic contracts, such as agreements for child custody and visitation if one of the parents is not located in the United States.[124] If state courts cannot even consider foreign law, those courts could not assess the best interests of children if the custody agreements were negotiated in other countries and governed by foreign law.[125]

### *Establishment Clause*

The Establishment Clause of the US Constitution provides that "Congress shall make no law respecting an establishment of religion."[126] As discussed above, the federal appellate court in *Awad* held that the Oklahoma "Save Our State" Amendment violated the Establishment Clause. Applying the *Larson* test, the *Awad* court found that the Oklahoma Amendment favored one religion over another and that the disparagement of one religion could not withstand constitutional scrutiny because there was no "compelling interest" behind that choice.[127] To the extent that other proposed amendments contain similar language to the Oklahoma amendment, those proposals may also be found to violate the Establishment Clause.

---

122 As noted in the ABA report, foreign business parties would be encouraged either to avoid entirely "the U.S. party's preferred forum or to impose a high price in connection with some other term of the business deal in exchange for agreeing to resolve future disputes in the [United States]." Ibid.

123 Ibid.

124 *See* ibid.

125 *See* ibid.

126 U.S. Const. Amend. 1.

127 *Awad*, 670 F.3d at 1126.

*Free Exercise Clause*

The Free Exercise Clause of the US Constitution provides that "Congress shall make no law respecting an establishment of religion, or prohibiting the free exercise thereof."[128] As noted, the *Awad* court ruled that, because the Oklahoma Amendment violated the Establishment Clause, the court did not need to rule on the further claim that the Amendment also violated the Free Exercise Clause.[129] However, as the ABA noted in its report, laws that "explicitly seek to ban 'Sharia Law' from being considered by a state court . . . violate the First Amendment's Free Exercise Clause because they place a substantial burden on individuals' religious practices."[130]

A law imposes an unconstitutional burden on the free exercise of religion when it prevents individuals from performing religious acts or rituals that are religiously motivated and based on a sincerely held religious belief.[131] The religious acts or rituals cannot endanger the health or safety of other individuals, however.[132] At various times in debate, proponents of laws to restrict consideration of Islamic law or Shari'a have argued that Islam can endanger the rights of persons such as women, gays and non-believers. They point, for example, to the previously mentioned New Jersey trial court opinion (later reversed on appeal) where the trial court dismissed a criminal case against a Muslim husband being prosecuted for criminal sexual assault upon his wife.[133] They also argue that Islamic law mandates the death penalty for homosexuals as well as Muslims who try to convert to another religion than Islam.

Although the death penalty has been imposed in some countries for those offenses against Islam, the proponents of state legislation banning consideration of international law or Islamic law cannot show that similar penalties are even remotely possible in the United States. US courts will apply the US Constitution and its protection of fundamental rights. There is nothing to justify state legislation (or even a state constitutional amendment) prohibiting courts from considering any aspect of Islamic law because of extreme sanctions. "Moreover, prohibiting or singling out the lawful and peaceful religious practice of millions of U.S. citizens and residents is certainly not narrowly tailored to advance any state interest."[134]

128 U.S. Const. amend. 1.

129 *Awad*, 670 F.3d at 1119.

130 ABA House of Delegates Res. 113A, at 7 (2011).

131 *See* ibid.

132 *See* ibid.

133 *See* S.D. v. M.J.R., 2 A.3d at 427–8; *see also* ABA House of Delegates Res. 113A, at 3 (2011).

134 ABA House of Delegates Res. 113A, at 8 (2011).

*Full Faith and Credit Clause*

The Full Faith and Credit Clause of the US Constitution provides that: "Full Faith and Credit shall be given in each State to the public Acts, Records, and judicial Proceedings of every other State. And the Congress may by general Laws prescribe the Manner in which such Acts, Records and Proceedings shall be proved, and the Effect thereof."[135] As the ABA noted in its report, legislation and state constitutional amendments "violate the Full Faith and Credit Clause of the US Constitution to the extent that they seek to refuse to enforce a judgment from another state court if that state includes religious law, 'foreign' law, or 'international' law in making judicial decisions."[136] The Full Faith and Credit Clause requires states to recognize judicial proceedings from "every other State."[137] Although a state would not have to recognize any judgment that would violate its own public policy, states are not free as a matter of course to choose only particular states for the recognition of judgments.

## Conclusion

Legislation to prohibit courts from considering particular sources of law have passed in states such as Oklahoma, where there was no evidence of any court in that state ever applying Islamic law or Shari'a.[138] The voter referendum was not brought before the voters to cure any problem in that state. The federal appellate court rightly struck down Oklahoma's amendment to its state constitution as a violation of the Establishment Clause, and it could have used other constitutional provisions to strike down the law.

Proponents of legislation prohibiting courts from considering "Islamic law," "Shari'a law," or even a more generic prohibition such as prohibiting "religious law" or "cultural law," will continue to point to the New Jersey trial court case where a judge dismissed a criminal prosecution of a Muslim man charged with assaulting his wife. It is a good example to point to, but that trial court decision was "soundly rejected" on appeal.[139] The protections inherent in the court system were effective.

As the ABA noted in the conclusion to its own report, "[l]egislation that bars courts from considering foreign or international law or the entire body of law

135 U.S. Const. Art. IV, § 1.

136 ABA House of Delegates Res. 113A, at 9 (2011). Oklahoma's amendment, for example, would have allowed its state courts to uphold the decisions of courts in other states only if "the law of the other state does not include Sharia law, in making judicial decisions." *Id.* (citing Okl. Enr. H.J.R. No. 1056, sec. C).

137 U.S. Const. Art. IV, § 1.

138 *Awad*, 670 F.3d at 1130.

139 S.D. v. M.J.R., 2 A.3d at 427.

of a particular religion impose unconstitutional burdens on various constitutional rights, threaten to impinge American commercial interests, and are unnecessary additions to existing law."[140] As also noted in its report, federal and state courts in the United States "have more than sufficient legal tools to permit them to reject foreign law and refuse to enforce foreign judgments that do not meet our fundamental standards of fairness and justice."[141]

The American judicial system is under attack, but not from the religion of Islam. It is being attacked by persons who oppose court decisions that have, for example, abolished the death penalty for juvenile offenders or the mentally retarded, or that have protected the rights of gay and lesbian persons. As shown in this article, those decisions cited international and foreign law sources not to construe provisions of the US Constitution, but to show that the results were consistent with international human rights norms. Opponents of those results in those cases grabbed onto the citations to international and foreign law sources because they did not understand what the court was doing or because they wanted to misrepresent the methodology used by the courts. In many cases, opponents criticized the methodology of judicial decisions that they had not even read.

The judicial system in the United States is professional and independent. A court decision can be corrected on appeal if there is an error. If the appellate court errs, their decision is subject to further judicial review. The legislature, for its part, can fulfill its role as an independent branch of government by enacting appropriate legislation after a court has ruled. However, no one is served by legislative proposals that restrict in advance the sources of law that independent and professional judges can consult. Opposing these restrictions on courts supports the independence of the judiciary.

140 ABA House of Delegates Res. 113A, at 11 (2011).

141 *Id.* at 10. The ABA report also correctly notes that "Constitutional rights (such as those contained in the Bill of Rights) protect everyone in the United States, and all courts throughout the country are bound to respect them." *Id.*

# PART II
# The Protection of Cultural Difference within Human Rights Traditions

# Chapter 7

# Preserving Traditions or Breaking the Mold? Transnational Human Rights Processes in the People's Republic of China and Hong Kong[1]

Carole J. Petersen

## Introduction

As recently as the 1980s, human rights was a forbidden topic in the People's Republic of China[2] and the government condemned international attempts to monitor rights as improper intervention in domestic affairs.[3] Yet the Chinese government has now ratified six of the nine "core" United Nations (UN) human rights treaties, each of which requires China to submit periodic reports to a treaty-monitoring body.[4] China provides an important case study of the efficacy of this reporting process, partly because of its controversial human rights record, but also because it has significantly increased its participation in the UN human rights system. If the reporting process is effective, then we should be able to document some meaningful exchanges and also improvements in human rights as a result of the government's dialogues with treaty bodies.

---

1 This is a revised version of a paper presented at the International Workshop on Transnational Legal Processes and Human Rights, Chair of Comparative and Anglo-American Law, School of Law, University of Lucerne, 29–30 October 2010. The William S. Richardson School of Law at the University of Hawai'i at Manoa supported the research for this chapter and the author's participation in the workshop.

2 Chen, A.H.Y. 2006. Conclusion: Comparative Reflections on Human Rights in Asia, in *Human Rights in Asia: A Comparative Legal Study of Twelve Asian Jurisdictions, France and the USA*, edited by R. Peerenboom, C.J. Petersen and A.H.Y. Chen. London: Routledge, at 502.

3 Edwards, R.R. 1986. Civil and Social Rights: Theory and Practice in Chinese Law Today, in *Human Rights in Contemporary China*, edited by R. R. Edwards, L. Henkin, and A.J. Nathan. New York: Columbia University Press, at 52–3.

4 United Nations Treaty Collection, *Status of Treaties*, Chapter IV: Human Rights. Available at: http://treaties.un.org/Pages/Treaties.aspx?id=4&subid=A&lang=en [accessed: 1 December 2010].

One way to explore this question is to compare the impact of human rights treaties in Mainland China and the Hong Kong Special Administrative Region. Formerly a British colony (from 1842 to 1997), Hong Kong was returned to China on 1 July 1997 under the "one county, two systems" model. Culturally the two jurisdictions have much in common: the vast majority of Hong Kong residents are ethnically Chinese and many have relatives in Mainland China. Yet Hong Kong developed its own distinct identity while it was a British colony, one that includes a commitment to rule of law and basic civil liberties. The Chinese government agreed, in the Sino-British Joint Declaration (the treaty by which the British government promised to return Hong Kong to China in 1997), that Hong Kong could maintain its common law legal system and enjoy a "high degree of autonomy" after reunification.[5] China also agreed that Hong Kong would continue to be bound by all of the human rights treaties that the British government had applied to the territory during the colonial period. This body of international law includes the six core human rights treaties that bind Mainland China, and also the International Covenant on Civil and Political Rights (the ICCPR), which China has signed but not yet ratified.[6]

In some respects, Hong Kong's autonomy is more symbolic than real because its Chief Executive (the highest official in Hong Kong) is appointed by Beijing and China has deliberately slowed the pace of democratic reforms.[7] Yash Ghai has argued that the real purpose of the one country, two systems model was simply to allow for the continuation of Hong Kong's capitalist economic system.[8] However, the incorporation of international human rights treaties is one area in which the territory arguably enjoys meaningful autonomy because Hong Kong's regional government drafts separate reports and the treaty bodies issue separate concluding

5 Joint Declaration of the Government of the United Kingdom of Great Britain and Northern Ireland and the Government of the People's Republic of China on the Question of Hong Kong, Doc. U.K.–P.R.C., 23 I.L.M. 1371 (19 December 1984). Available at: http://www.cmab.gov.hk/en/issues/joint3.htm [accessed: 1 December 2010].

6 This is possible because the Basic Law of the Hong Kong Special Administrative Region (enacted in 1990 and brought into force in July 1997) states, at Art. 153, that "agreements to which the People's Republic of China is not a party but which are implemented in Hong Kong may continue to be implemented." Available at: http://www.basiclaw.gov.hk/en/basiclawtext [accessed: 1 December 2011]. Although the Basic Law is a national law enacted by the National People's Congress of the People's Republic of China, it has the status of superior law in Hong Kong and is considered to be Hong Kong's constitutional instrument. Chen, A.H.Y. 2000. The Interpretation of the Basic Law – Common Law and Mainland Chinese Perspectives, *Hong Kong Law Journal* 30, 380–81 (2000).

7 Martin, M.F. 2011. Prospects for Democracy in Hong Kong: the 2012 Election Reforms. Washington D.C.: Congressional Research Service, 2 February. Available at: fpc.state.gov/documents/organization/135008.pdf [accessed: 19 December 2011].

8 Ghai, Y.P. 1999. *Hong Kong's New Constitutional Order: The Resumption of Chinese Sovereignty and the Basic Law*, 2nd edn. Hong Kong: University of Hong Kong Press.

observations on Hong Kong. This separation of the reporting process makes it possible to compare the impact of human rights treaties in Hong Kong and Mainland China. However, in doing so, one must be mindful of the different contexts. In Hong Kong the tradition was to uphold civil liberties while ignoring and even perpetuating discrimination.[9] Thus in order to assess the impact of international treaties in Hong Kong, researchers should consider not only whether civil liberties have been maintained but also whether international law has helped women and minority groups to "break the mold" and claim their rights. In Mainland China the scope of inquiry is rather different because of the severe and continuing violations of civil liberties. Yet inequality is also a problem in Mainland China and there is a developing body of anti-discrimination law, which is partly inspired by the need to comply with ILO Convention 111 and other international standards.[10]

The next section of this chapter briefly introduces the UN system of human rights treaties and the treaty-monitoring bodies. The chapter then analyses Hong Kong first, noting the constitutional significance of human rights treaties but focusing primarily on the reporting process.[11] The chapter then offers a comparative analysis of the situation in Mainland China, including the government's approach to the reporting process and the reasons why international human rights treaties still have less impact in Mainland China than in Hong Kong.

## Human Rights Treaties and the Reporting Process

There are currently nine "core" treaties in the UN human rights system, each of which requires state parties to report regularly on steps taken to comply with their treaty obligations and any barriers to implementation. These reports are submitted to the relevant treaty-monitoring body, a panel of experts who are elected according to the terms of the particular treaty and serve in their personal capacities.[12] The

---

9 See generally, Petersen, C.J. 1996. Equality as a Human Right: the Development of Anti-Discrimination Law in Hong Kong, *Columbia Journal of Transnational Law* 34, 334–88; and Petersen, C.J. 2006. From British Colony to Special Administrative Region of China: Embracing Human Rights in Hong Kong, chapter 2 in *Human Rights in Asia* (op. cit., note 2).

10 Lee, Y. 2009. An Analysis of Employment Discrimination in China's Economic and Social Transition, in Taking Employment Discrimination Seriously: Chinese and European Perspectives, edited by Y. Li and J. Goldschmidt. Leiden: Martinus Nijhoff.

11 This chapter does not discuss the Macau Special Administrative Region, which is also governed under the one country, two systems model and files separate regional reports with treaty-monitoring bodies.

12 For information on the nine core UN human rights treaty bodies, see Office of the High Commissioner for Human Rights. Available at: http://www2.ohchr.org/english/bodies/treaty/index.htm) [accessed: 1 December 2010]. The Committee on Migrant Workers and the Committee on Enforced Disappearance are not discussed in this chapter because neither Hong Kong nor Mainland China currently reports to those committees.

seven treaty monitoring bodies to which China and/or Hong Kong currently report are:

- the Human Rights Committee, which monitors the ICCPR (Hong Kong reports to this treaty body; Mainland China does not report as it has not ratified the ICCPR);
- the Committee on Economic, Social and Cultural Rights, which monitors the International Covenant on Economic, Social and Cultural Rights;
- the Committee Against Torture, which monitors the Convention against Torture and Other Cruel, Inhuman or Degrading Treatment or Punishment;
- the Committee on the Elimination of Racial Discrimination, which monitors the International Convention on the Elimination of All Forms of Racial Discrimination;
- the Committee on the Elimination of Discrimination against Women, which monitors the Convention on the Elimination of All Forms of Discrimination against Women;
- the Committee on the Rights of the Child, which monitors the Convention on the Rights of the Child; and
- the Committee on the Rights of Persons with Disabilities, which monitors the Convention on the Rights of Persons with Disabilities.

Once a treaty body receives a government's periodic report, it schedules a formal review session (generally after first formulating a list of issues that it wishes to focus on and after requesting and receiving supplementary written information). At the conclusion of the formal review, the treaty body publishes concluding observations (or concluding comments) assessing the extent to which the treaty is being implemented and identifying ways in which the state party could improve. This is fundamentally a dialogue, a non-coercive enforcement process. Yet it constitutes a significant departure from traditional views on state sovereignty and the role of international law.[13] By binding itself to regularly report, each state party has conceded that the international community has a legitimate interest in ascertaining whether it respects international norms within its territory. For the Chinese government, that is a significant concession. Optional complaints mechanisms invite states to go further and recognize the competence of the monitoring body to adjudicate certain disputes between the state and individual citizens.[14] However, at this time, neither China nor Hong Kong is bound by these

13 For discussion of the relationship between sovereignty and international human rights norms, see Petersen, C.J. 2011. Bridging the Gap? The Role of Regional and National Human Rights Institutions in the Asia Pacific, *Asian–Pacific Law & Policy Journal* 13(1), 174–209.

14 Optional complaints mechanisms exist for the ICCPR, CERD, CRPD and CEDAW. The UN General Assembly has also adopted an Optional Protocol to the ICESCR (see GA Resolution A/RES/63/117, 10 December 2008); however, as of January 2012, it was not yet in force owing to insufficient ratifications.

individual complaints mechanisms, which means that the reporting process is the chief international enforcement mechanism.

The reporting process encourages civil society to participate in the enforcement of international norms. Non-governmental organizations (NGOs) can submit written reports on the implementation of the treaty and alleged violations. An NGO report is generally called a "shadow" or "alternative" report, because it shadows the government report and provides alternative points of view. Treaty-monitoring bodies depend upon NGOs to raise issues that governments would prefer to ignore.[15] Of course, the number and nature of NGO reports will vary from state to state. NGO reports are more effective if the state has a high degree of freedom of expression and an active NGO community. However, even if a government suppresses domestic NGOs, it is possible for organizations from outside the country to submit reports commenting on a government report. For example, Amnesty International and Human Rights Watch in China frequently submit shadow reports commenting on the official reports of the Chinese government.[16]

Significant resources are invested in this reporting process, not only by the UN, but also by governments and NGOs. As governments ratify more treaties, they need to collect more data and produce increasingly detailed reports. They also invest time and money in preparing their delegations to answer questions during the public review. This has led some governments to complain about the burden of reporting to multiple treaty bodies – an issue that may be partly addressed by harmonized reporting guidelines and the use of a core document that discusses common issues and can be submitted to more than one treaty body.[17] NGOs also invest considerable resources in drafting shadow reports and some send their own representatives to observe or participate in the review. Depending on the treaty body, NGOs can sometimes present their information orally, either during pre-sessional working group meetings or during the formal sessions. Some treaty bodies also allow NGO representatives to speak informally with members of the committee.

In the past 12 years, China (including Hong Kong) has been formally reviewed by: the Committee Against Torture (2000 and 2008); the Committee on the Elimination of Racial Discrimination (2001 and 2009); the Committee on the Elimination of Discrimination Against Women (1999 and 2006); the Committee

15 Conners, J. 1996. NGOs and the Human Rights of Women at the UN, in *The Conscience of the World: The Influence of Non-Governmental Organizations in the U.N. System*, edited by P. Willetts. Washington, DC: The Brookings Institution, 147–81.

16 For examples of shadow reports of these and other international NGOs, see the reports submitted to the Committee Against Torture when China was reviewed during the Committee's 41st Session in November 2008. Available at: http://www2.ohchr.org/english/bodies/cat/cats41.htm [accessed: 1 December 2011].

17 For information on the core document and efforts to harmonize reporting processes, see Compilation of Guidelines on the Form and Content of Reports to be Submitted by States Parties to the International Human Rights Treaties: Report of the Secretary-General, HRI/GEN/2/Rev.6 (3 June 2009). Available at: http://www2.ohchr.org/english/bodies/icm-mc/documents-system.htm [accessed: 1 December 2011].

on the Rights of the Child (2005); and the Committee on Economic, Social and Cultural Rights (2001 and 2005).[18] The Human Rights Committee also reviewed, in 1999 and 2006, the regional reports of the Hong Kong Special Administrative Region under the ICCPR.[19] The next review, by the Committee on the Rights of Persons with Disabilities, will take place in 2012 as both Hong Kong and China submitted their initial reports under the Convention on the Rights of Persons with Disabilities (CRPD) in August 2010.[20]

## The Impact of Human Rights Treaties in Hong Kong

In the early 1980s, when the British and Chinese governments were negotiating Hong Kong's future, the British needed to reassure the people (and the international community) that human rights would be protected after reunification. The Sino-British Joint Declaration thus provides that Hong Kong will maintain its own common law legal system and independent judiciary. It also includes many detailed provisions on human rights and states that the ICCPR and the International Covenant on Economic, Social and Cultural Rights (ICESCR), "as they apply to Hong Kong, will continue to apply to the Hong Kong Special Administrative Region."[21] A similar provision was placed in Article 38 of the draft Basic Law of the Hong Kong Special Administrative Region (which was published for public consultation in 1988) and in Article 39 of the final version, which now serves as Hong Kong's regional constitution.[22]

When the Joint Declaration was negotiated in the early 1980s, China was less engaged in the United Nations human rights system and may not have fully appreciated the potential impact of placing a reference to international treaties in a document that would ultimately have constitutional significance for Hong Kong. Indeed the British negotiators also probably did not expect these references to promote significant change in the territory because there was no expectation at

18 In 2010 Hong Kong completed its Third Periodic Report under the ICESCR (which was officially submitted to the Committee on Economic Social and Cultural Rights as Part II of China's Second Periodic Report) but, as of January 2012, it had not yet been scheduled for a review by the Committee. Available at: http://www.cmab.gov.hk/en/issues/prc_3.htm [accessed: 30 December 2011].

19 Hong Kong's third periodic report under the ICCPR was filed in May 2011 and is likely to be reviewed by the Human Rights Committee in 2013. Available at: http://www2.ohchr.org/english/bodies/hrc/hrcs_future.htm [accessed: 30 December 2011].

20 UNCRPD, Committee on the Rights of Persons with Disabilities – List of Issues to be taken up in connection with the Consideration of the initial Report of China and Hong Kong, CRPD/C/CHN/Q/1, 8 May 2012.

21 Sino-British Joint Declaration 1984, op. cit., note 5, at Annex I, Section XIII.

22 Hong Kong Basic Law 1990, op. cit., note 6 , Art. 39.

that time that the treaties would be incorporated domestically.[23] The local business community has always been extremely influential in Hong Kong's undemocratic system. The leaders of that community wanted basic civil liberties maintained and were happy to see detailed provisions in the Basic Law on property rights, access to information and religious freedom. However, they had little desire to endow workers and other marginalized groups with new rights (such as a right to gender or racial equality) that might disturb Hong Kong's laissez-faire economic system.

This conservative approach to rights might have continued well beyond the handover, had it not been for important developments during the transition period between the ratification of the Joint Declaration in 1985 and the resumption of Chinese sovereignty over Hong Kong in 1997. On 4 June 1989, the Communist Party sent tanks into Tiananmen Square, crushing the student protests and forever changing human rights in Hong Kong. One million Hong Kong people took to the streets to protest against the government's actions in Beijing. With only eight years left before the handover, the Hong Kong colonial government needed to rebuild confidence.[24] It proposed to enact a local Hong Kong Bill of Rights, incorporating international standards into domestic law.[25] Enacted in 1991, the Hong Kong Bill of Rights Ordinance was largely copied from the ICCPR. This was a prudent approach because the Chinese government had already agreed that the Basic Law would provide for the continued implementation of the ICCPR. By enacting a domestic Bill of Rights Ordinance in 1991, the local legislature gave the local judiciary (and the legal profession) an opportunity to become familiar with the substantive provisions of the ICCPR well before the handover.

While there have been controversies, in general Hong Kong has been diligent about upholding civil liberties in the post-1997 era. In a previous publication, I described the ICCPR as Hong Kong's "gold standard" because the courts enforce it and government lawyers readily acknowledge that a local law must be declared invalid if it cannot be interpreted in a way that is consistent with the ICCPR.[26] Even conservative groups generally support civil liberties in Hong Kong, as demonstrated by the massive turnout (more than 500,000 people) for the successful protest march against the controversial "Article 23 legislation" in July 2003. The march was endorsed by church leaders and ultimately compelled the

---

23 Ghai, Y.P. and Chan, J. 1993. Introduction, *The Hong Kong Bill of Rights: A Comparative Approach*, edited by Y.P. Ghai and J. Chan. Hong Kong: Butterworths.

24 Miners, N. 1981. *The Government and Politics of Hong Kong*, 5th edn. Hong Kong: Oxford University Press, 27.

25 Jayawickrama, N. 1992. Hong Kong and the International Protection of Human Rights, in *Human Rights in Hong Kong*, edited by R. Wacks. Hong Kong: Oxford University Press.

26 Petersen, C.J. 2007. Embracing Universal Standards? The Role of International Human Rights Treaties in Hong Kong's Constitutional Jurisprudence, in *Interpreting Hong Kong's Basic Law: The Struggle for Coherence*, edited by H.L. Fu, L. Harris, and S.N.M. Young. New York: Palgrave Macmillan.

government to withdraw a bill that might have threatened civil liberties.[27] Perhaps the best evidence of continued free speech is the annual candlelight vigil on 4 June, something that would generate immediate arrests in Beijing.

What is arguably more dramatic is the extent to which women and minority groups have used international treaties to challenge Hong Kong's traditional order. For example, the domestic incorporation of the ICCPR led directly to the repeal of criminal laws prohibiting gay sex, despite widespread support for the laws in the local community.[28] More recently, criminal laws that set an older age of consent for anal intercourse than for vaginal intercourse were found to violate the rights to equality and privacy.[29] Although sexuality is not expressly mentioned in the ICCPR, the court held that sexuality discrimination constitutes discrimination on the ground of "any other status" and is therefore prohibited by the ICCPR. The case is considered a landmark by some commentators because it gave sexuality discrimination "equal footing" with other prohibited grounds of discrimination.[30]

The right of sexual minorities to marry has proven more difficult. The Hong Kong Marriage Ordinance still does not permit same-sex marriage and the government currently interprets this ordinance as prohibiting a transgender woman from marrying her male partner. This is because the Hong Kong government relies upon the gender recorded at birth when determining whether to issue a marriage license, even if the applicant has undergone gender reassignment surgery and obtained new identity documents recording the acquired gender. In 2011, a transgender woman unsuccessfully sought judicial review of the government's interpretation of the Marriage Ordinance; her appeal to the Hong Kong Court of Appeal was recently dismissed.[31] However, both courts called for legislative reform of the Marriage Ordinance and the applicant may still appeal to the Hong Kong Court of Final Appeal. (Interestingly, the applicant did not argue that the government's interpretation of the Marriage Ordinance constituted unlawful disability discrimination, although the Hong Kong Disability Discrimination Ordinance (DDO) has been interpreted to prohibit discrimination on the basis of

---

27 Petersen, C.J. 2005. Hong Kong's Spring of Discontent: The Rise and Fall of the National Security Bill in 2003, in *National Security and Fundamental Freedoms: Hong Kong's Article 23 Under Scrutiny*, edited by H.L. Fu Hualing, C.J. Petersen and S.N.M. Young. Hong Kong: Hong Kong University Press.

28 Previous efforts to reform the law were abandoned owing to public opposition. Petersen, C.J. 1997. Values in Transition: The Development of the Gay and Lesbian Rights Movement in Hong Kong, *Loyola of Los Angeles International and Comparative Law Journal* 19, 337–62.

29 Leung TC William Roy v. Secretary for Justice [2005] 3 HKLRD 657 (Court of First Instance), [2006] 4 HKLRD 211 (Court of Appeal).

30 Lau, H. 2008. Sexual Orientation and Gender Identity: American Law in Light of East Asian Developments, *Harvard Journal of Law and Gender* 31, 67–8.

31 W. v. Registrar of Marriages [2010]5 HKC 359 (CFI), appeal dismissed 25 November 2011, CACV266/2010 (CA). Volume 41(1) of the *Hong Kong Law Journal* includes several articles commenting on the case.

gender dysphoria[32] and some transgender individuals have obtained remedies under the DDO through the conciliation process at the Hong Kong Equal Opportunities Commission (EOC).[33])

While local judicial enforcement is an important part of human rights protection in Hong Kong, the process of reporting to the UN human rights treaty bodies has also played a significant role. The reporting process allows Hong Kong to actively engage in transnational human rights processes, while still respecting China's territorial integrity. Hong Kong's report is officially submitted as part of China's report (generally described as an addendum), but it is drafted by the local government after consultation with the local community.[34] The government of Hong Kong also sends its own delegation to answer questions at each periodic review. Local NGOs regularly prepare shadow reports and send representatives to Geneva when Hong Kong is reviewed. The treaty bodies then issue separate comments on Hong Kong. In many cases these comments are surprisingly detailed, given that Hong Kong is only a tiny part of China and has far fewer human rights controversies. The concluding comments are read carefully by local legislators and NGOs, who use them to lobby for reforms.

The Hong Kong women's movement has been particularly successful in using international human rights treaties to promote equality. When the Hong Kong Bill of Rights was first proposed there was virtually no legislation prohibiting gender discrimination and there were many examples of discriminatory laws and policies, including a ban on female inheritance of much of the land in the territory.[35] Realizing that the government and business community would never support law reform without significant external pressure, a coalition of women's groups submitted a shadow report to the UN Human Rights Committee in 1991.[36] The report documented gender discrimination that violated the ICCPR and questioned why the Convention on the Elimination of All Forms of Discrimination Against

32 The Church of Jesus Christ of Latter-Day Saints Hong Kong Ltd v. Stewart J.C. Park AKA Jessica Park, HKCA1167/2001 (8 November 2001).

33 Information provided by the Hong Kong Equal Opportunities Commission, November 2011. For additional analysis on whether transgender discrimination should be approached as a form of disability discrimination, see Petersen, C.J. 2011. Gender Diversity and Human Rights Treaty Bodies: Is there a Role for the Committee on the Rights of Persons With Disabilities?, in *Equality and Justice: Sexual Orientation and Gender Identity in the XXI Century*, edited by A. Schuster. Italy: Editrice Universitaria Udinese, 161–76.

34 Hong Kong's reports on the human rights treaties that apply to Hong Kong are published by the Government's Constitutional and Mainland Affairs Bureau, Human Rights Reporting. Available at: http://www.cmab.gov.hk/en/issues/human.htm [accessed: 10 December 2010].

35 Petersen, C.J. 1996. Equality as a Human Right: the Development of Anti-Discrimination Law in Hong Kong, *Columbia Journal of Transnational Law* 34, 334–88.

36 Hong Kong Council of Women, Report on the Third Periodic Report by Hong Kong under Art. 40 of the International Covenant on Civil and Political Rights (submitted to the UN Human Rights Committee) (copy on file with the author).

Women (CEDAW) had not been applied to the territory when it was ratified by the UK. (Hong Kong had been left out of the UK's ratification at the request of the local government.) Feminist organizations also distributed the shadow report locally and the local legislature gradually started to support them. The business community successfully argued that the Bill of Rights Ordinance should not apply to the private sector. However, an independent legislator, Anna Wu, then introduced the Equal Opportunities Bill, which sought to prohibit discrimination on the grounds of sex, marital status, pregnancy, disability, sexuality, race and age.[37] Under pressure from the legislature, the government agreed to introduce two narrower compromise bills, which were enacted in 1995 as the Sex Discrimination Ordinance and the DDO. This landmark legislation cleared the way for the application of CEDAW, which was applied to Hong Kong in 1996.[38] The Court of First Instance has since held that the Sex Discrimination Ordinance should be interpreted consistently with the government's obligations under CEDAW.[39]

The application of CEDAW to Hong Kong provided additional opportunities for women to participate in transnational human rights processes. In 1999 a coalition of women's organizations drafted their first CEDAW shadow report. The coalition included religious organizations, survivors of sexual violence, a lesbian rights group and a sex worker advocacy group.[40] The EOC also submitted a shadow report, which disagreed with some of the government's positions.[41] NGO representatives also traveled to New York, where they held an informal briefing for CEDAW Committee members and attended the review of Hong Kong's report. Several issues raised by NGOs were highlighted in the Committee's Concluding Comments.[42] For example,

37 Equal Opportunities Bill 1994, Hong Kong Government Gazette, Legal Supp. No. 3, 1 July 1994, at C991–1275.

38 CEDAW was applied to Hong Kong by the UK, but with China's agreement, which was necessary because only one year remained before the handover, on 1 July 1997. However, this was not a problem as China had ratified the CEDAW in 1980.

39 In EOC v. Director of Education [2001] 2 HKLRD 690, the Court relied on CEDAW to declare unlawful an admission policy for elite co-educational schools that required higher scores from female applicants than from male applicants. For discussion of other cases, see Petersen, C.J. 2009. Stuck on Formalities? A Critique of Hong Kong's Legal Framework for Gender Equality, in *Mainstreaming Gender in Hong Kong Society*, edited by F.M. Cheung and E. Holroyd. Hong Kong: Chinese University Press, 401–39.

40 The shadow report was endorsed by: the Association for the Advancement of Feminism, the Hong Kong Women Workers Association, the Hong Kong Women Christian Association, the Hong Kong Federation of Women's Centres, the Association Concerning Sexual Violence Against Women, the Hong Kong Association for the Survivors of Sexual Women Abuse, the Family Ideal Community Education Project, Queer Sisters, the Hong Kong Human Rights Monitor and Zi Teng, a sex-worker advocacy group.

41 Hong Kong Equal Opportunities Commission, 1998. NGO Report on the Convention on the Elimination of All Forms of Discrimination Against Women.

42 Committee on the Elimination of Discrimination Against Women, Twentieth Session, Concluding Comments on the Initial Report on the Hong Kong Special Administrative Region,

the CEDAW Committee recommended that the Hong Kong government expand the scope of the Domestic Violence Ordinance and amend the statutory definition of rape so as to clearly prohibit marital rape.[43] The Committee also urged the government to establish a Women's Commission, to serve as a "high-level central mechanism with appropriate powers and resources to develop and coordinate a women-focused policy and long-term strategy to ensure effective implementation" of CEDAW.[44] When the delegation returned to Hong Kong, the Legislative Council held hearings and several legislators repeated the Committee's call for a Women's Commission.[45]

Although the Hong Kong government initially rejected many of the CEDAW Committee's Concluding Comments[46] it eventually agreed to establish a Women's Commission[47] and to introduce legislation expressly prohibiting marital rape.[48] When Hong Kong was next reviewed, in 2006, the CEDAW Committee welcomed these developments but questioned why the government had done little to reduce domestic violence.[49] The Hong Kong government had to explain these negative comments to the local legislature.[50] It eventually agreed to expand the scope of the

---

paras 308–36, UN Doc. A/54/38/Rev. 1 (3 February 1999) [hereinafter CEDAW Concluding Comments on Hong Kong 1999].

43 CEDAW Concluding Comments on Hong Kong 1999, at paras 323–8. Although a Hong Kong court might well have followed the decision of the English House of Lords in R v. R [1992] 1 A.C. 599, 614, and held that non-consensual sex between married persons constituted rape, the Committee highlighted the lack of clarity in the law and called for statutory amendments.

44 CEDAW Concluding Comments on Hong Kong 1999, at paras 317–18.

45 Hong Kong Legislative Council, Panel on Home Affairs, Minutes of Meeting, 8 March 1999, Legco Paper No. CB(2) 1650/98–99.

46 Government of the Hong Kong Special Administrative Region, 1999. Initial Response to the Concluding Comments (attached as Annex D to the Information Note provided by the Home Affairs Bureau to the Legislative Council Panel on Home Affairs for its meeting on 8 March), Lego Paper No. CB(2)1429/98–99(02).

47 Government of the Hong Kong Special Administrative Region, 2000. Progress Report for the Legco Panel on Home Affairs, submitted to legislators for discussion on 2 June (especially at paras 4 and 5); and Report of the Hong Kong Special Administrative Government on the Implementation of the Beijing Platform of Action (May 2000) (copy on file with the author).

48 Emerton, R. 2001. Marital Rape and the Related Sexual Offences: A Review of the Proposed Amendments to Part XII of the Crimes Ordinance, *Hong Kong Law Journal* 31, 415 (for analysis of the legislative effort).

49 Office of the UN High Commissioner for Human Rights, Concluding Comments of the Committee on the Elimination of Discrimination Against Women: China, UN Doc. CEDAW/C/CHN/CO/6, paras 35–6 (25 August 2006). Available at: http://www2.ohchr.org/english/bodies/cedaw/cedaws36.htm

50 Government of the Hong Kong Special Administrative Region, The Administration's Response to the Concluding Comments of the United Nations Committee on the Elimination of Discrimination against Women on the Second Report of the Hong Kong Special Administrative Region under the Convention on the Elimination of All Forms

Domestic Violence Ordinance and to give judges additional enforcement powers.[51] The government described these reforms in considerable detail in the report that it later prepared for Beijing Plus 15, demonstrating its desire to receive a positive assessment from the international community.[52]

The Convention Against Torture and Other Cruel, Inhuman or Degrading Treatment or Punishment (CAT) is another example of a treaty that has brought about significant changes in Hong Kong. Article 3 of the CAT provides that "no State Party shall return a person to another State where there are substantial grounds for believing that he would be in danger of being subjected to torture." This duty is particularly significant in Hong Kong because the 1951 Convention relating to the Status of Refugees and its 1967 Protocol do not apply in the territory.[53] Although both the UK and China are states parties to the Refugee Convention, the Hong Kong government has successfully resisted its application, arguing that Hong Kong is vulnerable to abuse because it is small, densely populated and relatively prosperous.[54] (The fact that both London and Beijing deferred to the local government's views on this issue is an interesting example of local autonomy.) There are also reservations in many of the human rights treaties that apply to Hong Kong for matters relating to immigration law and policy and a broad exception for this field in the Bill of Rights Ordinance. Thus, for many individuals fleeing abusive governments, Article 3 of the CAT provides the strongest legal basis for resisting deportation from Hong Kong.

Interestingly, the local Crimes (Torture) Ordinance does not expressly incorporate the obligation stated in Article 3 of CAT into Hong Kong's domestic law. However, in Hong Kong's 1999 report to the Committee Against Torture, the local government assured committee members that a claim of torture by a potential deportee would be carefully assessed and that a person with a well-founded claim

---

of Discrimination against Women, LC Paper No. CB(2)1014/06-07(06), prepared for a meeting of the Legislative Council's Panel on Home Affairs, 9 February 2007.

51 See Hong Kong Legislative Council, Bills Committee to Study the Domestic Violence (Amendment) Bill 2007. Available at: http://www.legco.gov.hk/yr06-07/english/bc/bc61/general/bc61.htm; Legislative Council's Bills Committee to Study the Domestic Violence (Amendment) Bill 2009. Available at: http://www.legco.gov.hk/english/index.htm.

52 Hong Kong Special Administrative Region of the People's Republic of China's (HKSAR), Response to the Questionnaire to Governments on Implementation of the Beijing Declaration and Platform for Action and the Outcome of the Twenty-Third Special Session of the General Assembly of the United Nations Economic and Social Commission for Asia and the Pacific (focused on developments between 2004 and 2009), para. 49.

53 Loper, K. 2010. Human Rights, Non-refoulement and the Protection of Refugees in Hong Kong, *International Journal of Refugee Law* 23(3), 404–39 (discussing Hong Kong's reluctance to be bound by the Refugee Convention and arguing that the duty of non-refoulement is part of customary international law).

54 See Judgment of Justice Hartman in *Yam v Director of Immigration* (HCAL 82/2007, 18 February 2008), para. 151, quoting the 28 February 2007 affirmation of Hong Kong's Principal Assistant Secretary for Security.

would not be deported.[55] This representation was put to the test in the case of Sakthvel Prabakar v. Secretary for Security.[56] A Sri Lankan man alleged that he was a victim of torture and would be subjected to torture again if returned to Sri Lanka. The Secretary for Security issued a deportation order but Mr. Prabakar successfully moved to quash it on the ground that no branch of the Hong Kong government had investigated the allegations of torture. The court cited numerous international materials, including the government's periodic report to the Committee Against Torture. The court also described the Committee's General Comment No. 1, as a "useful reference" regarding the matters that should be considered in a proper assessment of a torture claim. This judgment gave the international reporting process new meaning, as the Hong Kong government could no longer promise one thing to a treaty body while taking the opposite position in court. The government responded by creating a new "torture screening" mechanism to be administered by the Immigration Department.[57] Subsequent litigation challenged the procedures as they did not comply with the "high degree of fairness" required by the Court of Final Appeal.[58] The government had to temporarily halt screening and allow all torture claimants to remain in Hong Kong, while it developed enhanced screening procedures.[59] In 2011, the Legislative Council began studying a bill to establish a revised screening procedure for CAT claimants.[60]

The CAT has also been used by Zi Teng, the main organization lobbying for sex workers' rights in Hong Kong. Although a Hong Kong resident can legally engage in sex work in her own home, several related activities are prohibited, including

55 See Hong Kong Government, Report on the Hong Kong Special Administrative Region under the Convention Against Torture and Other Cruel, Inhuman or Degrading Treatment or Punishment (1999), para. 2.

56 [2005] 1 HKLRD 289 (Court of Final Appeal).

57 For recent statements by the government regarding efforts to revise the screening mechanism, see Office of the UN High Commissioner for Human Rights, 2008. Written replies by the Hong Kong Special Administrative Region to the list of issues (CAT/C/HKG/Q/4) to be taken up in connection with the consideration of the fourth periodic report of Hong Kong to the Committee Against Torture (CAT/C/HKG/4), UN Doc. CAT/C/HKG/Q/4/Add. 1 (26 September) [hereinafter Written Replies of Hong Kong to CAT 2008]. Available at: http://www2.ohchr.org/english/bodies/cat/cats41.htm [accessed: 20 December 2011], at paras 39–45.

58 *F.B. v. Director of Immigration* [2008] H.K.E.C. 2072 (C.F.I.).

59 Government of Hong Kong, Security Bureau, Torture Claim Screening Mechanism: Enhanced Mechanism and the Way Forward, LC Paper No. CB(2)370/09-10(03) (1 December 2009). Available at: http://www.legco.gov.hk/yr09-10/english/panels/se/papers/se1201cb2-370-3-e.pdf [accessed: 20 December 2011]. For commentary, see Loper, K. 2008. Toward Comprehensive Refugee Legislation in Hong Kong? Reflections on Reform of the "Torture Screening" Procedures, *Hong Kong Law Journal* 39, 253–9.

60 Hong Kong Legislative Council, Bills Committee on Immigration (Amendment) Bill 2011. Available at: http://legco.gov.hk/yr10-11/english/bc/bc59/general/bc59.htm [accessed: 24 January 2012].

soliciting for an immoral purpose and running a vice establishment.[61] These offences can be used to harass sex workers because the term "vice establishment" is defined broadly, as the use of premises "wholly or mainly" by two or more persons for the purpose of prostitution.[62] Thus, undercover police can make arrests if they find two sex workers sharing an apartment or discover that sexual services are being provided in a venue where several women work (such as a massage parlor). A sex worker also may not legally employ a security guard because that person would be guilty of knowingly living "wholly or in part on the earnings of prostitution of another."[63] This makes sex workers vulnerable to attack, as they are obliged to work alone if they want to avoid arrest.[64]

Zi Teng submitted a shadow report in 2006 (when Hong Kong was reviewed by the Committee on the Elimination of Discrimination Against Women) and in 2008 (when Hong Kong was reviewed by the Committee Against Torture).[65] These reports described abusive police searches and accused undercover officers of receiving free sexual services under false pretenses. The Security Bureau had claimed (in a local legislative hearing) that the police are only permitted to receive intimate "massage" services in order to gain evidence. However, Zi Teng cited 22 complaints from sex workers in which undercover police officers had allegedly received oral or penetrative sex before making arrests. After reviewing Zi Teng's report, the Committee Against Torture requested the Hong Kong government to supplement its report with information regarding the treatment of sex workers. The Hong Kong government insisted that there is an operational need for the police to conduct covert operations but it assured the Committee that it had recently revised its internal guidelines so that undercover police officers would be subjected to more "vigorous control" on the extent of body contact.[66] The government also developed new guidelines on body searches of sex workers and other people held in detention.[67]

While welcoming the guidelines, the Committee questioned why body searches are automatic for everyone in police custody and criticized the continued use of strip searches. It urged the government to find alternative means for routine screenings of persons in detention, to use body cavity searches only as a last resort, and to ensure that searches are performed with due regard for the individual's

61 Crimes Ordinance (1997) Cap. 200 §§139 and 147 (H.K.).

62 Crimes Ordinance (1997) §117 (3).

63 Crimes Ordinance (1997) §137.

64 Guzder, D. 2009. Hong Kong Alarmed Over Sex-Worker Murders, *Time*, 10 February. Available at: http://www.time.com/time/world/article/0,8599,1878395,00.html [accessed: 24 January 2012].

65 Zi Teng's report to the Committee Against Torture is published on the Committee's website, 41st Session, China, Hong Kong and Macau, under the heading "Information Provided to the Committee". Available at: http://www2.ohchr.org/english/bodies/cat/docs/ngos/ZiTengHongKong41.pdf [accessed: 21 December 2011].

66 Written Replies of Hong Kong to CAT 2008, para. 135.

67 Written Replies of Hong Kong to CAT 2008, paras 124–8.

privacy and dignity. The Committee also expressed concerns regarding the allegations of police abuse during undercover operations.[68]

Although Zi Teng's lobbying effort has thus far only resulted in policy changes (and not substantive law reform), the process of submitting alternative reports has certainly helped it to gain allies in the Legislative Council and in the general human rights movement. For example, Human Rights Monitor,[69] the Civil Human Rights Front, the Hong Kong Human Rights Commission and the Society for Community Organization[70] have all mentioned the rights of sex workers in their shadow reports. This has helped to place the rights of sex workers in the mainstream of human rights and policy discourses in Hong Kong.

Although space does not allow a detailed discussion, another important example of treaty-inspired law reform is Hong Kong's new law prohibiting race discrimination in the private sector.[71] This almost certainly would not have been enacted without persistent (and increasingly firm) pressure from the Committee on the Elimination of Racial Discrimination and several other treaty-monitoring bodies. Although the law is weaker than the laws that prohibit sex and disability discrimination in Hong Kong, it is still a positive development.[72] It is also possible that the Race Discrimination Ordinance will be strengthened in the future; several NGOs criticized the law during the 2009 review by the Committee on the Elimination of Racial Discrimination and the Committee called for amendments in its Concluding Observations on Hong Kong.[73]

---

68 Concluding Observations of the Committee against Torture Hong Kong, UN Doc. CAT/C/HKG/CO/4 (19 January 2009) [hereinafter Concluding Observations of the Committee against Torture Hong Kong, 2009], para. 11 .

69 Hong Kong Human Rights Monitor, 2008. Shadow Report for the UN Committee against Torture on the implementation of the Convention against Torture and other Cruel, Inhuman or Degrading Treatment or Punishment in the H.K. Special Administrative Region, the People's Republic of China (18 April) at 44–60. Available at: http://www2.ohchr.org/english/bodies/cat/docs/ngos/HRMHongKong41.pdf [accessed: 18 December 2011].

70 Hong Kong Human Rights Commission and Society for Community Organization, Report to the United Nations Committee Against Torture on the Second Report by the H.K. Special Administrative Region under Art. 19 of the Convention Against Torture and Other Cruel, Inhuman or Degrading Treatment or Punishment (April 2008), para. 26. Available at: http://www2.ohchr.org/english/bodies/cat/docs/ngos/uncat_apr2008_CH_41.pdf [accessed: 18 December 2011]. See also the alternative report by the Civil Human Rights Front, at 1 (17 April 2008), available at: http://www2.ohchr.org/english/bodies/cat/docs/ngos/CHRFHongKong41.pdf) [accessed: 18 December 2011].

71 Race Discrimination Ordinance (2008) Cap. 602, Laws of Hong Kong.

72 For commentary, see Petersen, C.J. 2011. International Norms and Domestic Law Reform: The Difficult Birth of Hong Kong's Racial Discrimination Law, *Directions* 6(2) 13–21; and Loper, K. 2008. One Step Forward, Two Steps Back: The Dilemma of Hong Kong's Racial Discrimination Legislation, *Hong Kong Law Journal* 38, 15–30.

73 Concluding Observations of the Committee on the Elimination of Racial Discrimination: China (including Hong Kong and Macau Special Administrative Regions), UN Doc. CERD/C/CHN/CO/10-13 (15 September 2009), paras 27–8.

The treaty that has arguably had the least influence in Hong Kong is the ICESCR. In theory this treaty is incorporated into Hong Kong law by Article 39 of the Basic Law, which refers to the ICESCR with the same language that was used to incorporate the ICCPR. However, there is a widespread perception among Hong Kong judges that the ICESCR does not contain justiciable rights.[74] The Committee on Economic, Social and Cultural Rights has endeavoured to counter that perception[75] and the General Assembly adopted an Optional Protocol to the ICESCR in December 2008, which will empower the Committee to receive and consider individual communications when it comes into force.[76] However, the Optional Protocol to the ICESCR is unlikely to be accepted by China or Hong Kong. The other problem is that the provisions of the ICESCR have not been copied into a single domestic ordinance in Hong Kong (whereas the ICCPR was largely copied into the Bill of Rights Ordinance). The Committee on Economic, Social and Cultural Rights has urged Hong Kong to enact such a law,[77] but the government has declined. NGOs do submit shadow reports and there is some evidence that the government considers the Committee's comments when formulating policies. However, it is clear that economic and social rights are not really viewed as "rights" in Hong Kong (unless they arise in the context of a discrimination lawsuit). Rather, these issues are considered a matter of executive and legislative policy, largely insulated from emerging trends in international human rights law. This will probably continue as long as the influential business classes occupy a privileged position in Hong Kong's undemocratic political system.

While this is necessarily a summary of a broad range of developments in Hong Kong, it hopefully demonstrates that the realization of rights in this part of China has been profoundly affected by the incorporation of international norms, the ability of NGOs to submit shadow reports to treaty bodies and the government's desire to receive reasonably positive comments. The next section of

---

74 For a critique of these judicial decisions, see Petersen, C.J. 2007. Embracing Universal Standards?, op. cit., note 27.

75 The Committee's Third General Comment, entitled "The Nature of States' Parties' Obligations", interprets Art. 2(1) in a manner that includes a duty to immediately implement some of the treaty's obligations. See, also Lyon, B. 2002. A Post-Colonial "Agenda" for the United Nations Committee on Economic, Social and Cultural Rights, *American University Journal of Gender, Social Policy & the Law* 10, 535–79.

76 Optional Protocol to the International Covenant on Economic, Social and Cultural Rights, G.A. Res. A/RES/63/117, UN Doc. A/63/435 (10 December 2008). Available at: http://www2.ohchr.org/english/bodies/cescr/index.htm [accessed: 25 January 2012] [hereinafter "ICESCR"]. The Optional Protocol to ICESCR was opened for signature in 2009 and will enter into force three months after receiving its tenth ratification; as of 25 January 2012, it had acquired 39 signatories but only seven state parties.

77 See, e.g. the Concluding Observations of the Committee on Economic, Social and Cultural Rights on the Initial Report of the Hong Kong Special Administrative Region, 11 May 2001, E/C.12/1/Add. 58, para. 15.

the chapter analyzes the impact of human rights treaties in Mainland China and the reasons why transnational human rights processes are less influential there than in Hong Kong.

## Mainland China and Transnational Human Rights Processes

As noted in the introduction to this chapter, the central government of China has steadily increased its participation in the UN human rights system. By 1992, China had ratified the Convention on the Elimination of All Forms of Racial Discrimination (CERD); the CEDAW; the CAT; and the Convention on the Rights of the Child (CRC). China also signed the ICESCR in 1997 and became a State Party in 2001. In 2008 it became the first country in East Asia to ratify the CRPD. Although China is still only a signatory to the ICCPR, in 2009 it stated that it would undertake reforms to "prepare the ground for approval of the ICCPR."[78] The Chinese government has also begun to report on some of the rights protected in the ICCPR in the course of the Human Rights Council's "universal periodic review."[79]

The Chinese government does not apologize for the fact that it still places collective rights (including the right to stability and economic development) ahead of individual liberties. In theory, the end of the Cold War allowed the international community to move beyond this dichotomy and to recognize the indivisibility and interdependence of rights. In practice, however, the Chinese government believes that international critiques of its record still focus too heavily on civil liberties. This position was articulated in the Bangkok Declaration, drafted at the 1993 preparatory meeting of Asian governments for the Vienna World Conference on Human Rights.[80] The Chinese government took a particularly firm stand in this discussion, condemning internationally imposed human rights standards as an infringement upon state sovereignty.[81] The Vienna Declaration that was ultimately adopted at the 1993 World Conference affirmed the universality principle but also recognized that "all rights are universal, indivisible, and interdependent and

78 Information Office of the State Council of the People's Republic of China, National Human Rights Action Plan of China 2009–10, issued 13 April 2009, at V(1). Available at: http://www.china.org.cn/archive/2009-04/13/content_17595407.htm [accessed: 19 December 2011].

79 China was reviewed in February 2009 under the Universal Periodic Review mechanism and the documents (including China's report and stakeholder submissions) are published. Available at: http://www.ohchr.org/EN/HRBodies/UPR%5CPAGES%5CCNSession4.aspx [accessed: 1 December 2011].

80 Final Declaration of the Regional Meeting for Asia of the World Conference on Human Rights (1993). Available at: http://law.hku.hk/lawgovtsociety/Bangkok%20 Declaration.htm [accessed: 19 December 2011].

81 Davis, M.C., 1995–6. Human Rights in Asia: China and the Bangkok Declaration, *Buffalo Journal of International Law* 2, 215–29.

interrelated."[82] This more holistic approach to rights may partly account for the Chinese government's willingness to ratify more human rights treaties.

It is difficult to assess the impact of treaty ratification on domestic laws and policies in Mainland China, in part because the law-making process is far less public than in Hong Kong. In 2004, China amended its Constitution to expressly refer to human rights and Chapter Two now sets forth the "fundamental rights and duties" of citizens, including freedom of religion, expression, association and assembly.[83] However, unlike the Hong Kong Basic Law (which is regularly enforced by the courts), China's national Constitution is primarily symbolic and the rights stated there are not judicially enforceable without separate implementing legislation. Even when such legislation is adopted, enforcement is challenging, particularly in politically sensitive areas. China lacks an independent judiciary and the government has shown little interest in developing one. While the legal profession has become more independent, lawyers who dare to represent clients in human rights cases face regular harassment and intimidation.[84] Until this changes, local attempts to enforce human rights will necessarily be less effective in Mainland China than in Hong Kong.

The limits on local enforcement make the international human rights monitoring processes all the more important for Mainland China. Yet how should the treaty-monitoring bodies assess China's reports and its progress since it began participating in the reporting process? On one hand, there is no question that the quality of life has improved in the past 20 years for a large percentage of China's population. The majority of citizens also enjoy greater freedom and access to information than they did in the 1980s. However, there are still many sensitive topics that cannot be freely discussed and the government does not hesitate to assert its control over political dissidents and others who challenge the one-party state.[85] The conviction of Liu Xiaobo, one of the signatories to "Charter 08" and

82 Vienna Declaration and Program of Action, adopted by the United Nations World Conference on Human Rights, 25 June, 1993, UN Doc. A/CONF.157/24 (Part I), paras 1–5.

83 Constitution of the People's Republic of China, as amended at the Second Session of the Tenth National People's Congress, 14 March 2004, Chapter Two, especially Arts 35 and 36. Available at: http://english.gov.cn/2005-08/05/content_20813.htm) [accessed: 18 December 2011].

84 Cohen, J.A. 2011, First, They Came for the Lawyers, *China Digital Times*, 15 July 2011. Available at: http://chinadigitaltimes.net/2011/07/jerome-a-cohen-first-they-came-for-the-lawyers [accessed: 18 December 2011]. See also Human Rights Watch 2008. "Walking on Thin Ice": Control, Intimidation and Harassment of Lawyers in China. Available at :http://www.hrw.org/search/apachesolr_search/thin%20ice%20lawyers%20china?topic=710&region=137 [accessed: 18 December 2011].

85 This is acknowledged even by those scholars who argue that China's human rights record deserves a more positive assessment than it typically receives in international reports. See, e.g., Peerenboom, R. 2006. Human Rights in China, in *Human Rights in Asia*, op. cit., note 2, especially 413–18.

the winner of the Nobel Peace Prize in 2010, is but one example.[86] Although these well-known prosecutions have a direct impact upon only a small percentage of the population, they have a general chilling effect on civil society. There are also very serious violations of the rights of Tibetans and other ethnic minority groups. These are the people who need the protection of human rights law and transnational processes. Is China's engagement in the UN system of human rights making any difference for political dissidents and other groups who are potentially in conflict with the Chinese Communist Party?

One of the first books to shed light on this question was published by Ann Kent.[87] She provided detailed analysis of the interactions between China's delegation and the Committee Against Torture in 1989 (when China submitted its very brief initial report, which was deemed inadequate) and in 1992 (when China belatedly responded to the Committee's request for a supplementary report). Kent also studied the review in 1995, when China submitted its second periodic report to the Committee Against Torture. Kent documented how the government went through a "steep learning curve" in this period, as it mastered the procedural requirements and came to accept that the Committee has a right to ask challenging questions.[88] Kent also acknowledged that China has undertaken certain legal and policy reforms to comply with the CAT (such as providing access to a defense attorney). These reforms should not be discounted as they probably have helped to reduce torture. However, her overall conclusion was that there were huge gaps between the new laws and actual practices, primarily because China simply declined to make substantive changes to comply with the CAT.[89] Kent's follow-up study in 2007 drew similar conclusions.[90] Indeed, Kent went so far as to claim that the Chinese government's support for the CAT is purely theoretical, as it perceives the treaty "as posing unacceptable challenges to its sovereignty" and thus consistently resists the internalization of its core values.[91] Kent has also argued that Beijing has de-emphasized civil and political rights in its human rights discourse during the past two decades, which does not bode well for those who hope that China is planning to ratify the ICCPR. [92]

86 For recent coverage, see Mirsky, J. 2011. Liu Xiaobo's Plea for the Human Spirit, *New York Times*, 30 December.

87 Kent, A. 1999. *China, The United Nations, and Human Rights: The Limits of Compliance*. Philadelphia, PA: University of Pennsylvania Press.

88 Kent A. 1999, at 91–104.

89 Kent A. 1999, at 104.

90 Kent A. 2007. *Beyond Compliance: China, International Organizations, and Global Security*. Stanford, CA: Stanford University Press, 212–19.

91 Kent A. 2007, at 218.

92 See e.g., Kent, A. 2011. China's Human Rights in "the Asian Century," in *Human Rights in Asia*, edited by T.W.D. Davis (Cheltenham: Edward Elgar), 187–211, especially 193.

Ming Wan has also published a study of the impact of human rights treaties on law-making in China.[93] To some extent, he shares Kent's skepticism regarding Beijing's motives, concluding that the Communist Party views human rights treaties primarily as a tool of foreign policy, a way to "meet the West half way" while avoiding any genuine reform that might threaten party rule.[94] He even raised the possibility that Beijing's engagement with international human rights may be simply "a cynical exercise of legal formalism designed to fool" the international community.[95] However, Ming Wan ultimately identified at least 30 recent laws and amendments that have human rights applications, either because they place limits on the criminal justice and administrative systems (which are often the source of human rights violations) or because they establish rights for certain groups, such as women and persons with disabilities. He also provides concrete examples of cases in which citizens have obtained remedies, including two cases against local police. Other authors have also pointed to the significant increase in the demand for legal services from people who are litigating to enforce their rights, a trend that has been largely tolerated by the Communist Party in less sensitive fields, such as discrimination.[96] Indeed, the very fact that so many cases are being filed demonstrates that Chinese citizens are not uniformly cynical about the impact of recent law reform. However, Ming Wan believes that the legal rights that have been created in China were primarily driven by the government's domestic agenda, rather than by any desire to comply with international treaty obligations. Chen Dingding reached a similar conclusion, arguing that any increased emphasis on human rights is more directly related to internal changes in the Chinese government and in Chinese society than to pressure from international sources.[97]

Indeed, it appears that the Chinese government has rarely (if ever) changed its position on an important issue in order to implement a recommendation of a treaty body. In some cases, Beijing has rejected the same recommendation on multiple occasions.[98] For example, the Committee on Economic, Social and Cultural Rights has "strongly urged" China to withdraw its reservation from Article 8 of the

---

93 Wan, M. 2007. Human Rights Lawmaking in China: Domestic Politics, International Law, and International Politics, *Human Rights Quarterly* 29, 727.

94 Ibid. at 753.

95 Ibid. at 728.

96 Fu, H.L. 2009. Access to Justice in China: Potential, Limits and Alternatives, 15 September. Available at: http://ssrn.com/abstract=1474073) [accessed: 1 December 2011]. See also the disability discrimination cases litigated with assistance from Yirenping. Available at: http://www.yirenping.org/english/index.htm [accessed: 15 December 2011].

97 Chen, D. 2005. Explaining China's Changing Discourse on Human Rights, 1978–2004, *Asian Perspective* 29(3), 155–82. See also Chen, D. 2009. China's Participation in the International Human Rights Regime: A State Identity Perspective, *Chinese Journal of International Politics* 2(3), 399–419.

98 For a compilation of concluding comments relating to China, issued by treaty bodies and special mandate holders, see Compilation Prepared by the Office of the High Commissioner for Human Rights, in Accordance with Paragraph 15(b) of the Annex

ICESCR (on the right to form trade unions).[99] The Committee has also noted with concern the many reports from the Tibetan Autonomous Region and the Xinjiang Uighur Autonomous Region regarding restrictions on the teaching of minority languages, history, culture and the free exercise of religion, which the Committee addressed as a cultural right.[100] Similar problems were identified in the Concluding Comments of the Committee on the Elimination of Racial Discrimination, which has repeatedly urged the Chinese government to review policies that have led to large-scale migration of Han Chinese into autonomous areas.[101] The change in the demographic balance (combined with the widespread feeling that Han settlers are receiving most of the benefits of government investments in these areas) is a major factor causing unrest among China's ethnic minorities. There is very little indication that China puts much weight, if any, on the views of the treaty bodies on these issues. Rather, it appears that domestic considerations are the primary (perhaps the only) factor influencing the government's approach to what it considers entirely "internal" matters.

To be fair, many governments resist recommendations by treaty bodies. For example, the Hong Kong government has stubbornly refused to change the infamous "two week rule" (an immigration policy that makes migrant domestic workers more vulnerable to abuse), despite repeated requests from more than one treaty body that it change the policy.[102] Yet, as noted earlier in this chapter, Hong Kong also provides numerous examples of reforms that were facilitated by the international reporting process. More than once, the Hong Kong government has swallowed hard and taken the medicine prescribed by one of the human rights treaty bodies. Perhaps this is because the Hong Kong government cares deeply about its international reputation: as an unelected government of a small territory, its main claim to legitimacy is that rule of law and human rights have been maintained since the handover in 1997. In contrast, China now enjoys so much power and influence that it may feel that it can afford to ignore treaty body recommendations

to Human Rights Council Resolution 5/1, A/HRC/WG.6/4/CHN/2, 16 December 2008 (prepared for the Human Rights Council, Working Group on the Universal Periodic Review).

99 Concluding Observations of the Committee on Economic Social and Cultural Rights: People's Republic of China (including Hong Kong and Macau), UN Doc. E/C.12/1/Add. 107 (13 May 2005), para. 55.

100 Concluding Observations of the Committee on Economic Social and Cultural Rights: People's Republic of China (including Hong Kong and Macau), UN Doc. E/C.12/1/Add. 107 (13 May 2005), para. 38.

101 Concluding Observations of the Committee on the Elimination of Racial Discrimination: China (including Hong Kong and Macau Special Administrative Regions), UN Doc. CERD/C/CHN/CO/10-13, 15 September 2009, para. 13.

102 Lee, P.W.Y. and Petersen, C.J. 2006. Forced Labour and Debt Bondage in Hong Kong: A Study of Indonesian and Filipina Migrant Domestic Workers. Hong Kong: Centre for Comparative and Public Law Occasional Paper No. 16. Available at: http://www.law.hku.hk/ccpl/pub/occasionalpapers/index.html [accessed: 1 December 2011].

(much like the United States, which also produces long detailed reports but has rarely, if ever, changed a policy or law as the result of the reporting process).

The other key difference between Hong Kong and China relates to the role of civil society in the reporting processes. In Hong Kong, NGOs enjoy freedom of expression and are fully involved in the process – they comment on the government's initial outline of the report, they submit alternative (shadow) reports to the treaty bodies, and they use the concluding observations as lobbying tools. Hong Kong's local legislature also promotes accountability by holding hearings and asking the government to follow up on the treaty bodies' recommendations. In contrast, in Mainland China, the government strictly controls the reporting process and there is no legal right to criticize the Communist Party. As a result, it is difficult for civil society to play a meaningful role in the reporting process for human rights treaties.

Until recently there were no alternative reports from organizations within China; all of the NGO reports relating to China were either published by Hong Kong organizations or international groups, such as Amnesty International and Human Rights in China. In the recent reviews, a few alternative reports have been filed from organizations located in Mainland China but these do not appear to be independent reports. For example, when the Committee Against Torture last reviewed China (in November 2008) an alternative report was submitted by the Society for Human Rights Studies, which describes itself as the "largest national nongovernmental organization in the field of human rights in China" and as a member of the UN Conference of Nongovernmental Organizations.[103] However, its website contains links to government reports defending China's record in Tibet and ethnic minority areas, and its comments to the Committee were predictably bland and sympathetic to the government.[104] Not surprisingly, the Committee's concluding observations relied more heavily upon the international NGOs than on this local report. The Chinese government reacted with anger, claiming that the country rapporteurs on the Committee had displayed a "strong bias against China, paid no heed to the facts", and made "slanderous and untrue allegations."[105]

In the 2009 review by the Committee on the Elimination of Racial Discrimination there were three NGO reports from within China (all of which

---

103 See the "about us" section of the website of the China Society for Human Rights Studies. Available at: http://www.chinahumanrights.org [accessed: 19 December 2011].

104 China Society for Human Rights Studies, 2008. Challenges and Problems on Chinese Work Against Torture (submitted to the Committee Against Torture, 41st session, 30 September). Available at: http://www2.ohchr.org/english/bodies/cat/cats41.htm [accessed: 19 December 2011].

105 Comments by the Government of the People's Republic of China to the concluding observations and recommendations of the Committee Against Torture, CAT/C/CHN/CO/4/Add. 1, 17 December 2008, at 2.

are available on the Committee's website).[106] The report from the China Society for Human Rights Studies made a few mild suggestions for implementing the treaty. The report by the Research Center for Ethnic Issues in China was slightly more interesting as it referred to a few of the controversial issues (such as the danger that minority languages and culture will die out if minority children are not educated in their own language). However, all of the factual data in this report came directly from the State Commission on Ethnic Affairs. The most interesting shadow report from within China was submitted by the Institute of Human Rights and Humanitarian Law at the China University of Politics and Law. It reflected a degree of independent research and identified certain concrete deficiencies in the legislation. However, it also took pains to avoid the most controversial issues surrounding China's treatment of ethnic minorities. In its 2009 Concluding Observations the Committee on the Elimination of Racial Discrimination welcomed some of the new laws and policies (including the 11th Five-Year Program for the Ethnic Minority Cause, the Development Program to Help Ethnic Groups with Relatively Small Populations (2005–2010), the Grand Strategy for the development of China's West and the 11th Five-Year Program for the Action on Prosperity Promotion in Border Areas). However, the Committee appears to have put more weight on the comments from international NGOs (representing Tibetan, Uyghur and other ethnic minorities) and it suggested that the government should carefully consider the root causes of the July 2009 riots in East Turkestan. The Committee also expressed concern regarding the disproportionate use of force and detention against ethnic Tibetans and Uyghurs.

If the Chinese government really wants to decrease the influence of the international NGOs in the reporting process, then it should allow independent NGOs from within China to fully express their views, without fear of punishment. There are many organizations within China that could enrich the reporting process. For example, the Beijing Yirenping Center is dedicated to eliminating discrimination against carriers of contagious diseases (such as Hepatitis B and HIV) and has published several interesting research reports.[107] Women's Watch – China also engages in a variety of research and advocacy activities and describes itself as a "window that connects China to international society" because its members regularly participate in international meetings.[108] In September 2010 a "CEDAW Shadow Report Project Team" with representatives from this group took a study tour to Sweden to learn more about the reporting process. Similar training events

---

106 See records of the Committee on the Elimination of Racial Discrimination, 75th Session, August 2009. Available at: http://www2.ohchr.org/english/bodies/cerd/cerds75.htm (alternative reports appear under the heading "Information from other sources") [accessed: 19 December 2011].

107 See Introduction to Bejing Yirenping Center. Available at: http://www.yirenping.org/english/index.htm [accessed: 19 December 2011].

108 See the "Our Founding" section of the website of Women's Watch – China. Available at: http://www.womenwatch-china.org/en/about.aspx [accessed: 19 December 2011].

have been held in China and in Hong Kong, indicating that Mainland Chinese NGOs are eager to submit shadow reports the next time that China is reviewed by a treaty monitoring body.

Unfortunately, unless the political climate changes in China, it is highly unlikely that any local NGOs will feel confident enough to submit a really hard-hitting shadow report to a treaty body. The leaders of these NGOs know that they could pay dearly if they openly contradict the Chinese government in an international forum. Commentators from outside China tend to focus on the famous cases, such as the detention of Liu Xiaobo and Gao Zhisheng (a human rights lawyer who was detained and tortured). However, there are also many other examples of day-to-day intimidation that will deter NGOs from producing provocative shadow reports. For example, in April 2010 the Center for Women's Law Studies and Legal Services, which had been based at Peking University for 15 years, was told that it needed to find a new home. Legal aid organizations have often attached themselves to universities in China, as a way of keeping a low profile. This center apparently became too active and Peking University was reportedly pressured to end its sponsorship (along with three other organizations that had been based at the university). Guo Jianmei, the leader of the former Center, took the rare step of publishing a "good-bye" message, although much of the Center's work will hopefully carry on at the Qianqian law firm and in other organizations. In her message, Guo mentioned that being "cancelled" was not the greatest challenge that she and her colleagues had faced in the course of litigating against discrimination and she described physical threats.[109] Similarly, organizations that do work on behalf of persons with disabilities, such as Yirenping and the Beijing Aizhizing Institute of Health Education, have experienced increased harassment in recent years. Indeed, there is a general feeling that China became significantly more oppressive for independent NGOs in 2010 and 2011. This does not bode well for civil society's input into the reporting process.

The next opportunity to assess this process will probably be when the Committee on the Rights of Persons with Disabilities reviews the initial reports of China (including Hong Kong and Macau) on the implementation of the CRPD.[110] China actively helped to draft and promote this treaty and it was the first country in East Asia to ratify it. China also participated in the first meeting of States Parties to the CRPD, in October–November 2008, and successfully nominated a member of the first Committee on the Rights of Persons with Disabilities. It appears that

109 Jianmei, G. 2010. Goodbye, Peking University, 2 April (English translation by Human Rights in China). Available at: http://www.hrichina.org/public/contents/press?revision_id=173547&item_id=173519 [accessed: 1 December 2011].

110 Initial reports of China, Hong Kong, and Macau have been published by the Committee on the Rights of Persons with Disabilities. Available at: http://www.ohchr.org/EN/HRBodies/CRPD/Pages/Session7.aspx [accessed: 1 December 2011].

the Chinese government wants to be viewed as a leader in disability rights, which means that it may make a special effort to comply with CRPD.[111]

The Committee on the Rights of Persons with Disabilities will adopt its list of issues for the review of China at a closed session in April 2012 and it will probably complete the public review later in 2012. The CRPD review will provide a particularly important test of the reporting process because Beijing did not enter any reservations, although the treaty contains many provisions protecting civil liberties, political rights and access to justice. For example, Article 14 of the CRPD states that persons with disabilities must not be deprived of their liberty unlawfully or arbitrarily, and the existence of a disability shall in no case justify a deprivation of liberty. Article 13 requires state parties to ensure that persons with disabilities enjoy "effective access to justice" on an equal basis with others, including any procedural and age-appropriate accommodations that may be required to facilitate their effective role as participants in legal proceedings.[112] These provisions open the door for the Committee on the Rights of Persons with Disabilities to question China on detention procedures, civil commitment proceedings and conditions inside medical and detention facilities. The UN Committee Against Torture has already expressed concerns regarding Chinese criminal law, which allows authorities to administer compulsory medical treatment to persons with medical illness who commit crimes. In particular, the Committee Against Torture noted "with concern that this provision has been misused to detain some people in psychiatric hospitals for reasons other than medical."[113] China has since commenced the process of amending its Mental Health Care law, a process that was probably prompted by the upcoming review by the Committee on the Rights of Persons with Disabilities.[114] It is, however, too soon to predict whether the new law will comply with the CRPD. China's population policy also requires reform, as it has traditionally embraced eugenic theories that violate reproductive rights protected by the CRPD.[115] Yet China's initial report under the CRPD is strangely silent on the history of eugenic policies.

Article 29 of the CRPD further provides that persons with disabilities have the right to participate in political and public life and Article 21 provides that States Parties shall take all appropriate measures to ensure that persons with disabilities

111 For examples of China's support for the treaty, see Petersen, C.J. 2008. China's Ratification of the Convention on the Rights of Persons With Disabilities: the Implications for Hong Kong, 38 *Hong Kong Law Journal* 611–44.

112 CRPD, Art. 13(b).

113 Concluding Observations of the Committee Against Torture: China, 41st Session, CAT/C/CHN/CO/4, 12 December 2008, at 14.

114 Xinhua 2011. China to Enact Mental Health Care law in 2001. Available at: http://news.xinhuanet.com/english2010/china/2011-03/10/c_13771463.htm [accessed: 15 October 2011].

115 Petersen, C.J. 2010. Population Policy and Eugenic Theory: Implications of China's Ratification of the United Nations Convention on the Rights of Persons with Disabilities, *China: An International Journal* 8, 85–109.

can exercise the right to freedom of expression and opinion, including the freedom to seek, receive and impart information and ideas on an equal basis with others. Although Beijing will almost certainly interpret Article 21 as simply requiring accessible technologies, the Committee may interpret it more broadly and ask the Chinese delegation about controls on critical speech. The Committee will also expect to receive at least some shadow reports from independent NGOs on the Mainland, such as Yirenping. The China Federation of Disabled Persons will probably submit an alternative report, but this is essentially a public enforcement body, one that does good work but is notoriously pro-government.[116] If independent NGOs are not permitted to submit alternative reports then the Committee will continue to rely upon international NGOs, many of which have been documenting violations of the rights of persons with disabilities in China.[117]

There is also concern that China's increased economic and political influence may cause treaty-monitoring bodies to soften their critique. In theory, the members of the international treaty monitoring bodies are independent experts who do not represent their governments. This is the advantage that the treaty-monitoring bodies have over the Human Rights Council. In practice, however, Beijing's rapidly growing influence in the Asia–Pacific region may inhibit some committee members from questioning the Chinese delegation on sensitive issues. At the review of China in August 2009, a few members of the Committee on the Elimination of Racial Discrimination enthusiastically congratulated China on its detailed report and did not seem particularly interested in asking searching questions. Some observers were very concerned by this (although the Concluding Observations were still quite strong). It will be important to observe the attitudes of committee members, as well as the role of NGOs, when the Committee on the Rights of Persons with Disabilities delivers its review of China's initial report on the CRPD.

## Conclusions

The easiest conclusion to draw from this comparative study is that the Hong Kong government should continue to submit separate reports, allowing the treaty-monitoring bodies to conduct a distinct review of Hong Kong (and also of Macau) when they review China. One can imagine a time when the treaty bodies may decline to do this, as Hong Kong has a mere 7 million people and the resources of the UN human rights system are limited. However, abandoning the separate

116 The official website of the China Disabled Persons' Federation, which discusses programs to promote education and employment of persons with disabilities but avoids controversial issues. Available at: http://www.cdpf.org.cn/english [accessed: 1 December 2011].

117 See, for example, Human Rights Watch, 2003. Locked Doors: The Human Rights of People Living with HIV/AIDS in China, 3 September. Available at: http://www.unhcr.org/refworld/docid/3fe478e27.html [accessed: 16 December 2011].

reporting process would greatly diminish the impact of the UN human rights system in this Special Administrative Region of China.

At the moment, Hong Kong and Macau are the only regions in China entitled to participate in the reporting process in their own names. There are other regions, such as Tibet, which are theoretically autonomous and would also benefit from the opportunity to submit separate reports to treaty bodies, assuming that the report is drafted by local people and not overseen by the central government.[118] The Chinese government would not support this now, but it may be something that could be negotiated. After all, separate reporting certainly has not inspired any separatist movements in Hong Kong. Indeed, it arguably has had the opposite effect, by reassuring Hong Kong people that the promise of autonomy has some meaning.

It is far more difficult to draw conclusions on the impact of transnational human rights processes in Mainland China. On one hand, China should be congratulated for ratifying treaties, especially for ratifying the CRPD quickly and without reservations. However, Beijing's decreased reliance on reservations does not necessarily reflect a greater intent to comply with treaties. It may be that the Chinese government now perceives the international reporting process as being fairly weak and that it has therefore adopted a new strategy – one of ratifying without reservations and then simply denying that any conflicts exist between treaty obligations and the government's practices and policies. It falls to the treaty-monitoring bodies to seek a broad range of information from NGOs and to continually remind Beijing of its obligations.

118 For discussion of the different autonomy regimes in China, see generally Ghai, Y.P. 2000. Autonomy Regimes in China: Coping with Ethnic and Economic Diversity, in *Autonomy and Ethnicity: Negotiating Competing Claims in Multi-Ethnic States*, edited by Y.P. Ghai. Cambridge: Cambridge University Press.

# Chapter 8

# Combating Religious Defamation: An Exploration of Blasphemy in Islamic Thought and International Practice

Ali M. Abid

## Introduction

In 1999, Pakistan submitted the first resolution regarding the defamation of religions, entitled "Defamation of Islam," to the United Nations Human Rights Commission.[1] The submission was made on behalf of the Organization of the Islamic Conference (OIC) and its stated purpose was to combat "intolerance and misunderstanding, not to say hatred, of Islam and Muslims" and to counter the international media's depiction of Islam as "a religion hostile to human rights."[2] There was an immediate outcry from the Western states in the international community and throughout the scholarship against the resolutions as violating rights to freedom of expression and religion.[3] The fear is that these resolutions, aside from prohibiting speech that is protected under the International Covenant on Civil and Political Rights (ICCPR), will be used to support and extend domestic anti-blasphemy laws within Islamic states, laws which are already harshly criticized for violating human rights.[4] The countries defending these resolutions and their domestic blasphemy laws have alluded to Islamic law's supremacy over international law – ironically fulfilling the fears the resolutions were hoping to combat.[5] This debate has persisted over the last decade with new anti-defamation of religions resolutions being proposed by Pakistan and other OIC states nearly every year. This debate raises several questions: (1) whether the resolutions do indeed violate freedoms protected under international covenants; (2) whether the resolutions might actually support domestic blasphemy laws and what the consequences might be; (3) and – perhaps

---

1 Lorenz Langer, The Rise (And Fall?) of Defamation of Religions, 35 *Yale J. Int'l L.* 257, 258 (2010).

2 Comm'n on Human Rights, Draft Resolution on Racism, Racial Discrimination, Xenophobia and All Forms of Discrimination, U.N. Doc. E/CN.4/1999/L.40 (20 April 1999).

3 *See generally* Press Release, Comm'n on Human Rights, *infra* note 6.

4 Dobras, *infra* note 20, at 377.

5 Ibid.

most importantly – whether anti-blasphemy or defamation of religion laws are actually condoned within Islamic theology.

I find that the defamation resolutions do indeed violate the right to freedom of expression as protected under international accords, namely the ICCPR, and that, by comparing the defamation resolutions with similar domestic blasphemy laws in place in Pakistan, the possible human rights consequences are terrible. However, I do not find that Islamic theology condones these types of anti-blasphemy measures and that, in fact, drawing upon the primary sources of Islamic law, Islam has a far greater tolerance, even acceptance, of religious plurality than is evidenced by the practice of these Islamic states. Sadly, throughout Islamic history the schools of thought that would support such an open view have been suppressed by state powers. The rise of these anti-blasphemy laws and now these anti-defamation resolutions represents a fascinating use of two different transnational legal processes: international human rights mechanisms and Islamic law, or Shar'ia. I propose that, in addition to combating these resolutions by appealing to international human rights instruments, the opponents of the resolutions also take up arguing from within the Islamic tradition as well, that it would do immeasurable good for the West to be educated on the actual tenets of Islam and for the people of Islamic states to see how Islamic ideas can be used in connection with international human rights norms.

The next section outlines the history of the defamation resolutions and their content, after which I illustrate how the resolutions are in contravention of the right to freedom of expression guaranteed internationally. Following this I provide a case study of the blasphemy laws of Pakistan, how and why they were adopted, and their consequences. Next I examine the place of religious plurality and respect toward non-Muslims in Islamic theology and how Islamic theology has developed historically with respect to these ideas. Finally, I propose that opponents of the defamation resolutions argue by using the Islamic tradition and address certain objections regarding comparative ethics and the ability to affect change within a tradition from the outside.

## History of the Defamation Resolutions

The original resolution brought by Pakistan in 1999 was criticized for having too great a focus on Islam.[6] India, Germany and Japan, in particular, believed the resolution was far too specific with relation to Islam, that the problem of negative stereotyping was felt by all religions, and that the resolutions should be expanded to include not just Islam but all faiths, including minority religions

6 Press Release, Commission on Human Rights, Commission on Human Rights Establishes Intersessional Working Group to Review and Enhance Its Mechanisms, U.N. Doc. HR/CN/99/64 (29 April 1999).

within majority-Muslim countries.[7] Pakistan and other OIC countries countered this by saying that the problem they sought to address was quite specific to Islam and broadening the scope of the resolution would only dilute the effect it may have on the problem.[8] After long negotiations with Pakistan, a revised version of the resolution was put to the Commission, which prohibited the defamation of all religions but emphasized Islam in particular; this revised resolution was adopted by the Commission without a vote.[9] The resolution was geared toward preventing the "negative stereotyping of religions" and prohibiting any "media or other means . . . used to incite acts of violence, xenophobia, or related intolerance and discrimination towards Islam and any other religion."[10] An important feature of this resolution and those that followed it is the fact that religions themselves are the objects of protection not individual adherents.[11] The resolution did not say who would decide when a religion had been defamed.[12]

After the attacks on 11 September 2001 the international community and the OIC in particular became increasingly concerned with the rise of "Islamaphobia" throughout the West.[13] The Human Rights Commission passed a resolution called "Combating the Defamation of Religion" in 2002, and similarly titled resolutions from 2003 through 2010 have been passed in either the Human Rights Commission or Council and the General Assembly each year.[14] These new resolutions were also criticized by Western nations for their neglect of other religions and their specific focus on Islam.[15] However, each of the resolutions was amended just as the 1999 resolution was and passed through the Commission.[16]

In 2005, after the publication of several cartoons in Danish newspapers depicting the Prophet Mohammed, the anti-defamation resolutions' and Islam's clash with the international media drew a great deal of attention. In December 2005, the OIC held an Extraordinary Islamic Summit session in Mecca, where they expressed concern over what they perceived as attacks on Islam and the

7 Ibid.

8 Langer, *supra* note 1, at 258.

9 Ibid.

10 Comm'n on Human Rights Res. 1999/82, 55th Sess., 62d mtg U.N. Doc. E/CN.4/Res/1999/82 (30 April 1999) at Art. 3.

11 Langer, *supra* note 1, at 259.

12 Ibid.

13 Pujai Kapai and Anne S. Y. Cheung, Hanging in the Balance: Freedom of Expression and Religion, 15 *Buff. Hum. Rts. L. Rev.* 41, 53–4 (2009).

14 Combating Defamation of Religion, CHR Res. 2002/9, U.N. Doc. E/CN.4/RES/2002/9 (15 April 2002); Combating Defamation of Religions, CHR Res. 2003/4, U.N. Doc. E/CN.4/RES/2003/4 (14 April 2004); Combating Defamation of Religions, CHR Res. 2004/6, U.N. Doc. E/CN.4/RES/2004/6 (13 April 2004); and Combating Defamation of Religions, CHR Res. 2005/3, U.N. Doc. E/CN.4/RES/2005/3 (12 April 2005) (hereinafter "The Resolutions").

15 Kapai and Cheung, *supra* note 13, at 54.

16 Ibid.

desecration of the image of the Prophet Mohammed in the international media; at the session, they emphasized "the inapplicability of using the freedom of expression as a pretext to defame religions."[17] Yemen introduced a resolution that condemned the defamation of religions in the UN General Assembly; the resolution was adopted, but the vote was split along the same lines as those in the Human Rights Commission regarding the resolutions proposed by Pakistan there.[18] In 2007 and 2008 the OIC pushed resolutions through both the newly established Human Rights Council and the General Assembly.[19]

Despite previous criticisms, the 2008 version of the resolutions returned more of the focus to Islam.[20] Although the resolution spoke of maintaining a "careful balance" between all the rights expressed in the ICCPR, the freedom of religion, and secularism, it also expanded the scope of fighting the defamation of religions against the freedom of expression by equating the prohibition on racial hate speech (which is largely accepted internationally as a limitation on the freedom of expression) to the prohibition of stereotyping religions in the media and by political parties.[21] Fortunately, since the 2008 resolution, each defamation resolution has received less support. In 2010, the anti-defamation resolution presented to the Human Rights Council came within four votes of defeat, and there was no such resolution brought before the UN in 2011.[22] In particular, in December 2008, the freedom of expression rapporteurs for the UN, the Organization of American States, the African Commission on Human and Peoples' Rights, and the Organization for Security and Cooperation in Europe issued a joint statement urging states to stop supporting these resolutions because they do not accord with international standards for expression in free societies.[23] The UN Special Rapporteur on the Freedom of Religion or Belief has also insisted that these defamation resolutions are similarly violative of international human rights.[24]

---

17 Organization of the Islamic Conference, Final Communiqué of the Third Extraordinary Session of the Islamic Summit Conference, II (7–8 December 2005), available at http://www.oic-oci.org/ex-summit/english/fc-exsumm-en.htm.

18 Langer, *supra* note 1, at 260.

19 Ibid. at 261.

20 Rebecca J. Dobras, Is the United Nations Endorsing Human Rights Violations?: An Analysis of the United Nations' Combating Defamation of Religions Resolutions and Pakistan's Blasphemy Laws, 37. *Ga. J. Int'l and Comp. L.* 339, 376 (2009).

21 Ibid. at 377.

22 The Dangerous Idea of Protecting Religions from "Defamation": A Threat to Universal Human Rights Standards, *Policy Focus* (Update: Fall 2010), *United States Commission on International Religious Freedom*, 4, http://www.uscirf.gov/images/uscirf%20policy%20focus%20defamation%202010%20update.pdf; *3/24/2011: USCIRF Welcomes Move Away from "Defamation of Religions" Concept*, *United States Commission on International Religious Freedom*, http://www.uscirf.gov/news-room/press-releases/3570.html

23 Ibid.

24 Ibid.

These resolutions contain four common elements. First, since the 11 September attacks and even before, Muslims and Islam have been negatively portrayed in the international media and throughout the laws of several states.[25] Second, such intolerance and discrimination is rampant throughout the world and leads to the deprivation of Muslims' fundamental rights.[26] Third, using any form of media to incite acts of violence, xenophobia, intolerance, or discrimination should be condemned.[27] Finally, fourth, the states should prohibit the dissemination of any such intolerant or defamatory ideas and prevent the defamation of religions – particularly Islam.[28]

The criticisms of the resolutions in the Human Rights Commission and then the Human Rights Council can also be divided up into four different categories. First is the exceptionalism of Islam that has been discussed above; Western countries have said that the resolutions seem to imply that they sanction some forms of criticism against religions other than Islam that they would prohibit against Islam. They argue that this exceptionalism would be inconsistent with broad international norms of non-discrimination on the basis of religion. Second, the opposition has fears that the resolutions violate freedom of expression guarantees in international law as articulated in the Universal Declaration of Human Rights and the ICCPR.[29] Third, by protecting an entity such as religion instead of particular adherents to a religion, the resolutions are not protecting anything in particular at all, they do not fit within the tradition of the expansion of human rights, and this lack of individual protection opens the defamation resolutions up to abuse by those who would speak for the religions.[30] As an extension of this last point, the opposition is worried about the lack of clarity in these laws. Who will decide whether a religion has been defamed? What is the meaning of defamation when it applies to religion? How will certain minority religions be treated when their very tenets might be considered defamatory to the adherents of a majority religion?[31] Lastly, and somewhat related to this last concern, the opposition fears that these resolutions will be used by the governments in Islamic countries to buttress their own domestic anti-blasphemy laws and to suppress minority religions, and will ultimately lead to violations of human rights.[32] The rest of the chapter will examine each of these concerns, starting with an examination of the resolutions' harmony with the freedom of expression.

---

25 *See generally* The Resolutions, *supra* note 14.

26 Ibid.

27 Ibid.

28 Ibid.

29 *See generally*, Dobras *supra* note 20; and Press Release, Comm'n on Human Rights, *supra* note 6.

30 Ibid.

31 Ibid.

32 Ibid.

## Relationship to Right to Freedom of Expression

Article 19 of the Universal Declaration of Human Rights provides every individual with the right to freedom of opinion and expression; Article 18 provides the right of freedom of thought, conscience and religion.[33] Although the Universal Declaration of Human Rights is largely considered in the scholarship to be part of customary international law (despite it having come into existence as a nonbinding resolution in the UN General Assembly), the analysis in this chapter will focus on the articles of the ICCPR, which is a binding treaty to which all the relevant nations to this debate are signatories.[34] In the ICCPR, Article 18 provides protection for the freedom of thought, conscience and religion; its relevant provisions include the following:

> Article 18
> 1. Everyone shall have the right to freedom of thought, conscience and religion.
> . . .
> 3. Freedom to manifest one's religion or beliefs may be subject only to such limitations as are prescribed by law and are necessary to protect public safety, order, health, or morals or the fundamental rights and freedoms of others.[35]

Article 19 of the ICCPR governs the right to freedom of expression, providing:

> Article 19
> . . . .
> 2. Everyone shall have the right to freedom of expression; this right shall include freedom to seek, receive and impart information and ideas of all kinds, regardless of frontiers, either orally, in writing or in print, in the form of art, or through any other media of his choice.
> 3. The exercise of the rights provided for in paragraph 2 of this article carries with it special duties and responsibilities. It may therefore be subject to certain restrictions, but these shall only be such as are provided by law and are necessary:
> (a) For respect of the rights or reputations of others;
> (b) For the protection of national security or of public order (ordre public), or of public health or morals.[36]

Also relevant is Article 20(2) of the ICCPR, which states, "any advocacy of national, racial or religious hatred that constitutes incitement to discrimination,

33 Universal Declaration of Human Rights, G.A. Res. 217A, Art. 19, U.N. GAOR, 3d Sess., 1st plen. mtg, U.N. Doc A/810 (12 December 1948).

34 Dobras, *supra* note 20, at 342.

35 International Covenant on Civil and Political Rights, G.A. Res. 2200 (XXI), Art. 18, U.N. GAOR, 21st Sess., Supp. No. 16, U.N. Doc. A/6316 (16 December 1966) (hereinafter "ICCPR").

36 Ibid. at Art. 19.

hostility, or violence shall be prohibited by law."[37] The Human Rights Committee charged with reviewing and explaining the articles of the ICCPR stated that the requirement created of state parties in Article 20(2) along with the limitations placed on the freedom of expression in Article 19(3) signal and require state parties to protect these rights.[38] Furthermore, the Committee found that the limitation in Article 20(2) does not create a separate right that limits free speech on the grounds of respect for the beliefs or religions of others, but rather it limits the manifestation of incitement and hatred, including the manifestation of certain religious beliefs that may serve to incite.[39] This conduct is far more extreme than the conduct prohibited by the anti-defamation resolutions, which seem to apply to any offensive language. The Committee members found, as the drafters of the Article 20 also found, that lowering that bar may unduly infringe the freedom of expression.[40] Additionally, the UN Special Rapporteur on the Freedom of Opinion and Expression emphasized that the limitation in Article 20(2) is meant to protect individuals, rather than belief systems (it was created to address the type of incitement the Nazis used to persecute Jewish people).[41]

Some scholars also read into Article 19(3) that the limitations on the freedom of expression must be "necessary in a democratic society."[42] This phrasing comes from the following Articles 21 and 22, which only allow limitations on the right of assembly and association that are "necessary in a democratic society in the interests of national security, public safety, public order."[43] Whether such an additional requirement for a limitation can be fairly read into articles that do not contain it is a matter of some debate in the field,[44] but it does give us an understanding of the sort of limits the drafters of the ICCPR thought were appropriate for the rights provided for within the treaty.

The expression of negative stereotypes and the imparting of xenophobic ideas are prohibited by the Defamation Resolutions, but opponents of the resolutions point out that such ideas do not necessarily rise to the level of religious hatred or incitement to hostility as prohibited by Article 20, nor do they meet the requirements of Article 19(3).[45] In fact, the defamation resolutions seem to prohibit all anti-Islamic ideas regardless of the requirements the ICCPR places on limiting the freedom of expression.[46]

37 Ibid. at Art. 20.

38 Kapai and Cheung, *supra* note 13, at 49.

39 Ibid. at 50.

40 *Policy Focus, United States Commission on International Religious Freedom*, *supra* note 22, at 5.

41 Ibid.

42 Kapai and Cheung, *supra* note 13, at 49.

43 ICCPR, *supra* note 35, Arts 21–2.

44 *See generally* Kapai and Cheung, *supra* note 13.

45 Dobras, *supra* note 20, at 343.

46 Ibid.

The UN Human Rights Committee, which is assigned to interpret the provisions of the ICCPR and monitor their implementation, addressed the issue of the abuse of state power with respect to the freedom of expression in 1993.[47] They stated that, if a set of beliefs is accepted as the official ideology of a state, whether it be through official proclamations or through practice, it must not impair any of the freedoms found in Article 18 or 19 of the ICCPR and must not result in any discrimination against those who do not accept that ideology.[48] The recent rhetoric in the UN surrounding the passage of the Defamation Resolutions, however, seems to be altering these accepted interpretations of the provisions of Article 19(3); in 2007, when both the Human Rights Council and the UN General Assembly passed resolutions regarding the freedom of expression, they described the limitations on the right as such:

> provided by law and necessary for respect of the rights or reputations of others, protection of national security or of public order, public health or morals and *respect for religions and beliefs*. (Emphasis added.)[49]

This phrasing seems to directly push out blasphemous or defamatory speech from protection under the ICCPR by adding a new limitation to the freedom of expression that is not found in the very treaty that sets the outer bounds on what governments are allowed to prohibit.[50]

Another legal issue raised by the opponents of the Defamation Resolutions is the entire idea of what exactly constitutes defamation of a religion and how one would go deciding whether a religion has been defamed. Defamation traditionally, when it is applied to individuals, requires an element of falsity in what was expressed.[51] One concern is that, when a judge tried a case regarding the defamation of a religion, that judge would be put in a position of determining whether the defamatory statement were true or not.[52] So, if a Muslim were to make a statement that Mohammed was the last of the prophets, would that be defamatory to Baha'ism, which accepts prophets that came after Mohammed? Would the Baha'i belief be considered defamatory to Islam? Such cases would

47 Robert C. Blitt, Should New Bills of Rights Address Emerging International Human Rights Norms? The Challenge of "Defamation of Religion" 16 (University of Tennessee, Knoxville College of Law, Legal Studies Research Paper Series No. 90, 2010).

48 UN Human Rights Committee, General Comment No. 22: The Right to Freedom of Thought, Conscience and Religion, para. 10 (30 July 1993).

49 Blitt, supra note 47, at 17; UN General Assembly, "Combating Defamation of Religions," UN Doc. A/RES/61/164, (21 February 2007), and Human Rights Council, "Combating Defamation of Religions," UN Doc. A/HRC/Res/4/9/, 30 (March 2007).

50 Blitt, *supra* note 47, at 17.

51 L. Bennett Graham, Defamation of Religions; The End of Pluralism?, 23 *Emory Int'l L. Rev.* 69, 75 (2009).

52 Ibid. at 76.

draw the judiciary and the government into making decisions on theological issues, irrevocably discriminating between ideologies.[53]

All these fears regarding the possible ramifications of the Defamation Resolutions are grounded in history. The countries of the OIC that are pushing these defamation resolutions through the UN organs have very strict domestic blasphemy laws that, some fear, have been used to suppress the voices of dissidents and minority religions in contravention to the rights guaranteed under international law. The adoption of possible binding defamation of religions accords on the international stage, or their incorporation into customary international law might, many fear, lead to the expansion of blasphemy laws domestically. The country that has been principally presenting the resolutions in the Human Rights Commission – and then Council – has been Pakistan, and its own domestic blasphemy laws have long been criticized for their broad scope and harsh punishments. The next section analyzes the blasphemy laws of Pakistan, their origins, and the back and forth discussion that has existed between the Pakistani government and those in the international arena that criticize its law.

## Blasphemy Laws Of Pakistan

The blasphemy laws in Pakistan today are mainly the result of the presidency of General Muhammad Zia-ul-Haq.[54] The administration of General Zia is considered to be a time of intense Islamization that greatly transformed the role of the courts, giving them the power to review state laws for their conformity with Islam.[55] It was under his rule that the blasphemy laws in place in Pakistan since the time of British rule underwent radical changes. To analyze these changes and the purpose behind them it is important to review their history.

In 1860, in British India, the Crown found it necessary to install anti-blasphemy laws in order to maintain peace and tranquility within a colony that was home to a great multiplicity of religions and sects.[56] The law was geared toward protecting all religions and stated that "every man should be suffered to profess his own religion, and that no man should be suffered to insult the religion of another."[57] The intent requirement for the law was articulated as "the deliberate intention of wounding the religious feelings of another person."[58] This made it a specific

53 Ibid.

54 Osama Siddique and Zaya Hayat, Unholy Speech and Holy Laws: Blasphemy Laws in Pakistan – Controversial Origins, Design Defects, and Free Speech Implications, 17 *Minn. J. Int'l L.* 303, 319 (2008).

55 Ibid.

56 Ibid. at 336–7.

57 India Pen. Code, Act XLV of 1860 at a2 (Krishen Lal & Co. Law Publishers, 1929).

58 Ibid.

intent crime during British rule. In 1927 the intent requirement was changed to the "deliberate and malicious intention of outraging the religious feeling of any class of his Majesty's subjects," making the intent requirement even narrower and harder to attain.[59]

The statute remained on the books in Pakistan after independence and up until General Zia came to rule in 1978.[60] Upon its founding, Pakistan's leaders were divided roughly into thirds regarding what they wanted the role of Islam to be in the new nation. One group, led by the founder of Pakistan, Muhammad Ali Jinnah, comprising religious minorities and higher level civil and military leaders, wanted Pakistan to be secular and to adopt Western-style government in nearly all respects; the primary change between this and British rule would have been rule at home rather than rule by a distant European power.[61] The second group, the Modernists, led by the poet and national leader, Muhammad Iqbal, focused on bringing Islamic ethos and legitimacy into a Western style government by allowing the government to rule based on Islamic principles, but not bind itself to the Islamic legal precedents of the medieval period.[62] The third group, called the Men of Religion, wanted to completely replace Western style government with an Islamic one and to rely on the traditional schools of Islamic Shar'ia.[63] The final 1956 constitution, however, wound up being a middle point between the Secularizing elite led by Jinnah and the Modernists led by Iqbal; aside from some preambular mentions of the sovereignty of God and calling the nation an Islamic state, the word "Shar'ia" was avoided and the instrumentalities of government remained Western in style.[64]

In the following 20 years, the stance of the Men of Religion gained power and Prime Minister Bhutto conceded to many of the religious right's demands in calling for the official application of Shar'ia law and declaring the Ahmadi sect not to be Muslims.[65] Bhutto, who was originally against the position of the Men of Religion, began to fear their ability to replace him in an upcoming election; when he made his declaration regarding Shar'ia law, he turned over the entire judicial functions of the state to these provincial Shar'ia courts in order to appease his enemies.[66] General Zia took control in 1978 and, with fundamentalist sympathies at heart, undertook the Islamicizing of the country to a much greater degree, particularly through the blasphemy law.[67] However, Zia soon realized that turning over the

59 Ibid. at 1341.

60 *Christophe Jaffrelot, A History of Pakistan and its Origins*, 246 (Wimbledon Publishing Co., 2002).

61 Ibid. at 238.

62 Ibid. at 239.

63 Ibid. at 240.

64 Ibid. at 241.

65 Ibid. at 245.

66 Ibid.

67 Ibid.

judicial power to the religious authorities was not in the best interests of the state. Therefore, to consolidate his power, he resurrected the state courts and charged them with the official application and interpretation of Shar'ia law.[68] The Men of Religion who originally supported Zia were very much against this move as they felt it was not about Islamizing the country, but just another way of expanding state control.[69] This is significant because it shows how state powers can use religious authority to consolidate state power rather than work toward religious ends; this is a recurring theme, as will be discussed in the following section.

During Zia's rule each of the provisions of the blasphemy law were changed or amended and the intent requirement was removed altogether.[70] Among the changes, there was the narrowing of sections so they only addressed the defilement of Islam's holy personages, adding in a section dealing specifically with derogatory remarks against the Prophet Mohammed, and another section making it a crime for the Ahmadi sect to use Islamic nomenclature to refer to the founders of their religion and their ritual practices.[71] The Ahmadis are members of a religious sect who consider themselves Muslim, although the Pakistani government has declared them not to be a part of the Islamic community.[72] The Ahmadis are forbidden under the blasphemy laws to describe various ritual practices of Islam that they also perform by their Islamic name; for example, they are prohibited from describing the call to prayer, the "adhan," the ablutions performed before pray, "wudhu," or to even call themselves Muslim.[73] In fact under the last two sections of the blasphemy law concerning the applicability of the death penalty, the Ahmadis could be subject to the death penalty merely for affirming their faith as Ahmadis or saying that Mohammed is not the last prophet, as it would be considered to blasphemous.[74]

In addition to the Ahmadis, Christians, Hindus, journalists, human rights advocates, attorneys defending blasphemy cases and Muslims with more moderate beliefs have all been tried for violation of the blasphemy law.[75] The lack of an intent requirement has resulted in the criminal trials of people who are mentally handicapped, of a humanities professor who was answering questions by students who were consciously trying to trick him into saying something that would violate the law, and Ahmadis who unwittingly printed common Islamic expressions of well-wishing on wedding cards that were distributed to their guests.[76] Although

68 Ibid. at 246.

69 Ibid.

70 Dobras, *supra* note 20, at 355.

71 Siddique and Hayat, *supra* note 54, at 338–9.

72 Ibid. at 339.

73 Ibid.

74 Dobras, *supra* note 20, at 350.

75 Ibid.

76 Siddique and Hayat, *supra* note 54, at 345 (regarding the case of Dr Sheikh, who was accused on the basis of a petition of 11 of his students, who had baited him in answering questions to ultimately say that before the age of 40 the Prophet Muhammad was not a Muslim – of course this was before his first revelation, so by many conceptions no

there are a few instances of appellate courts in Pakistan reading a *mens rea* requirement into the law, these instances have been rare and have not been applied again even in the courts that have at one time tried to use them.[77]

Another factor contributing to the horrifying effects of these blasphemy laws is the vagueness in the *actus reus*. The law reads, "whoever by words, either spoken or written, or by visible representation, or by any imputation, innuendo, or insinuation, directly or indirectly, defiles the sacred name of the Holy Prophet Mohammed (peace be upon him) shall be punished with death, or imprisonment for life, and shall also be liable to fine."[78] The vagueness of what constitutes defiling the name of the Prophet, how far innuendo or insinuation extend, and also how far "indirectly" extends, all raise serious concerns that the blasphemy law violates the principles of legality. This vagueness leaves the judgment of whether someone has defiled the name of the Prophet to the personal biases of whichever judge an accused comes before. Despite what may seem to the glaring issue of vagueness in the law, the issue has not been raised in the Pakistani courts.[79] Also mysteriously absent from Pakistani courts' jurisprudence on the matter is how the blasphemy law harmonizes with the Pakistani constitution's provisions protecting the freedom of expression.[80]

In *Zaheeruddin v. State*, the Supreme Court in Pakistan held that the Ahmadi sect could not challenge the constitutionality of the blasphemy law by using Article 20 of the Constitution, which guarantees freedom of religion.[81] The Court held that the Ahmadis would interfere with law and order and disrupt the peace and that their practice would interfere with the human rights of others and so they are not protected by Article 20.[82] Some scholars have said that the distinction the Court drew in this case, although not focusing on Article 19 – the free speech article – looks a lot like the "fighting words" doctrine found in US Constitutional Law.[83] However, following that analogy through reveals the frightening prospect that, in Pakistan, the very affirmation of a person's faith as Ahmadi counts as "fighting words". In Pakistan, the statute itself is not phrased in terms of the rights

one was a Muslim before Muhammad was 40 years old). Also, there is the case of Saifullah Khan v. State in the Peshawar High Court which relates to the case of a mentally unstable person being convicted. Ibid. On appeal the court found that it was improper for the Trial court to deny the accused bail. Ibid. The case of Nasir Ahmad v. State was the case in which the Ahmadis were prosecuted for phrases in private wedding cards. Ibid.

77 Ibid. There have been only been three cases in which the judiciary has attempted to read in a *mens rea* requirement to the blasphemy law. Nasir Ahmad v. State was one such case, but the appellate court only looked toward the low level of intent of the accused to determine whether to grant bail. Ibid.

78 Pak. Pen. Code § 295-C.

79 Siddique and Hayat, *supra* note 54, at 374.

80 Ibid. at 376.

81 Ibid. at 375.

82 Ibid.

83 Ibid.

of individuals, but rather toward actions that insult Islam, the concept divorced from its adherents.

The blasphemy laws as rewritten under Zia remain in place today. In the past decade, since the beginning of the War on Terror, the number of blasphemy charges has increased.[84] Amnesty International has declared many of those convicted under the laws to be prisoners of conscience who, along with the lawyers who defend them, are in danger for their lives.[85] Pakistan has been criticized internationally for its blasphemy laws, to which Pakistan has formulated a few discrete responses. First, Pakistan often contends that, under their constitution, Freedoms of Speech and Religion are derogable rights and may be restricted in the interests of public order and morality.[86] The international response to this has been that these rights are not derogable under the international instruments that Pakistan has signed and that they discriminate on the basis of religion.[87] Second, Pakistan has argued that Islamic law supersedes international human rights law.[88] Critics respond that Islamic law, Shar'ia, does not necessitate such a derogation from international human rights principles and that this is only the position of those in power and interpreting Shar'ia in Pakistan today.[89]

This last argument, regarding what Shar'ia law actually requires, leads to another level of analysis of the defamation resolutions. Usually this is the roadblock at which the examination of the issue ends. When people from a particular religious tradition offer up an interpretation of that religion, outsiders rarely delve in and rebut that interpretation using the arguments of that religious tradition. However, if we accept Pakistan's assertion that Islamic law supersedes International law, then we would be driven to accept that Islamic countries are incapable of entering into covenants with the rest of the world, particularly in the form of treaties such as the ICCPR. We have seen what the resolutions say, the way they conflict with rights of expression and religion in the ICCPR. We have seen where these resolutions originate from, including how they may be utilized domestically by the Islamic states pushing them through the UN. Now we will examine whether ultimately they come from Islamic theology, what Islam itself thinks of religious plurality in societies, justice across religious communities and the act of insulting or criticizing the religion. This analysis is important because it will go to the core of whether these two different transnational legal processes can exist harmoniously with one another.

---

84 Dobras, *supra* note 20, at 372.

85 Ibid.

86 Dobras, *supra* note 20, at 360–63.

87 Ibid.

88 Ibid.

89 Ibid.

## Basis In Islamic Theology

M. Cherif Bassiouni has remarked that, in Islam, "[t]here is no division of church and state; there is no division between matters temporal and religious, and between different aspects of law."[90] Some scholars writing on the topic of Islamic blasphemy laws have gone further and, in describing Muslim governments' proclivity toward authoritarianism, have said that "Muslims believe in one God, one prophet and one book, being ruled by one man [is] consistent with their mentality."[91] These blanket characterizations seem to suggest that Islam is incompatible with the demands of a pluralistic international community or democracy and that Islamic countries could not respect freedoms of religion and expression while staying true to their beliefs. Certainly, some leaders of Islamic countries that have strict blasphemy laws have argued exactly that.[92] However, too much depends on Islam's compatibility with these human rights to let the theological debate be settled by the leaders of these states or by those scholars who only work out what Islamic principles may be by looking at these contemporary blasphemy laws. In order to investigate Islam's treatment of these matters we must look at how Shar'ia gets formed and what the primary sources of Islamic law actually say.

Shar'ia, and indeed all Islamic practice, is based on the Koran and the Sunnah.[93] The Koran is the compilation of 114 revelations to the Prophet Mohammed from the Archangel Gabriel and is considered to be the very words of God, Allah – the same god of the other Abrahamic faiths of Judaism, Christianity and others.[94] The Sunnah is a compilation of the acts and practices of the Prophet Mohammed, which are considered to be examples for the Muslim community to follow in all matters of life; the compilation of the Sunnah has a long and complex history and the practices recorded in the Sunnah have different levels of veracity.[95] The ones considered the most reliable as to the Prophet's actual practices have been compiled into collections known as the Hadith.[96] The canonical collections of Hadith are those compiled by Sahih Bukhari and Sahih Muslim in the ninth century during the Abbasid dynasty.[97] Muslim communities have used these sources to decide what the Islamic law, or Shar'ia, is, and the process of personally interpreting and arriving at rightly guided decisions is called Ishtihad.[98] We will now engage

---

90 Blitt, *supra* note 47, at 9.

91 Siddique and Hayat, *supra* note 54, at 318; this statement was in specific reference to how General Zia took control and why religion was important for him to consolidate his power.

92 Dobras, *supra* note 20, at 363.

93 John L. Esposito (ed.), *The Oxford History of Islam*, 118 (Oxford University Press, 1999).

94 Ibid.

95 Ibid. at 132.

96 Ibid.

97 Ibid.

98 Ibid. at 128.

in some Ishtihad of our own with regards to the respect of other religions and plurality within Islam.

Many verses in the Koran speak of diversity within the family of Abrahamic faiths. Christian and Jews are described as "The People of the Book" throughout the Koran and Muslims are commanded to treat them with respect and fairness.[99] This is not all that comforting with respect to international norms requiring the respect of all religions as it excludes all the other faiths.[100] However, in earlier Surahs, those revealed to Mohammed during the early years of Prophecy in Mecca, there are commands to respect religious diversity without requiring monotheism or membership of any of the Abrahamic faiths.[101] Many Surahs, when speaking about respecting religious diversity, say that judgment should be reserved to God with regards to peoples' faiths; these reservations of judgment are aimed not just at Christians and Jews, but at everybody.[102]

The theologian Yusuf al-Qaradawi asserts that "the Muslim regards difference between people in religion to be a fact according to the will of God Almighty, Who bestowed on his creation this form of freedom and choice in action and omission," with reference to Surah 18:29.[103] Qaradawi's finding is in line with many of the aforementioned surahs, which state that religious plurality is a fact of the world, something that God has willed and it is not for Muslims to hold others accountable for their belief or unbelief.[104] However, this stance, that plurality will and must exist, does not mean that non-Muslims will be treated the same as Muslims in Islamic societies. For those guarantees we turn to later Medinan surahs, revealed when Mohammed was the head of a new Muslim community in Medina, which also included many pagan and Jewish tribes; specifically, Surahs 4, 5 and 60 advocate equal justice across communities, regardless of religious identity.[105]

During the Abbasid dynasty in the ninth and tenth centuries, the Islamic Caliphate extended itself across many different nationalities and its population adhered to a variety of different religions.[106] At this time the theologian Al-Tabari wrote extensively on the Medinan surahs' commands of equal justice across all cultural and religious boundaries.[107] In relaying the story of a Christian who was accused of insulting the Prophet Mohammed, Al-Tabari spoke highly of how equitable the law was because the Christian was acquitted owing to the evidentiary rules that apply equally no matter what religion the accused adheres

99 *See e.g.*, Surahs 2:62; 2:213; 4:163; 5:43; and 5:47 (trans. X).

100 Andrew F. March, *Islam and Liberal Citizenship*, 210 (Oxford University Press 2009).

101 Surahs 6:35; 6:149; 10:99–100; 11:118–19; and 109:1–6.

102 22:68–9.

103 March, *supra* note 100, at 214.

104 Surah 22:68–9.

105 Surahs 4:135, 5:8, and 60:7–8.

106 *The Oxford History of Islam*, *supra* note 93, at 340.

107 *March*, *supra* note 100, at 217.

to.[108] However, Al-Tabari did not question the law that prohibited insulting the Prophet.[109] A current Lebanese theologian and expert on the history and the historical exegesis of the Koran, the Ayatollah Fadl Allah, says that, throughout the history of the interpretation of the Koran, there has always been an equality in the way Muslims are supposed to relate to non-Muslims and other Muslims.[110] Thus, throughout the Koran there is evidence of support for current international human rights norms regarding plurality and the freedom of religion. Yet why then is this interpretation not used by the governments of those Islamic states, such as Pakistan, who have blasphemy laws that discriminate on the basis of religion and are pushing international resolutions regarding the defamation of Islam?

The answer, in part, lies in the history of Koranic exegesis since the time of the first Islamic community. Shar'ia is not just the logical analysis of the primary sources of the law upon every application, but rather, like the Common Law, it also consists of the application of the many centuries of intervening precedent and theories of interpretation that have resulted in the practices and laws we see today.[111] During the Umayyad dynasty in the late seventh and early eighth centuries there was a struggle between two rival schools of Koranic interpretation.[112] In the one corner there were the Rationalists, who believed that the Koran was "created," that the revelation was given out at a particular time and that time had passed. They concluded that the text of the Koran should be treated as the laws that God gave to a particular community at a particular time and that only its founding principles should be seen to govern the following Muslim communities.[113] In the other corner were the Traditionalists; they believed that the Koran was "uncreated" or coeternal with God and that its verses were the commands of God for the religious community for all time.[114] Soon the Umayyad Caliphs started taking sides in the debate; at first a couple of Caliphs zealously pursued the proliferation of the Rationalist school and violently punished the Traditionalists.[115] Then the Traditionalists, or the Ulema, gained the favor of subsequent Caliphs and consolidated their power by taking over the judicial functions of the state.[116] The Rationalists were so thoroughly persecuted following the Traditionalist takeover that in the following centuries, up until today, all the remaining schools of Islamic Shar'ia draw primarily from Traditionalist rather than Rationalist origins.[117]

---

108 Ibid.

109 Ibid.

110 Ibid.

111 *Oxford History of Islam*, *supra* note 93, at 130–35.

112 *Reza Aslan, No god but God: The Origins, Evolution, and Future of Islam*, 142 (Random House, 2005).

113 Ibid. at 153.

114 Ibid. at 154.

115 Ibid. at 142.

116 Ibid.

117 Ibid. This is not to say that Rationalism was wiped out from other aspects of Islamic thought. For most of the Abbasid and Ottoman Empires Islamic philosophy was a

There was multiplicity though, even within the Traditionalist schools, and the Ottoman Empire adopted perhaps the most liberal end of the Traditionalist spectrum in the Hanafi school.[118] However in the Arabian Peninsula, which was ruled by Muhammad ibn Saud, founder of the first Saudi state, the Hanbali school was immensely popular.[119] Hanbalism was the most conservative, fundamentalist branch of Traditionalism and it had lain low throughout the Umayyad and Abbasid Dynasties.[120] During the first Saudi State, however, it gained muchpopularity through the works of Muhammad Ibn Abd-al-Wahhab.[121] This school of thought goes by many names – Wahhabism, Hanbalism, Salafism, to name a few – but its key features remain constant throughout: Wahhabism supports reversion back to what al-Wahhab referred to as the founding principles of Islam, which meant to him the literal interpretation of all Koranic verses and the rejection of all innovation or "heresies" that have entered the practice of the faith since the time of Mohammed.[122] In practice this has led to the reading of far more Koranic verses as law than were considered law in different schools of Shar'ia; this has also led to the adoption of many draconian punishments that other schools see presented only as parables or analogies in the Hadith and the Koran.[123] As it is focused on ridding Islam of certain foreign traits and innovations, Wahhabism has sacrificed respect for plurality of interpretations and other faiths in exchange for reviving the purity of Islam. Wahhabism draws upon many of those surahs in the Koran that were meant to rally and support the early Meccan Muslim community in the face of persecution by the ruling pagan tribes at the time;[124] these surahs have a more "fire and brimstone" style of rhetoric in them.

The Saudi Royal family did a great deal to promote Wahhabism and built schools throughout their realm and throughout the greater Islamic world from Afghanistan to the most Western reaches of Ottoman expanse.[125] When the Ottoman Empire collapsed, so did the growth of Hanafism, and the various states that came out of the chaos experienced an influx of Wahhabi scholars into positions of power.[126] Although the spread of Hanbali-inspired Wahhabism is only one part of why Shar'ia has developed that way it has throughout the twentieth century, it

separate and parallel branch of Qur'anic exegesis and interpretation from the Shar'ia. The Islamic philosophers, particularly Ibn Rushd (1126–98) said that, in determining the truths of about the universe and indeed the practice of the religion, the verses of the Qur'an and the Sunnah were subordinate to results of human reason. Ibid. at 153.

118 *Oxford History of Islam*, *supra* note 93, at 124–30.

119 Ibid.

120 Ibid.

121 Ibid.

122 Ibid.

123 Ibid. at 114.

124 Ibid. at 115.

125 Ibid. The Hanafi school is still very popular throughout the Middle East, but with the end of the Ottoman Empire Hanafism lost its greatest source of support. Ibid. at 112.

126 Ibid. at 115.

is important in that it is a transnational phenomenon – similar to the transnational legal processes driving international human rights – and may help to explain the similarities across Islamic states that the West often ascribes to Islam as a whole.[127]

Despite this recent phenomenon, we have seen that there are provisions in the Koran that respect plurality to a great degree. The Koranic provisions for respect of plurality and the equality of justice and relationships across religious lines shows that Islam can be interpreted, not only within the requirements of international human rights instruments, such as the ICCPR, but also in pursuit of many of the same aims as those instruments. However, owing to the calamities and misfortunes of history, the persecution of the Rationalists and the spread of Wahhabism, this cosmopolitan interpretation is not as popular among the Islamic governments as it could or should be.

## A Proposal

In the centuries leading up to the religious defamation resolutions, a debate has been raging throughout the Muslim world about the place of non-Muslims within their communities. In the twenty-first century, with the rise of international institutions and the collapse of centralized power in the Islamic world, the debate has turned to how exactly Islam and Muslims must relate to the rest of the world – especially now that constant immigration and the exchange of ideas are inalterable facts of life. Unfortunately, for the West, most of this debate has been invisible to and walled off from outside involvement. The effect of this has been to limit the representation of what Islam is and what it could be to the example set by those currently in power in Muslim-majority countries, who have direct diplomatic relationships with the rest of the world. Unfortunately, this is exactly the wrong source of information about a religion, especially when it comes to how that religion treats blasphemy and the freedom of expression. Studies of blasphemy laws – in both Muslim and Christian countries – have found that they are used in the same ways as laws against treason and sedition; and they are used to the same effect, namely, to punish dissidents and consolidate the power of the state.[128] We have seen this earlier in how General Zia used acts of Islamization to consolidate his power in Pakistan.

The threat posed by a possible binding international instrument prohibiting the defamation of religions is unprecedented in its scope. It would allow the signatory countries to use the international accords to buttress and expand their own blasphemy laws, and doing it through a UN-approved resolution would provide all the more legitimacy. It would also, in a very real way, further limit the conception of Islam as a religion opposed to pluralism. There is an irony in that the very instruments that are being proposed to protect Islam from claims that the religion is

127 Ibid.

128 Blitt, *supra* note 47, at 9.

incompatible with human rights are in themselves violations of human rights. The further irony, that I find is less apparent to those commenting on the resolutions, is that the reaction *against* the resolutions is filled with exactly the same anti-Islamic rhetoric (claims that these resolutions prove Islam's incompatibility with human rights, etc.) that the resolutions are seeking to remedy, lending credence to the purported reason behind the resolutions in the first place.

The real problem then, it seems, is one of dialectics. There is a need for those who oppose the resolutions and the leaders of the Islamic world to agree on certain definitions and principles upon which their positions are based and be able to make arguments within each others' traditions. Too readily the West seems to adopt what the leaders of the Islamic world say is their religion to be that religion and too readily do those leaders make such self-righteous statements. However, it is not enough to say that we should listen to dissenting voices within the community to get a true picture of Islam, because those dissenting voices have no more right to speak on behalf of a religion than anyone else – including highly suspect state powers. How then do we proceed? The real solution lies at the heart of why the debate in the Islamic community has been walled off from outsiders in the first place; it is not merely because state powers are limiting outside influence, censoring output, etc., but rather it is the larger issue of who gets to comment on religious traditions and who does not. It is my proposal that those who oppose the current interpretations of Islam that are practiced and enforced by the states of the Middle East should pick up the tools of Islamic interpretation themselves and argue those points on the international arena. This policy would, of course, face many challenges.

Believers in a religious framework are less likely to adopt the arguments of "outsiders," those who do not believe but who are nevertheless making arguments about the believers' religion and what is and what is not condoned within it.[129] This reluctance exists because analysis and argument within a religious framework depend not solely on the ability of the speaker to reason through all the relevant texts and precedent, but also on the authority lent to their arguments when the listener knows that the speaker believes in the religion and is not working to subvert or undermine it.[130] One feels manipulated when one is being told to accept things for reasons that the speaker herself does not believe in. Scholars in the field of comparative ethics refer to this type of objection toward commenting within another's tradition as the "religious integrity objection."[131] Another objection to trying to find within the Islamic tradition a respect for plurality is that Islam, and indeed any religion, can be used to support almost anything; religions comprise a whole host of human aims and emotions and they can and have been used to justify every form of government or law that Muslims have ever found themselves

129 March, *supra* note 100, at 67.

130 Ibid.

131 Ibid. at 69.

under.[132] This type of objection has been referred to as a "banality objection," pointing to the banality of using religious texts to justify particular viewpoints and the arbitrary choice of one more agreeable interpretation over another less agreeable one.[133]

My rebuttal to these objections is not particularly advanced other than to say that they ignore many aspects of human nature. As to the religious integrity objection, I would say that, so long as the principle we are seeking to justify within the Islamic tradition, such as the right to freedom of religion, is something we also believe in, then it is not manipulative to use arguments to justify it even though we do not require them for own belief. In other words, so long as we are trying to support a view that we want to apply as equally to ourselves as to our audience and so long as we are using the methods of interpretation that our audience adheres to without distorting them, then our audience is likely to accept our argument as valid and possibly accept it. To argue otherwise would be to suggest that conversation is impossible because the other side is incapable of listening to reason; that would be a terrible form of xenophobia and nothing more. As to the banality objection, I have no answer other than to say that we should advocate whatever interpretation we feel is the most correct and most plausible and hope that it takes root. To those who actually believe in the universal nature of human rights, an interpretation of a religious system that would support that universality would not seem coequal to contrary interpretations or interpretations arbitrarily pursued and thereby not subject to the banality exception – it would be superior to those other interpretations. We should not let cynicism about whether we will succeed or whether our work will be undone by succeeding generations or succeeding interpretations keep us from working for the good now.

## Conclusion

The anti-defamation resolutions represent a fascinating moment in comparative ethics and transnational legal processes. These resolutions explicitly seek to govern dialogues across religious communities on an international arena. They set against each other alleged principles of Islam with those of international human rights and subject them to a vote. The cause of this seeming conflict has been the product of many centuries of debate within the Islamic world and a lack of dialogue between the Islamic world and the West. It is in this moment that we should take up with renewed sincerity an effort to understand and to speak into each others' religious traditions so that the divisions we see in the world may start to mend. Through the blasphemy laws of Pakistan, we have seen the very real consequences of having a lack of dialogue within a society and letting the scope of intercommunity dialogue be governed by the state. It is for these reasons that we should forget the cynicism

132 Ibid. at 70.

133 Ibid.

of those who say that dialogue is not possible and argue against those who say it should not even be allowed.

# Chapter 9
# African Courts and African Values: Harmonizing International Human Rights and Customary Law[1]

Lauren Fielder

## Introduction

Constitutional courts are frequently called on to resolve disputes involving two or more sets of values. In today's increasingly global world, these disputes may center on traditional or cultural values and international human rights norms. This is especially true in Africa, where a strong tradition of custom now intersects with international human rights law obligations. One area in which this tension can be explored is the clash between the right to culture and the right to gender equality. This tension manifests itself in many situations, including disputes over inheritance, child marriage, bride price, divorce law and polygamy. This chapter will examine how international human rights impact African courts faced with the challenge of balancing the right to culture and the right to gender equality. First, the chapter will look at the international human rights obligations to gender equality that most African states have signed up to, then will look at the right to culture and explain how it conflicts with these rights. Next, the legitimacy of the application of international human rights by constitutional courts will be examined. Finally, the chapter will examine traditional African values and explore how courts may be able to incorporate them into their decisions to harmonize the right to culture with international human rights law.

Two qualifications are needed. First, this chapter, when referring to Africa, means sub-Saharan Africa only. Second, as explained below, while there is great value to drawing connections between the cultures present in sub-Saharan Africa, there are also enormous variations, and exceptions can always be found.

---

1 Parts of case analysis in this chapter were discussed in Lauren Fielder, Customary International Law and the Internationalization of African Constitutional Law: A Way Forward in the Protection of Human Rights? in *Zukunft und Recht* 243 (Mannhart, A and Buergi, S, eds., Zurich, Schulthess, 2012) and Lauren Fielder, *African Constitutional Courts and Transitional Justice: A Tool for Reconciling Gender and Customary Law?*, in press (Yarwood, L, ed., Oxford, Routledge 2012).

## The Right to Culture

The right to culture is found in many African constitutions, and can be embodied in different ways. The major cases explored in this chapter illustrate two different approaches to constitutionally protecting the right to culture. For example, sections 30 and 31 of South Africa's constitution give the people the right to participate in the cultural life of their choice and enjoy and participate in their culture, yet these rights may not be exercised in a manner inconsistent with the Bill of Rights.[2] Contrast this with Zimbabwe's constitution, which gives African customary law a special prominence. Violations of certain rights, such as gender equality, arising from the application of customary law are exempt from constitutional scrutiny.[3] In Zimbabwe's constitutional construction, there is a division between customary law and civil law, which prevents the court from deciding whether there has been a breach of certain provisions in the constitution.[4]

The right to culture is embodied in part by African customary law. A customary law may be defined as "a normative order observed by a population, having been formed by regular social behavior and the development of an accompanying sense of obligation."[5] African customary laws cover many aspects of life, particularly personal and family law. These laws in practice tend to mirror and sustain social inequalities, such as gender inequality.[6] In most African societies, there are gross disparities between the power exercised by males and females.[7] This is manifested by, for example, inheritance laws favoring males and marriage laws.

---

2 South Africa's Constitution, section 30 and 31, 1996. In a similar vein, Uganda's Constitution in Article 37 ensures the right to culture and in Article 33 (6) women's rights, prohibiting "laws, cultures, customs or traditions which are against the dignity, welfare or interest of women or which undermine their status." Uganda Constitution, Articles 33 and 37. Ghana's constitution has a comparable approach, which recognizes the right to participate in one's own culture unless these practices "dehumanize of injure the physical or mental well-being of a person." Celestine Nyamu, *Constitutional Barriers to Challenging Women's Equality in Family Property Arrangements*, 94 Am. Soc'y Int'l L. Proc, 289, 289 (2000), *citing* Ghana Constitution, Article 26. Malawi's constitution is similar in this respect; ibid. at 289.

3 Zimbabwe's Constitution, section 23(3)(b) exempts customary laws from its anti-discriminatory provision in section 23(2). Zambia is another example of a state whose constitution affords fewer protections for women. Nyamu, *supra* note 2, at 289.

4 David M. Bigge and Amelie von Briesen, *Conflict in the Zimbabwean Courts: Women's Rights and Indigenous Self-Determination in Magaya v. Magaya*, 13 Harvard H. Rts. J. 289, 294 (2000).

5 Gordon R. Woodman, *A Survey of Customary Laws in Africa in Search of Lessons for the Future*, in The Future of African Customary Law 9, 10 (Fenrich, F. et al., eds, Cambridge, Cambridge University Press, 2011).

6 Ibid. at 12.

7 Ibid.

Yet, customary law has great value and significance for Africans. Culture is an "irreducible social good and an intrinsic feature of individual identity that should not be surrendered in the assimilationist imperative."[8] African customary law is thought to reflect the ancestors' values,[9] making it worthy of respect and deference. It is also a living law, with a flexibility that can meet the needs of a changing society, constantly changing and modernizing. This dynamic feature of customary law potentially makes it an excellent vehicle for the protection of other rights, including women's human rights.[10]

African customary law is a part of an increasingly larger legal order, creating legal pluralism, a situation where a population observes more than one set of laws.[11] This is giving rise to increasing numbers of controversies,[12] where these laws intersect and conflict.

## International Treaty Law Overlay

In many cases, states have signed and ratified international agreements that oblige them to respect certain principles that may influence cases concerning gender equality and the right to custom.[13] The International Convention on Civil and Political Rights (ICCPR)[14] contains general non-discrimination principles in Articles 2(1) and 3, provisions for equality in marriage in Article 23(4)[15] and equal protection of the law guarantees in Article 26. The International Convention on Economic, Social and Cultural Rights (ICSECR)[16] contains non-discrimination provisions in Articles 2 and 3 that nearly mirror those found in the ICCPR. The Convention on

8 Michelle A. McKinley, *Cultural Culprits*, 24 Berkeley J. Gender L. & Just. 91, 94 (2009).

9 Fatou K. Camara, *From Contemporary African Customary Laws to Indigenous African Law: Identifying Ancient African Human Rights and Good Governance Sensitive Principles, a Tool to Promote Culturally Meaningful Socio-Legal Reforms*, in The Future of African Customary Law 494, 494 (Fenrich, J. et al., eds, 2011).

10 See also Nyamu, *supra* note 2, at 393.

11 Woodman, *supra* note 5, at 18.

12 Abdulmumini A. Oba, *The Future of Customary Law in Africa*, in The Future of African Customary Law 58, 65 (Fenrich, J. et al., eds, 2011).

13 States also have provisions in their constitutions guaranteeing the right to gender equality.

14 *Opened for signature* 16 December 1966, Article 2(1), 999 U.N.T.S. 171, *reprinted in* 6 I.L.M. 368 (1967).

15 States parties to the present Covenant shall take appropriate steps to ensure equality of rights and responsibilities of spouses as to marriage, during marriage and at its dissolution. In the case of dissolution, provision shall be made for the necessary protection of any children.

16 933 U.N.T.S. 3, G.A. Res. 2200A (XXI), U.N. Doc. A/6316 (16 December 1966).

the Rights of the Child (CRC)[17] also contains an anti-discrimination provision in Article 2(1) that prohibits gender discrimination against female children.

The Convention on the Eradication of Discrimination Against Women (CEDAW)[18] is a treaty that is focused on the equality of women and has been a successful tool for the realization of women's rights around the world.[19] One very important feature of CEDAW is that it holds governments directly responsible for what happens in the private sector.[20] This is an important departure from earlier treaties that address discrimination against women. It is also noteworthy in that it incorporates affirmative action provisions.[21] Some highly relevant provisions that deal with the tension addressed in this paper are the following: its definition of discrimination in Article 1, its requirement that harmful cultural practices be modified in Article 5,[22] a provision to eliminate discrimination in the economic and the social arenaa found in Article 13, a section affording special protections for rural women in Article 14, equal protection guarantees in Article 15 and far-reaching provisions on equality and family life in Article 16. In addition, the treaty body established by the convention has issued important recommendations with

---

17 28 I.L.M. 1448 (20 November 1989).

18 *Opened for signature* 1 March 1980, Articles 2, 2(e), 2(f), 1249 U.N.T.S. 14, *reprinted in* 19 I.L.M. 33 (1980).

19 Johanna Bond, *Gender, Discourse, and Customary Law in Africa*, 83 S. Cal. L. Rev. 509, 524 (2010).

20 Christine Chinkin, *Gender Mainstreaming in Legal and Constitutional Affairs: A Reference Manual for Governments and Other Stakeholders, Commonwealth Secretariat* 28–29 (2001), *available at* http://www.genderandtrade.org/shared_asp_files/uploadedfiles/%7B7712A695-36F7-4302-B422-B7AB9E05B843%7D_LegalConstitutionalAffairs.pdf. One major substantive problem with the enforcement of CEDAW is the fact that large numbers of states added reservations to their ratifications, even core provisions, often to shield family law, customary and/or religious law from their obligations. Bond, *Gender*, *supra* note 19, at 527, noting that approximately 40 states have made roughly 105 reservations to important treaty provisions. Ibid. at note 99, *citing* Anne F. Bayefsky, *General Approaches to the Domestic Application of Women's International Human Rights Law*, in Human Rights of Women: National and International Perspectives 351, 352 (Cook R.J., ed., Philadelphia, PA, University of Pennsylvania Press, 1994).

21 Bond, *supra* note 19, at 524, *citing* Article 4, calling for temporary measures aimed at achieving de facto equality. Ibid. at note 83.

22 Article 5:

> States Parties shall take all appropriate measures:
> (a) To modify the social and cultural patterns of conduct of men and women, with a view to achieving the elimination of prejudices and customary and all other practices which are based on the idea of the inferiority or the superiority of either of the sexes or on stereotyped roles for men and women;
> (b) To ensure that family education includes a proper understanding of maternity as a social function and the recognition of the common responsibility of men and women in the upbringing and development of their children, it being understood that the interest of the children is the primordial consideration in all cases.

regard to gender equality. For example, General Recommendation 21 addresses equality in marriage and provides that "[w]hatever form [the family] takes, and whatever the legal system, religion, custom or tradition within the country, the treatment of women in the family both at law and in private must accord with the principles of equality and justice for all people."[23]

In addition to the above-mentioned international treaties, there are several important regional treaties to consider. The African Charter on Human and People's Rights (African Charter)[24] "embodies a conscious effort to filter traditional human rights through an African lens."[25] This convention deals with gender discrimination in Article 18(3) and incorporates rules set forth in other treaties.[26] The Protocol to the African Charter on Human and Peoples' Rights on the Rights of Women in Africa (African Women's Protocol) is another treaty with enormously important provisions for gender equality.[27] This treaty, which was the result of a working group on African women's rights, "embodies a progressive vision of women's rights on the continent, one which African women played a significant role in creating."[28] Article 2 calls for an end to discrimination and includes a requirement that states include provisions in their constitutions and legislation to give effect to this requirement. Similar to the provision found in CEDAW, Article 2(2) mandates that social and cultural practices that are harmful or discriminatory to women must be eliminated.[29] Article 6 ensures that women enjoy equality in marriage, and Article 17 gives women the right to participate in the formation of culture.[30] Article

---

23 Bond, *supra* note 19, at 526, *citing* U.N. Comm. on Elimination of Discrimination Against Women, General Recommendation No. 21, para. 13 (1994).

24 (27 June 1981), Article 8, O.A.U. Doc. CAB/LEG/67/3/Rev. 5, *reprinted in* 21 I.L.M. 58 (1982).

25 Bond, *supra* note 19, at 535.

26 "The State shall ensure the elimination of every discrimination against women and also ensure the protection of the rights of the woman and the child as stipulated in international declarations and conventions" (27 June 1981), Article 18, O.A.U. Doc. CAB/LEG/67/3/Rev. 5, *reprinted in* 21 I.L.M. 58 (1982).

27 11 July 2003, OAU Doc. CAB/LEG/66.6.

28 Bond, *supra* note 19, at 540.

29 Article 2(2):

> States Parties shall commit themselves to modify the social and cultural patterns of conduct of women and men through public education, information, education and communication strategies, with a view to achieving the elimination of harmful cultural and traditional practices and all other practices which are based on the idea of the inferiority or the superiority of either of the sexes, or on stereotyped roles for women and men.

30 Article 17 Right to Positive Cultural Context:

> 1. Women shall have the right to live in a positive cultural context and to participate at all levels in the determination of cultural policies.
> 2. States Parties shall take all appropriate measures to enhance the participation of women in the formulation of cultural policies at all levels.

20 protects widows (who have been in many cases subject to harmful practices such as cleansing rituals)[31] and Article 21 specifies that widows and daughters are entitled to an equitable share of property. Finally, the African Charter on the Rights and Welfare of the Child (African Children's Charter) provides special anti-discrimination protection for female children in Article 3.[32]

## Concern with Human Rights – Legitimacy of International Human Rights in Africa

When African courts apply international human rights law in their decisions, it may cause legitimacy problems, even when the state is obligated to do so under its treaty requirements. This is problematic because the legitimacy of the courts is of vital concern. African courts have suffered greatly from legitimacy problems and dysfunctional constitutional processes, causing instability of the government. This instability has far-reaching consequences that can even threaten peace and security.[33]

Legitimacy problems stem, in part, from the role that the courts played in colonial administration.[34] Post independence, legitimacy problems have arisen from the fact that the African courts have at times perpetuated the abuses of the government.[35] This colonial and post-colonial history led to the public perception of the "judicial system as corrupt and biased in favor of the powerful, and the result is an African public that is both distrustful of judicial power and doubtful of the relevance of courts to the lives of the ordinary citizen."[36] It is not just citizens

---

31 Bond, *supra* note 19, at 545.

32 African Charter on the Rights and Welfare of the Child, adopted July 1990 (entered into force 29 November 1999) OAU Doc. CAB/LEG/24.9/49 (1990).

33 Charles Manga Fombad, *Constitutional Reforms and Constitutionalism in Africa: Reflections on Some Current Challenges and Future Prospects*, 59 Buff. L. Rev. 1007, 1094 (2011), listing the examples of the recent situations in the Ivory Coast, Sudan, the Democratic Republic of the Congo, Somalia, Kenya and Zimbabwe. Ibid. Conversely, Constitutionalism stabilizes governments. Ibid. at 1108.

34 H. Kwasi Prempeh, *Marbury in Africa: Judicial Review and the Challenge of Constitutionalism in Contemporary Africa*, 80 Tul. L. Rev. 1239, 1240 (2005–2006).

35 For example, for South Africa, D.M. Davis, *Constitutional Borrowing: The Influence of Legal Culture and Local History in the Reconstitution of Comparative Influence: The South African Experience*, 1 Int'l J. Const. L. 181, 182 (2003), *stating that*, "[t]he judiciary in colonial Africa was, in fact, the handmaiden of the colonial administration." Ibid.

36 Prempeh, *supra* note 34, at 1300. This mistrust is not limited to the courts, however. Law is often synonymous with the misuse of power in Africa. Werner Menski, Comparative Law in a Global Context 25 (2nd edn, Cambridge, Cambridge University Press, 2006).

who have criticized courts in Africa. When courts have attempted to exercise judicial review, they have encountered ferocious opposition from governments.[37]

As discussed above, most African states have ratified the major human rights treaties, such as the ICCPR, ICSECR and CEDAW, and regional human rights treaties, which obligate state parties to avoid gender discrimination.[38] What is problematic from a legitimacy perspective about courts basing judgments on these treaty obligations is that international human rights are seen to be a Western, imperialistic construct. For example:

> African courts have demonstrated a particular unwillingness to privilege international understandings of human rights over local customary practices, due in part to domestic political restrictions, the potential appearance of disrespect for local traditions and "African Values" and the fear of perceived legal impositions from the west.[39]

There is also the fear that international human rights alter culture,[40] leading to the widespread negative perception of human rights in Africa, and a fear that human rights will drown out the voices of Africa.[41] In addition, the civilizing mission approach of colonization makes it hard for some contemporary Africans to accept human rights.[42] For example, a leading African expert on human rights and traditional government, Manfred Hinz, writes that:

> [i]n training programmes of the Human Rights and Documentation Centre at the University of Namibia, we have always paid special attention to the perception of human rights by those who attended our programmes. Some of these perceptions we had to listen to were: human rights are western concepts; human rights interfere with the values of our culture; human rights are there to protect criminals; human

---

37 G. Devensih, *The Independence and Effectiveness of Constitutional Courts in Sub-Saharan Africa: The South African Experience*, 6 U. Botswana L.J. 3, 5 (2007). Former South African President Paul Kruger described judicial review as "a principle invented by the devil." Ibid.

38 Vice President Akua Kuenyehia, *Women, Marriage, and Intestate Succession in the Context of Legal Pluralism in Africa*, 40 U.C. Davis L. Rev. 385, 401 (2006). See also the section "International Treaty Law Overlay", *supra.*

39 Valerie Knobelsdorf, *Zimbabwe's Magaya Decision Revisited: Women's Rights and Land Succession in the International Context*, 15 Colum. J. Gender & L. 749, 790 (2006), *citing* footnotes 182 and 183.

40 Makau Wa Mutua, *The Politics of Human Rights: Beyond the Abolitionist Paradigm in Africa*, 17 Mich. J. Int'l L. 591, 591 (1996).

41 Menski, *supra* note 36, at 380.

42 Ibid. at 25, discussing that colonization is a barrier to the acceptance of human rights.

> rights prevent us from doing the job. Human rights are, so it has been said by a distinguished and well-respected traditional leader, monsters.[43]

Human rights have an implication for African law as well. African law, especially African customary law, has been denied the validity of its culture-specific legal norms on the basis of human rights.[44] This is one element of a generalized disrespect for African law. Skepticism about the existence of an African jurisprudence stems from the mistaken belief that African customary law is only custom and not law at all.[45] This can be explained by Eurocentricism and the lack of understanding about African ideas about law.[46] It is important to understand that Africans have a longstanding understanding of natural justice, the law and legal systems despite the fact that indigenous practice may have not developed in abstract theoretical terms.[47] African customary law has the same functional capacity as other law.[48]

Because of this skepticism about international human rights law, it is understandable that African courts are wary of using it in their decisions. One such example of a court's hesitance to apply international human rights is the *Magaya* decision from Zimbabwe.[49] The *Magaya* case concerned a dispute over an estate. In this case, a local court appointed Venia Magaya heir to her father's estate. Ms Magaya's younger half-brother, Nakayi Magaya, appealed the case on the grounds that African customary law prohibits a woman from inheriting property when there is a man in the family entitled to claim it. The appellate court was persuaded by this agreement and reversed Ms Magaya's heirship. Nakayi Magaya promptly removed Ms Magaya from the home she had lived in for over 20 years and moved her into a one-room shack in a neighbor's yard. He sold the house and used to proceeds to buy himself a car. Ms Magaya appealed to the Supreme Court of Zimbabwe, claiming that her constitutional right to equality was breached.[50] The Supreme Court upheld the appellate court's decision on the grounds that violations of equality arising from the application of customary law are exempt from constitutional scrutiny.[51] The Court explained that, in Zimbabwe's

---

43 Ibid. at 13, *quoting* Manfred O. Hinz, *Jurisprudence and Anthropology*, Vol. 26 Nos 3–4, Anthropology Southern Africa 114, 114 (2003).

44 Menski, *supra* note 36, at 381.

45 Clever Mapaure, *Reinvigorating African Values for SADC: The Relevance of Traditional African Philosophy of Law in a Globalising World of Competing Perspectives*, 1 SADC L J 149, 153 (2011), *stating that* "the thrust of the theory, therefore, is that, even if Africans had indigenous systems of social control, such systems substantially lacked any trace of legality, legal concepts, or legal elements." Ibid.

46 Ibid. at 154.

47 Ibid. at 154.

48 Ibid. at 154.

49 *Magaya v. Magaya*, (1999) 3 L.R.C. 35 (Zimb. Sup. Ct.).

50 Zimbabwe's constitution, section 23(2) prohibits discrimination on the basis of sex.

51 Zimbabwe's constitution, section 23(3)(b) exempts customary laws from its anti-discriminatory provision in section 23(2).

constitutional construction, there is a division between customary law and civil law, which prevented the court from deciding whether there had been a breach of the anti-discrimination provisions in the constitution.[52] In so holding, the court refused to consider case-specific concerns and international human rights law obligations, even though Ms Magaya argued that "the case struck at the heart of her internationally recognized human rights, and that denying her heirship would run contrary to basic principles of gender equality and individual rights."[53] The Court's decision focused on the nature of African society and declined to consider comparative constitutional decisions and regional and international agreements, which arguably would have outweighed these cultural considerations.[54]

This decision came despite the fact that the Chief Justice of the Zimbabwe had stated in another case in close temporal proximity to the Magaya decision that "judiciaries should make a greater conscious effort towards the protection and active enforcement of fundamental human rights and freedoms, and should always endeavor, wherever possible, to construe domestic legislation so that it conforms with the developing international jurisprudence of human rights."[55] However, the approach taken by the court is because section 111B of Zimbabwe's constitution explains that treaties do not have effect as domestic law unless they have been incorporated into domestic law by an act of parliament.[56]

## Harmonizing African Culture and International Human Rights

Are human rights and African culture incompatible? A better preliminary question would be are "international" human rights and African culture incompatible? Certainly, a study of traditional African values shows a widespread and deeply entrenched set of rights. Courts can and should turn to these values in resolving issues involving the application of international human rights. In doing so, courts may be able to harmonize custom and customary law with international human

---

52 Bigge and von Briesen, *supra* note 4, at 294.

53 Knobelsdorf, *supra* note 39, at 752 (2006).

54 Ibid. For example, Zimbabwe is party to numerous international human rights treaties, including CEDAW. Ibid. at 787.

55 Fareda Banda, *Global Standards: Local Values*, 17 Int'l J. L. Pol'y & Fam. 1, 11 (2010), *citing* Zimnat Insurance Co Ltd v. Chawanda (1990) ZLR 143, 154.

56 Constitution of Zimbabwe , *stating that*:

> 111B Effect of international conventions etc.
>
> (1) Except as otherwise provided by this Constitution or by or under an Act of Parliament, any convention, treaty or agreement acceded to, concluded or executed by or under the authority of the President with one or more foreign states or governments or international organizations –
>
> (a) shall be subject to approval by Parliament; and
>
> (b) shall not form part of the law of Zimbabwe unless it has been incorporated into the law by or under an Act of Parliament.

rights law. This is not unlike the principle present in many legal systems that deals with what to do when there is a conflict between domestic legislation and international law. This principle of statutory construction calls for interpretation of the domestic legislation in a way that does not conflict with the international law if there is more than one reading of the domestic legislation.[57] Applying this approach to the situation at hand, courts should choose a construction of African customary law that does not conflict with international law, while at the same time looking for ways to rest their decisions on a foundation that is African. African law, encompassing African values, "is a workable system which has better attributes, relatively, for African cultures."[58]

### *African Values*

There are similar values across African communities. "[I]n the comparative sense, a whole lot of similarities are clearly and interestingly exhibited among . . . different societies."[59] There has been and continue to be cultural themes and patterns that are unique to and similar among peoples in Africa.[60] In addition, there are categories and processes of thought that are unique to Africa.[61] Different states "are linked by shared values that are fundamental features of African identity and culture."[62] A brief and non-exhaustive list of several prominent values are set out below.

*Dignity* The concept of human dignity is of paramount importance among African values.[63] This covers the sacredness of human life and respect for humanity.[64] Members of the community are viewed as brothers and sisters whose lives should be preserved and protected.[65] Dignity is a cornerstone of many African constitutional protections and features prominently in the African Charter on Human and Peoples' Rights. Article 5 of the African Charter provides that "[e] very individual shall have the right to the respect of the dignity inherent in a human

57 For example, in US law, this is known as the "Charming Betsey Cannon."

58 Mapaure, *supra* note 45, at 154.

59 William Idowu, *Law, Morality and the African Cultural Heritage: The Jurisprudential Significance of the Ogboni Institution*, 14(2) Nordic J of African Studies 175, 180–81 (2005).

60 James E. Lassiter, *African Culture and Personality: Bad Social Science, Effective Social Activism, or a Call to Reinvent Ethnology?*, 3(2) African Studies Quarterly 1, 1 (1999).

61 Ibid. at 2.

62 Ibid. at 2, *citing* J. M. Nysani, The African Psyche 56–7 (1997).

63 Benson O. Igboin, *Colonialism and African Cultural Values*, 3(6) African Journal of History and Culture 96, 99 (2011).

64 Ibid.

65 Ibid.

being and to the recognition of his legal status."[66] Other rights are seen to flow from this right to dignity: "[a]ll forms of exploitation and degradation of man, particularly slavery, slave trade, torture, cruel, inhuman or degrading punishment and treatment shall be prohibited."[67]

*Community orientation* Because 80 percent of sub-Saharan Africans live in rural areas, the communal lifestyle has great meaning and value.[68] For Africans, security and value come from personal identification with the community.[69] The rationale for this idea is that the community is permanent while the individual is transitory.[70] Communal values call for the appreciation of the community and guide social interaction toward a common goal.[71] "[T]he pursuit of human dignity is not concerned with vindicating the right of any individual against the world."[72] There is the idea of brotherhood that goes beyond a Western conceptualization and calls for a patriotic response and disposition towards each other.[73] Therefore, what happens to one happens to the community.[74]

The family is the essential element of social life in Africa, whose cohesion is fundamental to the unity and functioning of the community.[75] The nuclear family is part of the extended family, with all members having rights and duties to the others.[76] In some African languages, there exist no words for extended family members, such as aunts, uncles and cousins.[77] Marriage is seen as very important as it is seen to be a connection between two extended families.[78]

*Concept of duties* African values emphasize concepts of duty and service.[79] Correspondingly, rights are not seen as entitlements free of corresponding duties. This is reflected in Articles 27–29 of the African Charter of Human and Peoples' Rights. Article 27 outlines the broad principle that every person has duties towards

66 (27 June 1981), Article 5, O.A.U. Doc. CAB/LEG/67/3/Rev. 5, *reprinted in* 21 I.L.M. 58 (1982).

67 Ibid.

68 Josiah A.M. Cobbah, *African Values and the Human Rights Debate: An African Perspective*, 9(3) Human Rights Quarterly 309, 327 (1987).

69 Macaulay A. Kanu, The Indispensability of the Basic Social Values in African Traditions: A Philosophical Appraisal, at 154, available at http://www.ajol.info/index.php/og/article/viewFile/57930/46296

70 Ibid.

71 Igboin, *supra* note 63, at 99.

72 Cobbah, *supra* note 68, at 322.

73 Igboin, *supra* note 63, at 99.

74 Ibid. at 99.

75 Ibid. at 100.

76 Ibid.

77 Kanu, *supra* note 69, at 156.

78 Ibid.

79 Idowu, *supra* note 59, at 181.

the family, society, state and international community and mandates that individual rights must be exercised with due regard for the rights of others.[80] Article 28 requires that "[e]very individual shall have the duty to respect and consider his fellow beings without discrimination, and to maintain relations aimed at promoting, safeguarding and reinforcing mutual respect and tolerance."[81] Finally, Article 29 sets out a more detailed list of duties toward the family, the community, national solidarity and African unity.[82]

There are four main principles underlying African duties: respect, restraint, responsibility and reciprocity.[83] Respect means respect for the community, family and elders.[84] The respect is manifested in greetings and other gestures that recognize seniority and hierarchy.[85] This seniority bears no relation to other attributes.[86] This respect for authority and elders smoothens social relations in African society.[87] The elders are seen to be the repository of communal wisdom and, thus, the leaders of the community.[88] The practical effect of this is that elders have the role of safeguarding customs and traditions.[89] The duty of restraint encompasses sacrifices that one makes for the family and community and world at large. It means that personal freedom is limited by the requirements of the group.[90] This principal facilitates communalism within the family and wider society.[91] Responsibility means that every person is responsible for others in the family and community. It provides a network of security with its imposition of burdens of obligations.[92] All who are capable of working must do so.[93] Included in this duty is an "ethics of care," which ties obligation to an expected relationship of care and concern between citizens that is distinct from a vertically imposed obligation of the state.[94] Reciprocity means that acts of generosity will be reciprocated in the

80 (27 June 1981), Article 27, O.A.U. Doc. CAB/LEG/67/3/Rev. 5, *reprinted in* 21 I.L.M. 58 (1982).

81 (27 June 1981), Article 28, O.A.U. Doc. CAB/LEG/67/3/Rev. 5, *reprinted in* 21 I.L.M. 58 (1982).

82 (27 June 1981), Article 29, O.A.U. Doc. CAB/LEG/67/3/Rev. 5, *reprinted in* 21 I.L.M. 58 (1982).

83 Cobbah, *supra* note 68, at 321.

84 Ibid.

85 Ibid.

86 Ibid.

87 Kanu, *supra* note 69, at 155.

88 Ibid. at 156.

89 Ibid.

90 Cobbah, *supra* note 68, at 321.

91 Ibid.

92 Ibid. at 322. See also Kanu, *supra* note 69, at 154.

93 Kanu, *supra* note 69, at 154.

94 Nkiruka Ahiauzu, *African Jurisprudence as Particularist Jurisprudence*, available at www.chinalawsociety.com.

long and short term.[95] Therefore, "entitlements and obligations form the very basis of the kinship system."[96] This includes the value of hospitality, very important in African society, which mandates sharing with others who are in need.[97]

*Ubuntu – humanity towards others* Ubuntu is a concept that encompasses many of the above-described African values. The term has many connotations and cultural implications.[98] It is a jurisprudential concept that means "humanity towards others."[99] Ubuntu emphasizes the value of the life of others and human dignity and respect,[100] and encompasses the idea of reconciliation.[101] It recognizes the interconnectedness of people to each other and their community.[102] The concept is also a "moral and political exhortation and an expression of hope for a better future."[103]

Ubuntu has an important place in African law as it has been formally adopted into the domestic law of a state.[104] The South African Interim Constitution of 1993 was the first official document to incorporate the term.[105] It was included in the epilogue to the Constitution, which provided a basis for amnesty and the Truth and Reconciliation Committee.[106] Ubuntu is now seen in South Africa as an "active and central" constitutional principle.[107] It has been mentioned in many South African cases, at all levels of the judiciary, notably in the famous case prohibiting the death penalty, *S v Makwanyane*.[108] In this case, the Court defined Ubuntu as the following:

> Generally, *ubuntu* translates as humaneness. In its most fundamental sense, it translates as *personhood* and *morality*. Metaphorically, it expresses itself in *umuntu ngumuntu ngabantu,* describing the significance of group solidarity on survival issues so central to the survival of communities. While it envelops the key values of group solidarity, compassion, respect, human dignity, conformity

95 Cobbah, *supra* note 68, at 322.
96 Ibid.
97 Kanu, *supra* note 69, at 155.
98 T.W. Bennett, *Ubuntu: An African Equity*, 14(4) PER/PELJ 30, 30 (2011).
99 Mapaure, *supra* note 45, at 160.
100 Ibid.
101 Ibid.
102 Ibid.
103 Ibid. at 161.
104 Bennett, *supra* note 98, at 30.
105 Ibid. at 32.
106 Drucilla Cornell and Nyoko Muvangua, Law in the uBuntu of South Africa 15, *available at* http://www.isthisseattaken.co.za/pdf/Papers_Cornell_Muvangua.pdf. Cornell and Muyangua point out that the direct reference to Ubuntu was left out of the permanent South African Constitution, except for a "shadow," where para. 22 of Schedule 6 preserves the Epilogue to the Interim Constitution. Ibid.
107 Ibid. at 8.
108 *S v Makwanyane & Another* 1995 (6) BCLR 665 (CC).

> to basic norms and collective unity, in its fundamental sense it denotes humanity and morality. Its spirit emphasises respect for human dignity, marking a shift from confrontation to conciliation.[109]

*Case Illustrating the Use of African Values in Tension Between Right to Culture and Right to Gender Equality*

*Bhe v. Magistrate* is actually a set of companion cases that concerned African customary inheritance laws that favored men. In its analysis of the issues presented in these cases, the South African Constitutional Court discussed the positive aspects of customary law as a dynamic system of law that is constantly evolving to meet the changing circumstances of the community. [110] In doing so, the Court emphasized its continuing commitment to the preservation and advancement of customary law in South Africa.[111] The Court made reference to African values, specifically Ubuntu, the dominant value in African traditional culture, which calls for communality, consensus building and the inter-dependence of members of the community.[112] The Court explained that the obligation to care for family members is "vital and fundamental" in the African social system, implicating another important African value.[113] The Court emphasized that, despite culture's important role in society, customary law must always be consistent with the Constitution.[114] The Court then explained that African women and descendants who are not first-born males are a vulnerable group and that the application of the customary law system of primogeniture violates their rights to equality and dignity.[115] This, reasoned the Court, is because primogeniture excludes women from inheritance, and is based on a system of patriarchy that keeps women in a position of subservience and subordination.[116]

---

109 Ibid. at 15, *quoting S v Makwanyane & Another* 1995 (6) BCLR 665 (CC) at para. 308.

110 Christa Rautenbach, Willemien du Plessis and Gerrit Peinaar, *Is Primogeniture Extinct Like the Dodo, or is There Any Prospect of it Rising From the Ashes? Comments on the Evolution of Customary Succession Laws in South Africa*, 22 S. Afr. J. on Hum. Rts 99 (2006).

111 Johanna E. Bond, *Constitutional Exclusion and Gender in Commonwealth Africa*, 31 Fordham Int'l L.J. 289, 338 (2008), and *Bhe*, pp. 24–5, para. 41.

112 *Bhe v. Magistrate, Khayelitsha* 2005 (1) BCLR 28, 1(CC). *See discussion above*, in the section "Concept of duties".

113 Rautenbach, et al., *supra* note 110, at 99, and *Bhe v. Magistrate, Khayelitsha* 2005 (1) BCLR 28, para. 45 (CC).

114 *Bhe* at 24–5, para. 41.

115 *Bhe* at 56, paras 91–2. Note that dignity is another important traditional African value.

116 *Bhe* at 49, para. 78.

In deciding the case, the Court made reference to international and comparative law, stating that the South African Constitution is not alone in the emphasis it places on the right to equality.

The right is cherished in the constitutions and the jurisprudence of many open and democratic societies. A number of international instruments, to which South Africa is a party, also underscore the need to protect the rights of women, and to abolish all laws that discriminate against them as well as to eliminate any racial discrimination in our society.[117]

In addition, the Court referred to provisions of the Convention on the Rights of the Child, the ICCPR and the African Charter on the Rights and Welfare of the Child in confirmation of the 'best interests of the child principle' in the South African Constitution.[118] After carefully balancing the rights to equality and custom,[119] the Court held that the primogeniture rule applied in customary law is inconsistent with the South African Constitution's guarantee of equality.[120]

*Dialogue Between African Courts*

If the first step is for courts to increasingly use African values to interpret international human rights, an important second step is for African courts to engage in a comparative dialogue with each other to develop an internationalization of African constitutional law that incorporates these African values. The effects of this dialogue would be an emerging African jurisprudence and an influence on the further development of international human rights law in the world at large. Because there are great similarities between African societies, and because there are problems in Africa that are different from problems faced in other areas of the world, courts should not have to reinvent the wheel when hearing cases involving culture and international human rights. There is great value in developing a comparative jurisprudence in which African courts borrow from each other horizontally. The reality is that African courts rarely borrow from each other with the exception of receiving law from the South African Constitutional Court. In addition, the South African Constitutional Court has done little to embrace African jurisprudence,[121] rarely citing cases from other African courts or regional judicial tribunals.[122] This is despite several important decisions citing the need for bringing

117 *Bhe* at 31.

118 Frans Viljoen, International Human Rights Law in Africa 559 (2007), *citing Bhe v. Magistrate, Khayelitsha* 2005 (1) BCLR 1 (CC).

119 *Bhe* at 45, para. 70.

120 *Bhe* at 64, para. 109.

121 Davis, *supra* note 35, at 194.

122 Charles Manga Fombad, *Internationalization of Constitutional Law and Constitutionalism in Africa*, Am. J. Comp. L., at 28, in press.

traditional African jurisprudence to matters before the court.[123] While it seems that limited access to decisions would be a barrier to borrowing, availability of these decisions is becoming less and less of an issue, since decisions of many courts are available on the internet.[124] Further empirical research is needed to collect and analyze African court cases that make reference to African principles.

## Conclusion

Globalization and the Western construction of international human rights law "are living realities which Africa cannot ignore."[125] International human rights law developed for most of its history without southern voices. Yet, African states have largely obligated themselves to uphold this body of law, including equality for women as embodied in many international human rights treaties. This equality is infringed in many circumstances where customary law governs the relationship between men and women. Courts must intervene to ensure that women can exercise their rights. African courts can add legitimacy to their decisions when balancing the right to culture and the right to gender equality by interpreting their international human rights obligations in the light of long-standing African values. Courts can borrow from the decisions of other state constitutional courts in making this interpretation, building a pan-African jurisprudence that will further stabilize constitutionalism in the region and finally give Africa a place at the table in the development of global human rights law.

123 Davis, *supra* note 35, at 194, *citing S v Makwanyane & Another* 1995 (6) BCLR 665 (CC).

124 Fombad, *supra* note 122 at footnote 90. Fombad points out that free access to decisions from the high courts of Angola, Botswana, Lesotho, Kenya, Madagascar, Malawi, Mauritius, Mozambique, Namibia, Seychelles, South Africa, Swaziland, Tanzania, Uganda, Zambia and Zimbabwe is available through the Southern African Legal Information Institute (SAFLII); http://www.saflii.org. The same organization provides access to decisions of COMESA, the East African Court of Appeal, the East African Court of Justice and the SADC Tribunal. Ibid.

125 Maupare, *supra* note 45, at 151.

## Chapter 10

# Exercising Religious Rights in European Classrooms: Value Conflicts between the National, the Supranational and the Transnational

Kyriaki Topidi

### Introduction: Theorizing Conflicts of Values in Religious Legal Claims

"Conflicts of values are an intrinsic part of human life and there is no single right answer in choosing between them."[1] Religion and the exercise of the freedom of belief are most of the time presented in the light of a value conflict in multicultural settings. This happens because cultural identity, of which religious belief is an integral part, remains "contested, temporal and emergent."[2] Until recently, the most debated value-oriented controversies concerned ethnic and cultural identities.[3] Religion was not part of these controversies, as it was perceived as a *forum internum* matter.

The separation of religion from the state has been the predominant normative paradigm in the European continent when attempting to pre-empt or respond to such conflicts. The European multicultural state has sought to create and protect the "neutral" public sphere by showing political and judicial commitment to a scheme of individual rights that includes freedom of religion. Whenever religious claims surface, there are, according to Koenig, three basic normative strategies in order to pursue them: the first relies on the right to equality (and by extension non-discrimination); the second is based on the right to difference and is articulated in the form of claims for exemption; and the third one engages with radical struggles for recognition, but is largely beyond the scope of this chapter.[4] For example, a claim by schoolgirls of the right to wear a headscarf in public schools becomes

1 Peter G. Danchin, "Of Prophets and Proselytes: Freedom of Religion and the Conflict of Rights in International Law," 49 *Harv. Int'l L.J.* 249, 2008 at 253.

2 Andrea Büchler, *Islamic Law in Europe?*, Ashgate, Farnham, 2011, at 7.

3 Matthias Koenig, "How Nations-States Respond to Religious Diversity," in Bramadat P. and Koenig M. (eds), *International Migration and the Governance of Religious Diversity*, McGill–Queen's University Press, Montreal, 2009, 293–322, at 298.

4 Ibid., at 300.

problematic insofar as it is perceived as a 'contestation of secular state authority' in the context of Koenig's first strategy. Claims for partial recognition of autonomous legal systems leading to multireligious jurisdiction and hence to legal pluralism, pose a challenge at an even higher degree to statehood and are therefore deemed highly contested for the same reason.[5] Unsurprisingly, legal pluralism has been and remains heavily critiqued in Europe.

There are nevertheless many and quite varied theories and approaches to legal pluralism per se in the context of the exercise of religious rights. Legal pluralism as a marker of the "presence of more than one legal order in the same social field"[6] confirms the transnationalization of law as combined with the effects of migration in the European continent.[7] At the very least, legal pluralism conceptually functions as a "product" emanating from diverse sources of law. Menski identifies four such sources: the state, society, religion/ethics/morality and international human rights law.[8] The multiplicity of legal understandings, norms and aspirations inevitably leads to culture-based conflicts, which Koenig's first strategy cannot address.[9] In essence, the choice of a given socio-legal environment is likely to produce variable legal outcomes for the same recurring religious rights conflicts. This is a reality that the right to equality on its own cannot rectify legally, socially or politically.

An alternative, 'third way' solution is what Danchin labels accommodative *value pluralism*.[10] This option shifts the normative underpinning from a clearly non-discrimination basis to one closer to collective rights claims. Still, this option is not without shortcomings. The major drawback that has emerged as a result of *value pluralism* when applied by courts at various levels of jurisdiction and geographical settings is that it prevents judicial actors from bringing consistence, regularity or coherence to their decision-making in conflicts between the religious and secular spheres, including in the field of education.[11]

Transposing this debate to public education, it becomes immediately obvious that religious diversity in public schools and universities seems *a priori* unattainable owing to the assumption that these institutions are considered essential to forming national citizens in accordance with the specific *de minimis* requirement of a specific legal culture. The aim of this study is to nuance this assumption by demonstrating the inconsistencies in the current approach to religious diversity

5 Ibid., at 301.

6 John Griffiths, "What is Legal Pluralism?," 24(1) *Journal of Legal Pluralism* 1–55, 1986, at 1.

7 Büchler, op. cit., at 15.

8 Werner Menski, *Comparative Law in a Global Context: The Legal Systems of Asia and Africa*, Cambridge University Press, Cambridge, 2006.

9 Büchler op. cit., at 73.

10 Danchin, op. cit., at 253.

11 In the US legal context, for example within the Establishment Clause jurisprudence, despite the existance of the Lemon test (*Lemon v. Kurtzman*, 403 U.S. 602, 612–13, 1971), neutrality has not been applied in a standardized way. For more on this point, see Danchin op. cit., at 304.

in Europe drawing from domestic as well as supra-national judicial findings on the matter, with a view to the feasibility of a religiously 'richer' educational environment. The study furthermore observes the tensions that arise from a transnational perspective with regards to the development of norms in this area domestically and supra-nationally in Europe.

Structurally, the chapter begins with a discussion of neutrality and secularism from the perspective of the legal duties that the current scheme of European jurisprudence entails for the state in the area of education, with parallel consideration of the role that European Convention on Human Rights (ECHR) jurisprudence has played in adding content to Article 9 ECHR when exercised in the classroom. Further on, the chapter will move on to the empirical consideration of the cases of Switzerland and the UK as playing fields of religious education rights, with emphasis on the 'internal' routes that religions in education have found and how they relate to the supra-national legal framework in Europe. The choice of the two cases is justified by their obvious divergence in their separation of religion–state arrangements, but as importantly by the difference in the method that they adopt in establishing a 'dialogue' with the supranational level of legal norms. In the light of the critical observations that arise out of these case studies, the chapter will then engage in alternative strategies for addressing religious rights claims in the classrooms, in order to reach the conclusion that transnational law and its workings can provide a 'safer' environment for the reconceptualization and reconsideration of the clashes between the national and the supranational but also for the conflicts of values arising out of the de facto cultural diversity in European classrooms. Inevitably, the consideration of evidence in both countries places emphasis on claims arising predominantly from the Islamic faith to illustrate more comprehensively the controversies of the types of claims presented.

## Mis-understandings of Neutrality and Secularism

The constitutional implications of the separation of church and state in Europe vary according to the type of neutrality stipulated in domestic constitutions and the ensuing interpretations provided by the highest courts. This choice very much affects and guides the types of religious rights available and applicable in educational settings.

An active neutrality constitutional setting, based on "the duty of the State to provide both positive and negative freedom of religion without discrimination," as is the case for example in Hungary,[12] allows for state funding for church-operated schools based on the two-fold duty of the state to promote religious activities and to ensure that parents retain the right to choose the type of education that they want

12 Decision of the Hungarian Constitutional Court 4/1993 (II.12) AB, as quoted in Renata Uitz, "Aiming for State Neutrality in Matters of Religion: The Hungarian Record," 83 *University of Detroit Mercy Law Review* 761–87, 2006, at 767.

in accordance with their beliefs for their children (Article 67(2) of the Hungarian Constitution).[13] The justification for such a finding placed emphasis on the fact that, by providing education, churches perform public service tasks and therefore these activities can be characterized as worthy of public funding.[14]

On a pan-European level, however, there is still no clear guidance on the implications and limits of interference with the exercise of the right to freedom of religion in a secular constitutional setting. Relatively recent cases concerning, for example, the prohibition on students wearing the headscarf or having beards while attending university classes have rendered the rights to freedom of religion or belief as a "potential tool for the repression of religious liberty rather than as a means of upholding it."[15] This is mainly because the state is seen as the primary actor responsible for the preservation of general public order and religious pluralism, yet this preservation is achieved through the elimination of forms of public manifestation of religious belief in public institutions, such as schools and universities. *A priori* and macroscopically, this suggests a very difficult circulation of religious rights norms between the national and the supranational.

Regarding religion in an educational context, state neutrality is an essential element, especially on the level of primary education. According to the Human Rights Committee, offering religious classes as part of the curriculum is consistent with state neutrality as long as the school provides opt-outs for those students who do not wish to attend those classes. State funding of denominational schools would also be compatible with state neutrality, as long as the state does not discriminate between schools. The Organization for Security and Co-operation in Europe's Toledo Guiding Principles on Teaching about Religions and Beliefs in Public Schools[16] as well as the UNESCO Declaration of Principles of Tolerance[17] conclude that lessons about religions and beliefs that are part of the regular curriculum and are taught in a neutral fashion are acceptable and even may enhance tolerance for the diverse panoply of religious convictions. European jurisprudence has not, however, fully aligned itself to this appreciation of religious diversity in the classroom.

---

13 11/1997 (IV.25) AB decision.

14 Uitz, op. cit., at 768.

15 Malcolm Evans and Peter Petkoff, "A Separation of Convenience? The Concept of Neutrality in the Jurisprudence of the European Court of Human Rights," 36(3) *Religion, State and Society* 205–22, 2008, at 208.

16 http://www.osce.org/odihr/29154.

17 Adopted on 16 November 1985, at the 28th Session of the UNESCO General Conference, available at http://www.unesco.org/webworld/peace_library/UNESCO/HRIGHTS/124-129.HTM.

### *Religious Diversity in Education: Duties of the State in the European Legal Landscape*

The duty of neutrality of the European state usually implies a neutral and impartial stance towards religious beliefs. It also requires states to abstain from assessments of the legitimacy of religious beliefs or of the ways in which they are expressed.[18] A characteristic field of application of the duty concerns the display of religious symbols: if an individual considers a certain symbol of religious significance to them, this conviction cannot be disputed. At the same time, additional implications that arise from the duty of neutrality call the state, also according to European Court of Human Rights (ECtHR) case law and the ECHR, to ensure that believers and non-believers enjoy their right, while learning at school, without being confronted with or disturbed by beliefs or convictions that they do not necessarily share. However, this duty is not uniformly applied in all cases.

In the field of education, this duty calls for a sensitive balance between the positive and negative aspects of the exercise of the freedom of religion, particularly in the light of parents' right to educate their children in accordance with their religious and/or philosophical beliefs (Article 2 of Protocol 1). The state is therefore required to provide space for the exercise of religious rights at school and can only restrict the right at issue in the presence of compelling reasons to do so (e.g. public interest), especially in schools where state authorities enjoy a power of coercion.

Article 2 of Protocol 1 does not impose a duty on states to set up institutions of higher education, but only to provide for an effective right to access to these institutions.[19] Nor does it confer a right to go to any particular school.[20] Also, the right to education is not absolute: limitations are permitted in the realm of state regulation,[21] with emphasis on the limitation pursuing a legitimate aim (e.g. such as maintaining public order or protecting the rights and freedoms of others). Interferences with Article 9 ECHR, however, must be "necessary in a democratic society." The question of necessity introduces a broad debate on the characteristics of such necessity and at the same time begs the question as to whether the term "necessary" suggests a higher burden of proof to be discharged by the state. Necessity certainly does not signify approval of the majority of the population, as courts must consider and respect the rights of minorities.[22] It does, on the other

18 *Manoussakis and Others v. Greece*, Judgment of 26 September 1996, at para. 47. See also the case of *Moscow Branch of the Salvation Army v. Russia*, No. 72881/01 at para. 92 where the Strasbourg Court stressed that "the freedom of religion . . . excludes any discretion on the part of the State to determine whether religious beliefs or the means used to express such beliefs are legitimate."

19 *Sahin v. Turkey and Efstratiou v Greece* (Application No. 24095/94), at para. 137.

20 Ibid., at para. 63.

21 Ibid., at para. 154.

22 Ibid., at para. 108.

hand, require proportionality to the aim pursued and the meeting of a pressing social need.

Finally, the duty of the state in protecting religious beliefs in education extends to the guarantee of mutual respect between the diverse religious groups, particularly when presenting their different ideas and opinions.[23]

In the light of the spectrum of the duties of the state, the conventional *forum internum–forum externum* dichotomy, as a tool of regulation of the exercise of the right to religion, is no longer a satisfactory paradigm for at least two reasons in the field of education: first, because it maintains an artificial distinction between what one believes in and what one is allowed to be seen to believe in;[24] second, because the division line between the private and the public sphere appears increasingly blurred. The public manifestation of religion in schools cannot be easily isolated from the content of education that stems out of a certain faith system.[25]

### *The Role of the European Court of Human Rights in Adjudicating Claims on Religious Expression*

It has been often stated that "the US way to be secular – or modern – is to be religious – while the European way of being religious is to be secular."[26] In this light, the Council of Europe's ECtHR has defined the freedom of religion as follows:

> (f)reedom of thought, conscience and religion is one of the foundations of a democratic society within the meaning of the Convention. It is, in its religious dimension, one of the most vital elements that go to make-up the identity of believers and their conception of life, but it is a precious asset for atheists, agnostics, skeptics and the unconcerned. The pluralism indissociable from

---

23 Malcolm D. Evans, "Religious Symbols: An Introduction," in Silvio Ferrari and Rinaldo Cristofari (eds), *Law and Religion in the 21st Century: Relations between States and Religious Communities*, Ashgate, Farnham, 2010, 291–6, at 295.

24 The incoherence of this becomes obvious when compared with ethnicity/race rights claims: race and ethnicity are perceived as inseparable (in the sense of believing and belonging to as well as being a member of given group). For more on this point see Peter Petkoff, "Religious Symbols between Forum Internum and Forum Externum," in Silvio Ferrari and Rinaldo Cristofari (eds), *Law and Religion in the 21st Century: Relations between States and Religious Communities*, Ashgate, Farnham, 2010, 297–304.

25 Petkoff, op. cit., brings an interesting analogy on the wearing of the headscarf as a religious symbol: in January 2004, the Declaration of the European Council of Fatwas and Research stated: "wearing the headscarf is a devotional commandment and a duty prescribed by Islamic Law, and not merely a religious and political symbol. Islamic women consider this to be an important part of their practising of the teachings of their religion. This adherence is a commandment that has not been made conditional on any (specific) public place" (at 299).

26 Winnifred Fallers Sullivan, "We are All Religious Now. Again," 76(4) *Social Research* 1181–98, 2009, at 1183.

a democratic society, which has been dearly won over the centuries, depends on it.[27]

The right in itself is of course not absolute, as mentioned already: the state may step in to protect the rights of others or other constitutionally protected liberties.

Against a rich variety of arguments and proposed solutions from domestic courts, the ECtHR has insisted on a tactic of "decisional minimalism,"[28] when it comes to religious human rights claims. This is because the Court has found that "(i)t is not possible to discern throughout Europe a uniform conception of the significance of religion in society . . . even within a single country such conceptions may vary."[29] In practice, the Strasbourg court has built its decisions on pragmatic arguments and has cautiously avoided complex legal theorizing in order to minimize political damage and severe judicial errors.[30] It also utilizes the techniques of the *margin of appreciation* or the concepts of *reasonableness* and *proportionality* to shift attention from *stricto sensu* legal reasoning towards the prevalent values in a given national context.[31] Particularly regarding legal pluralism, the ECtHR's stance remains that parallel religiously inspired legal systems are incompatible with secularism and equality.[32]

The recent and widely criticized Grand Chamber judgment, in the case of *Lautsi v. Italy*,[33] highlights pertinently the difficulties of adjudicating religiously related claims in the realm of education. The common question of whether the presence of a crucifix in a public school classroom violated one's freedom of conscience and right to have one's children receive an education in conformity with his/her philosophical beliefs led to confusion as to what exactly is the duty of the state: to create an "a-religious" order that serves pluralism by relegating religious rights to the absolutism of the individual sphere or rather to present and support spiritual and moral values that are the common heritage of a state.

On the other hand, the ECtHR when considering the question as to whether mandatory Turkish religious education courses were compatible with the right to education as guaranteed by the ECHR[34] did not hesitate to find a violation in the applicant's right to education[35] in conformity with her religious belief when it

27 *Kokkinakis v. Greece*, at para. 31 (1994).

28 The term is borrowed from Cass Sunstein, *One Case At a Time: Judicial Minimalism on the Supreme Court*, Harvard University Press, Cambridge, MA, 9–23, 2001.

29 *Otto Preminger Institute v. Austria*, 295 A ECtHR (ser. A) at 14 (1994).

30 See, for example, the relatively recent *Lautsi v. Italy* (Grand Chamber) decision.

31 See *Sahin v. Turkey and Efstratiou v Greece* (Application No. 24095/94) and *Valsamis v. Greece* (Application No. 21787/98).

32 Cf. *Refah Partisi and Others v. Turkey*, Application Nos 41349/98, 41342/98, 41344798, Judgment of 13 February 2003 at 127, 128.

33 Application No. 30814/06, Judgment of 18 March 2011.

34 *Zengin v. Turkey*, Application No. 1448/01, Judgment of 19 October 2007.

35 Article 2 of the First Additional Protocol stipulates that: "No person shall be denied the right to education. In the exercise of any functions which it assumes in relation to

ruled that the absence of instruction on the elements of the applicant's and her father's faith (in this case Alevism) was not compensated for because of the lack of objectivity and pluralism in the contents of the school subject "Religious Culture and Ethics."

In sum, the Court's approach at times embraces a "fundamentalist" degree of secularism by imposing on individuals a secular behavior in the public domain, particularly affecting the manifestation of religious beliefs through symbols (e.g. in clothing).[36] Without renouncing the human rights ideals reflected in the Convention and in particular the principle of freedom of religion, the Court avoids general rules and consequently fails to create consistent interpretation of the content of the right. It also places barriers to the circulation and efficient transfer of norms between the various jurisdictions by placing a wall of legal obscurity vis-à-vis the interpretation of religious rights and their compatibility with the broader human rights culture that courts have been developing in this continent.

Comparing this approach with other, non-European jurisdictions that have been faced with questions relating to the exercise of religious freedom at school, they have shifted their focus from objective to subjective criteria. They have focused on the sincerity of the belief that a student claims, which then leads to the discussion of the possible justification of the interference with the right,[37] just as is the case before the ECtHR.

Taking each situation separately and avoiding negative qualifications, as is often the case for Muslim headscarf cases in schools and elsewhere, the narrower approach to religious rights cases allows for the concretization of competing interests in the spirit of diversity and tolerance.[38] The doctrine of reasonable accommodation appears essential in non-European settings but is still largely missing from the European one.

---

education and to teaching, the State shall respect the right of parents to ensure such education and teaching in conformity with their own religious and philosophical convictions."

36 Ingvill Thorson Plesner, "The ECtHR between Fundamentalist and Liberal Secularism," 1–3, www.strasbourgconsortium.org/commentaries.php.

37 See indicatively the cases of *Pillay v. MEC for education, KwaZulu Natal and Others*, CCT 51/06 (South Africa) or *Multani v. Commission Scolaire Marguerite–Bourgeoys* (Supreme Court of Canada, 2 March 2006) as discussed in Hans-Martien Th.D. ten Napel and Florian H.K. Theissen, "The ECtHR on Religious Symbols in Public Institutions –A Comparative Perspective: Maximum Protection of the Freedom of Religion through Judicial Minimalism?," at 317–20, in in Silvio Ferrari and Rinaldo Cristofari (eds), *Law and Religion in the 21st Century: Relations between States and Religious Communities*, Ashgate, Farnham, 2010. These cases may be contrasted, for example, with the ECtHR case of *Karaduman v. Turkey* (1993), which concerned the refusal to a university graduate of a certificate asserting her qualifications because she would not submit a photograph without a headscarf, as required. The ECtHR held that "Article 9 of the Convention does not always guarantee the right to behave in the public sphere in a way which is dictated by such a belief" (para. 108).

38 Ibid., 319–320.

In the European space, it is, however, difficult to deny that the Strasbourg Court contributes in significant ways through positive as well as negative findings in cases concerning religious beliefs and education in conditioning the ways in which religion is perceived, interpreted and adjusted in the individual jurisdictions of its Member States. Elizabeth Shakman Hurd argues a step further by claiming that this is the beginning of a new form of horizontal religious governance.[39] It is indeed true that a state's authority to draw a line and designate the space where religious rights can be exercised is no longer exclusive: courts, constitutions and transnational bodies contribute to the exchange of norms and concepts, creating webs of understandings that are becoming decreasingly easy to study in isolation. The *transnational embedding* of religious norms and rights has already been identified as a crucial characteristic of the various modes of religious belonging, particularly for migrants,[40] yet it is still too early to depict, let alone predict, the ways in which the transnational element affects the practices of religious governance in Europe. The two examples that follow, drawn from Switzerland and the UK, are explored in order to give further content to the ways in which religious rights in education constitute a very challenging laboratory for the transnational 'circulation' of rights.

## Religion and Education in Switzerland

### *Background and Constitutional Framework*

Religious diversity in Switzerland is a twentieth-century phenomenon, owing largely to Catholic, Muslim and Hindu migrants. Article 15 of the Swiss Constitution guarantees the freedom of religion for both individuals and groups.[41]

As state law prevails over religious law, a system of state recognition of religious congregations has been set up with varying degrees of rights attached to each form. The only denomination to achieve public-legal recognition (*öffentlich-rechtliche anerkennung*) is the Catholic Church of the canton of Zurich since 1963.

---

39 Elizabeth Shakman Hurd, "Emergent Patterns in Global Religious Governance," ReligioWest Conference Paper, EUI, November 2011.

40 Koenig, op. cit., at 314.

41 Article 15 of the Swiss Constitution stipulates:

(1) The freedom of faith and conscience is guaranteed.

(2) Every person has the right to freely choose his or her religion or non-denominational belief and to profess them alone or in community with others.

(3) Every person has the right to join or belong to a religious community and to receive religious education.

(4) No person may be forced to join a religious community, to conduct a religious act or participate in religious education.

The Federal State grants to all 26 cantons the right to define their relationship with the various religious communities present on their territories. In essence, a variety of schemes, ranging from a strong link between state and church (e.g. in Protestant cantons), to a degree of autonomy (e.g. in Catholic cantons) and even to complete separation of church and state (e.g. the cantons of Geneva and Neuchatel), describe this relationship.

With regards to the recognition of immigrant religions, three predominant patterns exist: the *private-legal* type of recognition that does not entail any privileges but allows the formation of political and religious groups; *public-legal* status, resulting in the right to collect taxes from followers and the right to state support in tax collection, with rights also to erect places of worship and integrate religious lessons in school curricula; and finally the recognition of a system of faith as a *state religion*, which is synonymous to constitutional recognition.[42] The last type of recognition carries a high threshold, which has resulted in no minority religious minority being publicly recognized in Switzerland, other than the Jewish communities in Bern and St Gallen.

### *Patterns of Recognition of Religion in Education*

The Swiss legal system is based on the principles of neutrality, understood as impartiality yet with the underlying assumption that Christian churches enjoy a distinct position. For non-Christian communities, neutrality is conducive to "distance, tolerance and non-interference of the state in the religious sphere."[43] At schools, this conceptualization of neutrality has so far led to the protection of members of religious minorities against forced conversion into other faiths.[44] The Swiss Basic Law and the Swiss State value cultural plurality, resist assimilatory practices and make the connection between cultural and religious diversity and social cohesion and progress.

Yet the visibility of religious structures and religious claims for Muslims, in particular, despite the "openness" of the Swiss legal system, has been persistently linked to the general and recurring issue of Muslim fundamentalism.[45] The headscarf issue, differently from other European countries, has not generated

---

42 For more on this point see Joanna Pfaff-Czarnecka, "Accommodating Religious Diversity in Switzerland," in Bramadat P. and Koenig M. (eds), *International Migration and the Governance of Religious Diversity*, McGill–Queen's University Press, Montreal, 2009, 225–57, at 231.

43 Ibid., at 233.

44 Ibid., at 234.

45 A typical illustration of this trend can be observed in the recent successful initiative to ban minarets in Switzerland. On 29 November 2009, the Swiss people voted in a popular referendum in favor of an absolute prohibition of the construction of minarets on Swiss territory. The vote was 57.8 percent in favor, and 23 of the 26 cantons were in favor of the prohibition.

the levels of contestation encountered elsewhere. Students are allowed to wear religious symbols at schools and universities, although public officials, including teachers, are not. The ban includes Christian symbols as well.

A noticeable exception to this trend is the case of *Dahlab v. Switzerland*,[46] involving a claim of a Muslim Swiss teacher, who wished to wear the headscarf while teaching young children at a public school in the canton of Geneva. The case reached the ECtHR and provided it with the opportunity to stress the court's understanding of neutrality. More specifically, the Court noted that: "it is very difficult to assess the impact that a powerful external symbol such as the wearing of a headscarf may have on the freedom of conscience and religious of a very young children."[47]

It went on to state that: "it cannot be denied outright that the wearing of a headscarf might have some kind of proselytizing effect, seeing that it appears to be imposed on women by precept which is laid down in the Koran and which, as the Federal Court noted, is hard to square with the principle of gender equality."[48]

These often-quoted excerpts from the judgment confirm that, in the eyes of the European Court, the headscarf worn in public schools might have a proselytizing effect and is incompatible with gender equality and tolerance and respect for others.[49] These findings are largely unsubstantiated insofar as there is no scientific evidence that shows the detrimental effect of the headscarf on children from a teacher. It is also doubtful whether the dismissal of a teacher for wearing the headscarf fosters tolerance and understanding between children of different faiths. The assumption of the headscarf as a symbol of gender inequality appears also not to subscribe to the legal understandings of discrimination as difference in treatment arising in similar situations: as not all women wear the headscarf after all, it is unclear who the legal comparator should be in each case.

More controversial, according to Pfaff-Czarnecka, have proved pupil claims for school dispensation from swimming lessons on the basis of religious reasons, which have been dealt with in purely domestic legal instances in Switzerland. The Supreme Court in 1993 granted one such exemption to a 12-year-old Muslim girl on the basis of the argument that it would not affect the content of her education

---

46 Application No. 42393/98, Judgment of 15 February 2001.

47 The original language of the decision reads: "il est bien difficile d'apprécier l'impact qu'un signe extérieur fort tel que le port du foulard peut avoir sur la liberté de conscience et de religion d'enfants en bas âge," under LAW, at para. 1.

48 The original language of the decision reads: "Comment dès lors pourrait-on dans ces circonstances dénier de prime abord tout effet prosélytique que peut avoir le port du foulard dès lors qu'il semble être imposé aux femmes par une prescription coranique qui, comme le constate le Tribunal fédéral, est difficilement conciliable avec le principe d'égalité des sexes," under LAW, at para. 1.

49 Manisuli Ssenyonjo, "The Islamic Veil and Freedom of Religion, the Rights to Education and Work: a Survey of Recent International and National cases," 6(3) *Chinese Journal of International Law*, 653–710, 2007, at 701.

significantly.[50] The spirit of the decision was guided by the intention to avoid imposing an unnecessary choice between religious convictions and education on the student.[51] It furthermore signaled a broader willingness to reconcile the exercise of state authority with that of parental authority so as to avoid value conflicts.

Political opposition and intense public debate on the same topic sparked again in 2006–2007, but in the direction of significantly less sensitivity towards non-Christian religions. Requirements to cover the body were met by the provision of special full-body swimming costumes, allowing Muslim students to participate in sports lessons. No noticeable legal cases emerged out of this clash in the post-1993 period. The tolerant spirit of the Courts was superseded by a conservative political appreciation of the question.

Accommodative practices in Switzerland emerge therefore as fluctuating, without constant framing parameters. This is in part due to the variety of institutional and parallel legal frames observed at the levels of governance in the country. Moreover, the state rests on the consent and continuous participation of the people and is inevitably re-negotiated.[52]

Paradoxically, what in the 1990s appeared as reasonably accommodative ceased to be considered as such in the second part of the 2000s. The content of the concept of neutrality in education has therefore shifted. Religion continues to be considered as private but not to the degree of assimilationist culturalism. Instead, it fosters "multiple belonging" but rests on the firm basis of "civic commonality" of the type that aims at integration.[53]

## Religion and Education in the UK

### *Background*

An analysis of the physiognomy of religious rights in education in Britain presupposes an understanding of the country as a "community of communities."[54] The governance of religion in Britain is conditioned on and set against the background of migration mainly in the period between 1950 and 1970. The implications of this assumption lead toward a better and fuller *a priori* appreciation of the country's internal plurality, which needs to be reflected within the structure of a (shared) educational system.[55] Bhikhu Parekh is nevertheless right to caution

50 Pfaff-Czarnecka, op. cit., at 246.

51 BGE 119 Ia 178.

52 Pfaff-Czarnecka, op. cit., at 249.

53 Both terms in brackets borrowed from Pfaff-Czarnecka, op. cit., at 252–3.

54 Bhikhu Parekh, "The Future of Multi-ethnic Britain: Reporting on a Report," 90(362) *The Round Table* 691–700, 2001, at 695.

55 The 2001 Decennial Census for England, Wales and Scotland as well as Northern Ireland produced Christian, Muslim, Hindhu, Sikh, then Jewish, Buddhist, Jain, Baha'i

against the complicating factor of "shifting" boundaries of such communities. He points out that "(u)nlike nations, communities are porous, open, loosely structured and capable of both containing and joining an ever-widening circle of communities."[56] Accordingly, the need accordingly to build that system with an eye for a "constantly evolving body of values" does not come as a surprise.

Having an established church in Britain, the historical presence and legal character of the faith have penetrated the culture and institutions in the country. At the same time, it could be argued that this presence indirectly guarantees a certain degree of public space for religion.[57] For minority religions, in particular Muslims, the struggle for equality and "recognition" stems from individuals who possess UK citizenship, which is not necessarily a given in other countries (e.g. Germany). This indirect "legitimization" of religious claims has also resulted in the transformation of non-majoritarian religious groups into valuable social partners for the secular institutions of the country, which acknowledge diversity, while paradoxically relying heavily on integration strategies and the discourse of shared values of "Britishness."[58]

In essence, the UK remains a state that has never been a nation-state and that currently fits best under the Habermasian label of "post-nation state," requiring rules of contestation of religious rights and values within education that reflect its multicommunal character. An often-used and widely explored area of empirical demonstration of the application of legal pluralism in the country's legal system is family law. Although not strictly related to education, the enactment of the *Divorce (Religious Marriages) Act* of 2002 has signaled the possibility that a religious dissolution of a marriage may be recognized by English courts, provided it occurs prior to the pronouncement of a civil divorce. Similar legal developments give shape to the operation of "parallel" legal systems. Particularly for Islamic law, the system remains normatively effective but not officially recognized. It purports to selectively endorse aspects of Islamic law while at the same time adapting them to the British social reality.[59] One obvious repercussion of this symbiotic relationship has been the adaptation, re-interpretation and at times re-conceptualization of Islamic law. This evolution cannot nevertheless be isolated from the historical-legal experience of statutory legal pluralism under the British Empire (especially

and Zoroastrian as the largest groups of respondents, in this order of size (cf. Paul Weller "Religions and Governance in the United Kingdom: Religious Diversity, Established Religion and Emergent Alternatives," in Bramadat P. and Koenig M. (eds), *International Migration and the Governance of Religious Diversity*, McGill–Queen's University Press, Montreal, 2009, at 168–9).

56 Ibid., at 695.

57 Weller, op. cit., at 179.

58 Ibid. at 183.

59 Büchler, op. cit., at 17.

in India). As a transnational normative phenomenon, it gives a "post-modern answer to legal modernity."[60]

*Education and Religion*

The legal framework in the UK unambiguously recognizes religious freedoms by virtue of the ECHR as reflected in the Human Rights Act 1998.[61] Yet, when courts are faced with the question of the exercise of religious rights through manifestations such as the wearing of religious symbols in the classroom by a religious minority member, they have difficulties in implementing and enforcing the content of the right. They tend to take a restrictive stance with regards to the manifestation of religious belief through symbols, such as clothing. Recent case law places emphasis on claims emanating from the Muslim religious minority, particularly the wearing of the headscarf, despite the absence of national rules on school uniforms.[62]

In the case of *R (on behalf of Begum) v. Denbigh High School Governors*,[63] the pupil, Ms Begum, invoked her right to wear a *jilbab* (garment covering the majority of the body, including arms and legs) instead of a less strict religious dress that the school's policy had allowed female students to wear (the *shalwar kameeze*) as part of the school uniform policy.[64] Upon Shabina Begum's refusal to comply with the school's uniform policy, the school authorities prevented her from entering the school premises. The pupil and her family challenged this decision, which made its way to the House of Lords.[65] The Court found in favor of the school authorities. Interestingly, three of the judges sitting did not think that there was sufficient link with Article 9 ECHR on freedom of religion, and used the "specific situation" rule.[66] Nevertheless, the common ground of all judges remained the fact

60 Ibid. at 17.

61 The Race Relations Act 1976 prohibited discrimination on racial grounds in employment and education but extended its protection scope only to those groups that were both a distinct religious group as well as an individual race. Consequently only groups such as the Sikhs and Jews were covered.

62 Schools are permitted to have their own policies on uniforms "sensitive to the needs of different cultures, races and religions" (Department for Education and Skills, School Uniform Guidances, June 2004).

63 (2004) EWHC 1389 Admin.

64 The school had provided three alternatives catering for the needs of Muslim students, one of which was the shalmar kameeze.

65 For an overview of the procedural evolution on the case at first instance and on appeal see Amy Jackson, "A Critical Legal Pluralist Analysis of the Begum Case," Research Paper No. 46/2919, Osgoode Hall Law School Research Paper Series.

66 The content of this rule stipulates that there is no interference with the right to manifest one's religious belief where an individual has voluntarily accepted a role that does not accommodate that practice or observance and there are other means open to observe the religion without undue hardship or inconvenience.

that wearing certain religious clothing in school can disturb the peace and social balance, if it is not subject to certain limits. Thus the limitation would have been justified under Article 9(2), in any case. As for the alleged violation of Article 2 of the First Protocol, according to the Court, the interruption of her education was due to her unwillingness to observe the school's uniform policy.

Following the Begum case, the related question of wearing of a *niqab* (a veil that covers the face and head leaving only the eyes exposed) was raised.[67] The 12-year old Muslim student, basing her claim on the fact that her three sisters had been allowed to wear this veil in the same school, challenged the school board's decision to deny the girl the right.

The High Court, in finding for the school, replicated the House of Lords findings in Begum by arguing that the plaintiff's freedom of religion remained protected because she maintained the option of changing schools if she chose. Yet the question still stood: regardless of the presence of an alternative, was the school decision permissible and above all justifiable under the ECHR? A common argument in this respect stems from the fact that the use of religious clothing should not become an obstacle for student integration, in which case its use can be legitimately restricted. The court's conclusion is indeed justifiable by educational and security concerns, but it reminds us of the repeated attempts of courts to "align" religious beliefs with "mainstream Muslim opinion" by excluding all religious practices that escape the "average" practice of a given faith system. This attempt also runs contrary to the exclusion of "discretion on the part of the State to determine whether religious beliefs or the means used to express such beliefs are legitimate."[68]

A third case, this time concerning a teaching assistant wishing to completely cover her face while teaching, asked the same question.[69] Her request was denied by school authorities, on the basis that, without visual contact, her teaching would be severely undermined. The Employment Tribunal did not support the plaintiff's claim that she was the victim of religious discrimination, as she failed to prove that she had been treated less favorably than non-Muslim teachers. The Tribunal identified as the relevant comparator in her case a person not of the Muslim religion who covered her face for some reason. It therefore concluded that Ms Azmi was refused the permission to wear her veil on objective criteria that it constituted a barrier for the learning process, and her ability to communicate with students. Likewise, there was no ground to find indirect discrimination, as the school's actions were proportionate and guided by the public interest. The Employment Appeals Tribunal found as much.

---

67 *R (on the application of X) v. Headteachers and Governors of Y School*, (2007), EWHC (Admin) 298.

68 *Manoussakis and Others v. Greece*, 26 September 1996 at para. 47.

69 *Azmi v. Kirklees Metropolitan Council*, (2007) UKEAT, Appeal No. 0009/97/ MAA (25).

All three cases suggest the obvious: there is clear interference on behalf of courts and the state into the strictly personal decision of manifesting one's religious liberty. More disturbing, however, is the contrast between cases involving Muslim students and cases such as the one involving in July 2008 the exclusion by Aberdare Girls School in South Wales of a Sikh pupil for refusing to take off her religious bangle. The High Court overturned the school's decision because "in this case there is clear evidence it was not a piece of jewelry but to Sarika was, and remains, one of the defining focal symbols of being Sikh." The claim was successful because it was based on the Race Relations Act 1976 rather than Article 9 ECHR. Muslim women have not so far enjoyed similar legislative protection. The Court even pointed out that there is "an enormous difference" between this case involving a "very small" bangle and the rulings allowing schools to ban the *niqab* or *jilbab*.

In a sense, the Begum case made clear that the question of the wearing of the veil is resolved once and for all, as following the case as a precedent in the UK context, no interference with the claimant's right under Article 9(1) ECHR is to be found, and even if there were one, it would be found justifiable under 9(2).[70] However, wearing the headscarf for Muslim women in the UK and elsewhere is part of their identity, a spiritual and an essentially personal choice. Insisting on the issue of religious identity through its manifestation is genuinely limiting the broader vista of the right to work and the right to be educated for groups that are vulnerable to marginalization of their economic, social and cultural rights.[71]

## Easing the Tension: Alternative Strategies for Religious Rights Exercise in European Classrooms

### *Constitutional Pluralism*

Is constitutionalism compatible with (legal) pluralism? In other words, can the essential core of constitutional protection afforded to the individual be "safe" vis-à-vis parallel (and diverging) value-oriented systems of faith that are being treated as fully fledged legal systems? If the starting point of this "alliance" is the marriage between diversity and constitutionalism, then the co-existence can begin to take shape. The work of James Tully specifically explores this possibility.[72] He argues in favor of "an intercultural dialogue in which the culturally diverse citizens of contemporary societies negotiate agreements on their forms of association over

70 *R (on the application of X) v. Headteachers and Governors of Y School*, (2007), EWHC (Admin) 298, at 100.

71 Many European Muslims, especially women are victims of discrimination in employment, housing or education, inevitably leading to social exclusion (cf. Ssenyonjo, op. cit., 2007, 656–7).

72 James Tully, *Strange Multiplicity: Constitutionalism in an Age of Diversity*, Cambridge University Press, Cambridge, 1995.

time in accordance with . . . mutual recognition, consent and cultural continuity."[73] A constitutional pluralist vista of religious rights will bring new legal responses to diversity in education: it will move beyond the human rights paradigm and anti-discrimination because a diversity-sensitive conceptualization of justice will shift the constitutional commitment at the root and basis of the process and not at the end, as a deliverable. It will also make space and create opportunities for the different arguments to participate in the constitutional process. Participatory constitutionalism will therefore keep open for debate the implications for rights to diverse religious identities. Finally, but as importantly, it will facilitate "exchange" and transnational movement of norms between the domestic and the supranational.

Recognizing religion as an identity marker of constitutional significance, neutrality understood as the relegation of religious rights to the private sphere no longer has meaning. The ECtHR very characteristically maintains a positivist assessment of what "religious" means: it signifies the non-secular broadly perceived.[74] Why is this so? Anderson gave an answer by explaining that legal pluralism challenges "first, . . . the centralist notion that law only emanates from the state; secondly, . . . (the) monist ideas of the systematic coherence and singularity of law; and thirdly . . . the positivist view that we can trace a legal order as something 'out there' apart from the agents who created it."[75]

More concretely, constitutional pluralism as an approach and as an alternative to simple non-discrimination religious diversity management strategies has a certain number of advantages, as identified by Bharma.[76] First, it is more conducive to social coherence and the effective exercise of rights. This is so because it reduces the scope of prohibition of identity-markers (such as religion) and at the same time does not hinder societal continuity within diversity. It furthermore leads to new perspectives on the role and duties of schools and universities towards students.

In Bharma's terms, "a failure to value diversity is divisive and fractures societies."[77] This diversity is an essential feature of the post-modern state that values heterogeneity. This process is indeed part of the school's duties in the sense that a constitutional pluralist view of religious freedoms would require from schools the development of civic responsibility while protecting (vulnerable) students from extreme forms of thought and belief. The exclusion of students on the basis of religious beliefs as manifested through dress, symbols or other expressions impedes the development of civic responsibility, suggesting homogeneity as the immediate synonym of social cohesion. Acceptance of difference, however, remains conditioned by our accepted concept of justice at a given point in time,

73 Ibid., at 30.

74 Evans and Petkoff, op. cit., at 209.

75 G.W. Anderson, *Constitutional Rights After Globalization*, Hart, Oxford, 2005, at 39.

76 Meena K. Bharma, *The Challenges of Justice in Diverse Societies: Constitutionalism and Pluralism*, Ashgate, Farnham, 2011 at 210.

77 Ibid., at 210.

with emphasis nevertheless on diversity. In other words, constitutional pluralism, because it is premised on an active, participatory type of governance, provides an alternative for the consideration of the increased levels of religious diversity in the classrooms.

*Autonomy Regimes in Education*

The concept of *transformative accommodation* reflects the idea that individuals may choose the jurisdiction under which they will subject certain selected matters for resolution, most usually aspects of marital law, mediation and certain forms of conflict resolution. This option boldly put forward by the Anglican Archbishop Rowan Williams in February 2008, while reflecting on Shari'a and English law,[78] raised a number of concerns and heated reactions. The clash between Western European understandings of secularism and the exercise of the right to religion is clear and head on. The so-called empirical reality of Europe yet shows that Shari'a, in particular, lives increasingly within the unofficial Muslim systems and bodies, and certainly not in courtrooms or within national legal systems.[79] This shift is not without concerns, however. Women's rights but also the broader issue of compatibility between Islamic law, in this case, and the European legal system and International Human Rights law, bring to the fore the question of whether the institutionalization of legal pluralism could remedy these important shortcomings, through integration in the common "majoritarian" legal system.[80]

The closest application in the current educational practice of such a kind of *transformative accommodation* is available in the Israeli context. More specifically, and in the absence of a written constitution and consequently of an express constitutionally stipulated state–religion relationship, and also given the special role assigned to religion as an essential identity marker in the country, autonomy regimes have found their place in the Israeli normative landscape.

Along with other areas, such as marriage, divorce and women's rights, education has been designated as an area where a complex system of religious and secular legal provisions and proceedings have developed.[81] The system of "autonomy regimes" clearly moves in the direction of applying *in concreto* the

78 http://www.archbishopcanterbury.org/1575.

79 Lisbet Christoffersen, "Is Shari'a Law, Religion or Combination? European Legal Discourses on Shari'a," in Jorgen S. Nielsen and Lisbet Christoffersen (eds), *Shari'a As Discourse: Legal Traditions and the Encounter with Europe*, Ashgate, Farnham, 2010, 57–75, at 63.

80 Ibid., at 64.

81 In Israel, there are two separate educational systems: the Jewish and the non-Jewish, which operate autonomously yet requiring the non-Jews to study Jewish religion and history but not the Jews to study the Koran, the Gospels or Arab history (cf. Kevin Boyle and Juliet Sheen (eds), *Freedom of Relief and Belief: A World Report*, 1997, at 440 as quoted in Danchin, op. cit., at 306).

idea of value pluralism. Alternatively, legal recognition of religious and other "personal" laws has begun to become more common.[82]

The compatibility of Shari'a with European legal systems remains nevertheless thorny despite progressive Islamic voices that call for a deconstruction of traditional and conservative Shari'a and its reinterpretation in accordance with the currently applicable human rights standards.[83]A second option, applied in the French context but with a considerably less pronounced cultural element, suggests the "ethicization" of the minority religion, abandoning the legal framework while insisting on the system of belief as an ethical viewpoint exclusively.[84]

## Conclusion

In sum, two broad options present themselves in the area of education and religious diversity: either the state imposes a near monopoly over education or it pursues education policies based on legal and practical accommodation of religious diversity in the classroom. In the first case, the demand for the pluralization of curricula will increase as social spaces become more diverse. Empirical evidence on the impact of religious schools on a comparative basis does not seem to support the idea that separate religious education damages or diminishes liberal democratic values.[85] The work of Jose Casanova, who compared the fate of Muslim communities in North America and Europe, has concluded that denominationalism is working better.[86] In the second case, fairness (i.e. non-discrimination) and religious neutrality suffice to sustain the vast variety of legal claims in this area.

Case law emerging from both case studies, especially on Islamic religious beliefs and the limitations that arise from it, at the very least, needs to be examined on an individual, case-by-case basis. Human rights concerns as well as the rights of others are legitimate parameters of adjudication. Targeting, however, the veil exclusively as a form of manifestation of belief, instead of looking at the socio-economic, legal and political conditions surrounding a given category of individuals (assuming that choices of Muslim women are a real concern in

---

82 Cases include Bangladesh, India, Malaysia, Nigeria, Pakistan, South Africa, Sri Lanka, Tanzania and Uganda.

83 Abdullahi Ahmed An-Na'im, *Islam and the Secular State: Negotiating the Future of Sharia*, Harvard University Press, Cambridge, MA, 2008.

84 Manni Crone, "Shari'a and Secularism in France," in in Jorgen S. Nielsen and Lisbet Christoffersen (eds), *Shari'a As Discourse: Legal Traditions and the Encounter with Europe*, Ashgate, Farnham, 2010, 141–55 at 143.

85 Will Kymlicka, "The Governance of Religious Diversity: The Old and the New," in Bramadat P. and Koenig M. (eds), *International Migration and the Governance of Religious Diversity*, McGill–Queen's University Press, Montreal, 2009, 323–34 at 325–6.

86 Jose Casanova, "Immigration and the New Religious Pluralism: A EU/US Comparison," in Thomas Banchoff (ed.), *Democracy and the New Religious Pluralism*, Oxford University Press, New York, 2007, 59–83.

Europe), shifts the debate from its real center of gravity and essence to the margin of its superficial and largely symbolic manifestation.[87]

From a cultural perspective, case law in the UK and Switzerland as well as at the European level is constant in its reluctance to give protection to Islamic practices. In Dahlab, the Court stated that "it appears difficult to reconcile the wearing of an Islamic headscarf with the message of tolerance, respect for other and, above all, equality and non-discrimination that all teachers in a democractic society must convey to pupils."[88]

Moreover, as evidenced in *Sahin v.Turkey* (at para. 115), courts have the tendency to create a direct yet highly disputable link between the wearing of the hijab and terrorism.[89] In this case, the Strasbourg court noted that "it does not lose sight of the fact that there are extremist political movements in Turkey which seek to impose on society as a whole their religious symbols and conception of a society founded on religious precepts." The applicant, however, was not shown to belong to any fundamentalist group. From a feminist perspective, a similar reductionist argumentation is in operation that claims that wearing the headscarf is contrary to the principle of equality, assuming a flattening homogeneity among Muslim women on the reasons for which they decide to wear the hijab.

Human rights are not, however, fixed concepts or legal constructs that are exclusively the product of abstract agreement. They are instead objects and subjects of perpetual evolution, contestation and transnational formation. Danchin is right when he labels human rights as "mediators" between facts and value judgments,[90] despite the theoretical gaps that this assumption creates for the need for an objective character of rights. Globalization, lived through the historical and social experiences of migration to European countries, creates the spaces for the development of human rights in cosmopolitan, universally relevant patterns. At the same time, the local domestic level continues to sustain the essentialist categories of ethnic and religious origin,[91] leaving out the broader dimensions and ramifications of cultural belonging. While the search for universally applicable principles, particularly in relation to the subjectivity and irrationality of religion(s), is and remains a legitimate quest for the international lawyer, the typology of religious rights conflicts also suggests the path of toleration as an alternative to balancing competing claims of similar or equivalent validity both nationally as well as internationally.[92] This path entails emphasis on accommodation and a continuous quest for overlapping consensus between religious communities and their claims discourse.

87 Ssenyonjo, op. cit., at 710.

88 *Dahlab v. Switzerland* (2001), Application No. 42393/98, judgment of 15 February 2001, the LAW, Section 1.

89 Ssenyonjo, op. cit., at 666.

90 Danchin, op. cit., at 315.

91 Büchler, op. cit., at 8.

92 Ibid., at 320.

Toleration, however, as a 'response' to contemporary religious pluralism in education, is not an obvious and obstacle-free option, despite its moral virtues.[93] It presupposes a smooth transition from the private sphere, which is after all its habitual domain, to the public sphere. The legal framework has to cater for this transition and the principle of non-discrimination is not always sufficient, especially since non-interference leaves its place to positive notions of acceptance and recognition.[94] Another difficulty with the use of toleration is located at the level of its understanding as a "public recognition of differences."[95]

This toleration does not necessarily and exclusively lead to legal pluralist solutions. It could also suggest the creation of what Büchler calls "a compendium of values"[96] that resonates a new form of constitutionalism. These values would operate on two levels: first, they would set the limits of religious rights in education and, second, they would identify within education the extent(s) to which religious convictions have to be taken into account.[97]

Some authors argue that international law should be revisited in order to formulate a new understanding of universal claims that places religion at its center.[98] The European experience in religious rights in education, as well as in other fields of social activity, offers a more nuanced picture: the modern understanding of religion as "private, voluntary, individual and believed"[99] does not address the reality of claims such as wearing the headscarf in the classroom or the state funding of religious schools or even the presence of religious symbols in public schools. The classic judicial responses to these issues are inconsistent and unsatisfactory from both an individual as well as a collective rights perspective.

If, as Berger claims, "modernity fosters pluralism," rather than secularization,[100] our legal systems should focus on which values education should rely on, in order to respond adequately to the increasing normative force that religion is acquiring globally. Legal pluralism and all direct or indirect attempts to introduce it in the European continent demonstrate precisely the intensity of transnationalization

93 Toleration is understood in this context as approached by Galeotti in her work, namely as public acceptance of claims for different practices, behavior, religious and cultural symbols, etc. (cf. Anna Elisabetta Galeotti, "Contemporary Pluralism and Toleration," 10(2) *Ratio Juris* 223–35, 1997, at 223).

94 Galeotti, op. cit., at 226.

95 Ibid., at 224.

96 Buechler, op. cit., at 22.

97 A related legal experience has been undertaken in Canada in the area of family law through the attempt to institutionalize arbitration courts drawing on Shari'a as a transnational legal source.

98 See, for example, Mark C. Modak-Truran, "Law, Religion and Human Rights in Global Perspective," 22 *Mississippi College Law Review* 165–71, 2002–2003.

99 Winnifried Fallers Sullivan, "Religious Freedom and the Rule of Law: Exporting Modernity in a Postmodern World?," 22 *Mississippi College Law Review* 173, 2003.

100 Peter L. Berger, "Globalization and Religion," 4 *The Hedgehog Review* 7, 10, 2002, at 11.

of law, the increasing number of (conflicting) authorities in action within the European legal sphere on religious rights and the effects of legal fragmentation as a result of migration in Europe. This type of legal fragmentation suggests an equivalent type of fragmentation within each European state, as the Swiss and British case studies, among others, show. Indirectly, thus, diasporic or other social spheres call more and more for transnational responses to their claims.

The role of Shari'a councils in the UK, as quasi-judicial institutions with substantial normative authority, exemplifies this evolution.[101] Family law, especially with regards to the Islamic faith, has been so far an area of legal pluralist intensity, but education appears to be another social setting calling for the need for a "post-modern answer to legal modernity." The danger of having different bodies of legal rules in education, as well as in other areas, triggered by religious rights claims, raises the level of the complexity of legal conduct expected by citizens and can be contrary to the principle of equality. Shachar's "multicultural vulnerability" therefore cannot be excluded.[102] The emergence of transnational law and practice on these issues could provide some answers on how to reconcile in Europe the perennial struggle between the national and the supranational as well as between the majorities and the minorities. State-supported religiously informed education is not *ipso facto* incompatible with globalization, beyond universalism and false generalizations.

101 Büchler, op. cit., at 76. The British government has resisted the introduction of a system of separate personal law (cf. *One Law For All* Campaign, 2010).

102 The term denotes in Shachar's words 'the ironic fact that individuals inside the group can be injured by the very reforms that are designed to promote their status as group members in the accommodating, multicultural state." Ayelet Shachar, *Multicultural Jurisdiction: Cultural Differences and Women's Rights*, Cambridge, Cambridge University Press, 2001, at 3.

# PART III
# Transnational Economic Entities, Human Rights and Cultural Identity

Chapter 11

# Narrating Indigenous Rights, Indigenous Rights Professionals and Agreements between Mining Corporations and Indigenous Communities: *à qui l'homme sauvage?*

Deval Desai[1]

## Introduction

> The subject of the present discourse, therefore, is more precisely this. To mark, in the progress of things, the moment at which right took the place of violence and nature became subject to law, and to explain by what sequence of miracles the strong came to submit to serve the weak, and the people to purchase imaginary repose at the expense of real felicity. (Rousseau 2006b: 82).

This chapter is a critical study of agreements conducted between transnational mining companies and indigenous communities to share the benefits of mining subject to indigenous rights claims. Viewing these agreements as tools in the transnational context of human rights, I argue that they are discursively shaped by a range of actors engaging with them, seeking to inscribe values within them, and seeking to mobilize them both as instrument and as end. These national and transnational parties – International Financial Institutions (IFIs), non-governmental organizations (NGOs), multinational enterprises (MNEs), academics and policy-makers (all of whom can be seen in Environmental Resources Management

1 I am grateful to David Kennedy, Michael Woolcock, Varun Gauri, Nicholas Menzies, Caroline Sage, Andrea Shemberg, Michael Jarvis, Moya Tilly Sarner, Nina Sologubenko and participants in the University of Lucerne's *Transnational Legal Processes and Human Rights Workshop* for valuable discussions on various aspects of this paper, and to Kyriaki Topidi, Lauren Redman and Amanda Perry-Kessaris for helpful comments on earlier versions. A different version of this paper is published as Deval Desai, "A qui l'homme sauvage?: Text, Subtext and Context in Agreements between Mining Corporations and Indigenous Communities," in Amanda Perry-Kessaris (ed.), *Socio-legal Approaches to International Economic Law: Text, Context, Subtext* (London: Routledge, 2012).

2010) – are concerned with various aspects of the intersections between negotiated agreements and indigenous rights. As a result, the chapter engages with international and domestic movements for indigenous rights, and explores these agreements as both a process of norm socialization and a tool of global governance for mining and the construction of indigenity.

The indigenous rights framework for these agreements begins with the International Labour Organization (ILO Convention 169),[2] which deals with indigenous and tribal peoples in independent countries. The Convention outlines the rights due to indigenous peoples, with Part II of the Convention dealing with land rights. Land is seen as both a temporal asset and a spiritual good. Article 13(1) provides legal weight to the narrative that land is of sacred importance to indigenous communities, while Articles 14 and 15 deal with the profane, providing for rights of ownership and of participation in the use and benefits of subsoil resources. The United Nations Declaration on the Rights of Indigenous Peoples[3] also considers temporal and spiritual aspects of indigenous communities' relationships to land and the right to use its resources in the preamble and Articles 25–26. The Declaration has little legal force, as highlighted by the representatives to the UN from the United States, Australia, Canada, Colombia, the UK, Guyana and Turkey, all of whom stressed its non-binding nature. While adopted by the General Assembly, Australia, Canada, New Zealand and the United States voted against the Declaration.[4] However, as with the ILO Convention, the Declaration stresses land rights, resource rights and the spiritual nature of land; these are shibboleths of what might loosely be called the indigenous rights movement.

These instruments have been applied to case law, embedding their narratives in judicial imaging of indigenous peoples. Recent indigenous rights cases in the Inter-American Court of Human Rights (IACHR), for example, have been influenced by these ideas. The IACHR heard expert opinion recounting "the indigenous worldview" in the *Awas Tingni* case, an influential 2001 decision.[5] This "worldview" was supposedly encapsulated in international indigenous rights law, including the Convention and the Declaration. In its holding, the Court stated that "land must be recognized and understood as the fundamental basis of [indigenous] cultures, their spiritual life, their integrity, and their economic survival," from

---

2 *ILO Convention 169*, 27 June 1989, 28 I.L.M. 1382. While the convention is binding on ratifying countries, only 22 have done so; *see* Table of Ratifications for ILO Convention No. C169, http://www.ilo.org/dyn/normlex/en/f?p=NORMLEXPUB:11300:0::NO:11300:P11300_INSTRUMENT_ID.312314:NO.

3 United Nations Declaration on the Rights of Indigenous Peoples, 13 September 2007, adoption by General Assembly Resolution 61/295.

4 United Nations Department of Public Information, General Assembly Adopts Declaration on Rights of Indigenous Peoples (Press Release GA/10612, 13 September 2007), http://www.un.org/News/Press/docs/2007/ga10612.doc.htm.

5 Inter-American Court of Human Rights, *The Case of the Mayagna (Sumo) Awas Tingni Community v. Nicaragua*, Judgment of 31 August 2001 (Ser. C) No. 79 (2001) at para. 83d.

which stemmed indigenous communities' claims over land.[6] This was, however, without reference to the Convention or other international indigenous rights instruments. The IACHR explicitly adopted the international instrument-based "worldview" in the *Saramaka* case of 2007.[7] The people in question were not indigenous in that they could not trace their roots back to pre-colonial times (as they were descendants of slaves brought to Suriname). However, the Court decided to treat them as such as their primary cultural modality was "a strong spiritual relationship with the ancestral territory they have traditionally used and occupied. Land is more than merely a source of subsistence for them; it is also a necessary source for the continuation of the life and cultural identity of the Saramaka people."[8] This was rooted *inter alia* in the Convention.[9] The Saramaka were thus afforded rights over their traditional lands, territories and resources, including mining and logging concessions, while the state was put under a duty to recognize and secure their land rights.

At the international level, agreements are valorized by the UN (United Nations 2007: 175) and emerging in the theory (Environmental Resources Management 2010; Otto 2010) and practice (International Finance Corporation 2012) of IFIs. Agreements are also important at the national level. In Australia and Canada they are widespread: in the Northern Territory in Australia they are mandatory under ss 40–42 of the Aboriginal Land Rights (Northern Territory) Act 1976 (in which they are known as Mining Agreements) and voluntary but commonplace (Langton and Mazel 2008: 42) under the provisions of ss 24–44 of the Native Title Act 1993. In Canada, they are known as Impact and Benefit Agreements and are negotiated either because settled land claims agreements between the Crown and Aboriginal groups specifically require them before mining can take place, or as a voluntary measure to avoid future litigation if a land claim is not yet settled.

Similar agreements, situated in very different public law frameworks, exist outside of these two countries. In the Philippines, indigenous communities are granted rights over land under ss 3(f) and 11 of the Indigenous Peoples' Rights Act 1997 if they have had physical and/or spiritual ties to it since "time immemorial." Under s. 4 of the Mining Act 1995, the government is required to recognize and protect indigenous rights when granting mining concessions, although the community has no veto power and these provisions are rarely applied (Xanthaki 2003). In South Africa, once indigenous communities have registered their claims over land, the Mineral and Petroleum Resources Development Act 2002 requires mining companies to consult with communities to prepare statutorily mandated social, labor and environmental plans. In Papua New Guinea, the Land Groups Incorporation Act 1974 requires indigenous groups to apply to a registrar and

6 Ibid. at para. 149 *et seq.*

7 Inter-American Court of Human Rights, *Case of the Saramaka People v. Suriname*, Judgment of 28 November 2007 (Ser. C) No. 172 (2007).

8 Ibid. at para. 82.

9 Ibid. at para. 92 *et seq.*

show their historic and customary relationship to the area claimed. Once land is registered, concessionaires must now use a "development forum" to "apply for access to landowners, who have a clearly defined right to negotiate a package with the government and the company" (McPhail 2000: 47–8). In Indonesia, indigenous groups' land rights are superseded by concessionaires. Consequently, mining agreements tend to be the result of a decision taken by the mining company in response to non-legal stimuli; for example, PT Kelian Equatorial Mining entered into negotiations with a local community following protests at its mine. (Ballard 2001: 33). While these agreements vary to a great extent, they do share a basic *telos*: they are negotiated agreements to share the risk and reward from mining between mining companies and indigenous communities who assert jural rights or claims over land (Llewellyn and Tehan 2004: 4). For simplicity, negotiated agreements will be defined as formal risk-allocation agreements of mining's impacts and benefits (as defined by applicable law).

For the purposes of this chapter, negotiated agreements are encapsulated in two discursive frames, which are reflected in the narratives of the indigenous in the national and international indigenous rights instruments outlined above. The first is rooted in the Rousseaulian *homme sauvage* (roughly translated as natural man and often used synonymously with the "noble savage"), as outlined in his *Discourse on Inequality*. The *Discourse*, a literary work as much as a political tract,[10] sketches in essay form the Rousseaulian social evolution of man. Part I of the essay lays out Rousseau's conception of man in the state of nature. From *homme sauvage*, Rousseau charts man's socialization in Part II as he asserts and enforces (property) rights, a condition that leads to "crimes, wars and murders": "The first man who, having enclosed a piece of ground, bethought himself of saying *This is mine*, and found people simple enough to believe him, was the real founder of civil society" (Rousseau 2006b: 100). Finally, he concludes that the moral inequalities this socialization engenders might effectively be mitigated by some form of social contract. Natural man has two exalted characteristics that inform the use of these agreements. First, he is close to the land. Second, he is best placed to *know what to do with the land* in order to protect his lot and way of life. Thus he operates in harmony with nature and is the reified signifier of natural balance (Rousseau 2006b: 83–4). He is free from and unencumbered by the trappings of human society, able to pursue his natural desires without indulging them to an immoral extent: "[E]xcesses of every kind [in contemporary society] . . . are too fatal proofs that the greater part of our ills are of our own making, and that we might have avoided them nearly all by adhering to that simple, uniform and

10 The *Discourse* is found in the syllabi of undergraduate French literature courses as well as in political philosophy ones: the universities of Oxford (https://weblearn.ox.ac.uk/access/content/group/modlang/general/handbooks/11-12/Prelims/French/Frenchprelimhb11-12.pdf), Houston (http://gator.dt.uh.edu/~hagen/hum3320.pdf) and Florida (http://www.leeannhunter.com/wp-content/uploads/2010/07/LIT_2120.1464.pdf) are but three easily accessible examples at the time of writing.

solitary manner of life which nature prescribed" (Rousseau 2006b: 85). He is also sustained and nourished by nature: "I see him satisfying his hunger at the first oak, and slaking his thirst at the first brook; finding his bed at the foot of the tree which afforded him a repast: and with that, all his wants supplied" (Rousseau 2006b: 83).

Literature at the juncture of nature and the indigenous, often drawing on (Rousseaulian) strands of art (Ellingson 2001: 11–20), ethnography (van der Ploeg 1993; Posey et al. 1984), environmentalism (Kramer et al. 1997; Terborgh 1999) and (non)governmental policy (Alcorn 2010; Waitt 1999), is the "inheritor of the tendency . . . to romanticize the indigenous as noble savages or primitives living in harmony with their environment" and "describe[s] indigenous people . . . [as] corrupted by the problematic or ugly manifestations" of modern society (Horne 2001: 85, 89; there is also a significant literature analyzing this tendency: Stearman 1994; Conklin and Graham 1995; Nygren 1999; Nadasdy 2005; Hames 2007). This grants to indigenous communities moral legitimacy, pursuing as they do the nobility of living in a state of nature, in contrast to the corrupting influence of mining. It also ties indigenous peoples and their fortunes to the earth as a wine is tied to its *terroir*.

The second narrative takes as its launching point these indigenous ties to land. It conceives of them as rights or claims in some fashion; indigenous communities can thus leverage these (with some help) in order to obtain what they desire from mining companies, be it material benefit or simply to be left alone. Further, this leverage is best applied directly to mining companies in the form of negotiations for a formal legal agreement that reifies these desires.

A central interlocutor that shapes the discourse is a group that I shall refer to as the "indigenous rights professionals." Following Kennedy's characterization of the "human rights professional" (Kennedy 2002: 101), this is a term of art that refers to third parties (from individuals to NGOs) who act out of a sense of "compassion" or moral compunction to further the well-being of indigenous communities against the interests of the state or other private parties. This term has a wide meaning, encompassing individuals, groups and organizations who fight for indigenous communities through legal and non-legal means, and a narrow meaning, focusing on those who privilege legal solutions (giving full legal meaning to the word "rights").

Kennedy (2002: 101) indicates that the change-mechanisms deployed by the human rights professional are both an "emancipatory vocabulary" and an "institutional machinery." Within the spacious confines of the former definition of the indigenous rights professional, it is apt to focus on the use of emancipatory vocabulary, as the professionals will be bound by their common use of language more than their shared institutional outlook, which will conflict depending on their level of formality, politicization, legalism, professionalization, etc. However, when operating within the straits of the second definition, with its focus on law, one can imply both a common vocabulary and an institutional machinery. Within the campaign-vocabulary of the wider group of indigenous rights professionals, the operations of mining companies on indigenous land obtain a privileged place. Transnational corporation (TNC) activity has spawned substantial protest, sometimes leading to violence and even deaths as indigenous communities, supported by NGOs, protest against mines on their land (Ballard 2001). Such protest is not simply an expression of rejection of mines; it has its own, specific language. It is associated with such key words as "rights" (Ballard 2001), "local development" (Policy Forum 2008: 2), "sustainability" (Downing et al. 2002: 3), "environment" (Cawood and Minnitt 2002: 294), "culture" and even "spirituality."[11] This language contributes to a particular imaging of indigenous communities: they are not defined by simple opposition to mines; rather, they have positive demands of their own. In other words, they are no longer linguistically passive and reactionary, but rather are able to assert personhood through the ability to make active, verbal demands (albeit with the assistance of the indigenous rights professional).

The demands of the community vary, but tend to have a similar discursive framework. Leaving aside for the moment those groups who wish to oppose mining *in absolutis*, demands generally contain the following proscriptions:

1. that mining be sensitive to the desires of the indigenous community (including consultations with them);
2. that mining share the benefits of operation with the local community – it is to this requirement that the concepts of "local development" and "sustainability" have relevance; and
3. that mining preserve, or at least take into account, the unique (i.e. desirable to preserve) culture and ways of life of the indigenous community

If the narrower definition of the indigenous rights professional is taken, the third proscription is modified to the following:

4. that mining not infringe on the human and indigenous rights (as defined in national and international law) of the indigenous community.

In order to help indigenous communities achieve these ends, the indigenous rights professional can deploy various tools to influence the behavior of TNCs, including political pressure, legal pressure, social pressure, direct economic pressure (such as blockades of mines[12]) and indirect economic pressure (such as brand impairment through publicity campaigns). One mechanism by which legal pressure is applied is the negotiated pre-operational agreement between indigenous communities and mining companies. Such agreements can deal with anything from simple revenue-sharing to the full panoply of "sustainable development" (including local employment quotas, detailed environmental protection, etc.). These agreements have become increasingly popular in recent years and, just as importantly,

11 Art. 13, *ILO Convention 169*, 27 June 1989, 28 I.L.M. 1382.

12 Diego Cevallos, Mexican Peasants Seek Ways to Block Canadian-Run Mine (25 August 2008), http://www.tierramerica.info/nota.php?lang=eng&idnews=2836&olt=385.

have become the subject of study amongst the academic and indigenous rights professional communities.

This chapter is a critical analysis of these agreements and their perceived role as a transnational tool of indigenous rights realization, exploring narratives of law, actors and the indigenous rights professional. It seeks to stimulate a reflexive and self-aware worldview on the part of those who advocate for legal empowerment as an emerging and non-state tool of global governance, showing the law and legal empowerment actors to be active participants in this process, rather than neutral tools to be deployed.[13] It also engages with concepts of indigenity, juxtaposing their unique natural narrative with the weight of global governance such empowerment tools seek to make them bear. By drawing out these implications through the use of the literary device of the *Discourse*, the chapter also makes a limited methodological intervention. Identifying the literary narrative(s) underpinnings of legal text and legal practice, and subjecting it to scrutiny using literary analytical tools, is not new in the study of law (Thomas 1991; Bruner 2003). Yet its application to the role of law in development, and particularly notions of governance, is novel. It allows for a broader range of source material and knowledge claims to be used in critiquing and shifting the discursive basis of the role of law in development.[14]

## Narratives of Law

> Thus, as the most powerful or the most miserable considered their might or misery as a kind of right to the possessions of others, equivalent, in their opinion, to that of property, the destruction of equality was attended by the most terrible disorders. Usurpations by the rich, robbery by the poor, and the unbridled passions of both, suppressed the cries of natural compassion and the still feeble voice of justice, and filled men with avarice, ambition and vice. Between the title of the strongest and that of the first occupier, there arose perpetual conflicts, which never ended but in battles and bloodshed. (Rousseau 2006b: 107)

The predominant feature of narratives of law in these agreements is that a formal legal instrument is a desirable thing in upholding indigenous rights. These agreements formalize the interaction between indigenous community and TNC, which benefits all parties. "Law provides an important means of formalizing

13 *See*, for a clear articulation of the 'neutral' legal empowerment perspective, Golub (2003), which sees, at 25 *et seq.*, "the use of legal services and related development activities" as increasing freedom, choice and "disadvantaged populations' control over their lives." This can be contrasted with a more avowedly political or even ideological conception of legal empowerment: *see*, for example, Baxi (1982).

14 *See*, on the nature of expertise in legitimating different types of knowledge claim, Kennedy (2000), Dezalay and Garth (2002). On the role of the arts in offering critiques of formalism, *see* Lasser *et al.* (1999).

relationships that have been forged at an economic and policy level, but also as an instrument that defines what those relationships are, and how they are to be managed to achieve goals of economic empowerment and development" (Godden et al. 2008: 25). Indeed, this narrative of formality avers not only that formality is desirable, but also that some formalities are better than others: "While an agreement-based or partnership model can take many forms, and it is not unproblematic, it now appears to offer more scope to resolve longstanding issues of indigenous economic and cultural sustainability [than complex public-law processes]" (Godden et al. 2008: 24–5; citation omitted). The implication is that these agreements are more flexible and somehow *less formal* than the byzantine processes of public law. Indeed, they are often contrasted with litigation, which is seen as a formal, legal (and possibly time-consuming) approach (Langton and Mazel 2008: 43). Indigenous rights commentators see agreements as a means to formalize and thus encourage informal virtuous behavior by TNCs:

> If corporations, whether strictly as part of their corporate social responsibility obligations or as more wide-ranging "social licence to operate" seek to negotiate with indigenous and local communities ways to transform resource wealth into social and economic development, then, it is important to determine what provisions might be incorporated into agreements, and as well to ensure that there are measures for adequate evaluation of agreements and their implementation. (Godden et al. 2008: 28)

Whether TNCs act formally or informally is irrelevant if they continue to do the same things irrespective of the level of legalism. Continuing with the example of corporate social responsibility (CSR) provides a nuanced analysis. The scope of behavior-modification engendered through formalization seems to be a question of context. In richer countries, "[i]f it is accepted that the regular business activities of a business are conducted within the boundaries of a legislative framework it seems as if there is general consensus that CSR requires a business to voluntarily go beyond compliance." By contrast, in poorer countries, it is argued that "it is necessary to encourage the private sector to a larger extent to adhere to its social responsibilities" (Kloppers and du Plessis 2008: 95); in other words, government regulation or some other legal pressure (such as legal liability under an agreement) may be required to ensure corporate engagement with social and economic development. However, it may be that, in certain situations in the developing world, a mining TNC would be willing to contribute more to local development in the absence of a legal minimum than if one existed (say, for example, if that minimum was set artificially low in order to attract investment). Indeed, indigenous communities may find *legal* obligations hard to enforce (for example, where enforcement capacity is weak), while the company, having been put on a legal footing, may have no incentive nor desire to engage in otherwise-acceptable CSR practices.

Further, legalism may have an effect on the *trust* between indigenous community and TNC. Mining agreements require all parties to deal with each other legally and thus at arms' length; that is, it *institutionalizes* an otherwise informal good and the very act of institutionalization may weaken the mutual quality of the trust. Informal CSR operations by TNCs can take place in an environment that particularizes and that engages with names and faces. In that sense, informal activity can build up trust between the parties (a scarce resource in relationships between TNCs and indigenous communities: CDA Collaborative Learning Projects 2005: 6), whereas formal dealings require trust to be placed in legal–economic institutions (Stiglitz 2000: 63–5; Dixit 2007: 60–61). Trust may be a more desirable good than formalization in certain circumstances; on the other hand, it may harm the community as the trust may be misplaced. Whatever the outcome of formalization in a particular situation, it is clear that it is no panacea and may in fact be undesirable in certain circumstances. In this way, formal agreements may limit the *discursive* space that the *TNC-as-benevolent-agent* can occupy. Fetishizing formality can also reduce the space available to the indigenous community to act. Pursuing legal means to regulate its relationship with a TNC can exclude from consideration a range of other tools at the community's disposal, both before and after the signing of the agreement.

In general, by privileging the legal space, indigenous communities reduce their *political* space. They may be restricted in their political speech through confidentiality clauses,[15] struggle with legal and negotiation costs and have their solidarity undermined by the TNC's use of divisory negotiation tactics (Sosa and Keenan 2001). Importantly, they are often bound by arbitration, stabilization and choice of law clauses. Arbitration clauses are *de rigueur* in mining agreements and arbitration is established as the preferred primary forum for disputes.[16] Although arbitration does not preclude access to public law remedies or appeals on matters of public law, it is the first port of call for disputes and may exhaust some of the resources of an indigenous community, making it difficult to pursue

15 *See* the Raglan Agreement (draft version, Canada, 1995) at http://pubs.aina.ucalgary.ca/makivik/CI236.pdf [henceforth the "Raglan Agreement"], at 115; and the Plain Language Summary of the Participation Agreement Between Diavik Diamond Mines Inc.and Dogrib Treaty 11 Council (Canada, 2000) at http://www.reviewboard.ca/upload/project_document/EA01-004_877_1154722210.PDF [henceforth the "Diavik Agreement"] at 6. *See* also Sosa and Keenan (2001: 19) for the effect confidentiality can have on inter-community knowledge transfers and solidarity.

16 *See*, for South Africa, the Deed of Settlement between the Richtersveldt Community and Alexkor, http://www.dpe.gov.za/parliamentary-263, at 3; for the Philippines, the memorandum of agreement between Mindex Resources Development and the Mangyan community at 9; for Canada, the Raglan Agreement at 97–101 and the Diavik Agreement at 6; for Australia, the Argyle Diamond Mine Participation Agreement – Indigenous Land Use Agreement (Australia, 2005), at http://www.atns.net.au/objects/Agreements/Argyle%20ILUA.pdf, at 27.

an alternative resistance strategy.[17] Stabilization clauses "freeze" or stabilize the law of the state over the life of the investment project (Shemberg 2008; Mann 2008). They have proved controversial in the context of investor–state agreements as they restrict the effectiveness of state legislation designed to affect rights. Similar concerns can be raised as regards mining agreements: agreements between indigenous communities and TNCs and/or ones involving the state could freeze the law pertaining to indigenous rights. Choice of law clauses could enable mining companies to simply standardize their mining agreements, applying the same law across the board, to the detriment of many indigenous groups. Alternatively, they could choose the most expedient and favorable law to apply to the agreement, arbitraging (and strategizing) differences in public laws and institutions (as has been done with stabilization clauses).

The political implications of such a formalist turn suggest that legalism and institutionalization should be a sequence of dynamic choices rather than a *fait accompli*. They are *strategies* rather than ends in themselves. Rather than formalize for the sake of it, one must ask, as Rousseau does, whether the "still feeble voice of justice" is sufficient to suppress "[u]surpations by the rich [and] robbery by the poor."

## Narratives of Actors

> The body of a savage man being the only instrument he understands, he uses it for various purposes, of which ours, for want of practice, are incapable: for our industry deprives us of that force and agility, which necessity obliges him to acquire. If he had had an axe, would he have been able with his naked arm to break so large a branch from a tree? . . . Give civilised man time to gather all his machines about him, and he will no doubt easily beat the savage; but if you would see a still more unequal contest, set them together naked and unarmed, and you will soon see the advantage of having all our forces constantly at our disposal, of being always prepared for every event, and of carrying one's self, as it were, perpetually whole and entire about one. (Rousseau 2006b: 84)

### *Indigenous communities*

The role of indigenous communities in mining agreements is imbued with imagery and vocabulary from Rousseau's *homme sauvage*, as evinced by the language of

17 On the impact of legal relationships on violent and non-violent protests against mines in Papua New Guinea, *see* Filer (2008) and Filer (1997: 102) (arguing that the subsequent institutionalized process of contest was "moderate" and consumed other avenues of resistance). I do not argue that violence may be more effective or desirable as a means of resistance; I simply note the exclusionary aspects of legal formalism in resistance to mines.

the international and national legal frameworks for these rights. Natural man has two exalted characteristics that inform the use of these agreements. First, he is close to the land. The community of indigenous rights professionals has implied from this concept a transcendental link to land from what was in Rousseaulian terms a special but temporal attachment. Second, he is best placed to *know what to do with the land* in order to protect his lot in and way of life. Thus man operates in harmony with nature and is the reified signifier of natural balance (Rousseau 2006b: 83–4). There are considerable narrative tensions between the Rousseaulian conception of natural man and a formal, private law mining agreement. These tensions operate over the following oppositions: cultural uniqueness | legal same-ness and naturalness | professionalization.

The cultural uniqueness | legal same-ness opposition is based on a tension between legal narratives of private law aspects of agreements, which render indigenous actors the same as everyone else in the legal sphere (e.g. bound by the same rules of contract and the same microeconomic behavioral model that is applied to non-indigenous groups) and the special imaging of indigenous communities in international and national law that leads to the grant of rights over land to them. The naturalness | professionalization opposition is closely related. It contraposes the natural aspect of the *homme sauvage* (his affinity to and peaceful co-existence with nature) and the narrative of formal law. Mining agreements, at any stage in their lifecycle, require parties to operate as *legal* actors. This presumes some affinity and, crucially, hability with the language, vocabulary and praxis of law. This law is antithetical to the Rousseaulian construction of natural man: it is "modern," "dominant," "alienated," as opposed to a proprietary legal system of an indigenous community that forms part of their "unique" culture and is thus tied to the land (Cobo 1986: 30). Indigenous groups that see mining agreements as the most efficient tool to share the benefits from corporate activity on their land are in a double bind. Their indigenity is predicated on their image, as portrayed to the non-indigenous community, as different and distinct of culture and institutions. However, the process of pursuing these agreements requires language, expertise and institutional structures borrowed from the non-indigenous community, demystifying the indigenous community and reducing the space of difference between the community and TNC (Kingsbury 2002: 189–90).

This use of Lacan seeks to situate identity as *difference*. Using the binary opposition "moi (ego) | autre" in the imaginary order and its transition to "sujet | Autre" in the symbolic order, identity is first created in the same way as a child forms its ego through its identification with an image of the self perceived as "autre," be it a reflection in a mirror, or in an[]other's face (Lacan 1966: 90–95). The child sees its body as a unity, as presence, but is also alienated by and from the image of its body as "autre." The ego emerges at the moment of concurrent identification and alienation, and is formed by and from this specular image: the ego, like "l'autre," thus belongs to the imaginary order. Identity is at once self-aware and contraposed against an other: Lacan sought to find out "[à] travers les identifications typiques du sujet, comment *se constitue le je*, où *il se* reconnaît?"

(Lacan 1936: 86; emphasis added), the pronouns and verbal forms emphasizing the reflexive yet binary nature of self-identity. The other, by definition, is also non-identical to itself, as it is essentially bound to *its* "autre" – the "moi": "l'autre . . . n'est pas un autre du tout, puisqu'il est essentiellement couplé avec le moi" (Lacan and Miller 1978: 370).

The "moi" and "autre" themselves can only be conceived in terms of *difference* to the symbolic order's "sujet" and "Autre." Whilst the former pairing is associated with image, unity and presence, identity and resemblance, the latter pairing forms, as it were, their mirror image. The "Autre" designates a radical alterity, constructed by language, which cannot be assimilated by the self. The subject, "made and remade in his encounter with th[is Autre]" (Bowie 1988: 117), imagines himself the way others perceive him. Crucially, then, the (difference in) unity of the "moi" and "autre" in the imaginary order leads to the essential distance between "sujet" and "Autre" in the symbolic order as transmutation between the orders occurs through the language of "différences" that is central to Lacanian thought (Lacan 1973: 228).

Using Lacan in this way, if the act of negotiation begins from the first conscious contact between the indigenous community and TNC or from the first contact between indigenous rights groups and the indigenous community in preparation for discussions with the TNC, both parties mutually constitute identities and symbols with this act. As soon as this is translated into language (which may be instantaneous), the symbolic order comes to bear. For language, in the case of mining agreements, read narratives influenced by Rousseau and held by indigenous rights professionals and/or TNCs; read also law (often influencing and influenced by those narratives). This happens at the negotiation stage, when these narratives and the language of law are deployed by both parties and they begin the dynamic process of constituting the "moi/sujet | autre/Autre" oppositions that define them. The act of negotiation produces the "signifying chain of knowledge" (Schroeder 2008: 159) that codifies identity for the indigenous community (and TNC). For example, by deploying the language of indigenous rights when asserting indigenous rights over land (and thus providing an impetus to negotiate), with its embedded Rousseaulian narrative(s), indigenous communities are constituted as both linked on a binary axis with TNCs and symbolic of the natural (and vice versa), just as TNCs become symbolic of the unnatural (and vice versa).[18]

With regard to cultural uniqueness | legal same-ness, the law can now be seen as causing the creation of the "sujet | Autre" and codifying in the symbolic order the essential narrative difference between TNCs and indigenous communities.

18 The law *qua* language provides the medium of engagement with the symbolic order; yet the law also forms part of the symbolic order itself, defined by clients' (as defined in the broadest sense to mean *consumers* of the law) desires and borne out of the 'autre' of morality: *see* Schroeder (2008: 157). However, the symbolic nature of law itself does not affect its role in engaging the symbolic order for indigenous communities and may even reinforce this engagement.

Thus while the agreement may on the surface treat all individuals the same, it paradoxically embeds the uniqueness of the indigenous community as it is imbued with the narratives that can be traced back to Rousseau. A similar argument can be made for the resolution of the naturalness | professionalization tension: the very language that can only be accessed by a professional creates and reinforces the Rousseaulian identity of the indigenous community. The narrative of natural man thus becomes the discursive frame for the agreement. It can now be viewed as protecting the indigenous way of life through the construction of this identity, the assumption being that all parties will bear in mind this discursive imperative when forming and acting on the agreement. The gaps causing these tensions are not deleterious to the narrative of indigenous identity; rather, they are constitutive of it.

However, the use of (the language of) law to construct identity in this fashion must be examined critically. The law can lead to *political* concerns. The symbolic "sujet" of the indigenous community is a single representation of the entire community, ascribing a set of symbols to all members. It is thus clear that whatever politics may be embedded in the narrative are embedded in the law and thus indigenous identity. The political is relevant in two ways. Firstly, the political that is situated in this indigenous identity must be acknowledged, as indigenous rights professionals should be aware of the implications for communities and their space for negotiation with mining companies when deploying this narrative. For example, situating indigenous groups as natural implies a lack of desire for and an inability to value the unnatural (such as mining profits); this is political in the sense that it may legitimate interference in the distribution of indigenous proceeds from mining benefit-sharing. Secondly, this narrative of unitary homogeneity narrows the contours of the indigenous–political, especially the political space internal to indigenous groups, thereby denying heterogeneous expressions of identities within the social body and restricting the scope of the politics of identity (Conklin and Graham 1995). Relationships within and outwith the indigenous community are multifarious and intricate: "The relationships between mining companies and communities are complex. They are enacted in diverse ways, are experienced differently both within and across communities and companies" (Cheney et al., 2002: 8).

The identity narrative imposed on mining agreements limits these relationships. By restricting the expression of internal politics in this fashion, outcomes detrimental to the indigenous group can be reached: for example, negotiations can take place with an indigenous sub-group that is not representative of the whole. This is particularly important when free, prior and informed consent of an indigenous group is required, as the consent of a co-opted, non-representative subgroup can be portrayed as sufficient. Not only does a denial of internal politics make it easier for a TNC to negotiate with any person(s) it believes to be "representative" of the indigenous community, but it also decreases the space available to the rest of the community to reject the illegitimate representation. Indeed, such rejection often has to be presented as unnatural rather than politically illegitimate: members of the Siocon Subano Association framed their attempted rejection of purported representatives in terms of their not being indigenous or their past cooperation with (unnatural) mines.[19]

By using legal agreements and relying on negotiations, the indigenous community and both the narrow and wide indigenous rights professionals reduce the extant indigenous–political space. They embed a particular politics of identity, and restrict heterogeneous political expression. This can have a negative impact on the ultimate aim of benefit-sharing for the indigenous community, as it allows community capture and the co-option of leadership structures with restrictions on the political space in which members of the community can operate. Indigenous rights professionals should bear in mind the embedded politics in agreements *and* the existing contours of indigenous political space when strategizing about whether mining agreements are desirable.

### *TNCs*

The narrative of TNCs is closely tied to that of indigenous groups. As the "autre Autre" to indigenous groups' "moi | sujet" (and vice versa), they define and are defined by the community. Given that TNCs' identities are defined in this oppositional fashion and through the medium of law, this section will explore the embedded politics of that identity and how it limits other strategies aimed at a non-unitary view of the corporation.

Just as the indigenous community is narrativized as natural, in harmony with their environment, close to the land and a good manager of natural resources, so the TNC, viewed through the Lacanian *stade du miroir*, is the negative of these: unnatural, anti-environmental, not in symbiosis with the land and an exploiter of resources. TNCs are so unnatural that they only respond to that Rousseaulian construct of social man, the law. The law thus plays a formative and institutional role, creating a TNC's identity and motivating its behavior within the parameters of that identity.

By implication, the importance of formalization means that TNCs do not respond to informal stimuli or pressures, congruent with a narrow indigenous rights view of the narrative of formality. Homologous to this idea is the presumption that a TNC's only focus is on profits and the bottom line: a view, sketched broadly, that holds that TNCs are market actors, responsive simply to profit and loss, requiring their activities to be checked by institutions that can impose costs such as regulation and monetary penalties. This sees businesses as *passive* – a receptor of norms only if it is financially desirable (Reich 2007: 50–52, 70–87, 114–30). TNCs are thus

19 *See*, for example, the controversy over the Siocon Council of Elders who signed a memorandum in the Philippines in the face of significant 'internal' opposition: Mines and Communities, *Pro-TVI Member of the Siocon Council of Elders Admits Misrepresentation and Pays Penalty to Legitimate Chieftain* (23 June 2007), http://www.minesandcommunities.org/article.php?a=6073 and Siocon Subano Association Inc., Open Letter (20 February 2005), www.tviphilippines.com/stakeholders/SSAI_NGOs_letter.pdf.

apolitical at best (Micklethwaite and Wooldridge 2005: 161–91) and amoral at worst (Stephens 2002: 54–9). A slightly more nuanced view (Shavell 2004: 595–8) is that their behavior is driven by utility (including the non-monetary utility of its employees and agents), although it struggles to go far beyond expressing the utility of a company in balance sheet or profit-and-loss terms.

As explored in the narrative of indigenous communities, the narrative of TNCs has an embedded politics. Although the TNC is portrayed as apolitical, applying a theory of corporate self-interest to the mining agreement model is an attempt to construct a particular image of the corporation: viz. businesses are not required to internalize norms of behavior (such as benefit-sharing), but institutions are required to incentivize them through the market or through laws. Incentivizing corporate behavior in this manner has a metapolitical and ethical dimension. To accept the theory of law as a cost presumes that the desired norms transmitted by laws do not need to be internalized by a company: as long as they are expressed in monetary terms they will be followed. Alternatively, it presumes that these norms can be internalized *through the market mechanism*. Underpinning both of these alternatives is the presumption that the market itself acts normatively: that the ethics of the market are such that other norms are unnecessary unless translated into market terms, and that the only political space needed is that which establishes market institutions (a notion problematized in a growing body of literature, such as Hirschman 1992: 105–63; Gneezy and Rustichini 2000; Strahilevitz 2000). The unitary nature of this view of the corporation also has a political dimension. Emphasizing profit-and-loss reduces the tools available to influence corporate behavior. It denies the non-financial points of leverage in a company that can be exploited (such as the ego or social reputation of a CEO: Mace 2004: 94; Clarke 2004: 24–30), limiting the tools available to other actors (indigenous groups, activists, policy-makers and others).

The narrative of the TNC in mining agreements, constructed with and in opposition to that of indigenous communities, intersects with the narrative of formalization. In doing so, it presumes that legal formality is desirable to modulate corporate behavior. However, this embeds a view of the company as a passive, market-driven actor, aggressively reducing the political space to act. Nevertheless, this view is in itself political, requiring states and institutions to expend political capital seeking socially desirable solutions. Further, it brings with it a particular politics of corporate identity, masking individual preference behind the forces of profit and loss. This restricts the multiple leverage points that an indigenous rights professional can use in a disaggregated model. Denying the political thus impacts the strategies that an indigenous rights professional can pursue.

## Narratives of the Indigenous Rights Professional

> The passage from the state of nature to the civil state produces a very remarkable change in man, by substituting justice for instinct in his conduct, and giving his actions the morality they had formerly lacked. (Rousseau 2006a: 10)

> As for men like me, whose passions have destroyed their original simplicity, who can no longer subsist on plants or acorns, or live without laws and magistrates . . . they will not therefore have less contempt for a constitution that cannot support itself without the aid of so many splendid characters, much oftener wished for than found; and from which, notwithstanding all their pains and solicitude, there always arise more real calamities than even apparent advantages. (Rousseau 2006b: 123)

### *Professionalization*

The indigenous rights professional is, as the name suggests, well-placed to fill the space of professionalization in the narrative of the indigenous community. The distinction between wide and narrow professional matters little here: both act as professionals, and are in a privileged position of capacity, language and knowledge when it comes to mining agreements and embedding into or realizing from them indigenous rights or goods. While professionals fill this role, neither they nor their literature ask the questions: "Should I be here? Should I be doing this?"

It is perhaps appropriate to consider the indigenous rights professional's role as a realizatory buffer-of-identity by imagining the impact of his absence on the indigenous community. Indigenous rights *academics* have warned of the impact that a mobilization of indigenous resources to engage with a TNC would have in the absence of an NGO. As Kingsbury (2002: 190) notes: "Th[e] transformation [in language, institution and organizational structure of an indigenous community] is usually toward the most successful organizational forms fostered in the law and practice of modern secular liberal societies, principally NGOs or corporations. These same organizational forms are also favored in the construction of international civil society and fostered by its practices" (citation omitted).

How, then, does the narrative of the *homme sauvage* persist despite engagement with the legal system? Rather than pursue an intellectual history (Ellingson 2001) or a study of the actors continuing to use the narrative (Hames 2007), the Lacanian approach outlined above directs attention towards identity creation *through* law, or more accurately through the professional identity that law requires. To use Lacan's mirror analogy, by deploying both Rousseaulian imagery and the law in all its forms, the indigenous rights professional is part of the mirror in which the indigenous community's reflection is seen. The professional embeds into indigenous identity the language/vocabulary of Rousseau, the ideational regime of natural man and the institutional regime of legal agreements. The space of difference between natural and social (legal) man is accepted by us, and, importantly, it is a space that the professional fills.

The mere presence of the professional in this "buffer zone" between natural and social man can create real problems for the indigenous community. As the narrative space the professional occupies restricts indigenous groups to the role of "natural man," there is little incentive for him to improve the capacity of the indigenous community. The community's future is determined by the professional's capacity, priorities and time, which may be in short supply: "Plan B [negotiation] preparations require time and money. The capacity of tribal groups to prepare a participatory Plan B varies greatly . . . Alternatively, organizations active in Plan A should be willing to stand behind their commitment and pay some of the costs" (Downing and Garcia-Downing 2001: 16).

The professional becomes the receptor of the community's values and the conduit for its desires; the community, meanwhile, must rely on the professional-as-middleman to translate these into something intelligible to social man. By using the language of empowerment, the professional can *disempower* the community by denying it access to that very language. The professional puts himself in a privileged position, giving himself great space to operate while limiting that of the community. In the context of a detailed study of the negotiation and implementation of mining agreements in Australia, O'Faircheallaigh (2003: 21) writes:

> [The] actual process of designing and drafting agreements is undertaken by non-Indigenous technical staff who typically work with specific Indigenous organisations for brief periods of time and indeed often move onto another negotiation as soon as one is completed. These individuals build a professional reputation by facilitating the conclusion of agreements (not their implementation over extended periods of time), and they are rarely still working with an Indigenous organisation by the time the consequences of implementation failure become apparent.

While O'Faircheallaigh here considers implementation, the same argument can be made for organizations that disengage from the negotiation process, leaving the community to fend for itself against the well-paid, well-trained lawyers a TNC can deploy.

If the professional or NGO disengages from the community once negotiations or an agreement have been put in place, it is difficult for the indigenous community to express itself in non-legal languages, particularly the political, as the space for expression no longer exists. (Dis)engaging with (from) the agreement requires a community to take a legal approach; confidentiality clauses, arbitration clauses and the like may create real barriers to the pursuit of other avenues of expression. Given the importance to the indigenous community of the professional's actions, it thus behooves him not only to consider all of his options and his strategies (legal and non-legal) fully to realize the duty he has taken on, but also to consider whether he should take the duty on at all. While he needs the narrative space to act, and he acts in good faith for the best interests of the community, he should consider *himself* to be part of the indigenous strategy and establish whether his very presence is a help or hindrance. To be or not to be, that should be the question.

*Legalism*

Whereas the narrative of professionalization begged the question "Should I be here?," the narrative of legalism, focused on substance, asks "If I should be here, what should I do?" In examining the predilection for law among professionals, there will clearly be a difference between wide and narrow. As a generalization, the wide professional will be more willing to see law strategically than the narrow, given the latter's focus on legal rights. There is consequently a static tension between the professional as strategic actor and rights-absolutist actor, and a dynamic tension between the professional as strategic litigator (using rights claims as part of a toolkit for change) and rights activist (supporting change inasmuch as it realizes legal rights).

As explored at the start of this chapter, the language of indigenous rights draws on a common narrative history (with Rousseau as a touchstone) and set of legal sources (exemplified by ILO Convention 169 and the recent UN Declaration). For these mining agreements to be legitimate inheritors of these traditions, they must construct the indigenous party using the pan-national language of indigenous rights. Thus a large indigenous rights NGO will feel itself better placed to engage with and fight for indigenous rights on a large scale and with an international scope if it does so through the medium of an hegemonic, standardized language. Thence the justificatory narrative of these agreements between indigenous peoples and TNCs being "empowering" (Godden et al. 2008: 25; Downing et al. 2002: 34): it is "empowering" in the sense that it makes it easier to deploy the emancipatory vocabulary of indigenous rights, given the limited parties to an agreement. This will in turn realize "empowerment" through political, social or economic consequences of legal action such as a mining agreement. This essentialist approach is problematic. From a practical standpoint, the one-size-fits-all approach ignores genuine nuances of the situation of indigenous groups; further, by limiting the public space and privileging the private space, it is easier to turn a discourse towards rights rather than public policy, which may be a more appropriate tool to provide benefits for the indigenous community.

From a narrative standpoint, law-as-empowerment ignores the "uniqueness" and autonomy of the indigenous group. In the same study, O'Faircheallaigh (2003: 14) found:

> There was a failure among many non-Indigenous policy-makers and officials both in the mining companies and government to recognise the power of "Aboriginal political agency", in other words the capacity of Aboriginal people to shape non-Indigenous processes and institutions to their own purposes . . . An example was the assumption by non-Indigenous officials that because the provisions of

> an agreement and the constitution and rules of a royalty association required payments to be distributed in a particular manner, this would in fact occur.

While the rhetoric of the professional may be emancipatory, his praxis is anything but, restricting the indigenous community's ability to construct multiple identities for itself and engage in "promising local political and social initiatives" (which may be where the professional's support is most useful: Kennedy 2002: 108), rather restricting it to imposed and unfamiliar legal and institutional "solutions."

Further, this ignores the political nature of the narrative construction of TNCs. The Kennedyian "emancipatory vocabulary," embedded in a mining agreement, narrates the TNC as oppositional to the community. The narrow professional thus ascribes to the company certain political characteristics: that it acts for money only, that it is unnatural and that it is not acting in the best interests of the community. The wide professional may recognize and be able to manipulate this politics, through various forms of legal and non-legal action (such as direct political pressure) and by widening or narrowing the TNC's political space as appropriate to its campaign (e.g. contingent on whether NGO wants greater state engagement).

However, the narrow professional reduces the space for non-legal solutions; further, he does so with a veneer of the apolitical: mining agreements simply represent the will of the parties and their enforcement is legal. This would indicate that a drive to implement indigenous rights norms should only be supported by those who believe that the "apolitical" system has a background politics that will function in their favor. Narrow professionals should be aware of the embedded politics in this situation and strategize accordingly (Muchlinksi 2003: 36–7). Indigenous rights professionals (Indigenous Support Services and ACIL Consulting 2001: 33–4) and academics (O'Faircheallaigh 2008) have stressed the importance of using mining royalties to protect the indigenous way of life (be it via the state or the contract). The indigenous rights professional will directly or indirectly be involved in ensuring royalties are disbursed for this purpose; this means he will be involved in their use to some extent, having input into (or in some cases determining) the disbursement of funds and thus the sort of "indigenous way of life" that is to be protected. O'Faircheallaigh (2008: 42), discussing such practices in Australia and using the language of aboriginal empowerment, argues for the role of the professional in the "[p]rovision of financial and other resources to support cultural heritage identification and management," without asking whether the professional also defines what legitimate cultural heritage is.

The impact of this is clear. When the law *is* applied strategically, it might be used to further the indigenous rights professional's narrative of indigenity under the guise of protecting their culture. Given its strategic nature, it can be assumed that both narrow and wide professionals might apply it in this way. By ensuring the enduring strength of the indigenous narrative, the professional concomitantly ensures both his place (as intermediary between the community and the wider world) and his space to operate. Crucially, this strategizing may be for the benefit of the narrative of the community but not of the community itself; its input remains limited as the language of law limits its access.

The narrative of legalism mainly concerns the narrow indigenous rights professional. It is apparent that the narrow professional rejects the language or praxis of strategizing. Instead of endogenizing social factors such as the capacity for protest, he sees law as the end in itself. However, there is an inherent contradiction in the approach: rejecting law-as-strategy is *in itself a strategy* to make law a trump card, to universalize the language of interaction between community and TNC and to privilege the position of the professional. The wide professional is well placed to see law as strategy, not hegemony, given that she will deploy it in the context of *other* strategies such as political pressure. Her answer to the question "What should I do?" may be "Whatever is necessary." However, with the World Bank and other IFIs engaging with these agreements, the narrow professional may become the norm at the expense of those who seek to retain a diverse toolbox. Moreover, the wide professional is handicapped by the narrative that she herself deploys: when she does make strategic use of the law, she may use it to further the *narrative* of the actors, to the detriment of the ends she seeks.

## Conclusion

> The moderns, understanding, by the term law, merely a rule prescribed to a moral being, that is to say intelligent, free and considered in his relations to other beings, consequently confine the jurisdiction of natural law to man, as the only animal endowed with reason. But, defining this law, each after his own fashion, they have established it on such metaphysical principles, that there are very few persons among us capable of comprehending them, much less of discovering them for themselves. (Rousseau 2006b: 80)

### *Observations*

*Mining agreements may become the norm*: mining agreements are mandated by some countries and are becoming common practice in others, including those without strong protections for indigenous land rights. TNCs may begin using them as standard practice to avoid the risk of future litigation. Their use by IFIs will also be determinative of their popularity going forward.

*Mining agreements have an embedded narrative of indigenity*: these agreements will be governed by, operate in and take on the characteristics of the international and national legal frameworks, including an indigenous narrative of spiritual and temporal relationships to land, influenced by Rousseau. This is, of course, a subject for further empirical study.

*Law is not always good, and agreements have a(n identity) politics*: agreements conceive of the indigenous community and TNCs in ways that both limit and expand their external political spaces (often through alterity). They also conceive of the actors as unitary, limiting their internal political spaces.

*The politics of an agreement is not always desirable, giving rise to strategic implications*: the politics of indigenity and corporate action is one of *passivity*. Law is the active mechanism that regulates the parties' relationships. By institutionalizing relationships and backgrounding the politics, parties cannot follow alternative strategies to achieve their ends.

*The indigenous rights professional has a vested interest in deploying agreements*: given the tensions between the narrative of indigenity and the language of law, the indigenous rights professional creates a space for himself *qua* professional to help (save? interfere with?) the indigenous community and provide it with benefits. The wide professional can bring legal experience, negotiating experience and general facility with professional interaction to the table, while the narrow professional brings all of that plus a specifically legal lexicon and knowledge. Agreements deploy the universalist vocabulary of indigenous rights; the wide professional may be more strategic about this language, but will deploy it when it allows him to reinforce the narrative of indigenity and create space for him to act *qua* professional.

*These vested interests can be to the detriment of the indigenous community*: the approach of the professional leads to the indigenous community becoming dependent upon her and a concomitant limitation on indigenous space to engage with TNCs. Given the professional's privileged position, she should act in the best interests of the community, utilizing every tool to get the best result rather than relying on legalism.

### *Contrat and Contract; or, Rousseau and Anti-legalism*

Mining agreements, as legal documents, have embedded "principles," be they metaphysical (as Rousseau asserts) or simply political. Yet the discourse of legalism is such that "very few persons . . . are capable of comprehending [it]." In this way, embedded principles dominate – the narrative of legalism, the narrative of indigenity, the narrative of professionalization. Yet a close reading of the *Discours* enriches our approach to mining agreements by implying that Rousseau sees law as the enemy of natural man. It is highly specialized and hard to comprehend. It is the first thing that social man sought. It is used to entrench power elites, "eternally fix[ing] the law of property and inequality . . . for the advantage of a few ambitious individuals" (Rousseau 2006b: 109). Although the indigenous rights professional positions himself as a buffer between the indigenous community and the depredations of modern society (i.e. the TNC), he applies a narrative that engages the community in the legal formalities of Rousseaulian society; indeed the community's identity as regards TNCs is constructed *through* that formal mechanism. Within the social constraints of law, communities cannot avail themselves of other means and political spaces to achieve their ends.

Law is not only the enemy of natural man, but one of the corrupting influences that induced his fall from the state of nature. Legally fortifying private property rights (an essential indigenous right!, cry the professionals) and deploying the law to manage individual or human behavior can only corrupt the *homme sauvage*. It may be that those who accept law-as-strategy can engage in a purposive, teleological approach that will mitigate the impact of modernity on communities. However, the tensions between the narrative of law-as-emancipation and that of natural man are perilous. In order to protect indigenity, the narrative must become reliant on the highly professional activist. If the professional fetishizes law, just as the narrative of natural man is fetishized, he risks undermining one, the other or both. The indigenous rights professional, so influenced by Rousseau and acting on a belief in the nobility of the *homme sauvage*, seeks to protect indigenous communities. Yet by applying such a legal, professional discourse, he in fact risks harming those very communities. There is a stark irony here. In attempting to realize natural man, he reifies Rousseau's narrative of social man: he applies law; its embedded characteristics serve his interests and may harm those of the community. Rousseau's determinist view of the fall of natural man may thus be actualized, the only difference being that the indigenous rights professional acts out of good faith, not selfishness.

The indigenous rights professional must always ask himself the titular question of this chapter: "A qui l'homme sauvage?" He must think critically about the *narrative* of natural man: how it corresponds to the indigenous community's actual situation, its strategic use, whether he is deploying it for the community or to serve his own ends and how it might harm the very people he seeks to help. He must also consider how it intersects with the narrative of law, and the inherent tension therein between natural and social. It is hoped that in doing so, he is required take a step back and think about his own role, asking the reflexive, essential meta-corollary: "A qui le professionnel des droits indigènes?"

## References

Alcorn, J. 2010. *Indigenous Peoples and Conservation* [Online: MacArthur Foundation Conservation White Paper Series]. Available at: http://production.macfound.org/media/files/CSD_Indigenous_Peoples_White_Paper.pdf [accessed 18 September 2012].

Baxi, U. 1982. *The Crisis of the Indian Legal System*. New Delhi: Vikas.

Ballard, C. 2001. *Human Rights and the Mining Sector in Indonesia: A Baseline Study*. Mining, Minerals and Sustainable Development at the International Institute of Environment and Development Working Paper No. 182 [Online]. Available at: http://www.rimmrights.org/Documents/indonesia_hr_baseline.pdf [accessed 18 September 2012].

Bowie, M. 1988. *Freud, Proust and Lacan: Theory as Fiction*. Cambridge: Cambridge University Press.

Bruner, J. 2003. *Making Stories: Law, Literature, Life*. Cambridge, MA: Harvard University Press.

Cawood, F.T. and Minnitt, R.C.A. 2002. Identification and Distribution of Mineral Rents in Southern Africa. *Journal of The South African Institute of Mining and Metallurgy*, 102, 289–98.

CDA Collaborative Learning Projects 2005. *Corporate Engagement Project: Report of Fourth CDA/CEP Visit to the Yadana Pipeline* [Online]. Available at: http://www.cdainc.com/cdawww/pdf/casestudy/cep_myanmar__fourth_visit_field_visit_report_Pdf.pdf [accessed 18 September 2012].

Cheney, H., Lovel, R. and Solomon, F. 2002. *People, Power, Participation: A Study of Mining–Community Relations*. Mining, Minerals and Sustainable Development/Ameef Working Paper [Online]. Available at: http://www.isf.uts.edu.au/publications/HC_RL_FS_2002.pdf [accessed 18 September 2012].

Clarke, T. 2004. Theories of Governance – Reconceptualizing Corporate Governance Theory After the Enron Experience, in *Theories of corporate governance: the philosophical foundations of corporate governance*, edited by T. Clarke. London: Routledge.

Cobo, J.M. 1986. *Study of the Problem of Discrimination Against Indigenous Populations*, UN Doc. E/Cn.4/ Sub.2/1986/7Add.4.

Conklin, B.A. and Graham, L.R. 1995. The Shifting Middle Ground: Amazonian Indians and Eco-Politics. *American Anthropologist*, 97, 695–710.

Dezalay, Y. and Garth B.G. 2002. *The Internationalization of Palace Wars: Lawyers, Economists, and the Contest to Transform Latin American States*. Chicago, IL: University of Chicago Press.

Dixit, A. 2007. *Lawlessness and Economics: Alternative Modes of Governance*. Princeton, NJ: Princeton University Press.

Downing, T.E. and Garcia-Downing, C. 2001. Plan B: What Is Going To Happen To My People? *Cultural Survival Quarterly*, 25(3), 8–17.

Downing, T.E. et al. 2002. *Indigenous Peoples and Mining Encounters: Strategies and Tactics*. Mining, Minerals and Sustainable Development at the International Institute of Environment and Development Working Paper No. 57 [Online]. Available at: http://pubs.iied.org/pdfs/G00548.pdf [accessed 18 September 2012].

Ellingson, T.J. 2001. *The Myth of the Noble Savage*. Berkeley, CA: University of California Press.

Environmental Resources Management 2010. *Mining Community Development Agreements – Practical Experiences and Field Studies. Final Report for the World Bank*. Washington, DC: Environmental Resources Management [Online]. Available at: http://www.sdsg.org/wp-content/uploads/2011/06/CDA-Report-FINAL.pdf [accessed 18 September 2012].

Filer, C. 1997. The Melanesian Way of Menacing the Mining Industry, in *Environment and Development in the Pacific Islands*, edited by B. Burt and C. Clerk. Canberra: National Centre for Development Studies, Australian National University; Port Moresby: University of Papua New Guinea Press.

Filer, C. 2008. Development Forum in Papua New Guinea: Upsides and Downsides. *Journal of Energy and Natural Resources Law*, 26, 120–49.

Gneezy, U. and Rustichini, A. 2000. A Fine is a Price. *Journal of Legal Studies*, 29, 1–18.

Godden, L., Langton, M., Mazel, O. and Tehan, M. 2008. Accommodating Interests in Resource Extraction: Indigenous Peoples, Local Communities and the Role of Law in Economic and Social Sustainability. *Journal of Energy and Natural Resources Law*, 26, 1–30.

Golub, S. 2003. *Beyond Rule of Law Orthodoxy: The Legal Empowerment Alternative*. Carnegie Endowment for International Peace Rule of Law Series Working Paper No. 41.

Hames, R. 2007. The Ecologically Noble Savage Debate. *Annual Review of Anthropology*, 36, 177–90.

Hirschman, A. 1992. *Rival Views of Market Society and Other Recent Essays*. Cambridge, MA: Harvard University Press.

Horne, W.C. 2001. Samuel Johnson Discovers the Arctic: A Reading of a "Greenland Tale" as Arctic Literature, in *Beyond Nature Writing: Expanding the Boundaries of Ecocriticism*, edited by K. Armbruster and K.R. Wallace. Charlottesville, VA: University Press of Virginia.

Indigenous Support Services and ACIL Consulting 2001. *Agreements between Mining Companies and Indigenous Communities: A Report to the Australian Minerals and Energy Environment Foundation* [Online]. Available at: http://www.icmm.com/document/1131 [accessed 18 September 2012].

International Finance Corporation 2012. *Performance Standard 7: Indigenous Peoples* [Online]. Available at: http://www1.ifc.org/wps/wcm/connect/1ee7038049a79139b845faa8c6a8312a/PS7_English_2012.pdf?MOD=AJPERES [accessed 18 September 2012].

Kennedy, D. 2000. Challenging Expert Rule: The Politics of Global Governance. *Sydney Law Review*, 27, 5–28.

Kennedy, D. 2002. The International Human Rights Movement: Part of the Problem?, *Harvard Human Rights Journal*, 15, 101-125.

Kingsbury, B. 2002. First Amendment Liberalism as Global Legal Architecture: Ascriptive Groups and the Problems of the Liberal NGO model of International Civil Society. *Chicago Journal of International Law*, 3, 183–95.

Kloppers, H. and du Plessis, W. 2008. Corporate Social Responsibility, Legislative Reforms and Mining in South Africa. *Journal of Energy and Natural Resources Law*, 26, 91–119.

Kramer, R.A., van Schaik, C.P. and Johnson, J. 1997. *Last Stand: Protected Areas and the Defense of Tropical Biodiversity.* New York: Oxford University Press.

Lacan, J. 1936. Au-delà du "principe de réalité." *L'Evolution Psychiatrique*, 3, 67–86.

Lacan, J. 1966. *Ecrits*. Paris: Seuil.

Lacan, J. 1973. *Les Quatre Concepts Fondamentaux de la Psychanalyse*. Paris: Seuil.

Lacan, J. and Miller, J.-A. 1978. *Le séminaire de Jacques Lacan: Le moi dans la théorie de Freud et dans la technique de la psychanalyse*. Paris: Seuil.

Langton, M. and Mazel, O. 2008. Poverty in the Midst of Plenty: Aboriginal People, the "Resource Curse" and Australia's Mining Boom. *Journal of Energy and Natural Resources Law*, 26, 31–65.

Lasser, M., Kennedy, D., Kennedy, D. and Berman, N. 1999. Critical Legal Theory, in *Law and the Arts*, edited by S. Tiefenbrun. Westport, CT: Greenwood Press.

Llewellyn, D. and Tehan, M. 2004. *"Treaties", "Agreements", "Contracts" and Commitments" – What's in a Name? The Legal Force and Meaning of Different Forms of Agreement Making*. Melbourne Law School Legal Studies Research Paper, No. 134.

Mace, M. 2004. Directors: Myth and Reality, in *Theories of Corporate Governance: the Philosophical Foundations of Corporate Governance*, edited by T. Clarke. London: Routledge.

Mann, H. 2008. *International Investment Agreements, Business and Human Rights: Key Issues and Opportunities*. IISD Research Paper [Online]. Available at: http://www.iisd.org/pdf/2008/iia_business_human_rights.pdf [accessed 18 September 2012].

McPhail, K. 2000. How Oil, Gas, and Mining Projects can Contribute to Development. *Finance and Development*, 37(4), 46–9.

Micklethwaite, J. and Wooldridge, A. 2005. *The Company*. New York: Random House.

Muchlinski, P. 2003. The Development of Human Rights Responsibilities for Multinational Enterprises, in *Business and Human Rights: Dilemmas and Solutions*, edited by R. Sullivan. Sheffield: Greenleaf Publishing.

Nadsady, P. 2005. Transcending the Debate over the Ecologically Noble Indian: Indigenous Peoples and Environmentalism. *Ethnohistory*, 52, 291–331.

Nygren, A. 1999. Local Knowledge in the Environment–Development Discourse: From Dichotomies to Situated Knowledge. *Critique of Anthropology*, 19, 267–88.

O'Faircheallaigh, C. 2003. *Implementing Agreements between Indigenous Peoples and Resource Developers in Australia and Canada*. Griffith University School of Politics and Public Policy Research Paper No. 13 [Online]. Available at: http://www.griffith.edu.au/business-commerce/griffith-business-school/pdf/research-paper-2003-implementing-agreements.pdf [accessed 18 September 2012].

O'Faircheallaigh, C. 2008. Negotiating Protection of the Sacred? Aboriginal–Mining Company Agreements in Australia. *Development and Change*, 39, 25–51.

Otto, J. 2010. *Community Development Agreement Model Regulations & Example Guidelines*. World Bank Report No. 61482 [Online]. Available at: http://www.eisourcebook.org/cms/files/attachments/worldbank/9point6-COMMUNITY-DEVELOPMENT-AGREEMENT-MODEL-REGULATIONS-&-EXAMPLE-GUIDELINES.pdf [accessed 18 September 2012].

Policy Forum. 2008. *The Demystification of Mining Contracts in Tanzania* [Online]. Available at: http://www.policyforum-tz.org/files/demystification.pdf [accessed 18 September 2012].

Posey, D.A., et al. 1984. Ethnoecology as Applied Anthropology in Amazonian Development. *Human Organization*, 43, 95–107.

Reich, R. 2007. *Supercapitalism*. New York: Knopf.

Rousseau, J.-J. 2006a. The Social Contract, in *The Social Contract, a Discourse on the Origin of Inequality, and a Discourse on Political Economy*, trans. G. D. H. Cole. Stilwell, KS: Digireads.com.

Rousseau, J.-J. 2006b. A Discourse on the Origin of Inequality, in *The Social Contract, a Discourse on the Origin of Inequality, and a Discourse on Political Economy*, trans. G. D. H. Cole. Stilwell, KS: Digireads.com.

Schroeder, J.-L. 2008. *The Four Lacanian Discourses: or Turning Law Inside-Out*. Abingdon: Birkbeck Law Press and Routledge-Cavendish.

Shavell, S. 2004. *Foundations of Economic Analysis of Law*. Cambridge, MA: Harvard University Press.

Shemberg, A. 2008. *Stabilization Clauses and Human Rights*. IFC/SRSG Research Paper [Online]. Available at: http://www.ifc.org/ifcext/enviro.nsf/AttachmentsByTitle/p_StabilizationClausesandHumanRights/$FILE/Stabilization+Paper.pdf [accessed 18 September 2012].

Sosa, I. and Keenan, K. 2001. *Impact Benefit Agreements Between Aboriginal Communities and Mining Companies: Their Use In Canada* [Online]. Canadian Environmental Law Association. Available at: http://s.cela.ca/files/uploads/IBAeng.pdf [accessed 18 September 2012].

Stearman, A.M. 1994. Revisiting the Myth of the Ecologically Noble Savage in Amazonia: Implications for Indigenous Land Rights. *Culture and Agriculture*, 14, 2–6.

Stephens, B. 2002. The Amorality of Profit: Transnational Corporations and Human Rights. *Berkeley Journal of International Law*, 20, 45–90.

Stiglitz, J. 2000. Formal and Informal Institutions, in *Social Capital: A Multifaceted Perspective*, edited by P. Dasgupta and I. Serageldin. Washington, DC: World Bank.

Strahilevitz, L. 2000. How Changes in Property Regimes Influence Social Norms: Commodifying California's Carpool Lanes. *Indiana Law Journal*, 75, 1231–96.

Terborgh, J. 1999. *Requiem for Nature*. Washington, DC: Island Press.

Thomas, B. 1991. *Cross-Examinations of Law and Literature: Cooper, Hawthorne, Stowe, and Melville*. Cambridge: Cambridge University Press.

United Nations 2007. *World Investment Report 2007*. U.N. Doc. UNCTAD/WIR/2007.

Van der Ploeg, J.D. 1993. Potatoes and Knowledge, in *An Anthropological Critique of Development: The Growth of Ignorance*, edited by M. Hobart. London: Routledge.

Waitt, G. 1999. Naturalizing the "Primitive": A Critique of Marketing Australia's Indigenous Peoples as "Hunter-gatherers". *Tourism Geographies*, 1, 142–63.

Xanthaki, A. 2003. Land Rights of Indigenous Peoples in South-East Asia. *Melbourne Journal of International Law*, 4, 467–96.

Chapter 12

# Corporate Responsibility and Human Rights in the Context of an International Constitutional Legal Framework: The Case of Angola

Angelica Anatolie Tsakiridis

This chapter directly addresses the question of the inadequacy and inconsistencies of sovereign nations' applications and interpretations of fundamental human rights norms and seeks to make a compelling case for so-called "international constitutionalization of human rights," where the direct consequences for violations of such rights will come to pass not only upon sovereign state actors, but also upon the multinational corporate actors (MNCs) who indirectly and directly support and/or encourage these violations.

The chapter uses as its case study atrocities committed on a massive scale during Angola's 21-year civil war between Angolan state and quasi-state ("rebel") actors. There, MNCs in the oil and gas industries directly and indirectly sanctioned and facilitated human rights atrocities against Angolan citizens, including rape, torture, displacement and extrajudicial killings, financed through direct and indirect payments to remain in the country and in joint ventures with Angola's parastatal oil corporation "Sonangol."

Further, the chapter addresses a theory of universal responsibility as the basis for international constitutionalization of human rights. The chapter posits that, in order to ensure durable, sustainable legal frameworks, the stakeholders who bear responsibility for implementation of this international constitutionalization concept should be diverse, and should have real power to administer meaningful consequences for violations. The analysis addresses the need to encourage local actors who are historically disenfranchised and therefore unengaged in traditional models for international planning and policy-making. The chapter discusses the notion that, to be effective, international accountability models must rooted in ethnically, socially, politically and economically diverse norms and expectations, in order to support transparent and fair outcomes.

There is a nexus between domestic instability and risk of the neglect of human rights concerns where measures for internal corruption, disparate political goals of elected (or de facto) leaders, a lack of transparency and poverty are high. However, the chapter seeks to clarify that, where internal conflict or insecurity exists, the financial influence or support through investment of outside MNCs can and does compound violations of international human rights norms. Therefore, a forum for international constitutionalism will play a critical role in neutralizing outside actors, like MNCs in this example, who are currently unaccountable to either local or existing international legal structures.

As such, this chapter connects the concept of universal responsibility with a primary focus on including MNCs' responsibility to individuals as a pivotal issue where the actions of corporations acting in concert with individuals, even sovereigns, leads to civil and criminal violations of the fundamental human rights. Where corporate muscle is used to subvert and commit mass violations of human rights, the crucial role of a system rooted in international constitutionalism should be to provide an unbiased platform to submit claims by (1) creating new systems that in the first place recognize a cause of action against MNCs and impose liability on MNCs for violation of those laws, and (2) cultivating a jurisprudence of international law that recognizes those claims, individuals or entities. Therefore, domestic and international legal systems should further universalize human rights norms to more effectively protect developing resource rich States from horrendous abuses by predatory MNCs.

## Background and Case Study: Angola

A brutal civil war spanning nearly 30 years ended in Angola in April of 2002. A peace accord was signed between the Angolan Armed Forces (MPLA) and the National Union for Total Independence (UNITA).[1] Despite the written end of armed conflict, atrocities committed against the Angolan citizenry continued through 2004.[2] Displacement of persons by both the official government of the MPLA and UNITA is estimated to have affected more than 4.6 million persons.[3] The displacement operations included the systematic destruction of villages, forced labor, sexual abuse of women and girls and sexual slavery. Other activities that Human Rights Watch examiners deemed to be torture-related atrocities were also committed by both the MPLA and UNITA.[4] These human rights violations were exacerbated by the MPLA's inability to provide social services for the victims,

1 See, e.g., The U.S. State Department Country Profile on Angola, 2004. Available at: www.state.gov/r/pa/ei/bgn/6619.htm (visited 4 April 2004).

2 See, e.g., HRW-sponsored research examining its extensive HRW Transparency Report (January 2004) and related findings regarding crimes against Angolan citizens committed by the MPLA and UNITA during the civil war. Available at: www.hrw.org/english/docs/2004/01/12/angola6925.htm (visited 4 April 2004).

3 Ibid.

4 See, e.g. "The Human Rights Watch Organization World Report on Angola, 2003" (published January 2004). Available at: www.hrw.org/wr2k3/africa1.html (visited 4 April 2004).

including clean drinking water, food, shelter and security.[5] Reintegration efforts were made by United Nations non-governmental organizations (NGOs) like the United Nations Commission on Human Rights (UNHCR), but as of April of 2004, more than 1 million Angolans remained homeless.[6]

It is estimated that several hundred thousand people lost their lives and over 4 million persons were displaced from their homes. The placement of more than 10 million landmines has taken many more lives, even in so-called times of peace.[7]

Angola is a country located on the Atlantic coast of Sub-Saharan Africa. It remained a Portuguese colony for more than 500 years, until Portugal withdrew in 1975. The two factions principally responsible for the war were Angola's acting and recognized governments, the MPLA and UNITA, which have been described as proxies for the war's financial sponsors – Cold war combatants.[8] The United States (and the apartheid government of South Africa) financed the rebel UNITA forces, providing training and arms, while the Soviet Union and Cuba funded and armed the MPLA.[9] The resultant years of war and continued instability facilitated the unchecked operation of the corrupt central government (the MPLA), which drained the country of its vast oil and mineral wealth.[10] A 2004 Human Rights Watch International (HRW) Transparency and Accountability report documented that between 1994 and 2002, over US$4.22 billion in profits and external payments into the country remained unaccounted for, and were, in essence, missing.[11]

The US State Department corroborated HRW findings in a 2004 report commissioned by the Bureau on African Affairs, when it examined financial data and payments made by US corporations to the Angolan government during that

5 Ibid.

6 See, e.g., Press Release "Reintegration Efforts in Angola," Human Rights Watch, 13 January 2004. Available at: www.hrw.org.

7 Angola's Diamond Mining Case Issue, available at www.american.edu (visited 21 July 2006).

8 Paul S. Orogun, "Cross-Border Raids, Regional Insecurity and Political Destabilization in sub-Saharan Africa: An Analysis of Armed Conflicts in Angola, Sierra Leone, and the Democratic Republic of Congo" (2002) available at: http://isanet.ccit.arizona.edu/noarchive/orogun.html.

9 See *supra* note 5.

10 The report, "Some Transparency, No Accountability, The Use of Oil Revenue in Angola and its Impact on Human Rights," was produced by the Human Rights Watch Organization in cooperation with several International NGOs, the IMF and the UN. It was released on 13 January 2004. The report comprises recommendations for Angola, the Oil Industry, the international community and the United States. It also details the various restructuring programs attempted in Angola since 1995, and the results of their failures. Available at: www.hrw.org/reports/2004/angola0104/angola0104.pdf.

See, e.g., *supra* note 5.

11 See, e.g., *supra* note 13.

same time period.[12] The report made findings on reported data for American oil giant ChevronTexaco, through its subsidiary operating in Angola, Cabinda Gulf Oil Company. Cabinda and Sonangol (the non-OPEC Angolan State oil company joint venture that includes British oil giants TotalFinaElf and ENI-Agip) partnered prior to the 2004 peace agreement to negotiate the current, deep-water oil drilling and made exploration payments thus far unreported in the United States for a future natural gas exploration project. They also provided material assistance to the MPLA in order to remain a 39.2 percent shareholder in Sonangol during documented periods of violence.[13] During the same period of examination, the United States purchased more than half of the total Angolan oil exports, while sending the largest portion of foreign humanitarian aid to the MPLA in Angola.[14]

The conflict caused a standstill of development in Angola, leaving the country virtually without internal infrastructure or resources for the citizens of the country. The acting Angolan government, however, did develop prosperous working relationships with foreign direct investors, including mineral and oil companies from the mid-1970s that continue to the present.[15] The Angolan government, vis-à-vis its parastatal oil company, Sonangol, developed working partnerships with various MNCs through an intricate, extra-territorial banking system.[16] This system channeled foreign direct investment directly into privately held government officials' accounts and refilled its war chest, while depriving the citizens of Angola of public safety, education and healthcare.[17]

Subsequent historical research has indicated that the MNCs cooperated with the MPLA by utilizing a system of so-called exploration payments, deemed "signature

12 See, e.g., "The U.S. State Department Bureau on African Affairs Economics Section Report on Angola," February 2004. The report details the oil production distribution reports required by US internal reporting regulations, in an examination of US oil influence on the Angolan economy. Available at: www.state.gov/r/pa/ei/bgn/6619.htm (visited 10 April 2004).

13 Ibid. See also, *supra,* note 13.

14 See, e.g., www.hrw.org/wr2k3/africa1.html. See also, www.opec.org. OPEC's stated mission includes "providing aid to developing countries and adding stability and harmony to the oil market by adjusting their oil output to help ensure balance between supply and demand."

15 Ibid.

16 2004 Human Rights Watch World Report: "Angola and Transparency International's 2004 Corruption Perception Index," available at: www.transparencyinternational.org.

Ibid. See also, *supra* note 5. The US State Department 2004 figures indicate that the country is rich in oil, diamonds and other minerals and natural resources, yet the per capita GDP is only US$951 per year. Annual oil exports total US$9.8 billion, and account for more than 90 percent of all annual exports. Petroleum products account for 90 percent of government revenues and Angola is the second largest producer of oil in Africa. Despite these bloated oil profits, Angola remains one of Africa's poorest and most troubled nations.

17 Ibid.

bonuses."[18] MNCs participated in these payment structures, and continue to own mineral and oil holdings in Angola to the present, despite prevailing international law and domestic regulatory laws of countries such as the United States (e.g. The Foreign Corrupt Practices Act, which statutorily prohibits the payment of such signature bonuses to foreign governments and/or governmental officials in exchange for privileges otherwise unattainable in that country). Signature bonuses paid in Angola can be described as lump-sum, untraceable payments made to the Angolan government in exchange for the right to explore or derive oil or minerals from within the country, or offshore drilling and exploration rights.[19] Evidence of the payments cannot be traced directly to Angola's central treasury; instead, these monies were paid to offshore bank accounts.[20] The Sarbanes–Oxley Act, a domestic statutory reporting regulation in the United States, requires disclosure of such payments as part of a corporation's internal controls and accounting reporting obligations; however, MNCs involved in such payments would be subject to statutory fines.[21] Critically, an October 2002 assessment report commissioned by the International Monetary Fund (IMF) revealed that corruption had literally caused the disappearance of more than US$4 billion in revenues, which totaled more than the amount of humanitarian aid sent to the country in the same year.[22] Angola repeatedly flouted IMF directives and its own domestic laws and accounting procedures, and refused to cooperate with IMF-sponsored "Oil Diagnostic Programs."[23]

Overt evidence of foreign cash payments is difficult to uncover; however, the measurable expansion of offshore drilling of deep-sea blocks controlled by Sonangol is evidence that Sonangol received lump sum payments by companies such as BP-Amoco (i.e. US$870 million in May of 1999, and signature bonuses by Exxon and TotalFinaElf), and supplemental audits commissioned by the IMF and Transparency International indicate direct financing of oil, gas, gem and mineral mining-related projects by these same MNCs. Transparency International commissioned international audit-house KPMG to examine an audit in 2002.[24] The KPMG report documented accounting discrepancies totaling more than US$192 million where foreign direct investment into Sonangol documented as deposit credits to Angola's central bank, Banco National de Angola (BNA), cannot

18 See *supra* note 5.

19 See *supra* note 6.

20 Ibid.

21 Sarbanes-Oxley Act of 2002, Pub. L. No. 107-204 (30 July 2002).

22 See, e.g., 18 October 2002 Internal Monetary Fund Assessment Report: "Angola." See also, Justin Pearce, "IMF: Angola's Missing Millions," BBC News Correspondent in Luanda, Angola. The IMF report also indicated that mismanagement of this scale had never before been reported by an institution with the status of the IMF, which pin-pointed Sonangol as the main source of the reporting discrepancies.

23 See, e.g., *supra* note 19.

24 See, e.g., *supra* note 13.

be accounted for in actual assets held by the bank.[25] The result is a a bare cupboard for funds cited as foreign aid payments and foreign direct investment payments, and strong evidence that the money was used to purchase future oil revenues to use as quick cash to purchase arms and participate in displacement activities outlined above.[26] Private MNCs who participated in this ongoing payment structure are direct participants in the accounting fraud uncovered by these NGOs, KPMG and the IMF assessments, where MNCs had knowledge of the diversions, and continued to finance the government over years with the same payment structures.

## Solutions

### *Universal Responsibility*

Where internal conflict or insecurity exist, financial influence or support through investment of outside MNCs can and does compound and magnify negative outcomes contrary to internationally accepted human rights norms. Using the model case study of MNC activities in Angola, it is possible to draw a causal link between this high level of corruption, financial mismanagement and the deteriorated condition of human life in Angola during the years of the civil war where: (1) the Angolan government failed to follow its own laws regarding traceability of oil revenues; (2) MNCs and the Angolan Government failed to designate or maintain meaningful procedures for verify payment by the MNCs; (3) MNCs and the Angolan government's Ministry of Finance/Treasury failed to keep accurate or reliable records; (4) MNCs and the Angolan government failed to make audits or overseer reports public; and (5) MNCs and the Angolan government failed to account for billions of dollars in oil revenues. These factors were directly responsible for the secondary issues of (1) the Angolan government's inability to provide humanitarian assistance to displace or injured persons; (2) the Angolan government's failure to demobilize soldiers or control police and/or military and paramilitary activities, resulting in a multitude of human rights violations; and (3) the failure of the government to improve internal infrastructure including education, judiciary, health and welfare for its own citizens.[27]

The gulf between the quality of life for the citizens of Angola and an inability to match expansive oil and mineral wealth to the public treasury remains a painful reminder of the devastating collateral effects of systematic corruption.[28] Angola ranks among the poorest countries in the world, despite having one of the most abundant stretches of fertile lands, the third largest supply of oil resources in

25 Ibid.

26 Ibid.

27 Ibid.

28 www.transparencyinternational.org.

Africa, and multiple yet-untapped mineral and precious metals mines.[29] The infant mortality rate hovers around 209/1000 live births, and it is on the bottom rung of the GDP ladder. Transparency International ranks Angola 168 out of 180 on its corruption scale analysis for 2009.[30]

MNCs took advantage of oil, gas, mineral and gem investment opportunities, providing foreign "direct" investment knowing that these investments were being used to buy munitions and support the displacement, torture and neglect of Angolan citizens. The governmental, paramilitary officials and MNCs alone benefited from the country's natural resources, its minerals and oil under the guise of exploration and development assistance. Paradoxically, in the mid-1980s, US Senator Jesse called for more funds to fight the so-called Communist threat breeding in Angola; the oil, gas and mineral lobbies flourished under US anti-Communist policies, all the while "acting extra-judiciously, under the guise of foreign investment, to thwart those very objectives."[31]

Scrutiny by Transparency International and other non-governmental organizations such as Global Witness cites the widespread, unchecked corruption of government officials, no internal controls and a lack of accountability as reasons for the Angola's continued poverty, abysmal human rights record, lack of infrastructure and deteriorating stability.[32]

The long duration and cycle of multiple false détentes between the MPLA and UNITA prompted renewed foreign investment initiatives each time the country seemed to end the fighting. International organizations like the IMF, World Bank, and the Organisation for Economic Co-Operation and Development (OECD), utilizing as a framework, the OECD Guidelines for Multinational Enterprises and Principles of Corporate Governance, have stepped in to organize future development and investment in Angola.[33] The OECD guidelines provided an outline of procedures and recommended policies for the investment practices of MNCs in accordance

29 Last updated 29 March 2006; available at: www.imf.org/external/country/cog/omdex.htm.

Kenneth L. Adelman, "Report from Angola," *Foreign Affairs*, April 1975. Available at www.foreignaffairs.org.

30 Twenty-three of the 50 largest oil companies in the world have representation in Washington, DC. An example of the power of this lobby comes in the form of the African Growth and Opportunity Act, aimed at increasing US trade with African Nations. The oil industry supported the bill and the coincidence of the Bush Administration in 2000. See, Shantha Bloeman, "Angola: A Case Study," Initiative for Policy Dialogue, Summary Report of the British–Angola Forum Conference, London 12–13 November 2002 (2003); available at www.progressio.co.uk. See also, Transparency International, Annual Report, 2009, available at: www.transparency.org (visited 11 October 2010).

31 Ibid. Quotation taken from Bill Witherall, "Corporate Governance and Responsibility: Foundations of Market Integrity," OECD Observer (2003); available at: http://www.oecdobserver.org/news. Bloeman, *supra*, note 30.

32 *Good Governance: The IMF's Role*, IMF Publications at p. 6 (1997).

33 www.hrw.org/reports/angola0104/angola0104.pdf. Ibid.

with members' desires to compel good governance.[34] "Good governance goes beyond common sense. It is a key part of the contract that underpins economic growth in a market economy and public faith in that system. The OECD Principles of Corporate Governance and Guidelines for Multinational Enterprises are two essential instruments for ensuring that this contract is honoured."[35]

Despite the international community's involvement in the country through encouraged transparency and dialogue, both warring factions managed to thwart efforts to support peace through stability. The money to refuel the war effort came, on UNITA's part, from illegal diamond mining, and on MPLA's part, from continuing extra-judicial dealings with foreign oil concerns and their governments.[36]

The IMF provides criteria for a country's receipt of IMF-backed loans. While reserving a right to remain free of the role of "investigative agency or guardian of financial integrity" within a participating financial institution, the IMF still addresses corruption issues in its country assessment.[37] This hands off approach is appropriate to the Fund's role as an economic facilitator, and not as a development agency. However, the consequences of such disconnect have materialized in the pervasive and totally uncooperative governmental system in place in Angola.

An example of the continuing transparency problem comes in the form of IMF rules for loans to the country. A 2001 IMF agreement provided that borrowing through loans must be limited to US$269 million per year.[38] Between the months of September and October of 2001 alone, more than US$3.5 billion were counted in the form of seven loans. Furthermore, an IMF-sponsored Oil Diagnostic was

34 Ibid.

35 Ibrahim F.I. Shihata, "Corruption – a General Review with an Emphasis on the Role of the World Bank," based on the keynote address of Mr Shihata at the Fourteenth International Symposium on Economic Crime, Cambridge (1996).

36 Transparency International, Corruption Perception Report, 2004; available at www.transparency.org. The score is calculated as follows: "Score relates to perceptions of the degree of corruption as seen by business people and country analysts and ranges between 10 (highly clean) and 0 (highly corrupt). Confidence range provides a range of possible values of the CPI score. This reflects how a country's score may vary, depending on measurement precision. Nominally, with 5 percent probability the score is above this range and with another 5 percent it is below. However, particularly when only few sources (*n*) are available an unbiased estimate of the mean coverage probability is lower than the nominal value of 90%. Surveys used refers to the number of surveys that assessed a country's performance. 18 surveys and expert assessments were used and at least 3 were required for a country to be included in the CPI."

37 Press release concerning the publication of the extensive HRW Transparency Report, 13 January 2004; available from: www.hrw.org/english/docs/2004/01/12/angola6925.htm.

38 "Angola: Displaced Still Suffering: Three Years after Civil War, Little Progress for Returnees," http://hrw.org/english/docs/2005/03/17/angola10322.htm (2005).

*OECD Guidelines for Multinational Enterprises: Report of the Chairman: Annual Report on the OECD Guidelines for Multinational Enterprises*, 2005 edn at p. 79.

not completed as agreed, and the Angolan Ministry of Finance has thus far refused attempts to account for oil revenues in an annual publication according to the IMF agreement.[39] In addition, profits from oil drilling and exploration payments provide a constant stream of collateral that expedites alternative loans and avoids the strict compliance measures necessary to comply with the IMF structures and agreements.[40]

*Defining Corruption*

The problem of corruption and the lack of transparency in the case study of Angola's oil, mineral and gem industries is confounded by the fact that MNCs have created little incentive for the Angolan government to comply with the political carrots held out by international bodies seeking to end conflict and promote development. Namely, the outward interests of the US and other governments, efforts by the IMF, World Bank and the OECD and the humanitarian interests of multiple United Nations (UN) and NGO organizations are in direct opposition to the economic interests of private companies profiting from the loose system of non-disclosure and bait-and-switch tactics used by the Angolan government to hide the source and funds themselves. The result is the circular system of continued disintegration of the Angolan society, and the potential for further civil conflict as the borders around Angola continue to be enmeshed in ongoing conflict, poverty and displacement and land struggles.

The definition of corruption is multi-pronged. The reduction of corruption is a favorable outcome to achieve the goals stated by both the IMF and the World Bank, despite their inability or unwillingness to take on the task of policing the individual nations. The cost to the goals of those organizations of ignoring the problem, however, is indisputable.

> With the greater liberalization of trade and investment, the gradual globalization of the market place and overwhelming advances in technology, corruption is becoming not only a common domestic problem, but an international problem as well. It is being recognized as a development issue in view of its possible impact on the cost of transactions, the volume of external flows, the stability

39 Ibid. Furthermore, the conclusory notes of the Report summarized the obligation of companies operating in so-called "weakly governed" states as a duty to pay strict attention to: "1) the amount of due diligence and managerial care that has to be taken to ensure that these standards are adhered to; and 2) the effort companies need to make to ensure that they can be held accountable for their performance in these weak governance zones (where such transparency-enhancing institutions as business associations, legal and accounting institutions, free press and civil society do not function well)." Ibid. at p. 90.

40 "A Glimmer of Light at Last?: Sub-Saharan Economies are Growing Faster but are they Really Getting Stronger?," *The Economist*, 22 June 2006.

> and predictability of the investment environment, and eventually the world's premier development financial institution.[41]

Corruption provides a mechanism for the continued marginalization and destruction of the economic and civil society.[42] The failure of purely economic incentives to motivate a steady transformation from a war-torn society to a viable and stable one can be measured, in large part, by the level of corruption.[43]

A committee report by the OECD in 2005 highlights this particular issue. "[W] hat is at stake is not simply the credibility or profitability of OECD investment, but the physical, social and economic well-being of millions of people throughout the developing world." "Home country and international organisations can play important – but only supporting – roles in assisting weak governance host countries to get on the path to reform."[44] The 2005 OECD member Nations Convention Report by the Chairman also concluded that companies are expected to adhere to international laws and widely held international standards such as "human rights, management of security forces, protection of local populations, corporate governance".[45]

The influence of third-party state actors such as the Peoples' Republic of China (PRC) cannot be ignored, and Angola and other African nations who had previously struggled to attract the glances of Western foreign direct investment suitors now look towards economic powers like China to support its internal activities for the future. The PRC is the third largest world economy and is the most populous nation on earth.[46] The main thrust of the PRC's interest in Angola, may be explained by dwindling Middle Eastern oil reserves, the bulging Chinese technology sector and the desire to secure energy and natural resources for its explosive economy and population. The US House of Representatives committee hearings identified the US policy-related concerns: "petroleum and minerals; trade and manufacturing, and democracy and transparency." These concerns were amplified by Angola's troubled history and potentially troubled future as it could became fair game to other nations.[47]

---

41 Ibid.

42 Ibid. at 4.

43 Ibid. at 5.

44 Ibid. at 10–11.

45 Ibid.

46 See, Angelica Tsakiridis, "Making the Case for Angola", April, 2006. LLM Thesis on file with the author.

47 Alien Tort Claims Act 28 U.S.C.A. 1350, "The district courts shall have original jurisdiction of any civil action by an alien for a tort only, committed in violation of the law of nations, or committed in violation of the law of nations or a treaty of the United States." Enacted 1789. The principle was recognized first in *Filariga v. Pena Irala*, 630 F. 2d 876 (2d Cir. 1980). *Kadic v. Karadzic*, 70 F. 3d 232, 236 (2d Cir. 1995), reiterated; "the ATCA validly creates federal court jurisdiction for suits alleging torts committed anywhere in the world against aliens in violation of the law of nations."

The report focuses on the emerging Chinese influence in Angola and other African countries and whether the relationships will pose a threat to US foreign policy in the region. While the sphere thus far has been deemed a non-threat, the actions of the PRC have prompted official concern in Angola, Sudan and Zimbabwe that they are "problematic politically" for that particular region.[48] The most pressing problem identified in the report was the divergence in foreign aid policies regarding Angola (et al.) between the PRC and the West. While traditional donors and international financial institutions (IFIs) like the IMF and the World Bank or bilateral agreements are trying to "alter the behaviors of governments by imposing political conditions, the PRC has a soft policy, that seeks to be 'flexible' and may not be among the factors that contribute to transparency and a future of democracy."[49]

Interestingly, the report cites President Hu's declaration in May of 2004, "China wants business, with no political conditions," as evidence of the no-holds-barred attitude towards trade and traditional organic laws.[50] While the West bristles with this seemingly anti-democratic rhetoric and ever-present no-rules "trade trumps transparency" attitude, the real question still lingers. Is the concern really for human rights and the future democratization of Angola, or is China dipping into a resource-rich reserve the United States and the other Western powers wanted for themselves, in a time when the Middle East is bursting politically at the seams and the Saudi oil wells are beginning to run their course?

China has formed a bilateral relationship with Angola, and now purchases more than 25 percent of the yearly output of crude oil.[51] The PRC contributed more than US$2 billion in "signature payments" in 2004, and as reported by the US State Department citing the NGO Global Witness's recent investigations, the money landed in the MPLA's campaign war chest.[52]

The emergence of China as a major trading influence in Africa and especially Angola has prompted a stir in the US foreign policy powers that be. The criticism, however, is that this renewed interest in human security, democracy and transparency issues has come too late for lives lost, and a nation floundering in a culture of corruption, violence and secrecy.

Despite the outward feather ruffling by the United States towards China and to a lesser extent India regarding Angolan and general African foreign investment policies, the mood at home has not reflected the genuine concern for human rights and social distortion owing to the long-time military dismemberment of the

48 Ibid.

49 Ibid. at 704, 2750.

50 Ibid.

51 Ibid. at 716, 2756.

52 Ibid. at 728, 2763. See, e.g. 729, 30, 2764, Moreover, "International law is a part of our law and must be ascertained and administered by the courts of justice of appropriate jurisdiction, as often as questions of right depending upon it are duly presented for their determination", quoting The Nereide, 9 Cranch 388, 423, 3 L.Ed. 769 (1815).

country. Research regarding human rights abuses in Angola alleged that there was a direct correlation with the multinational oil/mineral corporations funding and directly "aiding and abetting" the illegal activities of the Angolan government.[53]

## Constitutionalization of Human Rights

### *Domestic Reforms (with Special Reference to the United States)*

The international constitutionalization of human rights is a necessary step to ensure durable, sustainable legal frameworks and confirm participation by stakeholders who bear responsibility for implementation of this framework. It is the right time for a paradigm shift in recognized principles of international jurisprudence. The world financial crisis of 2007–2010 and public scandals including the British Petroleum (BP) oil spill in the Gulf of Mexico in early 2010 have opened a narrow opportunity for international cooperation in the face of public outcry about the lack of transparency and resource accountability shown by MNCs.

The time for action is now, when some visible activities undertaken by the US Obama Administration have made gains for human rights initiatives and indicated a more comprehensive, participatory role for the US in the UN, including an active role in the International Criminal Court and increased participation in the UN Humans Rights Council.[54] However, in the same breath in which the Obama Administration has engendered domestic transparency and regulatory reform legislation, subtle political messaging has been aimed at whittling down the already shifting legal pathways by which individual actors can address grievances against MNCs in the areas of human rights and corporate governance.

A forum, therefore, for the international constitutionalism of human rights will play a critical role in neutralizing outside actors, like MNCs in the Angola example, who are currently not accountable to either local or existing international legal structures.[55] Moreover, a more unified pathway will not be weakened by shifts in an individual sovereign's political or legal domestic framework.

---

53 www.worldbank.org/urban/symposium2003/docs/presentation/kennedy.pdf. Additionally, in light of the *John Doe I. v. Unocal* case, and a host of similar actions successfully alleging collaboration to commit tortious acts with foreign governments, the details of complicity in human rights violations committed by multinational-American oil and mineral corporations began to surface. 2002 WL 31063976 (9th Cir. 2002).

Ibid.

54 See, e.g., "US Makes Gains for Human Rights in Geneva," Barbara Crossette, 11 October 2010 published on *The Nation*; available at www.thenation.com.

55 The double standard has once again emerged. The oil and gas lobby was quick to alert the Bush administration of its displeasure with the liberal use of the Alien Tort Claims Act to bring actions against US companies in the United States for wrongs allegedly committed in other nations. The success of a handful of African-based cases in the US Circuits was blindsided by the precedent decision in the US Supreme Court. *Sosa v. Alvarez-*

*Alien Tort Statute* On 28 February 2012, one of the most important cases to assert the Alien Tort Statute, *Kiobel v. Royal Dutch Petroleum*,[56] was heard in oral arguments before the United States Supreme Court. On 5 March 2012, the Court ordered that the case be restored for reargument, and the parties were directed to file supplemental briefs addressing the following question: "Whether and under what circumstances the Alien Tort Statute (ATS), 28 U.S.C. §1350, allows courts to recognize a cause of action for violations of the law of nations occurring within the territory of a sovereign other than the United States."[57] The case, based on scheduling, should be reargued sometime in the autumn of 2012. The ultimate question posed by the judges during oral arguments, is whether or not the ATS has an extraterritorial application, that is, whether or not the ATS applies to wrongs committed outside of the United States.[58] During oral arguments, the attorney for the petitioners, Paul L. Hoffman, attempted to cover the ground left pocked by the lower court opinion concerning the application of the ATS, stating in his opening argument that the court had before them "the narrow issue of whether a corporation can ever be held liable for violating fundamental human rights norms

---

*Machain, et al.*, 542 U.S. 692, 124 S.Ct. 2739 (2004). Sosa involved the arrest of a Mexican citizen on Mexican soil by Mexican nationals allegedly hired by the United States' Drug Enforcement Agency (the plan designed on American soil) as retaliation for Sosa's alleged involvement in the torture and murder of an American DEA agent on Mexican soil in 2000. In an opinion authored by Justice Souter in June of 2004, the Court held that Sosa could not recover under the Alien Tort Claims Act and the Foreign Tort Claims Act for an act which took place on foreign soil, as the ATCA contains a "foreign country exception" to the rule, that acts to bar application of the doctrine to wrongs that arise in a foreign country. Former decisions had linked the actions of foreign companies' employees and decision-making that took place in the United States as viable exceptions to the "foreign country" rule. The court also expressed its displeasure with the Alien Tort Statue, as it seemed to borrow too heavily from "hybrid international norms." The Court has had a tumultuous relationship with any firm adherence to international laws or widely accepted norms, as they hold in Sosa, "We have no congressional mandate to seek out and define new and debatable violations of the law of nations," despite having recognized in a plethora of former cases that the "United States recognizes the law of nations." However ultimately, *Sosa* concluded that imposing liability on MNCs for violations of the law of nations had to be of such "specific, universal, and obligatory" nature so as to be considered a norm of customary international law.

56 Alien Tort Claims Act 28 U.S.C. 1350 et seq. See also, Order in Pending Case, *Kiobel v. Royal Dutch Petroleum Co.* (docket 10-1491) (2012). See also, *Esther Kiobel, Individually and on Behalf of Her Late Husband, Dr. Barinem Kiobel, et al., Petitioners. Royal Dutch Petroleum Co. et al.* (petition for cert pending no. 10-1491 (filed 2012).

57 Order in Pending Case, *Kiobel v. Royal Dutch Petroleum Co., supra.*

58 John Bellinger, "Stop Press: Supreme Court Orders Kiobel Reargued to Address Extraterritoriality," *Lawfare*, 5 March 2012; available at: http://www.lawfareblog.com/2012/03/stop-press-supreme-court-orders-kiobel-reargued-to-address-extraterritoriality/.

under the Alien Tort Statute."[59] The claim made by petitioner alleges that Royal Dutch Petroleum and its relevant subsidiaries, British and Dutch MNCs, aided and abetted Nigerian military forces and Nigerian police in committing gross human rights violations, including torture, extrajudicial killing, crimes against humanity and arbitrary arrest and detention in Nigeria.[60]

The mood of the court in February's oral arguments was painted by Justice Kennedy, in addressing the contents of an amicus filing on behalf of the respondent by Chevron Corporation, stating that "no other nation in the world permits its court to exercise universal civil jurisdiction over alleged extraterritorial human rights abuses to which the nation has no connection."[61] Clearly if the petitioners are unable to reaffirm what legal scholars and jurisprudence in this area of human rights have long since understood – that the ATS is applicable to wrongs committed outside of the United States – a decision turning over this long-held principle will foreclose on the ATS application in like cases where plaintiffs have been injured or suffer continuing injury but have no recourse in their home country and will have no ongoing basis in international law upon which to bring an action elsewhere.[62] The US Federal Court is the only forum in the world to recognize a cause of action and provide a forum for violations of international law committed by foreign persons upon other foreign persons extraterritorially.

The *Kiobel* case marks a narrowing of ATS applicability. The 2nd Circuit hovered over and targeted the inconsistent swath of case law in this area, finding that the jurisdiction of the courts was limited where the respondents were corporations accused of violations of international human rights law.[63]

The *Kiobel* case has been politically charged as well. Legal scholar (and amici curiae) John Bellinger notes, "This development [the March Order] will

59 Lyle Dennisen, "Argument Recap: Downhill From the Start," *Scotus*, 28 February 2012; available at: http://www.scotusblog.com/?p=139919.

60 See, e.g., *supra*, note 59.

61 Ibid.

62 *Filartiga v. Pena-Irala*, 630 F.2d 876 (2d Cir.1980), See also, "Supplemental Brief for the Petitioner, Professors Of Legal History William R. Casto, Charles Donahue, Robert W.Gordon, Nasser Hussain, Stanley N. Katz, Michael Lobban, Jenny S. Martinez, James Oldham and Anne-Marie Slaughter as Amici Curiae," *Kiobel v. Royal Dutch Petroleum Co.* (docket 10-1491) (2012).

63 *Kiobel v. Royal Dutch Petroleum*, 621 F.3d 111 (2d Cir. 2010). On 17 September 2010, a three judge-panel from the US Federal Court's Second Circuit Court of Appeals (New York) ruled 2–1 that the "limited jurisdiction" granted by the ATS was insufficient to cover human rights violations alleged by Nigerian citizens against British and Dutch MNCs including torture, murders and rapes by Nigerian soldiers of Nigerian villagers opposed to the MNCs oil exploration activities. The court, in a reply for the majority authored by Justice Jose Cabranes stated that "corporations, unlike individuals, may not be subject to criminal and civil liability for violations of international law."

put the Obama Administration in a difficult position."[64] Moreover, more than 16 representatives of foreign governments and trade interests have weighed in to support the respondent in Amicus Briefs since the Order was issued in March.[65] In its subsequent supplemental amicus brief filed in June 2012, the Obama Administration forcefully counters its brief partially supporting the respondents wherein the Administration describes the US position as "the United States cannot be thought responsible in the eyes of the international community for affording a remedy for the company's actions, while the nations directly concerned could."[66]

Further analysis of the US Government's legal brief highlights political policy concerns where, it proffers, "In *Sosa*, this Court recognized that allowing US courts to pronounce 'a limit on the power of foreign governments over their own citizens, and to hold that a foreign government or its agent has transgressed those limits,' would have 'potential implications for the foreign relations of the United States' and would risk 'adverse foreign policy consequences.'"[67] The Obama Administration has clearly backed away from its original stance in supporting the petitioner's rights; before the Supreme Court ordered a rebrief of the case, the Government had focused on the petitioner's narrow issue, as its lawyer had during oral arguments regarding the application of the ATS to corporate liability.

While the Government's brief leaves room for the Justices to make way for other ATS claims in the future, the *Kiobel* case signifies a continuing reluctance on the part of the United States to recognize the correlation between weak governance, corruption and non-transparency as cognizable violations of the law of nations.[68] The United States has long recognized causes of action for "torts committed in violation of the laws of nations or a treaty of the United States".[69] The Alien Tort Claims Act (ATCA) was originally enacted as part of the Judiciary Act of 1789; however, modern courts, like the court in *Sosa v. Alvarez-Machain*, expressed their frustration with the Alien Tort Statue, as it seemed to borrow too heavily from "hybrid international norms." The Court has had a tumultuous relationship

64 See, *supra*, note 61, "In its original amicus brief in support of the petitioners, the [Obama] Administration argued in favor of corporate liability."

65 John Bellinger, "European Governments File Supreme Court Amicus Briefs in Kiobel," *Lawfare*, 8 February 2012; available at: http://www.lawfareblog.com/2012/03/stop-press-supreme-court-orders-kiobel-reargued-to-address-extraterritoriality/.

66 "Supplemental Brief of The United Staes in Partial Support of Affirmance as Amici Curiae," p. 11, *Kiobel v. Royal Dutch Petroleum Co.* (docket 10-1491) (2012).

67 Ibid. at 22.

68 Ibid. at 11.

69 See also, *supra*, note 59. "The district courts shall have original jurisdiction of any civil action by an alien for a tort only, committed in violation of the law of nations, or committed in violation of the law of nations or a treaty of the United States." Enacted 1789. This principle was first recognized in *Filartiga v. Pena Irala*, 630 F. 2d 876 (2d Cir. 1980). The follow- up case, *Kadic v. Karadzic*, 70 F. 3d 232, 236 (2d Cir. 1995), reiterated that "[T]he ATCA validly creates federal court jurisdiction for suits alleging torts committed anywhere in the world against aliens in violation of the law of nations."

with any firm adherence to international laws or widely accepted norms, as they hold in Sosa: "We have no congressional mandate to seek out and define new and debatable violations of the law of nations," despite having recognized in a plethora of former cases that the "United States recognizes the law of nations."[70]

While ultimately, Sosa concluded that imposing liability on MNCs for violations of the law of nations had to be of such "specific, universal, and obligatory" nature so as to be considered a norm of customary international law, and there, Sosa's claim did not rise to this level of scrutiny, the Court's decision in *Kiobel* now on its docket will decide whether or not the ATS's jurisdiction even extends to cover the type of wrong alleged by its plaintiffs – gross human rights violations committed by the Nigerian government while being aided and abetted by the respondent.

*Regulatory policy limitations* Domestic policies and existing domestic forums are demonstrably inadequate to address wrongs committed by MNCs who facilitate corruption and promote illegal activities through direct or indirect investments or encouragement of foreign governments in the Angola example, and further exemplified by the claims made in Kiobel, *Wiwa v. Royal Dutch Petroleum* and *Presbetarian Church of Sudan v. Talisman Energy Inc.*[71] Domestic policy focuses heavily on regulatory solutions for the promotion and monitoring of corporate responsibility, rather than on providing a forum with appropriate redress to adjudicate claims made by individual victims of specific human rights abuses.

*US domestic legislation* US law does include anti-corruption regulations such as the Foreign Corrupt Practices Act (FCPA), which prohibits US persons (including MNCs) from making or receiving items of value to foreign governmental officials, candidates for office and officials of political parties for the purpose of obtaining or maintaining business. Violations of the FCPA include criminal and civil liability. Enforcement activities are mitigated by domestic resources and violations may be mitigated by evidence of internal due diligence and corporate compliance programs. Individuals like the claimants in *Kiobel*, however, would not be parties to a regulatory claim against an offending company, and thus are not appropriately protected by these types of regulations.

Similarly, legislators in the United States passed the Dodd-Frank Wall Street Reform and Consumer Protection Act in July of 2010. The stated aim of the legislation is:

> To promote the financial stability of the United States by improving accountability and transparency in the financial system, to end "too big to fail", to protect the

70 See, *supra* note 58.

71 See also, *Wiwa v. Royal Dutch Petroleum Company and Shell Transport and Trading Co.*, 2002 WL 31'9887 (S.D.NY.); *The Presbyterian Church of Sudan v. Talisman Energy, Inc.*, 244 F. Supp 2d 289 (S.D.N.Y. 2003).

American taxpayer by ending bailouts, to protect consumers from abusive financial services practices, and for other purposes.[72]

Despite the sweeping transformative goals espoused by the 2010 Dodd-Frank passage, key provisions necessary to enact legislation remain stalled as of the date of this publication. Critically, rules that have required drafting by the Securities and Exchange Commission, and those rules concerning anti-corruption and transparency in obtaining raw materials from conflict zones remain unwritten.[73] Regulatory compliance legislation suffers from a lack of consistent enforcement and a lack of confidence in its strength by both the public and the corporate community alike. MNCs have already expressed their displeasure and lack of confidence in Dodd-Frank legislation. They provided poll results at the NYSE Euronext's Annual Boardroom Summit: more than 400 board members answered questions regarding corporate governance requirements imposed by legislation like the Dodd-Frank Act, ultimately dismissing the requirements as being "not something investors were clamoring for." Polling determined that the "SEC whistle-blower financial incentive portion of the Dodd-Frank Reform Act will ultimately prove to be the most detrimental, long-term, to improving governance in the boardroom."[74] Of course the poll is not dispositive of the Act itself, rather the continued message to the public continues to be one of corporate invincibility, a sense of impunity for activities undertaken by MNCs. The failure of the United States Securities and Exchange Commission (SEC) to swiftly write and finalize the rules required for Dodd-Frank leaves the nation in a continued state of flux with regard to the regulation of corporate activities, and leaves room for doubt as to the US Government's message to its citizens and the world as to whether or not transparency and reform are indeed part of its real endgoals.[75]

The case study for Angola illustrates the consequences of unchecked corruption facilitated by unmonitored actions of MNCs. [76] Without clear, enforceable and

72 Dodd-Frank Wall Street Reform and Consumer Protection Act (Enrolled Final Version – HR 4173); available at: www.frwebgate.access.gpo.gov/cgi-bin.

73 Srah N. Lynch, "SEC Urges Staff To Rely On Economists When Making Rules in Wake of Criticisms," *Reuters*, 16 April 2012; available at: http://www.huffingtonpost.com/2012/04/16/sec-economists_n_1429769.html (visited 5 July 2012).

74 See, e.g., "Directors Vote Best and Worst of Dodd-Frank Act," from *Corporate Board Member*, 8 October 2010; available at www.boardmember.com

75 Jess Hamilton, "Dodd-Frank Rules Slow at SEC After Cost Challenge," *Bloomberg*, 5 March 2012. Available at: http://www.bloomberg.com/news/2012-03-06/dodd-frank-rules-slow-at-sec-after-court-cost-benefit-challenge.html (visited 5 July 2012).

76 Ibid. at 55. The UN Millennium Goals identified eight factors that continue to stunt developing countries. Angola, in the most recent assessments still ranks at the very bottom of these indices. The goals include the eradication of extreme poverty and hunger, universal primary education, gender equality and the empowerment of women, lessening child mortality and increasing women's health, combating the increasing spread of HIV/AIDS, malaria and other diseases, environmental sustainability and building global partnerships.

absolute rules structured as the international constitutionalization of human rights laws, at-risk citizens in countries like Angola are still subject to the unchecked activities of outside influences like MNCs, and the increasing influence of non-related interests such as China and India in the region.[77] A 2004 World Bank symposium report additionally posits that Angola exemplifies supercharged wealth inequity and the direct relationship between corruption and this inequity.[78]

The Angolan government failed to complete IFI standards and cease bifurcation of the obligations of its National Treasury Department with the state-owned and highly suspect Sonangol Oil Company.[79] Angola has vast resources; however, despite the deep, financially fruitful wells, more than 90 percent of the population lives in "extreme poverty with a continued threat of civil unrest."[80]

The World Bank monitors express their concerns for Angola's future financial stability as rooted in fulfilling the following goals: to plan; scrutinize, monitor, execute and create a valid public expenditure program.[81] Angola currently applies for loan assistance through the IFIs, but continues to elicit petroleum-backed subsidies from MNCs in the West and the East, as well as governments trying to secure oil futures such as the most recent dealings with China.[82] Without a firm commitment from governments that support the IMF and World Bank to create punitive criminal and civil financial incentives for MNCs who aid in continued corrupt tactics and secret financial dealings with Angola and other at-risk countries, the IFI programs will continue to fail. Therefore, constitutionalization of these human rights standards will create the enforceable standard, regardless of domestic inconsistencies and political maneuvering by powerful MNC lobbies.

---

While the IFIs recognize the goals, their challenge is not to monitor or achieve them. They merely facilitate economic progress and stability, which, theoretically, would naturally lead to the financing of measures to meet or exceed the Millennium Goals.

77 Ibid. Angola has experienced rapid resettlement of more than 4 million of its former refugees to under-serviced urban centers like Luanda. Furthermore, despite a preliminary GDP in early 2006 assessment that showed more than an 18 percent growth and the payoff of more than US$6 million in loans to the United States this year, experts at the World Bank and the IMF are concerned that these numbers are short term and inflated owing to the sudden interest of China, and the increase in oil production.

78 Ibid. at 34. The World Bank symposium report additionally posits that Angola exemplifies supercharged wealth inequity and the direct relationship between corruption and this inequity.

79 Ibid. at 55–8. Sonangol acts as a debt service ($X$), and the tax due by Sonangol is $Y$. If $Y < X$, the National Treasury actually transfers public monies *in favor of* Sonangol in an amount equal to $X$. If the $\Delta$ of $Y - X$, then it rolls over to the next month. This virtual shell-game has long thwarted real attempts to centralize and open up scrutiny of the oil revenues and Sonangol's undisputed claim to them.

80 Ibid. at 90. See also, www.publishwhatyoupay.org (September 2005).

81 Ibid at 97.

82 Ibid.

*Defining Transparency*

Although much of the developed world ranks in the top tier of transparency (e.g. the United States recently ranked 11th in the first "Revenue Watch Index" released 5 October 2010 by the Revenue Watch Institute in collaboration with Transparency International),[83] the case study in Angola highlights discrepancies in the fundamental revenues realized by the MNCs of these very same Western nations, whose activities directly profit Western financial markets with both profits and resources used within these economies.

The result is operation on two parallel, thematically oppositional platforms, one for democratization, transparency and the Rule of Law, and the other seeking to expand the hegemony of the economic powers (alongside competitive economic powers like the PRC) and maintain and expand MNC financial security and dominance. In order to achieve transparency and preserve the Rule of Law, including preserving fundamental human rights, the dichotomy of competing interests must merge.

On a micro level, Angola serves to demonstrate the harms of operating with two platforms. A 2004 World Bank assessment named the two competing Angolan powers: the Conventional one, the National Treasury Directorate; and the Nonconventional one, Sonangol.[84] The World Bank report clarified its goals as elimination of the Nonconventional Sonangol power in Angola as key to meeting development objectives and eradicating poverty and improving corruption perceptions.[85] The report emphasized weak governance, and lack of control over staff, spending, expenditures and personal cost, as well as there being no readily identifiable credible central banking system, as holes in the system.[86]

The World Bank sought to implement viable macro-economic reforms through increased transparency, credibility boosters, effective and formal budget preparation, execution, accounting, representation and centralized open control over the entire system.[87] The problem, however, was in the disconnect between governmental incentive, continued corruption, a single resource (oil), and the

83 See, e.g., The Revenue Watch Index, 2010. The Revenue Watch Institute/Transparency International. The Revenue Watch Institute has collaborated with Transparency International since 2007 with goals in promoting awareness among governments, private and state-owned companies, experts and activists of the importance of revenue transparency in countries where oil, natural gas and minerals play a major role in the economy. The study rated the openness of governments for the management of their oil, gas and mineral resources.

84 Angola Public Expenditure Management and Financial Accountability, World Bank Report No. 29036-AO (2005), available at: http://www-wds.worldbank.org/external/default/WDSContentServer/WDSP/IB/2005/03/10/000090341_20050310101310/Rendered/PDF/290360AO.pdf.

85 Ibid.

86 Ibid.

87 Ibid.

continued secret support of multinational corporations interested in maintaining control as well as the influence of newly economically powerful nations like China, who have few incentives to support the goals laid out by the Western IFIs. The current system allows Sonangol to act as a central bank, with its own commercial bank accounts and a questionable, corrupt and inefficient method of offsetting debits and credits month to month.[88] The evidence is in the continued extremity of Angola on the lowest rung of human poverty indices. Oil revenues account for a whopping 40 percent of the GDP and 80 percent of the government revenues. The bonuses or "signature payments" make up more than 95 percent of this figure, and that is the part that is not disclosed by multinationals, nor by foreign governments, so the payoff of a loan worth US$6 millions in disclosed IMF loans, in reality, means very little when Angola takes in billions of dollars per year, in undisclosed, non-transparent signature payments that never see the public treasury. (Figures for 2002 indicate that Sonangol took in more than US$1.2 billion in US-serviced oil-backed loans in direct contravention of the IFI standards.[89])

## Conclusion

The concept promoted here is the constitutionalization of human rights in accordance with existing legal frameworks (such as the International Criminal Court, The European Court of Human Rights and the Inter-American Court of Human Rights). These existing forums should maintain diversity` and, with the appropriate measures to constitutionalism human rights claims brought against MNCs, have real power to administer meaningful consequences for violations. This collaboration will encourage local actors who are historically disenfranchised and therefore unengaged in traditional models for international planning and policy-making. Effective, international accountability models must rooted in ethnically, socially, politically, and economically diverse norms and expectations, in order to support transparent and fair outcomes, and these forums connect victims to the wider world.

The case study in Angola draws attention to last three decades of MNC–state cooperation to exploit the land and people, and promote control of the precious natural resources in the hands of a few, uber-corrupt government officials. In order to become prosperous, to promote democracy and to engage in sustainable, measurable, transparent development, at-risk countries like Angola must adhere to an appropriate fiduciary framework for its internal resources, in this case oil revenues; however, the analysis may be broadened to examine the role of MNCs in other contexts where people are disenfranchised from government, and resources and revenues are in the hands of a few in partnership with MNCs.

88 Ibid.

89 Ibid.

Democratization and the elimination of corruption are a global responsibility, and without cogent, clear objectives underpinned by a reliable international jurisprudence, MNCs will continue to ghostwrite outcomes in high-risk nations that lack transparency in government and management of internal resources. Corruption and lack of transparency are direct corollaries to poverty, instability, insecurity and negative protections of fundamental human rights. MNCs who participate in these outcomes must be held responsible as actors subject to penalties where international constitutional rights are violated by (1) creating new systems that in the first place recognize a cause of action against MNCs and impose liability on MNCs for violation of those laws, and (2) cultivating a jurisprudence of international law that recognizes those claims, individuals or entities.

# Index